PRAISE FOR STATISTICS FOR PI
WHO (THINK THEY) HATE STATIS....

Thank you so much for a wonderful textbook; it's written with such an awareness of the reader (and an awareness that some people have self-limiting beliefs about their abilities with statistics!).

Dr. Jeremy Nguyen
Swinburne Business School
Swinburne University of Technology

Hello Dr. Salkind! Just wanted to thank you for putting together a great resource in your *Statistics for People* . . . I use it to teach my grad course in Quantitative Research Methods in Anthropology here at Northern Arizona University. We fondly refer to your book as "Haters."

Britton L. Shepardson, PhD
Lecturer & Assistant Chair
Department of Anthropology
Northern Arizona University

Dr. Salkind, thank you for writing a textbook that was very entertaining to read! Not only did I learn something, but I was not bored. In Chapter 13 (page 218), I was drawn in by the prospect of getting a new macaroni and cheese recipe—hence why I am writing to you. I am also enclosing my family's recipe for buffalo chicken mac & cheese (there is a lot of cheese and butter, but I am from Wisconsin). If you have time to try it, I'd love to hear what you think. I would also appreciate it if you could send me your recipe. Thank you for a great text (and a new recipe)!

—Andrea Green

I am enrolled at Capella online trying to get my master's in Educational Psychology. I only would like to share with you that your book is amazing—really easy to under-stand—and I especially like the little fun you add to it. It is delightful to read because that fun takes the anxiety away. Now I understand the title!

Norma Vargas
Instructor & Data Administrator
Houston Center for Literacy

Just a quick note to say "Thank You! I had my engineering analysis class last fall at Eastern Kentucky University and we used your book, *Statistics for People Who (Think They) Hate Statistics*. I learned so much and really appreciate it. I am currently doing some research and was reading another master's thesis on my subject and they were discussing "t-testing." I was so excited that I was able to grab my marked-up and high-lighted book to review. I just had to write and thank you for producing a great book that I am able to use beyond a classroom. Again, thank you for making statistics a practical tool for my everyday life!

—Mark A. Campbell, CFPS, SET-

As a statistics professional with a creative writing English BA, let me be just one of many to say thank you for your book. You have helped me find what I have been looking for my entire career, a passion. I thoroughly enjoyed your writing style, your explanation of theory and practical usage, the incorporation of Excel, chapter quizzes, and—most of all—the examples. I sincerely hope to find more of your work for my continued learning. Thank you again for your inspiration. You have made a running joke with my staff at the office more fun than ever: "I math do well!"

—Sam Johnson

I am taking statistics at the graduate level for a master's program—late in life I might add—and I hate statistics to the depth, breadth, and volume of all the oceans of all the earth combined. I do, however, love statisticians. They . . . you are the resource for all things sadistically statistical?! Even more, I love brownies. And the recipe is fabulous. Thanks. This text has helped me more than any other, and I would be remiss if I did not give credit to my current instructor. Were it not for his style and sense of humor, stats would be lost on me. I think I will make brownies for class! (Mayonnaise?! Really, whoda thunk!)

—Bruce Bailey
Lead C.D. Technician Hazelden Fellowship Club Intermediate

My name is Jessica Maes and I am currently working on attaining a master's degree in Curriculum and Instruction from New Mexico Highlands University. In the statistics class I am taking at this time, our required text is your book. I just wanted to take this time to tell you that your book has changed my perception and attitude toward statistics. I find that it is very well written, the language is completely user friendly, and the progression of new concepts within each chapter is fantastic. Although my class is only on Chapter 5 at this point, I have found my interest in the concepts and order in which you introduce them becoming greater. I THANK you with very much appreciation as I WAS someone who dreaded taking statistics and thought I hated it!

Very Grateful,
Jessica Maes

I am a full-time registered nurse of 19 years and have recently begun my journey of obtaining my Bachelor of Science in Nursing. Tomorrow is my first statistics class. I have just read your "note to student" and wanted to write to you and inform you that you have described my symptoms to a T. My classmates and I are extremely anxious about our course and what we are in for over the next three months. After reading these two pages, I wanted to tell you that you have alleviated some of my anxiety and allowed me to stop fretting about the unknown and begin to read on. Thank you for that. I am working a night shift tonight. Hopefully I will find time to read my required chapters with less anxiety and actually absorb some of the material I am reading. Thank you again. I will try and look forward to learning from your book, my excellent instructor, and my classmates.

Sincerely,
Lori Vajda, RN

It is easily the best book of its kind that I have come across. I enthusiastically recommend it for anyone interested in the subject—and even (and especially) for those who aren't!

—Professor Russ Shafer-Landau
University of Wisconsin

I just wanted to send a little "thank you" your way for writing an extremely user-friendly book, *Statistics for People Who (Think They) Hate Statistics*. I'm a psychology major doing an independent study over break (at Alverno College, a statistics course is a prerequisite for a class I'm taking this spring, Experimental Psychology). In other words, I'm pretty much learning this on my own (with a little guidance from my mentor), so I appreciate having a book that presents the material in a simple, sometimes humorous manner.

Sincerely,
Jenny Saucerman

Dr. Salkind's book is a "must read" for students who think they don't "do statistics." He writes clearly about statistical topics and has a unique way of making them fun. The book contains useful explanations, examples that help students understand the underlying concepts, and graphics that clarify the material without overwhelming the novice.

—Professor Nancy Leffert
Fielding Graduate Institute

I just wanted to let you know how much I enjoyed your book *Statistics for People Who (Think They) Hate Statistics* and how easily it jogged my faint memories of statistics (my work had been primarily in the clinical world before I returned to the academic world) and of SPSS. I am sure you hear from students all the time, but I wanted to let you know that even other academics find your book useful.

—Professor John T. Wu, EdD
Point Loma Nazarene University

Great presentations for a subject that tends to be esoteric—the text makes statistics alive and vibrant. I told my wife that the book reads like a novel—I can hardly put it down.

—Professor Kenrick C. Bourne
Loma Linda University

I love the clear description of the two-tailed test.

—Pepper
The author's dog

My students really appreciate your approach, which is making my job a lot easier.

—Professor Tony Hickey
Western Carolina University

Hello! First and foremost, I think your book is wonderful, and it is helping me tremendously in understanding concepts that, for instance, our chosen class textbook cannot. I am supplementing my class text with your book. Thanks so much!

—Melissa W.
Administrator

I love your book *Statistics for People Who (Think They) Hate Statistics*. I thought I did hate statistics; to be honest, I feared the concepts of stats, numbers, math, etc. . . . Ewwww! But thanks to your book, I understand it now (I get it). Your book gives me hope. I'm working on my PhD in nursing here in Baton Rouge, Louisiana, and I'm confident that I will ace my 100 percent online graduate stats class. This text is my professor and guidance during these late nights of studying (my best time to study). This book is loaded with helpful tips and clarity, and it's fun. I love the part about the 100 airline pilots and the flying proficiency test. The lowest value was 60—"don't fly with this guy." Love it—funny. Thanks, Dr. Salkind.

—Del Mars

I studied statistics 20 years ago and recently moved from administration into health research. Your book has been a big help in reviewing basic statistics. I love the book! Please write another.

—Susan Lepre, PhD
Bergen County Department of Health Services

Hello! I bought your book at Barnes and Noble among 30 books that I browsed for my statistics class. I was intrigued by the title... and it was so simple to understand with the stepladder format. I followed those steps, and boy, they really work! Thanks a lot!

—Anne Marie Puentespina, RN, BSN
Legal Nurse Consultant

For my beginning students, this is the book that fits their needs. It is clear, concise, and not intimidating. It's even fun. I strongly recommend it.

—Professor Lew Marglois
School of Public Health, University of North Carolina

I have loved statistics ever since my second undergraduate course. Your book *Statistics for People Who (Think They) Hate Statistics* has cleared up confusion and partial understandings that I have had for years. It is a must for anyone beginning or continuing their journey in this science. I love it and will use it for all of the foreseeable future.

—Ronald A. Straube
Performance Improvement Coordinator, Mission Texas Regional Medical Center

Statistics for People Who *(Think They)* Hate Statistics

Using Microsoft Excel 2016 ○ 4th Edition

*Outside of a dog, a book is man's best
friend. Inside of a dog, it's too dark to read.*

—Groucho Marx

For Doug and Nancy.

Statistics for People Who (*Think They*) Hate Statistics

Using Microsoft Excel 2016 ○ 4th Edition

Neil J. Salkind

Los Angeles | London | New Delhi
Singapore | Washington DC | Melbourne

FOR INFORMATION:

SAGE Publications, Inc.
2455 Teller Road
Thousand Oaks, California 91320
E-mail: order@sagepub.com

SAGE Publications Ltd.
1 Oliver's Yard
55 City Road
London EC1Y 1SP
United Kingdom

SAGE Publications India Pvt. Ltd.
B 1/I 1 Mohan Cooperative Industrial Area
Mathura Road, New Delhi 110 044
India

SAGE Publications Asia-Pacific Pte. Ltd.
3 Church Street
#10-04 Samsung Hub
Singapore 049483

Acquisitions Editor: Helen Salmon
Editorial Assistant: Yvonne McDuffee
eLearning Editor: Katie Ancheta
Production Editor: Libby Larson
Copy Editor: Paula Fleming
Typesetter: C&M Digitals (P) Ltd.
Proofreader: Scott Oney
Indexer: Will Ragsdale
Cover Designer: Candice Harman
Marketing Manager: Susannah Goldes

Library of Congress Cataloging-in-Publication Data

Names: Salkind, Neil J., author.

Title: Statistics for people who (think they) hate statistics: Using Microsoft Excel 2016 / Neil J. Salkind, University of Kansas.

Description: 4 edition. | Los Angeles: SAGE, [2017] | Includes index.

Identifiers: LCCN 2015040053 | ISBN 978-1-4833-7408-6 (pbk.: alk. paper)

Subjects: LCSH: Statistics. | Microsoft Excel Computer file)

Classification: LCC HA29 .S23652 2017 | DDC 519.5—dc23 LC record available at http://lccn.loc.gov/2015040053

This book is printed on acid-free paper.

16 17 18 19 20 10 9 8 7 6 5 4 3 2 1

BRIEF CONTENTS

PART V

DETAILED CONTENTS

PART II

PART III

PART IV

PART V

A NOTE TO THE STUDENT: WHY I WROTE THIS BOOK

This is the fourth edition of *Statistics for People Who (Think They) Hate Statistics, Excel 2016 Edition* (and also features the 2016 Macintosh version of Excel) and it was as much fun (really!) writing this revision as it was writing the earlier ones. I hope that the use of the book helps you and that the entire experience is interesting and productive.

What many of the students who study statistics, as well as people in various other roles (researchers, administrators, and professionals in many different fields), have in common (at least at the beginning of the course) is a relatively high level of anxiety, the origin of which is, more often than not, what they've *heard* from their fellow students. Often, a small part of what they have heard is true—learning statistics takes an investment of time and effort (and there's the occasional monster for a teacher).

But most of what they've heard (and where most of the anxiety comes from)—that statistics is unbearably difficult and confusing—is just not true. Thousands of fear-struck students have succeeded where they thought they would fail. They did it by taking one thing at a time, pacing themselves, seeing illustrations of basic principles as they are applied to real-life settings, and even having some fun (see the recipe for delicious brownies in Appendix F) along the way. That's what I tried to do in writing all the editions of *Statistics for People Who (Think They) Hate Statistics*, and I tried even harder in completing this latest revision.

After a great deal of trial and error, and some successful and many unsuccessful attempts, I have learned to teach statistics in a way that I (and many of my students) think is unintimidating and informative. I have tried my absolute best to incorporate all of that experience into this book.

What you will learn from this *Statistics for People . . .* is the information you need to understand what the field and study of basic statistics is all about. You'll learn about the fundamental ideas and the most commonly used techniques to organize and make sense out of data. There's very little theory (but some), and there are few mathematical proofs or discussion of the rationale for certain mathematical routines. And, for this Excel edition, you'll also learn how to better understand the world of statistics through the use of an easy-to-use, and powerful, tool.

Why isn't theory and other stuff in *Statistics for People Who (Think They) Hate Statistics?* Simple. Right now, you don't need it. It's not that I don't think it is important. Rather, at this point and time in your studies, I want to offer you material at a level I think you can understand and learn with some reasonable amount of effort, while at the same time not be scared off from taking additional courses in the future. I (and your professor) want you to succeed.

So, if you are looking for a detailed unraveling of the derivation of the analysis of variance F ratio, go find another good book from SAGE Publications (I'll be glad to refer you to one). But if you want to learn why and how statistics can work for you, you're in the right place. This book will help you understand the material you read in journal articles, explain what the results of many statistical analyses mean, and teach you how to perform basic statistical work.

And, if you want to talk about any aspect of teaching or learning statistics, feel free to contact me. You can do this through my email address at school (**njs@ku.edu**). You can also keep up on anything new regarding this edition (and all versions of *Statistics for People . . .*) at **http://edge.sagepub.com/salkindexcel4e**.

Good luck, and let me know how I can improve this book to even better meet the needs of the beginning statistics student.

AND A (LITTLE) NOTE TO THE INSTRUCTOR

I'd like to share two things.

First, I applaud your efforts at teaching introductory statistics. While the topic may be easier for some students than others, most find the material very challenging. Your patience and hard work is appreciated by all, and if there is anything I can do to help, please send me a note.

Second, the Excel® edition of *Statistics for People Who (Think They) Hate Statistics* is not meant to be a dumbed-down book similar to others you may have seen. Nor is the title meant to convey anything other than the fact that many students new to the subject are very anxious about what's to come. This is not an academic version of a book for dummies or anything of its kind. I have made every effort to address students with the respect they deserve, to not patronize them, and to ensure that the material is approachable. How well I did in these regards is up to you, but I want to convey my very clear intent and feeling that this book contains the information needed in an introductory course and, even though there is some humor involved in my approach, nothing about the intent is anything other than serious. Thank you.

Instructors can sign in at **edge.sagepub.com/salkindexcel4e** to access the test bank, PowerPoint® slides, chapter outlines, discussion questions, suggested activities, sample syllabi, SAGE journal articles, video and web resources, and data files to accompany this book

ACKNOWLEDGMENTS

Everybody, and I mean everybody, at SAGE deserves a great deal of thanks for providing me with the support, guidance, and professionalism that takes only an idea (way back before the first edition) and makes it into a book like the one you are now reading, and then makes it successful.

However, there are some people who have to be thanked individually for their special care and hard work. C. Deborah Laughton supported the original idea for this type of book, and Lisa Cuevas-Shaw encouraged the writing of this particular book, which uses Excel as a framework for teaching introductory statistics. Vicki Knight is the publisher who saw to it that this revision reached fruition, and she has provided the support and patience necessary to make this a reality. Her experience, insight, advocacy, and friendship are this author's dream. I am greatly appreciative. Very special thanks to Vicki who is moving on to a new chapter in her life for all the time, good counsel, hard work, and dedication to making this book, and my other SAGE publications, successful. I will be losing an editor, but I have gained a lifelong friend.

Others who deserve a special note of thanks are Yvonne McDuffee, editorial assistant; Katie Ancheta, e-learning editor; Susannah Goldes, marketing manager; and Libby Larson, production editor. Special thanks goes to Paula Fleming for her sharp eye and sound copyediting, which makes this material read as well as it does.

I also want to thank the following people for their help in providing feedback on the previous edition as well as this edition. Apologies to those I may have missed.

Jacqueline S. Craven, Delta State University

Patty Kero, University of Montana

David C. Kershaw, Slippery Rock University

Soomi Lee, University of La Verne

Yating Liang, Missouri State University

Robin Spaid, Morgan State University

Douglas Fairbanks Threet, Foothill College

Jed W. Utsinger, Ohio University

AND NOW, ABOUT THE FOURTH EDITION . . .

What you read above about this book reflects my thoughts about why I wrote this book in the first place. But it tells you little about this new edition.

Any book is always a work in progress, and the Excel edition of *Statistics for People Who (Think They) Hate Statistics* is no exception. Over the past 8 years or so, many people have told me how helpful this book is, and others have told me how they would like it to change and why. In revising this book, I am trying to meet the needs of all audiences. Some things have remained the same, and some have changed.

There are always new things worth consideration and different ways to present old themes and ideas. Here's a list of what you'll find that's new in *Statistics for People Who (Think They) Hate Statistics, Excel 2016 Edition.*

- There are a bunch of new exercises at the end of each chapter. Not only are there more exercises, but they also vary more in their level of application and (I hope) interest. These exercises use data sets that are available at **edge.sagepub.com/salkindexcel4e** and directly from the author at **njs@ku.edu**. The version of Excel that these were developed for is Excel 2016 for Windows and Excel 2016 for the Mac, but the files will work with earlier versions of Excel as well.

- At the end of each chapter is a Real-World Stats feature that provides an applied example of the content covered in the chapter. It's an attempt to further show the reader how statistics is, and can be, applied in the everyday world.

- The answers to the Time to Practice questions are now in a separate appendix (Appendix D). After going back and forth with students and faculty about the best placement, this seemed to be the winning location.

- A new Chapter 20 includes an introduction to dealing with large data sets using certain Excel functions and pivot tables. This is not a total treatment of data mining (which would be far too ambitious a task for a book at this level) but simply shows how certain database and other categories of functions and formulas can help make the data in big data sets easier to work with and the results more understandable.

- A new Appendix E presents some basic math instruction and some practice for those who need to brush up on that material.

- The fourth edition features the latest version of Excel, from Office 2016 (for the Windows platform) and the 2016 version for the Mac. There are some significant changes from prior versions, so students (and others) might want to look through Appendix A, which is a quick guide to some main features.

- There's a new Little Chapter 1c that is for people sticking with the 2011 version of Excel for the Mac. This chapter reviews StatPlus, an Excel add-on, that does many of the things that the Data Analysis Tools do. Note that the trial version is a free-bie but the complete version requires purchase.

- Online Resources for instructors at **edge.sagepub.com/salkind excel4e** include a test bank, PowerPoint slides, chapter outlines, discussion questions, suggested activities, sample syllabi, SAGE journal articles, video and web resources, and data files. Open-access study tools for students at **edge.sagepub.com/ salkindexcel4e** include data files, quizzes, flashcards, video and web resources, SAGE journal articles, action plan checklists and more.

- But wait, there's more! OK, folks (and especially Mac fans), hold on to your hat. As with the Windows version of Excel, now the Mac version offers the too-handy-to-be-true Data Analysis Tools (discussed throughout the book). The Mac Excel folks have been waiting for this for years. So, for almost every operation that you can perform with the Windows version of Excel, ditto × 10 for the Mac version of Excel. Finally.

- Instructors can sign in at **edge.sagepub.com/salkindexcel4e** to access the test bank, PowerPoint slides, chapter outlines, discussion questions, suggested activities, sample syllabi, SAGE journal articles, video and web resources, and data files to accompany this book.

- Open-access study tools for students at **edge.sagepub.com/ salkindexcel4e** include data files, quizzes, flashcards, video and web resources, SAGE journal articles, learning objectives, and action plan checklists.

Whatever typos and such have appeared in any edition of this book are entirely my fault, and I apologize to the professors and students who were inconvenienced by their appearance. You can find a list of typos from the previous printings and editions of this book at www.statisticsforpeople.com. And I so appreciate all the letters, calls, and emails pointing out these errors and making this fourth edition a better book for it. We have all made every effort in this edition to correct them and hope we did a reasonably good job. Let me hear from you with suggestions, criticisms, nice notes, and so on. Good luck.

Neil J. Salkind
University of Kansas
njs@ku.edu

ABOUT THE AUTHOR

Neil J. Salkind received his PhD from the University of Maryland in Human Development, and after teaching for 35 years at the University of Kansas, he remains as a Professor Emeritus in the Department of Psychology and Research in Education, where he continues to collaborate with colleagues and work with students. His early interests were in the area of children's cognitive development, and after research in the areas of cognitive style and (what was then known as) hyperactivity, he was a postdoctoral fellow at the University of North Carolina's Bush Center for Child and Family Policy. His work then changed direction and the focus was on child and family policy, specifically the impact of alternative forms of public support on various child and family outcomes. He has delivered more than 150 professional papers and presentations; written more than 100 trade and textbooks; and is the author of *Statistics for People Who (Think They) Hate Statistics* (SAGE), *Theories of Human Development* (SAGE), and Exploring Research (Prentice Hall). He has edited several encyclopedias, including the *Encyclopedia of Human Development*, the *Encyclopedia of Measurement and Statistics,* and the recently published *Encyclopedia of Research Design*. He was editor of *Child Development Abstracts and Bibliography* for 13 years and lives in Lawrence, Kansas, where he likes to letterpress print (see https://sites.google.com/site/bigboypressofks/ for more), read, swim with the Lawrence River City Sharks, bake brownies (see the recipe at http://www.statisticsforpeople.com/The_Brown.html), and poke around old Volvos and old houses

SAGE was founded in 1965 by Sara Miller McCune to support the dissemination of usable knowledge by publishing innovative and high-quality research and teaching content. Today, we publish over 900 journals, including those of more than 400 learned societies, more than 800 new books per year, and a growing range of library products including archives, data, case studies, reports, and video. SAGE remains majority-owned by our founder, and after Sara's lifetime will become owned by a charitable trust that secures our continued independence.

Los Angeles | London | New Delhi | Singapore | Washington DC | Melbourne

PART I

Yippee! I'm in Statistics

Not much to shout about, you might say? Let me take a minute and show you how some very accomplished scientists use this widely used set of tools we call *statistics*.

- Michelle Lampl is a physician and an anthropologist and the director of the Center for the Study of Human Health at Emory University. She was having coffee with a friend, who commented on how quickly her young infant was growing. In fact, the new mother spoke as if her son were "growing like a weed." Being a curious scientist (as all scientists should be), Dr. Lampl thought she might actually examine how rapid this child's growth, and that of others, was during infancy. She proceeded to measure growth in a group of children on a daily basis and found, much to her surprise, that some infants grew as much as 1 inch overnight! Some growth spurt.

  o *Want to know more?* Why not read the original work? You can find more about this in Lampl, M., Veldhuis, J. D., & Johnson, M. L. (1992). Saltation and stasis: A model of human growth. *Science, 258*, 801–803.

- Sue Kemper is the Roberts Distinguished Professor of Psychology at the University of Kansas and works on the most interesting of projects. She and several other researchers studied a group of nuns and examined how their early experiences, activities, personality characteristics, and other information related to their health during their late adult years. Most notably, this diverse group of scientists (including psychologists, linguists, neurologists, and others) wanted to know how well all this information predicts the occurrence of Alzheimer's disease. Kemper and her colleagues found that the complexity of the nuns' writing during their early 20s was related to the nuns' risk for Alzheimer's 50, 60, and 70 years later.

- ○ *Want to know more?* Why not read the original work? You can find more about this in Snowdon, D. A., Kemper, S. J., Mortimer, J. A., Greiner, L. H., Wekstein, D. R., & Markesbery, W. R. (1996). Linguistic ability in early life and cognitive function and Alzheimer's disease in late life: Findings from the nun study. *Journal of the American Medical Association, 275,* 528–532.

- Aletha Huston (a very distinguished professor emerita) from the University of Texas in Austin devoted a good deal of her professional work to understanding what effects television watching has on young children's psychological development. Among other things, she and her late husband, John C. Wright, investigated the impact that the amount of educational television programs watched during the early preschool years might have on outcomes in the later school years. They found convincing evidence that children who watch educational programs such as *Mr. Rogers* and *Sesame Street* do better in school than those who do not.

  - ○ *Want to know more?* Why not read the original work? You can find more about this in Collins, P. A., Wright, J. C., Anderson, R., Huston, A. C., Schmitt, K., & McElroy, E. (1997, April). *Effects of early childhood media use on adolescent achievement.* Paper presented at the biennial meeting of the Society for Research in Child Development, Washington, D.C.

All of these researchers had a specific question they found interesting and used their intuition, curiosity, and excellent training to answer it. As part of their investigations, they used this set of tools we call *statistics* to make sense out of all the information they collected. Without these tools, all this information would have been just a collection of unrelated outcomes. The outcomes would be nothing that Lampl could have used to reach a conclusion about children's growth, or Kemper could have used to better understand aging and cognition (and perhaps Alzheimer's disease), or Huston and Wright could have used to better understand the impact of watching television on young children's achievement and social development.

Statistics—the science of organizing and analyzing information to make it more easily understood—made these tasks doable. The reason that any of the results from such studies are useful is that we can use statistics to make sense out of them. And that's exactly the goal of this book—to provide you with an understanding of these basic tools and how researchers use them and, of course, how to use them yourself.

In this first part of *Statistics for People Who (Think They) Hate Statistics, Excel 2016 Edition,* you will be introduced to what the study of statistics is about and why it's well worth your efforts to master the basics—the important terminology and ideas that are central to the field. This part gives you a solid preparation for the rest of the book.

We'll also be getting right into the Excel material with two little chapters that follow Chapter 1—one chapter about formulas and functions (Little Chapter 1a) and one chapter about the use of the Data Analysis tools (Little Chapter 1b).

And this third edition uses Excel 2016 (for Windows and the Mac). Although you can use other versions of Excel and do fine, you'll be much better equipped to follow the material in these pages and do the exercises if you have the current version of this pretty cool application. It is probably available through the computer center or information technology department at your school or even at your local public library if you don't have access through the class that you might taking, so check out those possibilities before you buy it.

1

Statistics or Sadistics?

It's Up to You

Difficulty Scale ☺ ☺ ☺ ☺ ☺ (really easy)

WHAT YOU'LL LEARN ABOUT IN THIS CHAPTER

✦ What statistics is all about

✦ Why you should take statistics

✦ How to succeed in this course

WHY STATISTICS?

You've heard it all before, right? "Statistics is difficult," "The math involved is impossible," "I don't know how to use a computer," "What do I need this stuff for?" "What do I do next?" and the famous cry of the introductory statistics student, "I don't get it!" Well, relax. Students who study introductory statistics find themselves, at one time or another, thinking at least one of the above and quite possibly sharing the thought with another student, their spouse, a colleague, or a friend.

And all kidding aside, some statistics courses can easily be described as *sadistics*. That's because the books are repetitiously boring and the authors have no imagination.

That's not the case for you. The fact that you or your instructor has selected *Statistics for People Who (Think They) Hate Statistics, Excel 2016 Edition* shows that you're ready to take the right approach—one that is unintimidating, informative, and applied (and even a little fun) and that tries to teach you what you need to know about using statistics as the valuable tool that it is.

If you're using this book in a class, it also means that your instructor is clearly on your side. He or she knows that statistics can be intimidating but has taken steps to see that it is not intimidating for you. As a matter of fact, we'll bet there's a good chance (as hard as it may be to believe) that you'll be enjoying this class in just a few short weeks.

And Why Excel?

Simple. It's the most popular, most powerful spreadsheet tool available today, and it can be an exceedingly important and valuable tool for learning how to use basic and some advanced statistics. In fact, many stats courses taught at the introductory level use Excel as their primary computational tool and ignore other computer programs, such as IBM® SPSS® Statistics (SPSS)* and Minitab. Although we are not going to teach you how to use Excel (see Appendix A for a refresher on some basic tasks), we will show you how to use it to make your statistics learning experience a better one.

But like any program that takes numbers and consolidates and analyzes them, Excel is not a magic bullet or a tool to solve all your problems. It has its limitations. Unless you are an expert programmer and you can program Excel to do just about anything other statistics programs can (the language you would use is Visual Basic Applications or VBA), Excel may not look as pretty as other programs dedicated to statistical analysis or offer as many options. But at the level of introductory statistics, it is a very powerful tool that can do an awful lot of very neat things.

A bit of terminology about Excel before we move on: The first ever Excel-like computer application was called VisiCalc (thank you, Dan Bricklin and Bob Frankston) and was known as a spreadsheet. Okay, the Excel application is known as a spreadsheet program as well, but each individual sheet is known as a **worksheet**. And worksheets, when combined, constitute what is known as a **workbook**. Fun, huh?

A 5-MINUTE HISTORY OF STATISTICS

Before you read any further, it would be useful to have some historical perspective about this topic called statistics. After all, almost every undergraduate in the social, behavioral, and biological sciences and every graduate student in education, nursing,

---

*SPSS is a registered trademark of International Business Machines Corporation.

psychology, social welfare and social services, anthropology, and . . . (you get the picture) is required to take this course. Wouldn't it be nice to have some idea from whence the topic it covers came? Of course it would.

Way, way back, as soon as humans realized that counting was a good idea (as in "How many of these do you need to trade for one of those?"), collecting information became a useful skill.

If counting counted, then one would know how many times the sun would rise in one season, how much food was needed to last the winter, and what amount of resources belonged to whom.

That was just the beginning. Once numbers became part of language, it seemed like the next step was to attach these numbers to outcomes. That started in earnest during the 17th century, when the first set of data pertaining to populations was collected. From that point on, scientists (mostly mathematicians, but then physical and biological scientists) needed to develop specific tools to answer specific questions. For example, Francis Galton (a half-cousin of Charles Darwin, by the way), who lived from 1822 to 1911, was very interested in the nature of human intelligence. He also speculated that hair loss was due to the intense energy that went into thinking. No, really. But back to statistics.

To explore one of his primary questions regarding the similarity of intelligence among family members, he used a specific statistical tool called the correlation coefficient (first developed by mathematicians), and then he popularized its use in the behavioral and social sciences.

You'll learn all about this tool in Chapter 5. In fact, most of the basic statistical procedures that you will learn about were first developed and used in the fields of agriculture, astronomy, and even politics. Their application to human behavior came much later.

The past 100 years have seen great strides in the invention of new ways to use old ideas. The simplest test for examining the differences between the averages of two groups was first advanced during the early 20th century. Techniques that build on this idea were offered decades later and have been greatly refined. And the introduction of personal computers and such programs as Excel has opened up the use of sophisticated techniques to anyone who wants to explore these fascinating topics.

The introduction of these powerful personal computers has been both good and bad. It's good because most statistical analyses no longer require access to a huge and expensive mainframe computer. Instead, a simple personal computer costing less than $250 or a cloud account can do 95% of what 95% of the people need. On the other hand, less than adequately educated students (such as your fellow students who passed on taking this course!) will take any old data they have and think that by running them through some sophisticated analysis, they will have reliable, trustworthy, and meaningful outcomes—not true. What your professor would say is "Garbage in, garbage out"; if you don't start with reliable and trustworthy data, what you'll have after your data are analyzed are unreliable and untrustworthy results.

Today, statisticians in all different areas, from criminal justice to geophysics to psychology, find themselves using basically the same techniques to answer different questions. There are, of course, important differences in how data are collected, but for the most part, the analyses (the plural of *analysis*) that are done following the collection of data (the plural of *datum*) tend to be very similar, even if called something different. The moral here? This class will provide you with the tools to understand how statistics are used in almost any discipline. Pretty neat, and all for just three or four credits.

If you want to learn more about the history of statistics and see a historical time line, great places to start are Saint Anselm's College at www.anselm.edu/homepage/jpitocch/biostatshist.html and the University of California–Los Angeles at www.stat.ucla .edu/history/.

Okay. Five minutes is up, and you know as much as you need to know about the history of statistics. Let's move on to what it is (and isn't).

STATISTICS: WHAT IT IS (AND ISN'T)

Statistics for People Who (Think They) Hate Statistics, Excel 2016 Edition is a book about basic statistics and how to apply them to a variety of different situations, including the analysis and understanding of information.

In the most general sense, *statistics* describes a set of tools and techniques that are used for describing, organizing, and interpreting information or data. Those data might be the scores on a test taken by students participating in a special math curriculum, the speed with which problems are solved, the number of side effects when patients use one type of drug rather than another, the number of errors in each inning of a World Series game, or the average price of a dinner in an upscale restaurant in Santa Fe, New Mexico (not cheap).

In all of these examples, and the million more we could think of, data are collected, organized, summarized, and then interpreted. In this book, you'll learn about collecting, organizing, and summarizing data as part of descriptive statistics. And then you'll learn about interpreting data when you learn about the usefulness of inferential statistics.

What Are Descriptive Statistics?

Descriptive statistics are used to organize and describe the characteristics of a collection of data. The collection is sometimes called a **data set** or just **data**.

For example, the following list shows you the names of 22 college students, their major areas of study, and their ages. If you needed to describe what the most popular college major is, you could use a descriptive statistic that summarizes their most frequent choice (called the mode). In this case, the most common major is psychology. And if you wanted to know the average age, you could easily compute another descriptive statistic that identifies this variable (that one's called the mean). Both of these simple descriptive statistics are used to describe data. They do a fine job of allowing us to represent the characteristics of a large collection of data such as the 22 cases in our example.

Name	Major	Age	Name	Major	Age
Richard	Education	19	Elizabeth	English	21
Sara	Psychology	18	Bill	Psychology	22
Andrea	Education	19	Hadley	Psychology	23
Steven	Psychology	21	Buffy	Education	21
Jordan	Education	20	Chip	Education	19
Pam	Education	24	Homer	Psychology	18
Michael	Psychology	21	Margaret	English	22
Liz	Psychology	19	Courtney	Psychology	24
Nicole	Chemistry	19	Leonard	Psychology	21
Mike	Nursing	20	Jeffrey	Chemistry	18
Kent	History	18	Emily	Spanish	19

So watch how simple this is. To find the most frequently selected major, just find the one that occurs most often. And to find the average age, just add up all the age values and divide by 22. You're right—the most often occurring major is psychology (9 times), and the average age is 20.3 (actually 20.27). Look, Ma! No hands—you're a statistician.

What Are Inferential Statistics?

Inferential statistics are often (but not always) the next step after you have collected and summarized data. Inferential statistics are used to make inferences based on a smaller group of data (such as our group of 22 students) about a possibly larger one (such as all the undergraduate students in the College of Arts and Sciences).

A smaller group of data is often called a **sample**, which is a portion, or a subset, of a **population**. For example, all the fifth graders in Newark (your author's fair city of origin), New Jersey, would be a population (the population is all the occurrences with certain characteristics, in this case, being in fifth grade and attending school in Newark), whereas a selection of 150 of these students would be a sample.

Let's look at another example. Your marketing agency asks you (a newly hired researcher) to determine which of several names is most appealing for a new brand of potato chip. Will it be Chipsters? FunChips? Crunchies? As a statistics pro (we know we're moving a bit ahead of ourselves, but keep the faith), you need to find a small group of potato chip eaters who are representative of all potato chip fans and ask these people to tell you which one of the three names they like the most. Then, if you do things right, you can easily extrapolate the findings to the huge group of potato chip eaters.

Or let's say you're interested in the best treatment for a particular type of disease. Perhaps you'll try a new drug as one alternative, a placebo (a substance that is known not to have any effect) as another alternative, and nothing as the third alternative to see what happens. Well, you find out that more patients get better when no action is taken and nature (and we assume that's the only factor or set of factors that differentiate the groups) just takes its course! The drug does not have any effect. Then, with that information, you can extrapolate to the larger group of patients who suffer from the disease, given the results of your experiment.

In Other Words . . .

Statistics is a tool that helps us understand the world around us. It does so by organizing information we've collected and then letting us make certain statements about how characteristics of those data are applicable to new settings. Descriptive and inferential statistics work hand in hand, and which statistic you use and when depends on the question you want answered.

And today, a knowledge of statistics is more important than ever because it provides us with the tools to make decisions that are based on empirical (observed) evidence and not our own biases or beliefs. Want to know whether early intervention programs work? Then test whether they work and provide that evidence to the court where a ruling will be made on the viability of a new school bond issue that could pay for those programs.

TOOLING AROUND WITH THE DATA ANALYSIS TOOLS

An awful lot of what you need to know about using Excel can be found in Appendix A. However, certain Excel procedures are available only if you have the Data Analysis tools installed (and we use those tools in several chapters throughout the book). Please note that this Excel add-in is sometimes called the Data Analysis Toolpak and sometimes the Data Analysis tool or Data Analysis tools and sometimes the Analysis Toolpak. These are all different names for the same thing. We'll refer to it as Data Analysis tools to cover all the bases.

The Data Analysis tools are a spectacular Excel add-in. Add-ins are special sets of tools that are often not installed when Excel was originally installed.

How do you know whether Data Analysis tools are installed on the computer you are using? If the Data Analysis tools option doesn't appear on your Data tab as Data Analysis tools (as you see it appears in Figure 1.1) in the Windows version, you need to install it. Either ask your instructor to have it installed on the network level where Excel is installed or install it on your own machine by doing the following. In the Mac version, it appears as the Data Analysis option on the Tools menu, so Mac users have no need for any installation steps.

Figure 1.1   The Data Analysis Tools Option on the Data Tab

1. Click the File tab and then click Options.

2. Click Add-Ins and then in the Add-Ins box, select Analysis Toolpak (see, it's named different things in different places).

3. Click Go under Manage, at the bottom of the screen.

4. In the Add-Ins box, click the Analysis Toolpak check box and then click OK.

You are now ready to make your Excel activities even that much more productive and fun. You can learn how to use the Data Analysis tools in Little Chapter 1b.

WHAT AM I DOING IN A STATISTICS CLASS?

You might find yourself using this book for many reasons. You might be enrolled in an introductory statistics class. Or you might be reviewing for your comprehensive exams. Or you might even be reading this on summer vacation (horrors!) in preparation for a more advanced class.

In any case, you are a statistics student, whether you have to take a final exam at the end of a formal course or you're just in it of your own accord. But there are plenty of good reasons to be studying this material—some fun, some serious, and some both.

Here's the list of some of the things that my students hear at the beginning of our introductory statistics course:

1. Statistics 101 or Statistics 1 or whatever it's called at your school looks great listed on your transcript. Kidding aside, this may be a required course for you to complete your major. But even if it is not, having these skills is definitely a big plus when it comes time to apply for a job or for further schooling. And with more advanced courses, your résumé will be even more impressive.

2. If this is not a required course, taking basic statistics sets you apart from those who do not. It shows that you are willing to undertake a course that is above average with regard to difficulty and commitment. And, as the political and economic (and sports!) worlds become more "accountable," more emphasis is being placed on analytic skills. Who knows, this course may be your ticket to a job!

3. Basic statistics is an intellectual challenge of a kind that you might not be used to. There's a good deal of thinking that's required, a bit of math, and some integration of ideas and application. The bottom line is that all this activity adds up to what can be an invigorating intellectual experience because you learn about a whole new area or discipline.

4. There's no question that having some background in statistics makes you a better student in the social or behavioral sciences, because you will have a better understanding not only of what you read in journals but also of what your professors and colleagues may be discussing and doing in and out of class. You will be amazed the first time you say to yourself, "Wow, I actually understand what they're talking about." And it will happen over and over again, because you will have the basic tools necessary to understand exactly how scientists reach the conclusions they do.

5. If you plan to pursue a graduate degree in education, anthropology, economics, nursing, sociology, or any one of many other social, behavioral, and biological pursuits, this course will give you the foundation you need to move further.

6. There are many different ways of thinking about, and approaching, different types of problems. The set of tools you learn about in this book (and this course) will help you look at interesting problems from a new perspective. And, while not apparent now, this new way of thinking can be brought to new situations.

7. Finally, you can brag that you completed a course that everyone thinks is the equivalent of building and running a nuclear reactor.

TEN WAYS TO USE THIS BOOK (AND LEARN STATISTICS AT THE SAME TIME!)

Yep. Just what the world needs—another statistics book. But this one is different. It is directed at the student, is not condescending, is informative, and is as basic as possible in its presentation. It makes no presumptions about what you should know before you start and proceeds in slow, small steps, which lets you pace yourself.

However, there has always been a general aura surrounding the study of statistics that it's a difficult subject to master. And we don't say otherwise, because parts of it are challenging. On the other hand, millions and millions of students have mastered this topic, and you can, too. Here are 10 hints to close this introductory chapter before we move on to our first topic.

1. **You're not dumb.** That's true. If you were, you would not have gotten this far in school. So, treat statistics as you would any other new course. Attend the lectures, study the material, do the exercises in the book and from class, and you'll do fine. Rocket scientists know statistics, but you don't have to be a rocket scientist to succeed in statistics.

2. **How do you know statistics is hard?** Is statistics difficult? Yes and no. If you listen to friends who have taken the course and didn't work hard and didn't do well, they'll surely volunteer to tell you how hard it was and how much of a disaster it made of their entire semester, if not their lives. And let's not forget—we always tend to hear from complainers. So, we'd suggest that you start this course with the attitude that you'll wait and see how it is and judge the experience for yourself. Better yet, talk to several people who have had the class and get a good idea of what they think. Don't base your expectations on just one spoilsport's experience.

3. **Don't skip lessons—work through the chapters in sequence.** *Statistics for People Who (Think They) Hate Statistics, Excel 2016 Edition* is written so that each chapter provides a foundation for the next one in the book. When you are all done with the course, you will (I hope) continue to use this book as a reference. So if you need a particular value from a table, you might consult Appendix B. Or if you need to remember how to compute the standard deviation, you might turn to Chapter 3. But for now, read each chapter in the sequence that it appears. It's okay to skip around and see what's offered down the road. Just don't study later chapters before you master earlier ones.

4. **Form a study group.** This is a big hint and one of the most basic ways to ensure some success in this course. Early in the semester, arrange to study with friends or classmates. If you don't have any friends who are in the same class as you, then make some new ones or offer to study with someone who looks as happy to be there as you are. Studying with others allows you to help them if you know the material better, or to benefit from those who know some material better than you. Set a specific time each week to get together for an hour and go over the exercises at the end of the chapter or

ask questions of one another. Take as much time as you need. Studying with others is an invaluable way to help you understand and master the material in this course.

5. **Ask your teacher questions, and then ask a friend.** If you do not understand what you are being taught in class, ask your professor to clarify it. Have no doubt—if you don't understand the material, then you can be sure that others do not as well. More often than not, instructors welcome questions. And especially because you've read the material before class, your questions should be well informed and help everyone in class to better understand the material.

6. **Do the exercises at the end of the chapters.** The exercises are based on the material and the examples in the chapter they follow. They are there to help you apply the concepts that were taught in the chapter and build your confidence at the same time. If you can answer these end-of-chapter exercises, then you are well on your way to mastering the content of the chapter. Correct answers to each exercise are provided in Appendix D.

7. **Practice, practice, practice.** Yes, it's a very old joke:

   Q. How do you get to Carnegie Hall?

   A. Practice, practice, practice.

   Well, it's no different with basic statistics. You have to use what you learn and use it frequently to master the different ideas and techniques. This means doing the exercises in the back of Chapters 1 through 17 and Chapter 20 as well as taking advantage of any other opportunities you have to understand what you have learned.

8. **Look for applications to make it more real.** In your other classes, you probably have occasion to read journal articles, talk about the results of research, and generally discuss the importance of the scientific method in your own area of study. These are all opportunities to see how your study of statistics can help you better understand the topics under class discussion as well as the area of beginning statistics. The more you apply these new ideas, the fuller your understanding will be.

9. **Browse.** Read over the assigned chapter first; then go back and read it with more intention. Take a nice leisurely tour of *Statistics for People Who (Think They) Hate Statistics* to see what's contained in the various chapters. Don't rush yourself. It's always good to know what topics lie ahead as well as to familiarize yourself with the content that will be covered in your current statistics class.

10. **Have fun.** This might seem like a strange thing to say, but it all boils down to you mastering this topic rather than letting the course and its demands master you. Set up a study schedule and follow it, ask questions in class, and consider this intellectual exercise to be one of growth. Mastering new material is always exciting and satisfying—it's part of the human spirit. You can experience the same satisfaction here—just keep your eye on the ball and make the necessary commitment to stay current with the assignments and work hard.

And a short note for Mac users. Over the years, the Excel people at Microsoft have become increasingly kind to users of the Macintosh version. The latest versions of Excel for a Windows operating system and a Macintosh operating system are almost identical. And, as we have mentioned before, for the first time in the history of the galaxy, the Mac version now comes with the Data Analysis tools, the great convenience that the Windows version has provided for years.

One big difference between the Windows and the Mac version (and it really isn't that big) is the keystrokes that one uses to accomplish particular tasks. So, for example, instead of using the Ctrl+C key combination in Windows to copy highlighted text windows, the Mac uses the Apple or the Command key (the cool little key on the lower left of the keyboard with the four little squiggles) in combination with the C key to accomplish the same. This Apple key is also referred to (believe it or not) as the splat, the cloverleaf, the butterfly, the beanie, or the flower key. Using Excel in one operating system or the other (or both) requires a very similar set of tasks, and you should have no problem making the adjustment.

Plus, both the Windows and the Mac version of Excel can read each other's files, so you are safe exchanging files between one operating system and the other. All that said, if they really want to impress their friends, Mac users can go to System Preferences and reconfigure the keyboard to ensure that Windows and Mac keystrokes are exactly the same!

✛ *ICONS*

An icon is a symbol. Throughout *Statistics for People . . .* , you'll see a variety of icons. Here's what each one is and what each represents:

This icon represents information that goes beyond the regular text. At times we may want to elaborate on a particular point and find we can do so more easily outside of the flow of the usual material.

Here, we discuss some more technical ideas and tips to give you a sampling of topics beyond the scope of this course. You might find these interesting and useful.

Throughout *Statistics for People . . .* , you'll find a small-steps icon like the one you see here. This indicates that a set of steps is coming up that will direct you through a particular process. These steps have been tested and approved by whatever federal agency approves these things.

That finger with the bow is a cute icon, but its primary purpose is to help reinforce important points about the topic that you just read about. Try to emphasize these points in your studying, because they are usually central to the topic.

Many of the chapters in *Statistics for People . . .* provide detailed information about one or more statistical procedures and the computation that accompanies them. The computer icon is used to identify the "Using the Amazing Data Analysis Tools to . . ." section of the chapter.

The more Excel icon identifies additional information on the Excel feature that has just been mentioned or worked with in the text.

Appendix A, Excel-erate Your Learning: All You Need to Know About Excel, contains a collection of 50 basic and important (and time-saving) tasks that anyone who uses Excel should know.

Appendix B contains important tables you will learn about and need throughout the book.

And, in working through the exercises in this book, you will use the data sets in Appendix C. In the exercises, you'll find references to data sets with names like "Chapter 2 Data Set 1," and each of these sets is shown in Appendix C. You can either enter the data manually or download them from the publisher's site at http://edge .sagepub.com/salkindexcel4e or get them directly from the author. Just send a note to njs@ku.edu and don't forget to mention the edition for which you need the data sets.

Appendix D contains answers to end-of-chapter questions, Appendix E contains a primer on math for those who could use a refresher, and Appendix F offers the long-sought-after brownie recipe.

KEY TO DIFFICULTY ICONS

To help you along a bit, we placed a difficulty index at the beginning of each chapter. This adds some fun to the start of each chapter, but it's also a useful tip to let you know what's coming and how difficult chapters are in relation to one another.

☺ (very hard)

☺ ☺ (hard)

☺ ☺ ☺ (not too hard, but not easy either)

☺ ☺ ☺ ☺ (easy)

☺ ☺ ☺ ☺ ☺ (very easy)

KEY TO "HOW MUCH EXCEL" ICONS

To help you along a bit more, we placed a "How Much Excel" index at the beginning of each chapter. This adds even more fun (groan) to the start of each chapter, but it also lets you know how much Excel material is contained in the chapter.

How much Excel?

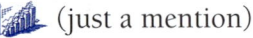 (just a mention)

 (some)

 (lots)

 (lots and lots)

(a ton)

GLOSSARY

Bolded terms in the text are included in the glossary at the back of the book.

SUMMARY

That couldn't have been that bad, right? We want to encourage you to continue reading and not worry about what's difficult or time-consuming or too complex for you to understand and apply. Just take one chapter at a time, as you did this one.

TIME TO PRACTICE

Because there's no substitute for the real thing, Chapters 1 through 17 and Chapter 20 each end with a set of exercises that will help you review the material that was covered in the chapter. As noted above, the answers to these exercises can be found near the end of the book in Appendix D.

For example, here is the first set of exercises (but don't look for any answers for these because these are kind of "on your own" answers— each answer is highly tied to your own experiences and interest).

1. Interview someone who uses statistics in his or her everyday work. It might be your adviser, an instructor, a researcher who lives on your block, a market analyst for a company, a city planner, or . . . Ask the person what his or her first statistics course was like. Find out what the person liked and didn't like. See if this individual has any suggestions to help you succeed. And most important, ask the person about how he or she uses these new-to-you tools at work.

2. We hope that you are part of a study group or, if that is not possible, that you have a telephone, e-mail, instant messaging, or webcam study buddy (or even more than one). And, of course, plenty of Facebook friends. Talk to your group or a fellow student in your class about similar likes, dislikes, fears, etc. about the statistics course. What do you have in common? Not in common? Discuss with your fellow student strategies to overcome your fears.

3. Search through your local newspaper (or any other publication) and find the results of a survey or interview about any topic. Summarize the results and do the best job you can describing how the researchers who were involved, or the authors of the survey, came to the conclusions they did. Their methods and reasoning may or may not be apparent. Once you have some idea of what they did, try to speculate as to what other ways the same information might be collected, organized, and summarized.

4. Go to the library (either in person or online) and find a copy of a journal article in your own discipline. Then, go through the article and highlight the section (usually the "Results" section) where statistical procedures were used to organize and analyze the data. You don't know much about the specifics of this yet, but how many different statistical procedures (such as t-test, mean, and calculation of the standard deviation) can you identify? Can you take the next step and tell your instructor how the results relate to the research question or the primary topic of the research study?

5. Find five websites that contain data on any topic and write a brief description of what type of information is offered and how it is organized. For example, if you go to the mother of all data sites, the US Census (www.census.gov), you'll find links to hundreds of databases, tables, and other informative tools. Try to find data and information that fit in your own discipline.

6. And the big extra-credit assignment is to find someone who actually uses Excel for daily data analysis needs. Ask why he or she uses Excel rather than a more specialized program such as SPSS or Minitab. Also, ask if there is anything specific about Excel that makes it stand out as a tool for data analysis. You may very well find these good folks in everything from political science to nursing, so search widely!

7. Finally, as your last in this first set of exercises, come up with five of the most interesting questions you can about your own area of study or interest. Do your best to come up with questions for which you would want real, existing information or data to answer. Be a scientist!

All You Need to Know About Formulas and Functions

Difficulty Scale ☺☺ (a little tough, but invaluable to stick with)

How much Excel? 📊 📊 📊 📊 (lots and lots)

WHAT YOU'LL LEARN ABOUT IN THIS CHAPTER

✦ The difference between formulas and functions

✦ How to create and use a formula

✦ The important Excel functions

✦ How to select and use a function

There may be nothing more valuable in your Excel magic tool box than formulas and functions. They both allow you to bypass (very) tedious calculations and get right to the heart of the matter. Both formulas and functions are shortcuts— and both work in different ways and do different things. Let's start with formulas.

WHAT'S A FORMULA?

You probably already know the answer to that question. A formula is a set of mathematical operators that performs a particular mathematical task. For example, here's a simple formula:

$$2 + 2 =$$

The operator + tells you to add certain values (a 2 and another 2) together to produce the outcome (4). This is a simple one.

Here's one that's a bit more advanced and one with which you will become more familiar in Chapter 16 of *Statistics for People . . .* :

$$Y = bX + a \qquad\qquad (1A.1)$$

This is the formula that is used to predict the value of Y' from our knowledge of the values of b, X, and a. We'll worry about what all those symbols mean later. For now, just know this is a formula that contains a bunch of symbols and mathematical operators and helps us compute numbers we need to make decisions.

Excel is a formula engine just ready to help make your learning of statistics easier.

Creating a Formula

A formula is created through these steps:

1. Click on the **cell** in which you want the results of the formula to appear.

2. Enter an equal sign, which looks like this: =. All formulas begin with an equal sign, no matter what else they contain.

3. Enter the formula. No spaces in formulas please—Excel does not like them.

4. Press the Enter key, and voilà! The results of the formula will appear in the selected cell.

For example, let's enter the formula that was shown earlier— 2 + 2—and see how these steps work.

As you can see in Figure 1A.1, we selected Cell A1.

Figure 1A.1   Selecting a Cell Into Which a Formula Will Be Entered

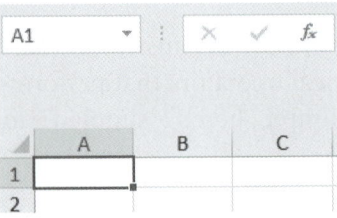

1. The equal sign is entered, as shown in Figure 1A.2. And, as you can see, the formula bar at the top of the column becomes active. Everything we enter in Cell A1 will appear in the formula bar. Also, note that Excel automatically enters the name of the last function used (in this example it is AVERAGE—much more about functions soon).

| **Figure 1A.2** | Entering the Equal Sign to Indicate the Beginning of a Formula |

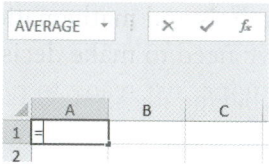

2. Enter the rest of the formula, which in this case is (2+4)/2, as you see in Figure 1A.3.

| **Figure 1A.3** | Entering the Formula in Cell A1 |

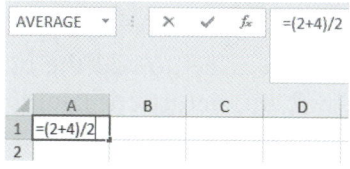

3. Press Enter, and the value of the formula is returned to the cell, as you see in Figure 1A.4. And, if you click on cell A1 (as we did in Figure 1A.4), you can see the formula located in that cell. In all cases, when a formula is entered into a cell, you see the results of that formula in the cell and the formula itself in the formula bar. In this case, the formula (2+4)/2 (shown in the formula bar) returns the result of 3.

| **Figure 1A.4** | The Value of a Formula Being Returned to the Cell |

A few notes:

- A formula always begins with an equal sign, which tells Excel that what follows is the formula.
- The formula itself always appears in the formula bar.
- The results of the formula (and not the formula itself) are returned to the selected cell.

This is the simplest example of how to use a formula. Formulas can become as complex as you need them to be.

 Want to see the formula behind the scenes in a worksheet? Just use the Ctrl+` key combination to toggle between formulas and the results of those formulas. The ` key is to the left of the number 1 key near the top of the keyboard.

Operator, Operator—Get Me a Formula!

You have just seen that even the simplest formulas consist of operators. In this case, the only operators are a plus (+) sign and a division (/) sign, which direct Excel to add the two values you see in Figure 1A.3, divide by 2, and return the sum to Cell A1.

Addition and division are just two of the operations you can perform. The most important operations and the symbols you use to accomplish them are shown in the following table.

Operator	Symbol	Example	What It Does
Addition	+ (plus)	=2+5	Adds 2 and 5.
Subtraction	– (minus)	=5–3	Subtracts 3 from 5.
Division	/ (slash)	=10/5	Divides 10 by 5.
Multiplication	* (asterisk)	=2*5	Multiplies 2 times 5.
Power of	^ (caret)	=4^2	Takes 4 to the power of 2, or squares 4.

Beware the Parentheses

When you create a formula that goes beyond a very simple one, it is critical for you to consider the order in which operations are carried out and the use of parentheses.

Let's say that we want to find the average score on a weekly test given each Friday for a month and the scores range from 0 to 100.

Here are Willy's scores:

Week 1   78

Week 2   56

Week 3   85

Week 4   92 (Willy finally got it!)

We need to create a formula that will add all of the scores together and divide the sum by 4. We'll name the scores w_1, w_2, w_3, and w_4. Here's one way we might try it:

$$w_1 + w_2 + w_3 + w_4/4$$

Oops! This will work in the sense that it will produce a number, but it won't give you the outcome you want. What this does is add w_1, w_2, and w_3 together and then adds that sum to the value of (only) w_4 divided by 4. This is not what we want.

Rather, take a look at this formula:

$$(w_1 + w_2 + w_3 + w_4)/4$$

This is more like it. Here, the four values are summed and then that sum is divided by 4. This one works. The lesson? Watch your parentheses!

WHAT'S A FUNCTION?

You know that a formula is a simple set of symbols (such as numbers and operators) that performs some calculation and results in an outcome in the cell where the formula lives.

A **function** is nothing other than a predefined formula. The good people who created Excel developed a whole bunch of functions that can do many different things, but throughout *Statistics for People . . .* , we deal only with those that are relevant to the things we do in these chapters. Functions fall under the general Formulas tab on the ribbon, as you see in Figure 1A.5.

Figure 1A.5   The Formulas Tab on the Excel Ribbon

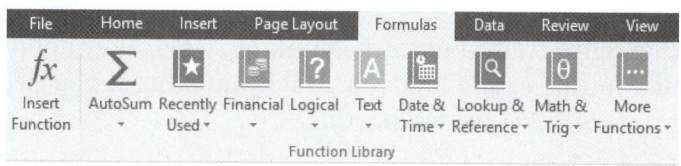

For example, there are groups of financial functions, logical functions, text functions, and others. But we're going to focus (mostly) on the functions that fall in the category of statistical functions and a few database functions. The group of statistical functions are visible on your screen only when you click on the More Functions drop-down box, which you see in Figure 1A.5, and then click Statistical. The group of database functions must be the black sheep of Excel because they don't have their own grouping on the Excel Ribbon. Instead, you have to click the Insert Function button on the left of the ribbon and then specify the group of database functions.

Functions that are relevant to the material covered in this book include AVERAGE (guess what that does) and T.TEST (guess, but you probably don't yet know). Some are too advanced for us to bother with, such as FISHER and GAMALIN. We'll leave those for the next course or for you to explore on your own.

Using a Function

Unlike a formula, a function is not created by you. You just tell it which values (located in which cells) you want to work with. Every formula contains two elements—the name of the function and the argument of the function. *Argument* doesn't mean the function is quarrelling over whose turn it is to wash the dishes. To understand what an Excel argument is, let's look at an example.

Here's a very simple function that averages a given set of numbers. In this example, this function averages the numbers in Cells A1 through A3:

=AVERAGE(A1:A3)

The *name* of the function is AVERAGE, and the *argument* is A1:A3—the cells on which you want the function to perform its magic. And as you can see, functions (like formulas) always, always, always begin with an equal sign.

Here's another function that produces the sum of a set of cells:

=SUM(A1:A3)

Simple, right? And, you may be thinking, "Well, why not just use a formula in this case?" and you could. But what if you need the sum of a set of 3,267 values like this?

=SUM(A1:A3267)

You really don't want to type in =(A1+A2+A3+A4 . . .) until you get to A3267, right? We thought not. Or what if you need a fancy-schmancy calculation that includes formulas that are very complex? Functions to the rescue!

So, let's get to the way that we use a function, and as an example, we'll use the AVERAGE function.

To use this (or any other function), you follow three steps:

1. Enter the function in the cell where you want the results to appear.

2. Enter the range of cells on which you want the function to operate.

3. Press the Enter key, and voilà! There you have the result located in the cell in which the function was created.

However, there are several ways to accomplish these three steps, and let's deal with those now.

Inserting a Function (When You Know the Function's Name and How It Works)

Here's the old-fashioned way.

1. Enter the function in the cell where you want the results to appear.

For example, in Figure 1A.6, you can see a data set of 10 values. We are going to find the average of those values using the AVER-AGE function. And, to make things a bit clearer, we entered a text label in the cell to the left of where we want the sum to appear.

Figure 1A.6 Creating a Data Set and the Location of the AVERAGE Function

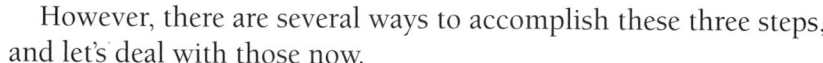

	A	B
1		Value
2		3
3		4
4		2
5		3
6		4
7		5
8		4
9		3
10		2
11		3
12	Average	

2. Type =AVERAGE(B2:B11) in Cell B12.

3. Press the Enter key, and presto: As you see in Figure 1A.7, the sum shows up in Cell B12, and in the formula bar, you can see the structure of the function.

Notice that the results of the function (3.3) are returned to the same cell (B12) where the function was entered. Pretty cool.

And not very difficult. And very convenient. Remember that you can do this with any function. But how do you know what the structure of the function is? That's where the next step comes in.

Figure 1A.7   The Completed AVERAGE Function

B12	▾	⋮	✕	✓	f_x	=AVERAGE(B2:B11)

◢	A	B	C	D	E
1		Value			
2		3			
3		4			
4		2			
5		3			
6		4			
7		5			
8		4			
9		3			
10		2			
11		3			
12	Average	3.3			

Okay—so how do you know what function to use? Well, certainly one way is through exploring different functions and finding out what they do (which you will do throughout *Statistics for People . . .*). Another is by using Excel Help (press F1 at any time and enter the terms on which you want help). And another way is to look at Table 1A.1 at the end of this little chapter, which gives you a heads-up on which functions we'll be mentioning (some in great detail and others just in passing) throughout the book and what they do.

Inserting a Function Using the Insert Function (fx) Command

Let's use the same example, the AVERAGE function, and assume you haven't used it before but know this is the one you want to use.

We're using the same data as shown in Figure 1A.6. First, erase the results of the function in Cell B12 by selecting the cell and hitting the space bar once and then Enter.

1. Select Cell B12.

2. Click the Formulas tab and the Insert Function command (*fx*). When you do this, you will see the Insert Function dialog box as shown in Figure 1A.8. In the Mac version, you see the Formula Builder dialog box, which does the same thing as the Insert Function dialog box in the Windows version.

Figure 1A.8 The Insert Function Dialog Box

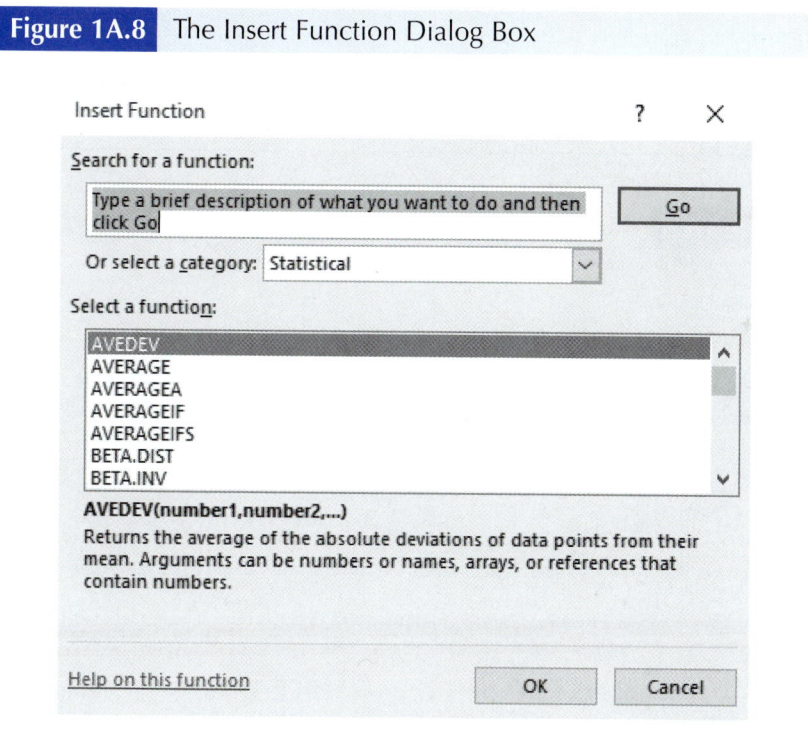

A very nice shortcut to the function command (*fx*) can be found on the Formula bar just to the left of where you see any information that is entered into a cell. Just click that, and you get the Insert Function dialog box.

3. Now you can do one of two things:

    a. Type a brief description of what you want to do, such as *average*, and click the Go button; or

    b. Find the function you want in the list of functions and double-click on it.

We selected option (b), and when we did, the Function arguments dialog box appeared, as shown in Figure 1A.9. Notice that Excel automatically assumed that we wanted to average all of the values above the current cell, and it completed the cell range in the Number 1 box.

Don't get too excited. A function's argument is not really an argument like a disagreement. An argument in mathematical terms is a set of premises, and that's exactly what you need to provide within the parentheses of any function—a set of premises that the function is to carry out.

Figure 1A.9 The Function Arguments Dialog Box

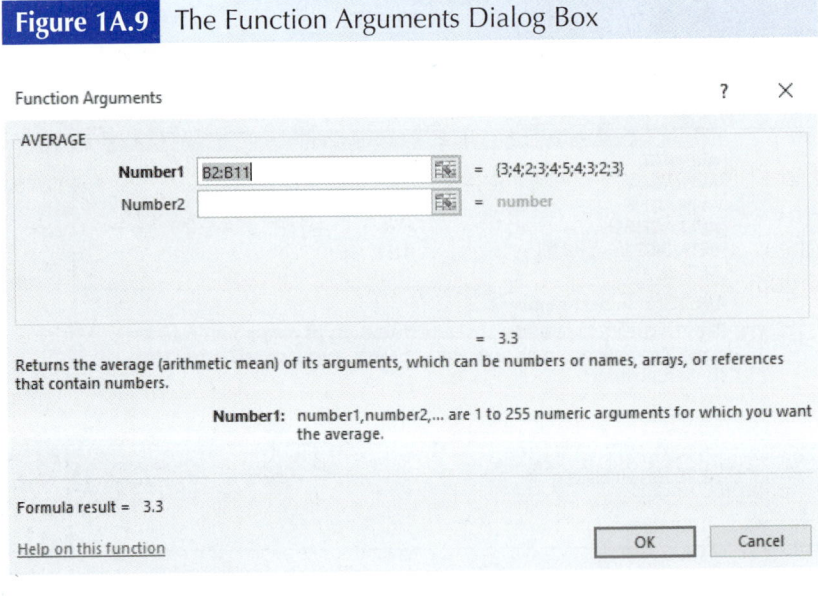

Let's take a look at the different elements in this dialog box.

- There's the name of the function, AVERAGE.
- Then there are text boxes where you enter the range of cells (the argument) on which you want the function to perform its

duty. Note that Excel is pretty smart and automatically enters the range of cells it thinks you want to average. Notice also that the actual numbers you want to average are listed to the right of the text box.

- In the middle of the dialog box is a description of what the function does, and above that is the value the function will return to the cell in which it is located (in this case, your average is 3.3).
- The syntax (or directions) of how to put the function together is given near the bottom, preceded by **Number 1**.
- The formula result is shown again at the bottom left.
- Finally, there is a link to a place to get help if you need it.

4. Click OK, and you will see the same result as you saw in Figure 1A.7. We entered the function using the Insert Function command instead of by typing its name, but we got the same result.

Inserting a Function Using Formulas → More Functions → Statistical

That really says it all. Just follow these three mouse clicks, and you will see a list of all the statistical functions that are available. Selecting any of them (such as AVERAGE) provides you with the same dialog box you see in Figure 1A.9.

Most functions can do a lot more than first appears. Excel functions are so useful because they are so flexible. For example, with the simplest of functions such as SUM, you can enter the following variations as arguments and get the following results.

If you enter the following formula . . .	Excel does this . . .
=SUM(3,4)	Adds the values to get 7.
=SUM(A2:A4)	Adds the values located in Cells A2 through A4.
=SUM(A2:A4,6)	Adds the values located in Cells A2 through A4 and also adds the value of 6 to that sum.
=SUM(A6:A8,4)	Adds the values located in Cells A6 to A8 and adds the value of 4 to that sum.

Now you know two ways to insert a function in a worksheet—by typing its name or selecting it through the Insert Function dialog box. And once a specific Function Arguments dialog box (like the one you see in Figure 1A.9) is open, you can just enter the cell addresses in the appropriate text box. However, you can also just click in the cell address box and then drag the mouse over the cell addresses you want to include in that box. This is good. But there's another nifty way to go about this. You can click on the Collapse button (which looks like this ▦), which will shrink the entire dialog box and allow you to select the cells you want using the mouse directly on the worksheet. Then click the Expand button, and the dialog box returns to its normal size with the cell addresses included.

If you insert a function by typing it directly into a cell (or even by typing a partial name), the 2016 version of Excel provides a list of similarly spelled functions as well as a tip about how to use your function, as you see in Figure 1A.10. Here we typed in =aver, and as we typed, Excel provided a list of various average functions plus a tip as to what the AVERAGE function does.

Figure 1A.10   Excel Helps You Choose the Right Function

11		3	
12	Average	=aver	
13		*f*x AVERAGE	Returns the average (arithmetic mean) of its arguments, which can be numbers or names, arrays, or references that contain numbers
14		*f*x AVERAGEA	
15		*f*x AVERAGEIF	
16		*f*x AVERAGEIFS	

Using Functions in Formulas

It's time to get a bit fancy. Now, formulas and functions are basically the same animal—they carry out instructions. There's just no reason why you can't include a function in a formula.

For example, let's say that you have three job evaluation scores (Eval 1, Eval 2, and Eval 3) as you see in Figure 1A.11. You also have a Fudge Factor (in column E), which is a value you can use to increase or decrease an employee's score at your discretion. For example, you want to increase employee GH's score by 3%, so you multiply the average evaluation score (from Eval 1, Eval 2, and Eval 3) by 1.03. Figure 1A.11 shows the formula that includes the AVERAGE function (which you will learn more about in Chapter 2).

Figure 1A.11	Using a Function in a Formula

F2 ▼ ⋮ ✕ ✓ *fx*   =AVERAGE(B2:D2)*E2

	A	B	C	D	E	F
1	Name	Eval 1	Eval 2	Eval 3	Fudge Factor	Final Score
2	HY	92	76	90	1.10	94.60
3	TT	73	70	80	1.02	75.82
4	HG	60	70	77	1.04	71.76
5	YU	70	67	67	1.09	74.12
6	NE	87	64	71	1.07	79.18
7	GH	77	74	67	1.03	74.85
8	QJ	96	69	99	1.03	90.64
9	US	93	84	83	1.10	95.33
10	TN	85	77	100	1.04	90.83
11	DF	67	64	77	1.09	75.57

As you can see in the formula bar shown in Figure 1A.11, the formula in Cell F2 looks like this:

=AVERAGE(B2:D2)*E2

And it reads like this: The contents of Cells B2 through D2 are averaged, and then that value is multiplied by the contents of Cell E2. We copied the formula from Cell F2 to Cells F3 through F11, and the results are shown in Column F.

We're Taking Names: Naming Ranges

It's certainly easy enough to enter cell addresses such as A1:A3—not much work involved there.

But what if you're dealing with a really large worksheet with hundreds of columns and rows and thousands of cells? Wouldn't it be nice if you could just enter a name that represents a certain range of cells rather than having to remember all those cell addresses? Desire it no more. Excel allows you to name a range, or a collection of cells.

For example, in Figure 1A.11, if you want to average the employees' second evaluations, instead of using the cell addresses C2:C11, why not just give the range of cells a name, such as eval2 or EVAL_2 (no spaces, please!)? Then, the average for that set of scores using the AVERAGE function would look like this—

$$=AVERAGE(EVAL\_2)$$

rather than like this—

$$=AVERAGE(C2:C11)$$

And if you can believe it, this only gets better—you can just paste that name into any formula or function with a few clicks. You don't even have to type anything!

Here's how to assign a name to a range of cells:

1. Highlight the range of cells you want to name.

2. Click the Name box at the left end of the formula bar (in the Mac version, it's the Define Name option on the Formulas bar).

3. Type the name that you want to use to refer to your selection, as shown in Figure 1A.12 (we used Eval_2). And again, no spaces please—Excel does not like them in name ranges.

Figure 1A.12   Naming a Selection of Cells as a Range

Eval_2	▼	⋮	✕	✓	*fx*	76

◢	A	B	C	D	E	F
1	Name	Eval 1	Eval 2	Eval 3	Fudge Factor	Final Score
2	HY	92	76	90	1.10	94.60
3	TT	73	70	80	1.02	75.82
4	HG	60	70	77	1.04	71.76
5	YU	70	67	67	1.09	74.12
6	NE	87	64	71	1.07	79.18
7	GH	77	74	67	1.03	74.85
8	QJ	96	69	99	1.03	90.64
9	US	93	84	83	1.10	95.33
10	TN	85	77	100	1.04	90.83
11	DF	67	64	77	1.09	75.57

4. Press Enter.

Using Ranges

Once a range is defined, you can use the name assigned instead of a cell range. If you remember that the data are named, you can just enter that name by using the drop-down menu now available in the Name Manager command area (on the Formulas tab), as shown in Figure 1A.13. Or you'll use the Apply Names option in the Mac version.

Figure 1A.13   Seeing Range Names

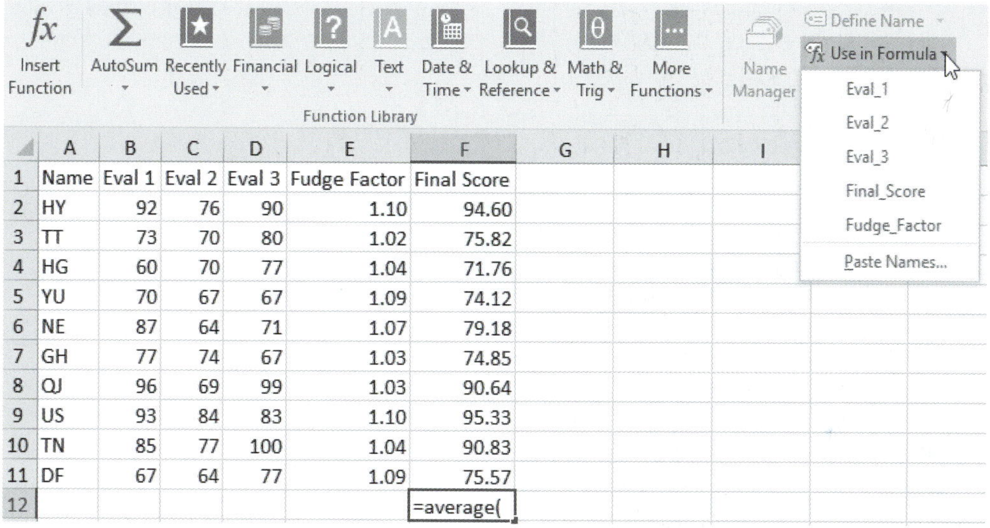

Let's use the ranges that were defined and compute the average of all the Fudge Factor scores.

1. Click on Cell F12, where the average will be placed.

2. Type =average(.

3. Click Formulas → Use in Formula, and you will see the Use in Formula drop-down menu, as shown in Figure 1A.14.

4. Click on Final_Score.

5. Type).

6. Click Enter and take a look at Figure 1A.15, where you can see how the name was used in the function rather than the cell addresses of F2 through F11.

Figure 1A.14   The Menu for Selecting a Range of Cells

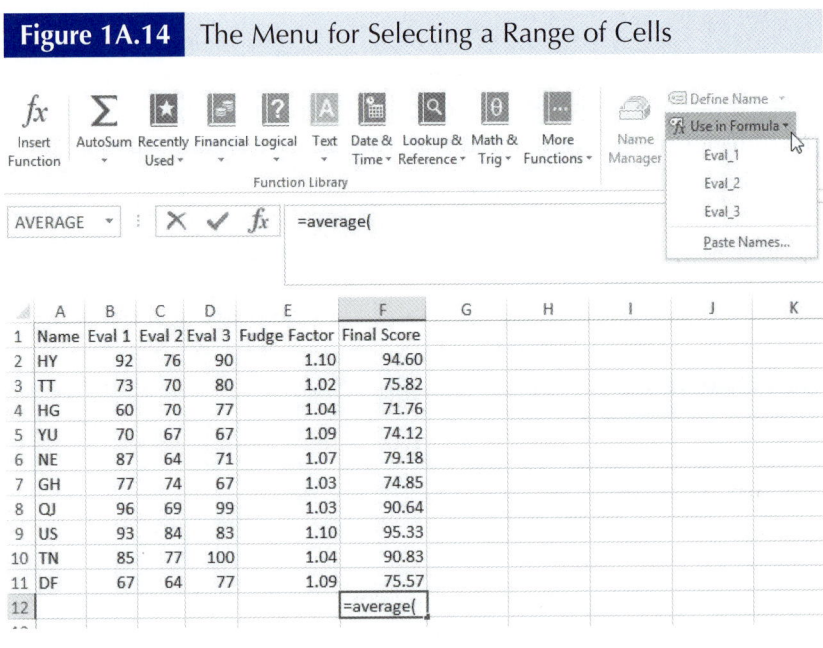

Figure 1A.15   Inserting a Cell Range Into a Function

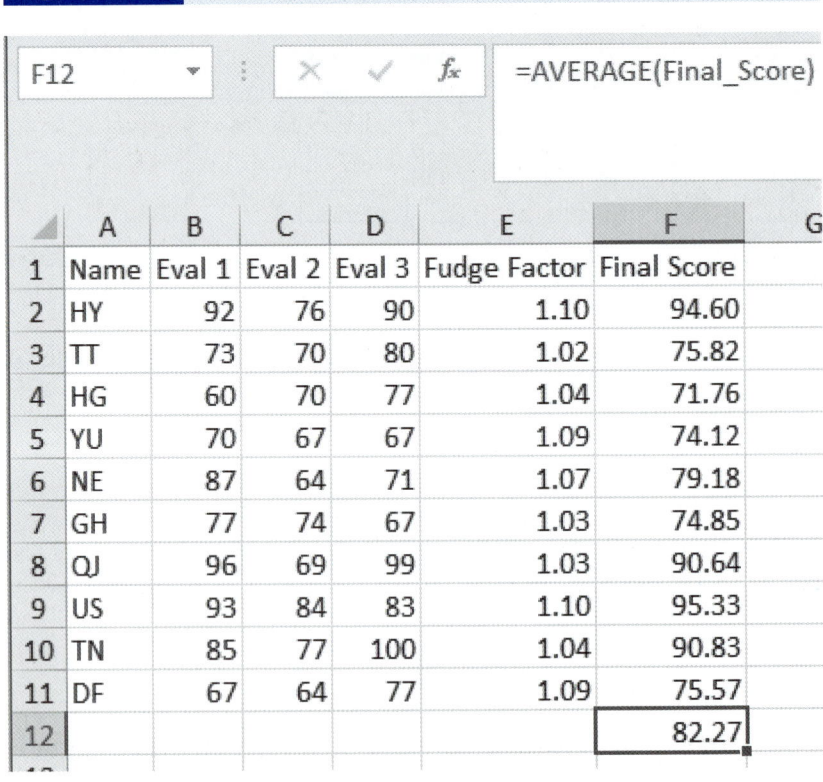

REAL-WORLD STATS

Real-World Stats will appear at the end of every chapter and, hopefully, will provide you with a demonstration of how a particular method, test, idea, or some other aspect of statistics is used in the everyday work of scientists, physicians, policy makers, government folks, and others.

In this first such feature, we look at a very short paper in which the author shares the argument for the National Academy of Sciences (first chartered in 1863, by the way!) to "whenever called upon by any department of the Government, investigate, examine, experiment, and report upon any subject of science or art." This charter, in turn, led to the formation of the National Research Council some 50 years later in 1916, another nonprofit that provides policy makers with information they need to make informed decisions. Often this "information" takes the form of quantitative data—also referred to as statistics—that assist people in evaluating alternative approaches to problems with a wide-ranging impact on the public. So, this article, as does your book and the class you are taking, points out how important it is to think clearly and use data to support your arguments.

Want to know more? Go online or go to the library, and look for . . .

Cicerone, R. (2010). The importance of federal statistics for advancing science and identifying policy options. *The ANNALS of the American Academy of Political and Social Science, 631,* 25–27.

SUMMARY

This may be a "little" chapter, but it contains some of the most useful tools that Excel has to offer. In fact, the uses of formulas and functions are limited only by your imagination. As you use Excel, you will find more and more ways to make these powerful tools work exactly the way you need them to.

TIME TO PRACTICE

1. Create formulas for the following in an Excel worksheet:

   a. Add the values of 3 and 5 to one another.

   b. Subtract the value of 5 from 10 and multiply the outcome by 7.

    c. Average the values 5, 6, 7, and 8.

    d. Find the sum of the squared values of 3, 4, and 5.

2. Use the AVERAGE function to add the values of 3, 5, and 7 and divide the total by 3.

3. What would the function look like for summing the values in Cells A1 through A5?

4. What would the function look like for averaging the values in Cells A1 through A5?

5. Create a worksheet with any five values in Cells A1 through A5, name the range of these cells Test_Scores, and enter a function in Cell A6 that computes the average. Can you think of another way to do this?

| Table 1A.1 | The Functions You'll Love to Love* | |

The Function Name	What It Does	The Chapter in Which You'll Read About It
AVERAGE	Returns the average of its arguments	2
CHISQ.DIST	Returns the one-tailed probability of the chi-square distribution	17
CHISQ.TEST	Returns the test for independence	17
CORREL	Returns the correlation coefficient between two data sets	5 and 16
COUNTIF	Counts the number of nonblank cells within a range given certain criteria	2 and 20
DAVERAGE	Returns the average for a set of entries contained in a database	20
F.DIST	Returns the F probability distribution	13
F.TEST	Returns the result of an F-test	13
FORECAST	Returns a value along a linear trend	16
FREQUENCY	Returns a frequency distribution as a vertical array	16
GEOMEAN	Returns the geometric mean	2
INTERCEPT	Returns where a regression line crosses the y-axis	16
KURT	Returns the kurtosis of a data set	4

The Function Name	What It Does	The Chapter in Which You'll Read About It
LINEST	Returns the parameters of a linear trend	16
MEDIAN	Returns the median of the given numbers	2
MODE.MULTI	Returns the most common values in a data set	2
MODE.SNGL	Returns the most common value in a data set	2
NORM.S.DIST	Returns the standard normal cumulative distribution	8
PEARSON	Returns the Pearson product moment correlation coefficient	5
QUARTILE.INC	Returns the quartile of a data set	2
SKEW	Returns the skewness of a distribution	4
SLOPE	Returns the slope of the linear regression line	16
STANDARDIZE	Returns a normalized value	8
STDEV.P	Calculates standard deviation based on the entire population	3
STDEV.S	Estimates standard deviation based on a sample	3
STEYX	Returns the standard error of the predicted y value for each x in the regression	16
T.DIST	Returns the Student's t distribution	11, 12
T.TEST	Returns the probability associated with a Student's t-test	11, 12
TREND	Returns values along a linear trend	16
VAR.P	Calculates variance based on the entire population	3
VAR.S	Estimates variance based on a sample	3
Z.TEST	Returns the probability of a one-tailed z value	10

*Some of the names of the functions that appeared in the Excel 2007 and 2010 versions (and earlier) have changed slightly. For example, TTEST became TEST (leaving the general Excel user, of course, clueless as to why the change occurred).

1B All You Need to Know About Using the Amazing Data Analysis Tools

Difficulty Scale ☺ ☺ (a little tough, but invaluable to stick with)

How much Excel? (a ton)

WHAT YOU'LL LEARN ABOUT IN THIS CHAPTER

✦ What the Data Analysis tools are and what they do

(Almost) everything you need to know about Excel, you can learn in Appendix A. But certain Excel procedures are available only if you have the Data Analysis tools (which used to be called the Data Analysis Toolpak) installed, and we use those tools in several chapters in this book. Excel refers to this set of tools as the Data Analysis Tools, but you will see it on your screen as Data Analysis tools (and same for the Mac). No worries; the set of tools, no matter its name, does the same thing. And remember, for the Windows version, the Data Analysis tools is an Excel add-in—a special set of tools that may not have been installed when Excel was originally installed.

How do you know if this add-in is installed on the computer you are using? If the Data Analysis tools item doesn't appear on the Data tab (usually at the right-hand side of the Data tab), you need to install it. Either ask your instructor to have this done on the network level where Excel nay be installed or install it on your own machine as discussed in Chapter 1. For the Mac version, the Toolpak is automatically installed.

The Data Analysis tools are easy to use. You just follow the instructions and identify the analysis you want to perform and the data on

40

which you want it performed, and you're done. Throughout *Statistics for People . . .* , we will show you in detailed steps how this is done.

One more note: As you already know from Table 1A.1, there are many functions, and some of these have counterparts in the Data Analysis tools. For example, you can perform a test for the difference between the means of two groups using a function (T.TEST) or using the Data Analysis tools (using the *t*-test tool—say that three times fast). That's all for the better. You will often have more than one way to analyze your data—always a nice position to be in.

A LOOK AT THE DATA ANALYSIS TOOLS

For now, let's just look at some output where we took a random sample of 5 numbers from a group of 25 numbers. In Figure 1B.1, you see the data in Column A; the sample of 5 numbers in Column C; and the Sampling dialog box that we used from the Data Analysis tools to tell Excel what to sample, how many to sample, and where to put the results. Much more about this later in the book, but we thought you'd like to see how this cool set of tools works.

Figure 1B.1   Using the Sampling Tool From the Data Analysis Tools

	A	B	C	D	E	F	G	H	I	J
1	Score									
2	50		42			Sampling			? X	
3	42		57							
4	45		55			Input			OK	
5	48		55			Input Range:	$A$2:$A$26			
6	59		59			☐ Labels			Cancel	
7	43					Sampling Method			Help	
8	42					○ Periodic				
9	60					Period:				
10	45					◉ Random				
11	41					Number of Samples:	5			
12	43									
13	42					Output options				
14	43					◉ Output Range:	$C$2:$C$6			
15	42					○ New Worksheet Ply:				
16	58					○ New Workbook				
17	60									
18	56									
19	60									
20	41									
21	50									
22	53									
23	51									
24	55									
25	53									
26	49									

For our purposes, we will be working with the following Data Analysis tools (we'll be working with about three fourths of them—the others are more advanced than we need). And in the appropriate chapter (such as Chapter 2), you will learn about particular tools (such as Descriptive Statistics):

ANOVA

Correlation

Descriptive Statistics

Histogram

Moving Average

Random Number Generation

Rank and Percentile

Regression

Sampling

t-test

Z-test

Now take a look at Figure 1B.2 and you can see a side-by-side comparison of the Windows and Mac Excel output from using the

Figure 1B.2	A Comparison of Data Analysis Tools Output for the Windows and Mac Versions of Excel

	A	B	C
1	Score	Score	
2	42		
3	51	Mean	49.1
4	45	Standard Error	1.83
5	40	Median	51
6	52	Mode	51
7	53	Standard Deviation	5.78
8	51	Sample Variance	33.43
9	45	Kurtosis	-0.99
10	54	Skewness	-0.24
11	58	Range	18
12		Minimum	40
13		Maximum	58
14		Sum	491
15		Count	10

	A	B	C
1	Score	Score	
2	42		
3	51	Mean	49.1
4	45	Standard Error	1.83
5	40	Median	51
6	52	Mode	51
7	53	Standard Deviation	5.78
8	51	Sample Variance	33.43
9	45	Kurtosis	-0.99
10	54	Skewness	-0.24
11	58	Range	18
12		Minimum	40
13		Maximum	58
14		Sum	491
15		Count	10

Descriptive Statistics options in the Data Analysis tools. As you can see, the output is virtually identical. The way each version is used is virtually identical as well.

DON'T HAVE IT? (INSTALLATION AGAIN!)

The Data Analysis tools is an Excel add-in for the Windows version. An add-in is a program that adds custom commands and features to Microsoft Office. Microsoft Office is Excel's mother ship. For the Mac version, there's no installation necessary.

To load the Data Analysis tools into Excel, follow these steps:

1. Click the File Tab and then click Options.
2. Click Add-Ins and then, in the Manage box, select Data Analysis tools.
3. Click Go.
4. In the Add-Ins dialog box, select the Data Analysis tools check box and click OK.

And you are done and ready to make your Excel activities even that much more productive and fun.

1C For Mac Lovers Who Are Still Using Version 2011

Rejoice!! And, for Mac Lovers Who Are New to Version 2016, Rejoice More!!!

A MAC ALTERNATIVE TO THE DATA ANALYSIS TOOLS

Mac users of Excel need no longer feel like second-rate citizens, because the 2016 version for the Mac does indeed offer the Data Analysis tools feature.

However, for those of you who have yet to upgrade to the newest 2016 version for the Mac, StatPlus (officially called StatPlus: Mac LE) from AnalystSoft is a free Excel add-in that performs many of the same types of analysis as do the Data Analysis tools. It is easy to install and easy to use, and it provides a valuable set of analytic tools. You can download it from http://www.analystsoft .com/en/products/statplusmacle/. An important note: There is a StatPlus Pro version that is not free of charge, and you may be asked to upgrade to that version. There are a good number of more advanced analytic procedures that you can only do using the Pro version, so while the free version gives you a good idea of how StatPlus works, to do everything, you'll need to upgrade. Ask you instructor to have your university buy a license for the Pro version so everyone can access it.

In previous editions of *Statistics for People . . .* (the Excel version), we have mentioned this tool, but this is the first time that we go into any detail about how it is used. And here's an early peek. In Figure 1C.1, you can see a set of sample data (10 test scores) and the results of a descriptive analysis using StatPlus—all on the same spreadsheet just the way the Data Analysis tools do it. And, of course, like any Excel information, it can be manipulated to appear as you need it—lines or columns deleted, table templates used, font size and style adjusted, etc.

Figure 1C.1	Sample StatPlus Output

	A	B	C	D	E	F
1	Score		Alpha value (for confidence interval)	0.02		
2	45			Variable #1 (Score)		
3	65		Count	10	Skewness	0.09384
4	78		Mean	62.4	Skewness Standard Error	0.61451
5	67		Mean LCL	49.21181	Kurtosis	2.61218
6	59		Mean UCL	75.58819	Kurtosis Standard Error	0.92244
7	61		Variance	218.48889	Alternative Skewness (Fisher's)	0.11128
8	67		Standard Deviation	14.78137	Alternative Kurtosis (Fisher's)	0.27868
9	55		Mean Standard Error	4.67428	Coefficient of Variation	0.23688
10	38		Minimum	38.	Mean Deviation	10.8
11	89		Maximum	89.	Second Moment	196.64
12			Range	51.	Third Moment	258.768
13			Sum	624.	Fourth Moment	101,005.9712
14			Sum Standard Error	46.7428	Median	63.
15			Total Sum Squares	40,904.	Median Error	1.85257
16			Adjusted Sum Squares	1,966.4	Percentile 25% (Q1)	57.
17			Geometric Mean	60.75875	Percentile 75% (Q2)	72.5
18			Harmonic Mean	59.04782	IQR	15.5
19			Mode	67.	MAD	6.

Getting Started With StatPlus

There are many ways to use StatPlus, but here's the most direct and pragmatic:

1. Open the worksheet of data you want to analyze in Microsoft Excel. If you have not already created a worksheet of data, then open a blank worksheet and enter the data you want to analyze.

2. Open StatPlus.

3. Perform the analysis you want.

Computing Descriptive Statistics

Here's how we computed the output you see in Figure 1C.1.

1. Open the worksheet containing the Excel data as you see in Figure 1C.2.

Figure 1C.2   Sample Excel Data

	A
1	Score
2	45
3	65
4	78
5	67
6	59
7	61
8	67
9	55
10	38
11	89

2. Open StatPlus.

3. Click Statistics → Basic Statistics and Tables → Descriptive Statistics. When you do this, you will see the Descriptive Statistics dialog box as shown in Figure 1C.3, where you will define the range that contains the data you want to analyze.

Figure 1C.3   Defining the Range for Analysis

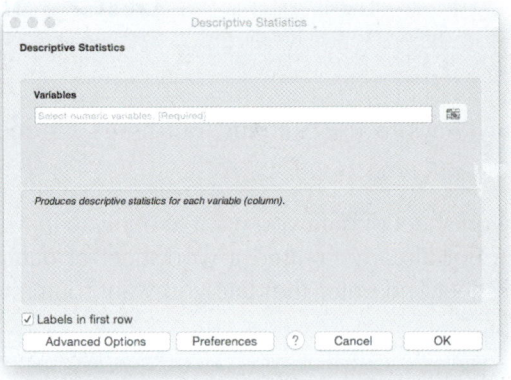

4. Select the range of data you want to analyze by either selecting the range in the worksheet (the easiest way), using the Collapse button, or entering the range using the keyboard. If you have column headings for the data, be sure to click the Labels in First Row check box in the Descriptive Statistics Window.

5. Click OK and you'll see results as shown in Figure 1C.1. Figure 1C.4 shows the same results after a good deal of cleanup using various Excel features.

Figure 1C.4 StatPlus Output After Format Changes

	A	B
1	**Score**	
2	Count	10
3	Mean	62.4
4	Variance	218.49
5	Standard Deviation	14.78
6	Minimum	38
7	Maximum	89
8	Range	51
9	Sum	624
10	Mode	67
11	Skewness	0.09
12	Kurtosis	2.61
13	Median	63.00
14	Percentile 25% (Q1)	57.00
15	Percentile 75% (Q2)	72.50

Options and Preferences

As you can see in Figure 1C.3, there are both Advanced Options and Preferences buttons in the box where you define the range containing the data to be analyzed.

The Advanced options contain different options for different analytic tools. For the Descriptive Statistics tool, you can select such options as plotting a histogram, creating a normal curve (nice!), and defining the range of intervals. Options change with the analytic tool being used.

The Preferences button reveals preferences that are constant for all StatPlus analytic tools and allows you to change font design and size, number of decimal places used, and even how missing data are handled.

What StatPlus Can Do

Since you're interested in StatPlus, here's what's covered in various chapters in the book and the corresponding StatPlus analytic tool. This should help you to figure out what to use when. You'll need either the basic version of StatPlus or the Pro version depending upon the analysis you want to complete.

Chapter in Statistics for People . . .	StatPlus Analytic Tool
Chapter 2. Computing and Understanding Averages: Means to an End	Basic Statistics and Tables → Descriptive Statistics
Chapter 3. Vive la Différence: Understanding Variability	Basic Statistics and Tables → Descriptive Statistics
Chapter 4. A Picture Really Is Worth a Thousand Words	Basic Statistics and Tables → Histogram
Chapter 5. Ice Cream and Crime: Computing Correlation Coefficients	Basic Statistics and Tables → Linear Correlation
Chapter 6. Just the Truth: An Introduction to Understanding Reliability and Validity	Basic Statistics and Tables → Linear Correlation
Chapter 7. Hypotheticals and You: Testing Your Questions	
Chapter 8. Are Your Curves Normal? Probability and Why It Counts	
Chapter 9. Significantly Significant: What It Means for You and Me	
Chapter 10. Only the Lonely: The One-Sample Z-Test	Basic Statistics and Tables → One Sample z test for Mean . . .
Chapter 11. t(ea) for Two: Tests Between the Means of Different Groups	Comparing Means (T-Test) . . .
Chapter 12. t(ea) for Two (Again): Tests Between the Means of Related Groups	Comparing Means (T-Test) . . .
Chapter 13. Two Groups Too Many? Try Analysis of Variance	Analysis of Variance (ANOVA)
Chapter 14. Two Too Many Factors: Factorial Analysis of Variance—A Brief Introduction	Analysis of Variance (ANOVA)
Chapter 15. Cousins or Just Good Friends? Testing Relationships and the Significance of the Correlation Coefficient	Basic Statistics and Tables → Linear Correlation
Chapter 16. Predicting Who'll Win the Super Bowl: Using Linear Regression	Regression → Linear Correlation
Chapter 17. What to Do When You're Not Normal: Chi-Square and Some Other Nonparametric Tests	Nonparametric Statistics → Chi Square X^2 Test

PART II

Σigma Freud and Descriptive Statistics

Snapshots

And you thought *your* statistics professor was tough.

One of the things that Sigmund Freud, the founder of psychoanalysis, did quite well was to observe and describe the nature of his patients' conditions. An astute observer, he used his skills to develop the first systematic and comprehensive theory of personality. Regardless of what you may think about the validity of his ideas, he was a good scientist. Back in the early 20th century, courses in statistics (like the one you are taking) were not offered as part of undergraduate or graduate curricula. The field was relatively new, and the nature of scientific explorations did not demand the precision that this set of tools brings to the scientific arena.

But things have changed. Now, in almost any endeavor, numbers count (as Francis Galton, the inventor of correlation and a first cousin to Charles Darwin, said as well). This section of *Statistics for People Who (Think They) Hate Statistics, Excel 2016 Edition* is devoted to how we can use Excel's most basic statistical functions to describe an outcome and better understand it.

Chapter 2 discusses measures of central tendency and how computing one of several different types of averages gives you the one best **data point** that represents a set of scores. Chapter 3 completes the coverage of tools we need to fully describe a set of data points with its discussion of variability, including the standard deviation and variance. When you get to Chapter 4, you will be ready to learn how distributions, or sets of scores, differ from one another and what this difference means. Chapter 5 deals with the nature of relationships between variables—namely, correlations—and the last of the chapters in this part, Chapter 6, focuses on reliability and validity, two topics that are critical in evaluating the assessment tools used in any research setting.

When you finish Part II, you'll be in excellent shape to start understanding the role that probability and inference play in the social and behavioral sciences.

2 Computing and Understanding Averages

Means to an End

Difficulty Scale ☺ ☺ ☺ ☺ (moderately easy)

How much Excel? 📊 📊 📊 📊 (a ton)

WHAT YOU'LL LEARN ABOUT IN THIS CHAPTER

◆ Understanding measures of central tendency

◆ Computing the mean for a set of scores using the AVERAGE function

◆ Computing the mode for a set of scores using the MODE function

◆ Computing the median for a set of scores using the MEDIAN function

◆ Using the Data Analysis tools to compute descriptive statistics

◆ Selecting a measure of central tendency

Y ou've been very patient, and now it's finally time to get started working with some real, live data. That's exactly what you'll do in this chapter. Once data are collected, a usual first step is to organize the information using simple indexes to describe the data. The easiest way to do this is through computing an average, of which there are several different types.

An **average** is the one value that best represents an entire group of scores. It doesn't matter whether the group of scores is the number correct on a spelling test for 30 fifth graders or the batting percentage of each of the New York Yankees for the entire season or the number of people who registered as Democrats or Republicans in the last 10 elections. In all of these examples, groups of data can be summarized using an average. You can also think of an average as the "middle" space or as a fulcrum on a seesaw. It's the point where all the values in a set of values are balanced.

Averages, also called **measures of central tendency**, come in three flavors: the mean, the median, and the mode. Each provides you with a different type of information about a distribution of scores and is simple to compute and interpret.

COMPUTING THE MEAN

The **mean** is the most common type of average that is computed. It is simply the sum of all the values in a group divided by the number of values in that group. So if you had the spelling scores for 30 fifth graders, you would simply add up all the scores and then divide that total by the number of students, which is 30. The formula for computing the mean is shown in Formula 2.1:

$$\bar{X} = \frac{\Sigma X}{n},$$

(2.1)

where

- the letter $\bar{X}$ with a line above it (also called "X bar") is the mean value of the group of scores or the mean;
- the Σ, or the Greek letter sigma, is the summation sign, which tells you to add together whatever follows it;
- the X is each individual score in the group of scores; and
- the n is the size of the sample from which you are computing the mean.

To compute the mean, follow these steps:

1. List the entire set of values in one or more columns. These are all the Xs.
2. Compute the sum or total of all the values.
3. Divide the total or sum by the number of values.

For example, if you needed to compute the average number of shoppers at three locations, you would compute a mean for that value.

Location	Number of Annual Customers
Lanham Park Store	2,150
Williamsburg Store	1,534
Downtown Store	3,564

The mean or average number of shoppers in each store is 2,416. Formula 2.2 shows how this was computed using the formula you saw in Formula 2.1:

$$\bar{X} = \frac{\sum X}{n} = \frac{2,150+1,534+3,564}{3} = 2,416 \qquad (2.2)$$

See, we told you it was easy. No big deal.

And Now . . . Using Excel's AVERAGE Function

To compute the mean of a set of numbers using Excel, follow these steps:

For some reason, the people who name functions would rather call the one that computes the mean AVERAGE than MEAN. Yikes—these same folks used the name MEDIAN to name the function that computes the median, and they assigned the name MODE to the function that computes the mode, so why not make everyone's life easier and assign the name MEAN to the function that computes the mean? If you find out, let us know.

1. Enter the individual scores into one column in a worksheet, such as you see in Figure 2.1.

Figure 2.1 Data That Will Be Used to Compute an Average Score

	A
1	2150
2	1534
3	3564

2. Select the cell (an intersection of a row and a column) into which you want to enter a formula to compute the average of the values in these three cells or compute the value of the AVERAGE function. In this example, we are going to compute the mean in Cell A5, and we'll show you the two ways to do this.

3. Create a formula in Cell A5 that would average the three values. The formula would look like this:

$$=(A1 + A2 + A3)/3$$

Or click on Cell A5 and type the AVERAGE function (which we did):

$$=AVERAGE(A1:A3)$$

And press the Enter key.

Another option: Use the Formulas → Insert Function menu option and the "Inserting a Function" technique we talked about in Little Chapter 1a to enter the AVERAGE function in Cell A5.

Whether you type in a function or enter it using the Formulas → Insert Function option, it looks the same and no one will ever, ever, ever know how you did it. Once it's there, whether typed or inserted, it does exactly the same thing.

As you can see in Figure 2.2, the mean was computed and the value returned to Cell A5. Notice that in the **formula bar** (where you can see the contents of a cell) in Figure 2.2, you can see the AVERAGE function fully expressed and the value computed as 2,416, just the way it looked when we did it manually.

Figure 2.2 Using the AVERAGE Function to Compute the Mean of a Set of Numbers

A5	▼	⋮	✕	✓	*fx*	=AVERAGE(A1:A3)

◢	A	B	C	D	E
1	2,150				
2	1,534				
3	3,564				
4					
5	2,416				

You may also want to explore the geometric mean (the function is **GEOMEAN**). The geometric mean is used when you have two or more metrics to describe different sets of data. For example, you may rank customer satisfaction with certain health care programs on a 1–10 scale but rank the quality of the same programs' health care outcomes on a 1–100 scale.

Here are some things to keep in mind about the mean:

- The mean is also sometimes represented by the letter *M* and is also called the typical, average, or most central score. If you are reading another statistics book or a research report and you see something like *M* = 45.87, it probably means that the mean is equal to 45.87. Also, remember that the population mean is represented by the Greek symbol μ (*mu*).
- In the formula, a small *n* represents the sample size for which the mean is being computed. A large *N* (like this) would represent the population size. In some books and in some journal articles, no distinction is made between the two.
- The sample mean is the measure of central tendency that most accurately reflects the population mean.
- The mean is like the fulcrum on a seesaw. It's the centermost point where all the values on one side of the mean are equal in weight to all the values on the other side of the mean.
- Finally, for better or worse, the mean is very sensitive to extreme scores. An extreme score can pull the mean in one direction or another and make it less representative of the set of scores and less useful as a measure of central tendency. How representative the mean is, of course, depends on the values for which it is being computed. More about this later.

You just learned (we hope!) how the mean is sensitive to extreme scores, meaning that one or more extreme values can throw off what would otherwise be a pretty good representation of what the whole set of scores looks like. So, what's an extreme score? That's a very good question and one without a very good answer. And this is a question that well illustrates that the study of statistics is not just the study of "yes or no" or "black and white" rules. There is plenty of room for nuanced decisions. An extreme score, on first look, is one that just looks much different from the majority, if not all, of the other scores in the group. It's an **outlier** or one that does not belong—one that just seems like it should not be there. There's no statistical formula or rule for determining this (although there's plenty of discussion about it among professional statisticians). Instead, you need to make a judgment call as to what scores might be anomalies or not even belong in a set of scores. Trust your judgment and take some risks—that's what science (and statistics) is all about.

The mean that we just computed is also referred to as the **arithmetic mean**, and you may read about other types of means, such as the harmonic mean. Those are used in special circumstances but need not concern you here. And if you want to be technical about it, the arithmetic mean (which is the one that we have discussed up to now) is also defined as the point at which the sum of the deviations about it is equal to zero (whew!). So, if you have scores like 3, 4, and 5 (where the mean is 4), the sum of the deviations about the mean (–1, 0, and +1) is 0.

In addition to the arithmetic mean (and many other kinds of averages), there's also the moving average, brought to you by the Data Analysis tools. Using the Moving Average tool, you can compute the average of a set of scores in chunks. For example, say you have the numbers 1, 4, 5, and 10. The average of these is 5.0. But a moving average taking two measures at a time (the average of 1 + 4, the average of 4 + 5, and the average of 5 + 10) equals 4.88. The moving average, in some cases, is a bit more accurate because it takes into account scores that are extreme or unique in the set (in this case, the 10). The Moving Average tool also generates a chart that plots the actual data against the averages for each point.

Remember that the word *average* means only the one measure that best represents a set of scores and that there are many different types of averages. Which type of average you use depends on the question that you are asking and the type of data you are trying to summarize. More about this later.

COMPUTING A WEIGHTED MEAN

You've just seen an example of how to compute a simple mean. But there may be situations in which one or more values occur more than once and you want to compute a weighted mean. A weighted mean can be computed easily by multiplying each value by the frequency of its occurrence, adding the total of all the products, and then dividing by the total number of occurrences.

To compute a weighted mean, follow these steps:

1. List all the values in the sample for which the mean is being computed, such as those shown in the column labeled Value (the value of X) in the following table.
2. List the frequency with which each value occurs.
3. Multiply the value by the frequency, as shown in the third column.
4. Sum all the values in the Value × Frequency column.
5. Divide by the total frequency.

For example, here's a table that organizes the values and frequencies of scores on a flying proficiency test for 100 airline pilots.

Value	Frequency	Value × Frequency
97	4	388
94	11	1,034
92	12	1,104
91	21	1,911
90	30	2,700
89	12	1,068
78	9	702
60 (don't fly with this guy)	1	60
Total	100	8,967

The weighted mean is 8,967/100, or 89.67. Computing the mean this way is much easier than entering 100 scores into your calculator or computer program.

How can we do this using Excel? Quite easily. Just follow these steps:

1. Enter the data you see in the above table in a new worksheet.

2. Create a formula like the one you see in Cell C2 to multiply the value by the frequency, as shown in Figure 2.3.

Figure 2.3   Using Excel to Compute a Weighted Mean

	A	B	C
1	Value	Frequency	Values x Frequency
2	97	4	=A2*B2
3	94	11	
4	92	12	
5	91	21	
6	90	30	
7	89	12	
8	78	9	
9	60	1	

3. Copy the formula down the column so that Cells C2 through C9 contain the multiplied values.

Remember that a cell contains information. Sometimes, that information is a formula, even though what you see is the results of that formula. You can use the Ctrl+` key combination to show the formulas or functions in a cell, rather than the results of that formula or function.

4. In Cells B10 and C10, use the SUM function to total the columns.

5. Now, placing the results in Cell C12, divide the total sum (in Cell C10) by the total frequency (in Cell B10), as you see in Figure 2.4. Ta-da! You did it again and arrived at a weighted average of 89.67, just as we showed above.

Figure 2.4	The Computation of a Weighted Mean

	A	B	C
1	Value	Frequency	Values x Frequency
2	97	4	388
3	94	11	1,034
4	92	12	1,104
5	91	21	1,911
6	90	30	2,700
7	89	12	1,068
8	78	9	702
9	60	1	60
10		100	8967
11			
12		Weighted Average	89.67

In basic statistics, an important distinction needs to be made between those values associated with samples (parts of a population) and those associated with populations. To do this, statisticians use the following conventions. For a sample statistic (such as the mean of a sample), Roman letters are used. For a population parameter (such as the mean of a population), Greek letters are used. So, the mean of the spelling score for a sample of 100 fifth graders is represented by $\bar{X}_5$, whereas the mean of the spelling score for the entire population of fifth graders is represented as μ_5, using the Greek letter mu.

COMPUTING THE MEDIAN

The median is also an average, but of a very different kind. The **median** is defined as the **midpoint** in a set of scores. It's the point that one half, or 50%, of the scores fall above and one half, or 50%, fall below. It's got some special qualities that we talk about later in this section, but for now, let's concentrate on how it is computed. There's no standard formula (but there is an Excel function, as we will see later) for computing the median.

To compute the median, follow these steps:

1. List the values in order, either from highest to lowest or lowest to highest.
2. Find the score exactly in the middle. That's the median.

For example, here are the incomes from five households:

$135,456

$25,500

$32,456

$54,365

$37,668

Here is the list ordered from highest to lowest:

$135,456

$54,365

$37,668

$32,456

$25,500

There are five values. The middle value is $37,668, and that's the median.

Now, what if the number of values is even? Let's add a value ($34,500) to the list so there are six income levels. Here they are:

$135,456

$54,365

$37,668

$34,500

$32,456

$25,500

When there is an even number of values, the median is simply the average of the two middle values. In this case, the middle two cases are $34,500 and $37,668. The mean of those two values is $36,084. That's the median for that set of six values.

What if the two middle values are the same, such as in the following set of data?

$45,678

$25,567

$25,567

$13,234

Then the median is the same as both of those middle values. In this case, it's $25,567.

And Now . . . *Using Excel's MEDIAN Function*

To compute the median of a set of numbers using Excel, follow these steps:

1. Enter the six individual incomes from above into one column in a worksheet, such as you see in Figure 2.5.

Figure 2.5 Data for Computing the Median

	A
1	Income Level
2	$ 135,456
3	$ 54,365
4	$ 37,668
5	$ 34,500
6	$ 32,456
7	$ 25,500

2. Select the cell into which you want to enter the **MEDIAN** function. In this example, we are going to compute the median in Cell B9.

3. Click on Cell A9 and type the median function as follows . . .

    = MEDIAN(A2:A7)

    . . . and press the Enter key.

    Or use the Formulas → Insert Function command we talked about in Little Chapter 1a to enter the MEDIAN function.

You can see in Figure 2.6 the value of the median, and in the formula bar, you can see the MEDIAN function.

Figure 2.6   Computing the Median Using the MEDIAN Function

A9	▼	⋮	✕	✓	*fx*	=MEDIAN(A2:A7)

	A	B	C	D
1	Income Level			
2	$ 135,456			
3	$ 54,365			
4	$ 37,668			
5	$ 34,500			
6	$ 32,456			
7	$ 25,500			
8				
9	$ 36,084			

Along with medians, you should know about **percentile points**. Percentile points are used to define the percentage of cases equal to and below a certain point in a distribution or set of scores. For example, if a score is "at the 75th percentile," it means that the score is at or above 75% of the other scores in the distribution. The median is also known as the 50th percentile, because it's the point below which 50% of the cases in the distribution fall. Other percentiles are useful as well, such as the 25th percentile, often called Q_1, and the 75th percentile, referred to as Q_3. So what's Q_2? The median, of course.

Now here's a cool trick. You can place a negative sign in front of a function and have it compute the negative value of that function such as =–MEDIAN or =–AVERAGE. Why would you want to do that? You may have a circumstance where a function is part of a larger formula and that value needs to be negative, or you may want, or need, to compute a negative value using that function.

Here comes the answer to the question you've probably had in the back of your mind since we started talking about the median. Why use the median instead of the mean? For one very good reason. The median is insensitive to extreme scores, whereas the mean is not.

When you have a set of scores in which one or more scores are extreme, the median represents the centermost value of that set of scores better than any other measure of central tendency. Yes, even better than the mean.

What do we mean by "extreme"? As discussed above, there's no strict definition of this term. It's probably easiest to think of an extreme score as one that is very different from the group to which it belongs. For example, consider the list of five incomes that we worked with earlier (shown again here):

$135,456

$54,365

$37,668

$32,456

$25,500

The value $135,456 is more different from the other four than is any other value in the set. We would consider that an extreme score.

The best way to illustrate the usefulness of the median as a measure of central tendency is to compute both the mean and the median for a set of data that contains one or more extreme scores and then compare them to see which one best represents the group. Here goes.

The average or mean of the set of five scores you see above is the sum of the set of five divided by 5, which turns out to be $57,089. On the other hand, the median for this set of five scores is $37,668. Which is more representative of the group? The value $37,668 is more representative, because it clearly lies more in the middle of the group and we like to think about the average as being representative or assuming a central position. In fact, the mean value of $57,089 falls above the fourth highest value ($54,365) and is not very central or representative of the distribution.

It's for this reason that certain social and economic indicators (mostly involving income) are reported using a median as a measure of central tendency, such as "The median income of the average American family is . . ." There are just too many extreme scores that would **skew**, or significantly distort, the mean if it were used to represent a central point in the set or distribution of scores.

You learned earlier that sometimes the mean is represented by the capital letter *M* instead of $\bar{X}$. Well, other symbols are used for the median as well. We like the letter *M,* but some people confuse it with the mean, so they use *Med* or *Mdn* for median. Don't let that throw you—just remember what the median is and what it represents, and you'll have no trouble adapting to different symbols.

You can use Excel's **QUARTILE.INC** function to compute the 25th, 50th, and 75th percentiles as well as other quartiles in a distribution.

Remember the median? It's the second quartile in Excel's grand plan.

Here are some interesting and important things to remember about the median.

- The mean is the middle point of a set of values, and the median is the middle point of a set of cases.
- Because the median cares about how many cases there are, and not the values of those cases, extreme scores (sometimes called *outliers*) don't count.

COMPUTING THE MODE

The third and last measure of central tendency that we'll cover, the mode, is the most general and least precise measure of central tendency, but it plays an important part in understanding the characteristics of a special set of scores. The mode is the value that occurs most frequently.

There is no formula for computing the mode. Instead, just follow these steps:

1. List all the values in a distribution, but list each value only once.

2. Tally the number of times that each value occurs.

3. The value that occurs most often is the mode.

For example, an examination of the political party affiliation of 300 people might result in the following distribution of scores.

Party Affiliation	Number or Frequency
Democrats	90
Republicans	70
Independents	140

The mode is the value that occurs most frequently, so in the above example, the mode is Independents. That's the mode for this set of values.

And Now . . . Using Excel's MODE.SNGL Function

To compute the mode of a set of numbers using Excel, follow these steps:

1. Enter the individual scores into one column in a worksheet as you see in Figure 2.7, where one column indicates party affiliation. Keep in mind that we have to enter numbers (not text) so that Excel can count the number of times each value appears. We did include a legend, though, in Column B so you can keep straight what value stands for what party.

Figure 2.7 Data for Computing the Mode

	A	B
1	Party	
2	1	1=Democrats
3	2	2=Republicans
4	3	3=Independents
5	3	
6	3	
7	2	
8	2	
9	1	
10	1	
11	1	
12	1	
13	1	
14	2	
15	2	
16	2	
17	2	
18	1	
19	1	
20	1	

2. Select the cell into which you want to enter the **MODE.SNGL** function. In this example, we are going to compute the mode in Cell B21.

3. Click on Cell B21 and type the MODE.SNGL function as follows . . .

=MODE.SNGL(A2:A20)

. . . and press the Enter key.

Or use the Formulas → Insert Function menu option and the "Inserting a Function" technique we talked about in Little Chapter 1a to enter the MODE function in Cell B21. You see the mode and the function in the formula bar in Figure 2.8.

Figure 2.8   Using the MODE.SNGL Function

| B21 | ▼ | ⋮ | ✕ ✓ | *fx* | =MODE.SNGL(A2:A20) |

	A	B	C	D	E
1	Party				
2	1	1=Democrats			
3	2	2=Republicans			
4	3	3=Independents			
5	3				
6	3				
7	2				
8	2				
9	1				
10	1				
11	1				
12	1				
13	1				
14	2				
15	2				
16	2				
17	2				
18	1				
19	1				
20	1				
21	Mode	1			

You can use the COUNTIF function (in the category of functions under Database) to count the number of occurrences of text, which would be a really simple way to find out the mode without having to use the MODE function. Simply create a list and then use the function, defining the input range and the values. In our example here, it would be something like =COUNTIF(A2:A20, "Democrats"), which would tally all the occurrences of the word *Democrats* and return it to the cell of your choice. Then, you would just select the largest value as the mode. You can use uppercase or lowercase letters or a mixture, but you need to include the quote marks ("").

Want to know what the easiest and most commonly made mistake is when computing the mode? It's selecting the number of times a category occurs, rather than the label of the category itself. In our example of the party affiliation of 300 people, the mode is Independents, but someone could easily conclude the mode is 140. The error would be in looking at the number of times the value occurred, not the value that occurred most often. This is a simple mistake to make, so be on your toes when you are asked about mode.

Apple Pie à la Bimodal

If every value in a distribution contains the same number of occurrences, then there really isn't a single mode (and Excel will return an incorrect value). But if more than one value appears with equal frequency, the distribution is multimodal. The set of scores can be bimodal (with two modes), as the following set of data using hair color illustrates.

Hair Color	Number or Frequency
Red	3
Blond	5
Black	8
Brown	8

In the above example, the distribution is bimodal because the frequency of the values of black and brown hair occurs equally. The two modes are black and brown. You can even determine that you have a bimodal distribution when the modes are relatively close together but not exactly the same, such as when 10 people have black hair and 9 have brown hair. The question becomes "How much does one class of occurrences stand apart from another?"

Can you have a trimodal distribution? Sure—when three values have the same frequency. It's unlikely, especially when you are dealing with a large set of data points, but certainly possible.

And Now . . . Using Excel's MODE.MULT Function

Guess what, folks! Excel 2016 also comes with a function that allows us to compute multiple modes. The old MODE, which only dealt with a single mode (and is still accessible in this later version of Excel), is now called MODE.SNGL, as you just learned. MODE.MULT is a bit tricky, so pay close attention. The MODE.MULT function is most useful when you have a large set of data and suspect that there may be more than one mode.

 To compute more than one mode of a set of numbers using Excel, follow these steps:

1. Enter the individual scores into one column in a worksheet as you see in Figure 2.9, where one column indicates hair color.

Figure 2.9   Data for Computing Multiple Modes

	A	B
1	Hair Color	
2	1	1=Red
3	1	2=Blond
4	1	3=Black
5	2	4=Brown
6	2	
7	2	
8	2	
9	2	
10	3	
11	3	
12	3	
13	3	
14	3	
15	3	
16	3	
17	3	
18	4	
19	4	
20	4	
21	4	
22	4	
23	4	
24	4	
25	4	

2. Select the cells into which you want to enter the **MODE.MULT** function. In this example, we are going to compute the modes in Cells
B26 through B29. We selected four cells just in case there are more
than one or two or three modes. Always select more cells than you
think there will be modes.

3. Enter the MODE function as follows . . .

=MODE.MULT(A2:A25)

. . . and press—all at once—the Ctrl+Shift+Enter keys. You need to
do this since you are creating an array.

Or use the Formulas → Insert Function menu option and the
"Inserting a Function" technique we talked about in Little Chapter 1a
to enter the MODE.MULT function in Cells B26 through B29. You see
the function in the formula bar in Figure 2.10; it is surrounded by
curly brackets because it creates an array. And, since there are only
two modes for this set of scores, N/A appears in Cells B28 and B29.

Figure 2.10 Using the MODE.MULT Function

| B26 | ▼ | : | × | ✓ | *fx* | {=MODE.MULT(A2:A25)} |

◢	A	B	C	D	E	F
22	4					
23	4					
24	4					
25	4					
26		3				
27		4				
28		#N/A				
29		#N/A				

We used the special Ctrl+Shift+Enter combination because we
created a vertical array of values in the selected cells as the result of
the formula. You can tell that it is an array by looking at the function
bar in Figure 2.10 and seeing that the function is surrounded by the
{} brackets.

USING THE AMAZING DATA ANALYSIS TOOLS TO COMPUTE DESCRIPTIVE STATISTICS

Now is our first chance to use the amazing Data Analysis tools that
we introduced in Little Chapter 1b.

This particular item in the Data Analysis tools, named Descriptive
Statistics, computes more values than we need. Because you can't be

selective about what the Data Analysis tools compute (but can edit the results, as you will shortly see), we'll show you all the results but deal only with those that we cover in this chapter. We'll follow the same procedure in later chapters.

To use the Data Analysis tools to compute descriptive statistics, follow these steps. We're using the data you see in Figure 2.11, which you also saw way back in Figure 2.5.

Figure 2.11	Data for the Data Analysis Tools Descriptive Statistics Option

	A
1	Income Level
2	$ 135,456
3	$ 54,365
4	$ 37,668
5	$ 34,500
6	$ 32,456
7	$ 25,500

1. Click the Data tab → Data Analysis, and you will see the Data Analysis dialog box shown in Figure 2.12.

Figure 2.12	The Dialog Box That Gets Us Started With the Data Analysis Tools

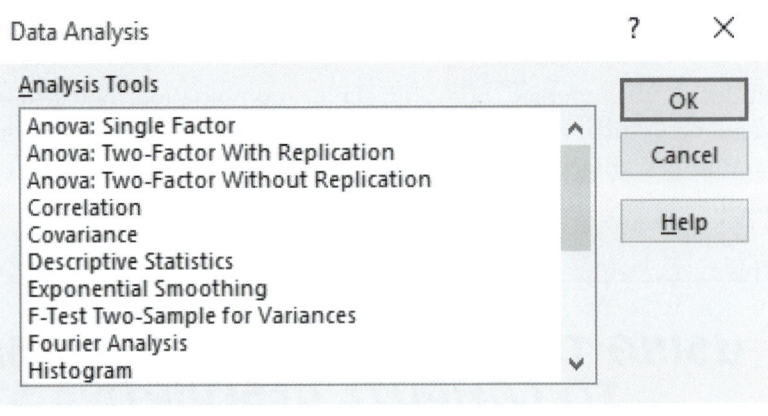

2. Click Descriptive Statistics and then click OK, and you will see the Descriptive Statistics dialog box, as shown in Figure 2.13.

Figure 2.13 Descriptive Statistics Dialog Box

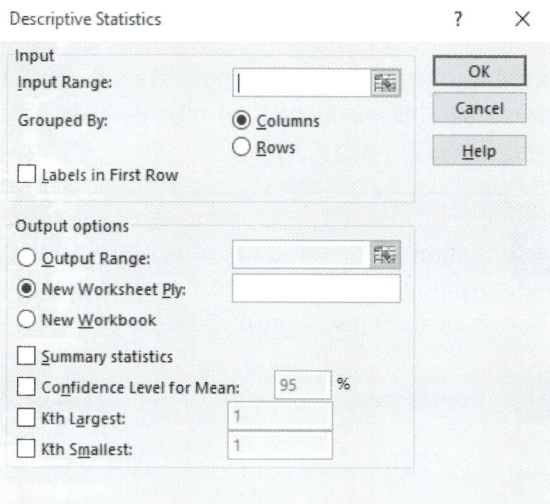

3. Enter the range of data you want Excel to use in the computation of the descriptive statistics in the Input Range box. Also include the column heading (so the heading shows up in the analysis). In this example (as you can see in Figure 2.11), the data we want to analyze are in Cells A1 through A7. Enter the range directly or use the Collapse button.

4. Click the "Labels in First Row" check box.

5. Now click the Output Range button, which is in the Output Options section of the dialog box, and enter the location where you want Excel to return the results of the analysis. In this example, we choose C1.

Click or Drag?

This is covered in Appendix A, but it's important enough to emphasize here as well. You can enter cell addresses in a dialog box in Excel in three ways.

Way 1. You can just enter them using the keyboard (such as by typing "A1").

Way 2. You can click and drag the mouse over the cells you want to select and then release the mouse, and the cell range (or cell) will appear in the range box.

Way 3. You can use the Collapse box (the one that looks like this: 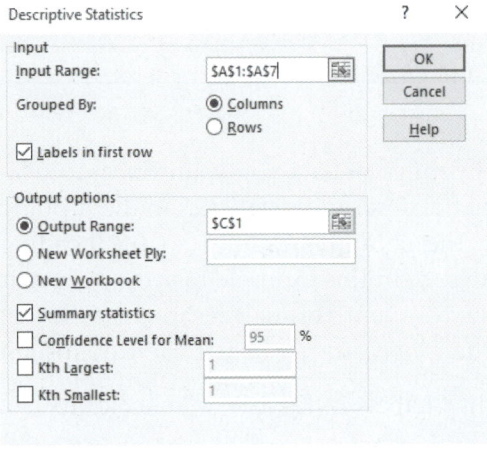). When you click this, it allows you to enter the range through dragging as well.

Which one's right for you? Whichever you find works best, but you have to know that typing cell ranges can get old very fast. Try to click and drag or use the Collapse box.

6. Click the "Summary statistics" check box in the Descriptive Statistics dialog box. The completed Descriptive Statistics dialog box is shown in Figure 2.14.

| **Figure 2.14** | The Completed Descriptive Statistics Dialog Box |

7. Click OK, and you will see the results, as shown in Figure 2.15.

| **Figure 2.15** | The Descriptive Statistics Data Analysis Tools Results |

	A	B	C	D
1	Income Level		*Income Level*	
2	$ 135,456			
3	$ 54,365		Mean	53324.17
4	$ 37,668		Standard E	16887.72
5	$ 34,500		Median	36084
6	$ 32,456		Mode	#N/A
7	$ 25,500		Standard D	41366.29
8			Sample Va	1.71E+09
9			Kurtosis	4.861219
10			Skewness	2.173756
11			Range	109956
12			Minimum	25500
13			Maximum	135456
14			Sum	319945
15			Count	6

Now this is pretty darn amazing. You get all this information with relatively few clicks. From here, you just have to get your ducks all lined up in a row (you know, everything lined up quite nicely). To make this work, do be sure that all the cell references are entered accurately.

You can see all kinds of useful information in Figure 2.15, from the mean (which is actually 53324.16667 but is rounded to 53324.17) of the six values (see how Count = 6?) to the median (36084) and a bunch of other stuff (some of it we will not be dealing with—see Statistics 2 in your course catalog). We'll show you how to make tables like this prettier and more pleasing to the eye later.

Make the Data Analysis Tools Output Pretty

It's later.

Once you use any tool in the Data Analysis tools and get some output, like what you see in Figure 2.15, you can (of course) leave it like it is or use other Excel tools to format it to better fit your needs. This output is absolutely part of the worksheet you created in the first place, so anything you do to the entire sheet also has an impact on this new output. In Figure 2.16, you can see we made several changes using simple Excel tools.

- We formatted the entire worksheet in Arial 12.
- We deleted the Mode cells because there is no mode.
- We used the Format → Column → AutoFit option to adjust the columns so that all the information fits on the worksheet.
- We added commas (formatted as "thousands") and rounded decimals to two places.

Figure 2.16 The New and Improved Descriptive Statistics Output

	A	B	C	D
1	Income Level		Income Level	
2	$ 135,456			
3	$ 54,365		Mean	53,324.17
4	$ 37,668		Standard Error	16,887.72
5	$ 34,500		Median	36,084.00
6	$ 32,456		Standard Deviatio	41,366.29
7	$ 25,500		Sample Variance	1,711,170,163.37
8			Kurtosis	4.86
9			Skewness	2.17
10			Range	109,956.00
11			Minimum	25,500.00
12			Maximum	135,456.00
13			Sum	319,945.00
14			Count	6.00

- We could have added other things and used more of Excel's bells and whistles (color, table formats, shading, etc.), but what you see does a fine job of showing the results of the analysis. Fancy is nice, but there's nothing wrong with simple and straightforward—words to live by.

WHEN TO USE WHAT

Okay, we've defined three different measures of central tendency and given you fairly clear examples of each. But the most important question remains unanswered. That is "When do you use which measure?"

In general, which measure of central tendency you use depends on the type of data that you are describing. Unquestionably, a measure of central tendency for qualitative, categorical, or nominal data (such as racial group, eye color, income bracket, voting preference, and neighborhood location) can only be given using the mode.

For example, you can't be looking at the most central measure that describes which political affiliation is most predominant in a group and use the mean. What in the world could you conclude—that everyone is half Republican? Rather, you could say that out of 300 people, almost half (140) are Independent; this seems to be the best way of describing the value of this variable. In general, the median and mean are best used with quantitative data, such as height, income level in dollars (not categories), age, test score, reaction time, and number of hours completed for a degree.

It's also fair to say that the mean is a more precise measure than the median, and the mode is a less precise measure than the median. This means that all other things being equal, use the mean, and indeed, the mean is the most often used measure of central tendency. However, we do have occasions when the mean would not be appropriate as a measure of central tendency—for example, when we have categorical or nominal data, such as hair color. Then we use the mode. So, here is a set of three guidelines that may be of some help. And remember, there can always be exceptions.

1. Use the mode when the data are categorical in nature and values can fit into only one class, such as hair color, political affiliation, neighborhood location, and religion. When this is the case, these categories are called *mutually exclusive*.

2. Use the median when you have extreme scores and you don't want to distort the average, such as (often) when studying income.

3. Finally, use the mean when you have data that do not include extreme scores and are not categorical, such as the numerical score on a test or the number of seconds it takes to swim 50 yards.

REAL-WORLD STATS

Few applications of descriptive statistics would make more sense then their use in a survey or poll, and there have been literally millions of surveys and polls (remember that recent minor election in 2012?). In an article by Roger Morrell and his colleagues, they examined Internet use patterns in 550 adults in several age-groups including middle-aged (ages 40–59), young-old (ages 60–74), and old-old adults (ages 75–92). With a response rate of 71%, which is pretty good, they found a few very interesting (but not entirely unexpected) outcomes.

- There are distinct differences in the way individuals use the Internet depending on their age.
- Middle-aged and older Web users are similar in their use patterns.
- The two primary predictors for not using the Internet are lack of access to a computer and lack of knowledge about the Internet.
- Old-old adults have the least interest in using the Internet compared with middle-aged and young-old adults.
- The primary content areas for people who learn how to use the Internet are using electronic mail and accessing information about health and traveling for pleasure.

This survey, which primarily used descriptive statistics to reach its conclusions, was done almost 15 years ago and many, many things have changed since then. The reason we include it here as an example of Real-World Statistics is that it is a good illustration of a historical anchor point that can be used for comparative purposes in future studies—a common use of descriptive statistics and such studies.

Want to know more? Go online or visit the library and look for . . .

Morrell, R. W., Mayhorn, C. B., & Bennett, J. (2000). A survey of World Wide Web use in middle-aged and older adults. *Human Factors: The Journal of the Human Factors and Ergonomics Society, 42*, 175–182.

SUMMARY

No matter how fancy-schmancy your statistical techniques are, you will still almost always start by simply describing what's there—hence, the importance of understanding the simple notion of central tendency. From here, we go to another important descriptive construct: variability, or how different scores are from one another. That's what we'll explore in Chapter 3!

TIME TO PRACTICE

1. Compute the mean, median, and mode for the following three sets of scores saved as Chapter 2 Data Set 1 in Appendix C. Do it by hand or using Excel. Show your work, and if you are using Excel, print out a copy of the output.

Score 1	Score 2	Score 3
3	34	154
7	54	167
5	17	132
4	26	145
5	34	154
6	25	145
7	14	113
8	24	156
6	25	154
5	23	123

2. Use the Data Analysis tools and Chapter 2 Data Set 2 to find out the average number of times children in three different classes ask a question each day of the week. What measure of central tendency did you use and why?

3. You are the manager of a fast-food store. Part of your job is to report to the boss at the end of each day which special is selling best. Use your vast knowledge of descriptive statistics to write one paragraph letting the boss know what happened today. Here are the data. Do this exercise by hand. Be sure to include a copy of your work.

Special	Number Sold	Cost
Huge Burger	20	$2.95
Baby Burger	18	$1.49
Chicken Littles	25	$3.50
Porker Burger	19	$2.95
Yummy Burger	17	$1.99
Coney Dog	20	$1.99
Total Specials Sold	119	

4. Under what conditions would you use the median rather than the mean as a measure of central tendency? Why? Provide an example of two situations in which the median might be more useful than the mean as a measure of central tendency.

5. List three variables, and how they are measured, for which you would use the mode as the most appropriate measure of central tendency.

6. You're in business for yourself and you have been fortunate to buy and own the website titled Havefun.com, where you sell every imaginable stupid toy (like potato guns) and games that everyone needs. You're reviewing your advertising budget for the third quarter (from July 1 through September 30) and need to compute the mean (what Excel refers to as the "average" and computes with the function named AVERAGE, remember?). Here are the sales data in dollars. Use Excel functions or formulas to compute the average sales by toy and by month.

Toy	July Sales	August Sales	September Sales	Mean Sales
Slammer	$12,345	$14,453	$15,435	
Radar Zinger	$31,454	$34,567	$29,678	
Potato Gun	$3,253	$3,121	$5,131	
Mean Sales				

7. Working with the data from Question 6, compute the median sales for all three toys.

8. Suppose you are working with a data set that has some very "different" (much larger or much smaller than the rest of the data) scores. What measure of central tendency would you use and why?

9. As the head of public health, you conduct a weekly census across age-groups of the number of cases of flu reported in your area. By hand, compute the mean and the median by week. Which do you think, given these particular data, is the most useful measure of central tendency and why?

	12/1 Through 12/7	12/8 Through 12/15	12/16 Through 12/23
0–4 years	12	14	15
5–9 years	15	12	14
10–14 years	12	24	21
15–19 years	38	12	19
Mean			
Median			

10. Working with Chapter 2 Data Set 3, use the Data Analysis Tools or StatPlus LE to find out all the descriptive statistics that are available for five scores (from 1 to 7) on a baking test for 10 culinary arts students. Make the output as coherent and attractive as you can.

3

Vive la Différence

Understanding Variability

Difficulty Scale ☺ ☺ ☺ ☺ (moderately easy, but not a cinch)

How much Excel? 📊 📊 📊 📊 (a ton)

WHAT YOU'LL LEARN ABOUT IN THIS CHAPTER

✦ Why variability is valuable as a descriptive tool

✦ Computing the range, standard deviation, and variance

✦ How the standard deviation and variance are alike and how they are different

✦ Using the Data Analysis tools to compute the range, standard deviation, and variance

---

WHY UNDERSTANDING VARIABILITY IS IMPORTANT

In Chapter 2, you learned about different types of averages, what they mean, how they are computed, and when to use them. But when it comes to descriptive statistics and describing the characteristics of a distribution, averages are only half the story. The other half is measures of variability.

In the simplest of terms, **variability** reflects how scores differ from one another. For example, the following set of scores shows some variability:

7, 6, 3, 3, 1

The following set of scores has the same mean (4) and has less variability than the previous set:

3, 4, 4, 5, 4

The next set has no variability at all—the scores do not differ from one another—but it has the same mean as the other two sets we just showed you:

4, 4, 4, 4, 4

Variability (also called spread or dispersion) can be thought of as a measure of how different scores are from one another. It's even more accurate (and maybe also easier) to think of variability as how different scores are from one particular score. And what "score" do you think that might be? Well, instead of comparing each score to every other score in a distribution, the one score that could be used as a comparison is—that's right—the mean. So, variability becomes a measure of how much each score in a group of scores differs from the mean. More about this in a moment.

Remember what you already know about computing averages— that an average (whether it is the mean, the median, or the mode) is a representation of a set of scores. Now, add your new knowledge about variability—that it reflects how different scores are from one another. Each is an important descriptive statistic. Together, these two (average and variability) can be used to describe the characteristics of a distribution and show how distributions differ from one another.

Three measures of variability are commonly used to reflect the degree of variability, spread, or dispersion in a group of scores: the range, the standard deviation, and the variance. Let's take a closer look at each one and how it is used.

COMPUTING THE RANGE

The range is the most general measure of variability. It gives you an idea of how far apart scores are from one another. The **range** is computed simply by subtracting the lowest score in a distribution from the highest score in the distribution.

In general, the formula for the range is

$$r = h - l, \qquad (3.1)$$

where

r   is the range;

h   is the highest score in the data set; and

l   is the lowest score in the data set.

Take the following set of scores, for example (shown here in descending order):

$$98, 86, 77, 56, 48$$

In this example, $98 - 48 = 50$. Thus, the range is 50.

There really are two kinds of ranges. One is the *exclusive* range, the one we just defined, which is the highest score minus the lowest score (or $h - l$). The second kind of range is the *inclusive* range, which is the highest score minus the lowest score plus 1 (or $h - l + 1$). You most commonly see the exclusive range in research articles, but the inclusive range is also used on occasion if the researcher prefers it.

The range is used almost always to get a very general estimate of how wide or different scores are from one another—that is, the range shows how much spread there is from the lowest to the highest point in a distribution.

So, although the range is fine as a general indicator of variability, it should not be used to reach any conclusions regarding how individual scores differ from one another. Remember, the range uses only two scores—a poor reflection of what's really happening in a larger set of scores.

As far as Excel is concerned, there is no function for computing the range, but you can compute it using the Descriptive Statistics option from the Data Analysis tools (just subtract the Minimum value in the output from the Maximum value shown in the output). For an example of the Descriptive Statistics output you can use, look back at Figure 2.15 in Chapter 2. Alternatively, you can create a simple formula that subtracts one value from the other and adds 1 (to compute an inclusive range) or doesn't add anything (for the exclusive range).

COMPUTING THE STANDARD DEVIATION

Now we get to the most frequently used measure of variability, the standard deviation. Just think about what the term implies; it's a *deviation* from something (guess what?) that is *standard*. Actually, the **standard deviation** (abbreviated as **s** or **SD**) represents the average amount of variability in a set of scores. In practical terms, it's the average distance of each score from the mean. The larger the standard deviation, the larger the average distance each data point is from the mean of the distribution.

So, what's the logic behind computing the standard deviation? Your initial thought may be to compute the mean of a set of scores and then subtract each individual score from the mean. Then, compute the average of that distance. That's a good idea—you'll end up with the average distance of each score from the mean. But it won't work (see if you know why even though we'll show you why in a moment).

First, here's the formula for computing the standard deviation:

$$s = \sqrt{\frac{\Sigma(X - \bar{X})^2}{n-1}}, \tag{3.2}$$

where

s is the standard deviation;

Σ is sigma, which tells you to find the sum of what follows;

X is each individual score;

$\bar{X}$ is the mean of all the scores; and

n is the sample size.

This formula finds the difference between each individual score and the mean $(X - \bar{X})$, squares each difference, and sums all the differences. Then, it divides the sum by the size of the sample (minus 1—be patient, we'll get to why) and takes the square root of the result. As you can see, the standard deviation is indeed an average deviation from the mean.

Here are the data we'll use in the following step-by-step explanation of how to compute the standard deviation.

5, 8, 5, 4, 6, 7, 8, 8, 3, 6

And here are the steps:

1. List each score. It doesn't matter whether the scores are in any particular order.

2. Compute the mean of the group.

3. Subtract the mean from each score.

Here's what we've done so far, where $X - \bar{X}$ represents the difference between the actual score and the mean of all the scores, which is 6.

X	$\bar{X}$	$X - \bar{X}$
8	6	8 − 6 = +2
8	6	8 − 6 = +2
8	6	8 − 6 = +2
7	6	7 − 6 = +1
6	6	6 − 6 = 0
6	6	6 − 6 = 0
5	6	5 − 6 = −1
5	6	5 − 6 = −1
4	6	4 − 6 = −2
3	6	3 − 6 = −3

4. Square each individual difference. The result is the column marked $(X - \bar{X})^2$.

X	$X - \bar{X}$	$(X - \bar{X})^2$
8	+2	4
8	+2	4
8	+2	4
7	+1	1
6	0	0
6	0	0
5	−1	1
5	−1	1
4	−2	4
3	−3	9
Sum	0	28

5. Sum all the squared deviations about the mean. As you can see above, the total is 28.

6. Divide the sum by $n - 1$, or $10 - 1 = 9$, so then $28/9 = 3.11$.

7. Compute the square root of 3.11, which is 1.76 (after rounding). That is the standard deviation for this set of 10 scores.

And Now . . . Using Excel's STDEV.S Function

To compute the standard deviation of a set of numbers (the *S* in the function name is for *sample*) using Excel, follow these steps:

1. Enter the individual scores into one column in a worksheet such as you see in Figure 3.1.

Figure 3.1 Data for the STDEV.S Function

	A
1	Score
2	8
3	8
4	8
5	7
6	6
7	6
8	5
9	5
10	4
11	3

2. Select the cell into which you want to enter the **STDEV.S** function. In this example, we are going to compute the standard deviation in cell A12.

3. Now click on cell A12 and type the STDEV.S function as follows . . .

   =STDEV.S(A2:A11)

   . . . and press the Enter key.

   Or use the Formulas → Insert Function menu option and the "Inserting a Function" technique we talked about in Little Chapter 1a to enter the STDEV.S function in Cell A12.

4. As you can see in Figure 3.2, the standard deviation was computed, and the value 1.76 (rounded off), which is the

same result we got manually, was returned to cell A12. Notice that in the formula bar in Figure 3.2, you can see the STDEV.S function fully expressed.

Figure 3.2	Computation of the Standard Deviation Using the STDEV.S Function

A12	▾	⋮	✕	✓	*fx*	=STDEV.S(A2:A11)

	A	B	C	D	E
1	Score				
2	8				
3	8				
4	8				
5	7				
6	6				
7	6				
8	5				
9	5				
10	4				
11	3				
12	1.76				

Now, here's a surprise. When you go to select the STDEV function from the Formulas → Insert Function options, you see that there are actually several functions that can compute the standard deviation. Two are especially important for us. One is named STDEV.S (the one we used in the example above), and the second is named **STDEV.P.** They both compute the standard deviation of a set of scores, so what's the difference?

   The one that we used, STDEV.S, computes the standard deviation for a set of scores from a sample. STDEV.P computes the standard deviation for a set of scores that is an entire population. What's the difference in the two values, and why use one rather than the other? More about this later, but for now, because STDEV.S is based on only a portion of the entire population (the definition of a sample, right?), it's more likely (we're talking probability here) to overestimate the true, real, honest-to-Pete value of the standard deviation for the entire population.

   When to use what? Use STDEV.S—you'll almost always be correct. But if a group of scores is defined as a population, then STDEV.P is the function that loves ya, baby.

What we now know from these results is that each score in this distribution differs from the mean by an average of 1.76 points.

Let's take a short step back and examine some of the operations in the standard deviation formula. They're important to review and will increase your understanding of what the standard deviation is.

First, why didn't we just add up the deviations from the mean? Because the sum of the deviations from the mean is always equal to zero. Try it by summing the deviations: $2 + 2 + 2 + 1 + 0 + 0 - 1 - 1 - 2 - 3$. In fact, that's the best way to check whether you computed the mean correctly.

There's another type of deviation that you may read about, and you should know what it means. The **mean deviation** (also called the mean absolute deviation) is the average of the absolute value of the deviations from the mean. You already know that the sum of the deviations from the mean must equal zero (otherwise, the mean probably has been computed incorrectly). Instead, let's sum the absolute values (the values regardless of the sign) of each deviation. Divide that sum by the number of data points, and you have the mean deviation. (Note: The absolute value of a number is usually represented as that number with a vertical line on each side of it, such as |5|. For example, the absolute value of –6, or |–6|, is 6.)

Second, why do we square the deviations? Because we want to get rid of the negative sign so that when we do eventually sum them, they don't add up to zero.

And finally, why do we end up taking the square root of the entire value in Step 7 of our manual calculation? Because we want to return to the same units with which we originally started. We squared the deviations from the mean in Step 4 (to get rid of negative values) and then took the square root of their total in Step 7. Pretty tidy.

Why n – 1? What's Wrong With Just n?

You might have guessed why we square the deviations about the mean and why we go back and take the square root of their sum. But how about subtracting the value of 1 from the denominator of the formula? Why do we divide by $n - 1$ rather than just plain ol' n? Good question.

The answer is that s (the standard deviation) is an estimate of the population standard deviation and is an **unbiased estimate** at that, but only when we subtract 1 from n. By subtracting 1 from the denominator, we artificially force the standard deviation to be larger than it would be otherwise. Why would we want to do that? Because, as good scientists, we are conservative. In fact, dividing by n − 1 is exactly what we are doing by using STDEV.S rather than the STDEV.P function in the earlier example.

Being conservative means that if we have to err, we will do so on the side of overestimating the standard deviation of the population. Dividing by a smaller denominator lets us do so. Thus, instead of dividing by 10, we divide by 9. Or, instead of dividing by 100, we divide by 99.

You can see this if you look at Figure 3.3, where we used both functions to compute the standard deviation. See how the unbiased one (1.76) is larger than the biased one (1.67)? That's because the one based on the sample (the unbiased one) intentionally overestimates the value.

Figure 3.3 A Comparison of the STDEV.S and STDEV.P Functions

	A	B
1		Score
2		8
3		8
4		8
5		7
6		6
7		6
8		5
9		5
10		4
11		3
12	STDEV.S	1.76
13	STDEV.P	1.67

Biased estimates are appropriate if your intent is only to describe the characteristics of the population. But if you intend to use the sample as an estimate of a population parameter, then it's better to calculate the unbiased statistic.

Take a look at the following table and see what happens as the size of the sample (the first column) gets larger (and moves closer to the population in size). The $n - 1$ adjustment has far less impact on the difference between the biased and the unbiased estimates of the standard deviation (the bold column in the table). All other things being equal, then, the larger the sample size, the less difference there is between the biased and the unbiased estimates of the standard deviation.

Sample Size	Value of Numerator in Standard Deviation	Biased Estimate of the Population Standard Deviation (dividing by n)	Unbiased Estimate of the Population Standard Deviation (dividing by $n - 1$)	Difference Between Biased and Unbiased Estimates
10	500	7.07	7.45	0.38
100	500	2.24	2.25	0.01
1,000	500	0.7071	0.7075	0.0004

The moral of the story? When you compute the standard deviation for a sample, which is an estimate of the population, the closer the sample size is to the size of the population, the more accurate the estimate will be.

What's the Big Deal?

The computation of the standard deviation is very straightforward. But what does it mean? As a measure of variability, all it tells us is how much each score in a set of scores, on the average, varies from the mean. But it has some very practical applications, as you will find out in Chapter 4. Just to whet your appetite, consider this:

The standard deviation can be used to help us compare scores from different distributions, *even when the means and standard deviations are different.*

Amazing! This, as you will see, can be very cool.

When dealing with the standard deviation, keep these facts in mind:

- The standard deviation is computed as the average distance from the mean. So, you first need to compute the mean as a measure of central tendency. Don't fool around with the median or the mode in trying to compute the standard deviation. The larger the standard deviation, the more spread out the values are, and the more different they are from one another.

- Just like the mean, the standard deviation is sensitive to extreme scores. When you are computing the standard deviation of a sample and you have extreme scores, note that fact somewhere in your written report.
- If s = 0, there is absolutely no variability in the set of scores, and they are essentially identical in value. This will rarely happen.

COMPUTING THE VARIANCE

Here comes another measure of variability and a nice surprise. If you know the standard deviation of a set of scores and you can square that number, you can easily compute the **variance** of that same set of scores. This third measure of variability, the variance, is simply the standard deviation squared. In other words, it's the same formula you saw earlier without the square root bracket, like the one shown in Formula 3.3:

$$s^2 = \frac{\sum(X - \bar{X})^2}{n - 1} \qquad (3.3)$$

If you take the standard deviation and never complete the last step (taking the square root), you have the variance. In other words, $s^2 = s \times s$, or the variance equals the standard deviation times itself (or squared). In our earlier example, where the standard deviation is equal to 1.76, the variance is equal to 1.76^2 or 3.10.

And Now . . . Using Excel's VAR.S Function

To compute the variance of a set of numbers using Excel, follow these steps:

1. Enter the individual scores into one column in a worksheet. We're going to use the same scores as those shown in Figure 3.1.

2. Select the cell into which you want to enter the **VAR.S** function. In this example, we are going to compute the variance in Cell B12.

3. Now click on Cell B12 and type the VAR.S function as follows . . .

=VAR.S(B2:B11)

. . . and press the Enter key.

Or use the Formulas → Insert Function menu option and the "Inserting a Function" technique we talked about in Little Chapter 1a to enter the VAR.S function in Cell B12.

4. As you can see in Figure 3.4, the variance was computed and the value returned to Cell B12. Notice that in the formula bar in Figure 3.4, you can see the VAR.S function fully expressed, and the value is computed as 3.11. This is almost the same result we got manually; the difference is a function of the internal formula that Excel uses to compute the variance and nothing more.

Figure 3.4 Using the VAR.S Function to Compute the Variance

B12	▼	⋮	✕	✓	*fx*	=VAR.S(B2:B11)

	A	B	C	D	E
1		Score			
2		8			
3		8			
4		8			
5		7			
6		6			
7		6			
8		5			
9		5			
10		4			
11		3			
12		3.11			

STDEV.S Is to STDEV.P as VAR.S Is to VAR.P

Sounds like an acronym love fest, right? Nope—just as there is a function for computing the standard deviation of a population (STDEV.P), so there is for the variance, and it is named **VAR.P.** In Figure 3.5, you can see that when the variance for a sample is computed (VAR.S), it is larger than its VAR.P cousin.

Figure 3.5	Comparing the VAR.S and VAR.P Functions

You are not likely to see the variance mentioned by itself in a journal article or see it used as a descriptive statistic. This is because the variance is a difficult number to interpret and to apply to a set of data. After all, it is based on squared deviation scores.

But the variance is important because it is used both as a concept and as a practical measure of variability in many statistical formulas and techniques. You will learn about these later in *Statistics for People Who (Think They) Hate Statistics, Excel 2016 Edition.*

The Standard Deviation Versus the Variance

How are standard deviation and the variance the same, and how are they different?

Well, they are both measures of variability, dispersion, or spread. The formulas used to compute them are very similar. You see the standard deviation and the variance (mostly) all over the place in the "Results" sections of journal articles.

They are also quite different.

First, and most important, the standard deviation (because we take the square root of the average summed squared deviation) is stated in the original units from which it was derived. The variance is stated in units that are squared (the square root is never taken).

What does this mean? Let's say that we need to know the variability of a group of production workers assembling circuit boards. Let's say that they average 8.6 boards per hour and the standard deviation is 1.59. The value 1.59 means that the difference in the average number of boards assembled per hour is about 1.59 circuit boards from the mean.

Let's look at an interpretation of the variance, which is 1.59^2, or 2.53. This would be interpreted as meaning that the average difference between the workers is about 2.53 circuit boards *squared* from the mean. Which of these two numbers, 1.59 circuit boards or 2.53 circuit boards squared, is easier to understand?

USING THE AMAZING DATA ANALYSIS TOOLS (AGAIN!)

Guess what? We already did this! See Figures 2.12 through 2.15 in Chapter 2 that show the Data Analysis tools performing a descriptive analysis, including the standard deviation, the variance, and the range. Now, that was easy, wasn't it?

REAL-WORLD STATS

If you were like a mega stats person, then you might be interested in the properties of measures of variability for the sake of those properties. That's what mainline statisticians spend lots of their time doing—looking at the characteristics and performance and assumptions (and the violation thereof) of certain statistics.

But we're more interested in how these tools are used, so let's take a look at one such study that actually focused on variability as an outcome. As you read earlier, variability among scores is interesting for sure, but when it comes to understanding the reasons for variability among actual performances and people, then the topic becomes really interesting.

This is exactly what Nicholas Stapelberg and his colleagues in Australia did when they looked at variability in heart rate as it related to coronary heart disease. Now, they did not look at this phenomenon directly. Instead, they entered the search terms "heart rate variability," "depression," and "heart disease" into multiple electronic databases and found that decreased heart rate variability is found in both major depressive disorders and coronary heart disease. Why might this be the case? The researchers think that both diseases disrupt control feedback loops that help the heart function efficiently. This is a terrific example of how looking at variability can be the focal point of a study rather than an accompanying descriptive statistic.

Want to know more? Go online or go to the library, and look for . . .

Stapelberg, N. J., Hamilton-Craig, I., Neumann, D. L., Shum, D. H. K., & McConnell, H. (2012). Mind and heart: Heart rate variability in major depressive disorder and coronary heart disease—a review and recommendations. *Australia New Zealand Journal of Psychiatry, 46,* 946–957.

SUMMARY

Measures of variability help us understand even more fully what a distribution of data points looks like. Along with a measure of central tendency, we can use these values to distinguish distributions from one another and effectively describe what a collection of test scores, heights, or measures of personality looks like. Now that we can think and talk about distributions, let's look at ways we can look at them.

TIME TO PRACTICE

1. Why is the range the most convenient measure of dispersion yet the most imprecise measure of variability? When would you use the range?

2. Compute the exclusive and inclusive ranges for the following items.

High Score	Low Score	Inclusive Range	Exclusive Range
7	6		
89	45		
34	17		
15	2		
1	1		

3. For the following set of scores, compute the range, the unbiased and the biased standard deviation, and the variance. Do these computations by hand.

31, 42, 35, 55, 54, 34, 25, 44, 35

4. For the following set of achievement scores, compute the unbiased standard deviation and variance. (Hint: Use STDEV.S and VAR.S.)

87, 87, 58, 78, 98, 69, 88, 71, 86, 91

5. Now compute the biased estimates for the data in Question 4.

6. Why are the unbiased estimates computed in Question 4 larger than the biased estimates computed in question 5?

7. This practice problem uses the data contained in the file named Chapter 3 Data Set 1 in Appendix C. There are two variables in this data set.

Variable	Definition
Height	Height in inches
Weight	Weight in pounds

Using Excel, compute the standard deviation and variance (both biased and unbiased) for height and weight.

8. You're one of the outstanding young strategists for Big Boy Airlines and are really curious to compare the number of passengers flying in the mornings versus the evenings out of the Kansas City, Missouri; Washington, DC; and Providence, Rhode Island, hubs for the last 2 days of last week. Here are the data. Compute the descriptive statistics that you will use in tomorrow's presentation to your boss and provide a few sentences of summary. Be on time!

	Thursday	Friday	Thursday	Friday	Thursday	Friday
Morning Flights	To Kansas City	To Kansas City	To Washington	To Washington	To Providence	To Providence
Number of Passengers	258	251	303	312	166	176

	Thursday	Friday	Thursday	Friday	Thursday	Friday
Evening Flights	To Kansas City	To Kansas City	To Washington	To Washington	To Providence	To Providence
Number of Passengers	312	331	321	331	210	274

9. You are conducting an experiment on the effectiveness of a reading intervention with young children and want to report the descriptive results to your colleagues. Some of the children received the intervention, and some did not. What do the averages and standard deviations tell you about the results? For this exercise, use the data in Chapter 3 Data Set 2.

10. Why would you chose to report the variance of a set of scores rather than the standard deviation?

4

A Picture Really Is Worth a Thousand Words

Difficulty Scale ☺ ☺ ☺ ☺ (pretty easy, but not a cinch)

How much Excel? 📊 📊 📊 📊 (lots and lots)

WHAT YOU'LL LEARN ABOUT IN THIS CHAPTER

✦ Why a picture really is worth a thousand words

✦ Creating a histogram and a polygon

✦ Using the Data Analysis tools to create a histogram

✦ Using the SKEW and KURT functions

✦ Using Excel to create charts

✦ Using Excel to modify charts

✦ Different types of charts and their uses

WHY ILLUSTRATE DATA?

In the previous two chapters, you learned about two important types of descriptive statistics—measures of central tendency and measures of variability. Together they provide you with the one best score for describing a group of data (central tendency) and a measure of how diverse, or different, scores are from one another (variability).

What we did not do, and what we will do here, is examine how differences in these two measures result in different-looking distributions. Numbers alone (such as $\overline{X} = 10$ and $s = 3$) may be important,

96

but a visual representation is a much more effective way to allow examination of the characteristics of a distribution as well as the characteristics of any set of data.

In the last edition of this book, we introduced pivot tables (ways of creating new tables from the same data) at the end of this chapter, but with this edition, we're saving that for Chapter 20 when we deal with large data sets. Coverage of pivot tables just seems to fit better there.

So, in this chapter, we'll learn how to visually represent a distribution of scores as well as how to use different types of graphs to represent different types of data.

TEN WAYS TO A GREAT FIGURE (EAT LESS AND EXERCISE MORE?)

Whether you create illustrations by hand or use a computer program, the principles of decent design still apply. Here are 10 to copy and put above your desk.

1. *Minimize chart or graph junk.* "Chart junk" (a close cousin to "word junk") is the result of using every function, every graph, and every feature of a computer program to make your charts busy, full, and uninformative. More is definitely less.

2. *Plan out your chart before you create the final copy.* Use graph paper to create a preliminary sketch even if you will be using a computer program to generate the graph. You can even print out graph paper for free at www .printfreegraphpaper.com.

3. *Say what you mean and mean what you say—no more and no less.* There's nothing worse than a cluttered (with too much text and fancy features) graph to confuse the reader. And there's nothing better than a graph that is simple and straightforward.

4. *Label everything so nothing is left to the misunderstanding of the audience.*

5. *A graph should communicate only one idea.*

6. *Keep things balanced.* When you construct a graph, center the titles and axis labels.

7. *Maintain the scale in a graph.* The scale refers to the relationship between the horizontal and vertical axes. This ratio should approximate the "golden," which is about 1:1.61, so a graph that is 3 inches tall will be about 4.8 or 5 inches wide (just about the size of a standard index card).

8. *Simple is best.* Keep the chart simple, but not simplistic. Convey the one main idea as straightforwardly as possible, with distracting information

saved for the accompanying text. Remember, a chart or graph should be able to stand alone; the reader should be able to understand its message by looking at it.

9. *Limit the number of words you use.* Too many words, or words that are too large, can detract from your chart's visual message.

10. *A chart alone should convey what you want to say.* If it doesn't, go back to your plan and try it again.

Want to read the best resource in the universe on how to make data visually attractive and informative? Get any of Edward R. Tufte's self-published and hugely successful books, such as *The Visual Display of Quantitative Information*, 2nd edition (Graphics Press, 2001, www.edwardtufte.com/tufte/books_vdqi). This book has become a classic for explaining how numerical data can be illustrated.

FIRST THINGS FIRST: CREATING A FREQUENCY DISTRIBUTION

The most basic way to illustrate data is through the creation of a frequency distribution. A **frequency distribution** is a method of tallying, and representing, how often certain scores occur. In the creation of a frequency distribution, scores are usually grouped into **class intervals**, or ranges of numbers.

47	10	31	25	20
2	11	31	25	21
44	14	15	26	21
41	14	16	26	21
7	30	17	27	24
6	30	16	29	24
35	32	15	29	23
38	33	19	28	20
35	34	18	29	21
36	32	16	27	20

Class Interval	Frequency
45–49	1
40–44	2
35–39	4
30–34	8
25–29	10
20–24	10
15–19	8
10–14	4
5–9	2
0–4	1

Here are 50 scores on a test of reading comprehension followed by the frequency distribution for these scores.

The Classiest of Intervals

As you can see from the above table, a class interval is a range of numbers, and the first step in the creation of a frequency distribution is to define how large each interval will be. In the frequency distribution that we created, each interval spans five possible scores such as 5–9 (which contains scores 5, 6, 7, 8, and 9) and 40–44 (which contains scores 40, 41, 42, 43, and 44).

How did we decide our intervals should contain 5 scores? Why not five intervals each consisting of 10 scores? Or two each consisting of 25 scores? Here are some general rules to follow in the creation of a class interval, regardless of the size of values in the data set you are using.

- Select a class interval that has a range of 2, 5, 10, or 20 data points. In our example, we chose 5.
- Also, select a class interval such that 10 to 20 such intervals cover the entire set of data. A convenient way to do this is to compute the range (see Chapter 3), and then divide by a number that represents the number of intervals you want to use (from 10 to 20). In our example, the range is 45 (47 − 2), and we wanted 10 intervals. Thus, $45 \div 10 \approx 5$, which is the size of

each class interval. If you had a set of scores ranging from 100 to 400 and wanted 20 intervals, you could calculate $300 \div 20 \approx 15$, and 15 would be the class interval.

- Begin listing the class interval with a multiple of that interval. In our frequency distribution, the class interval is 5, and we started the lowest class interval at 0.

Note that the largest interval goes at the top of the frequency distribution.

Once class intervals are created, it's time to complete the frequency part of the frequency distribution. That simply means counting the number of times a score occurs in the raw data and entering that number in the appropriate class interval.

In the frequency distribution above, the number of scores between 30 and 34 is 8. So, an 8 goes in the column marked Frequency for the interval 30–34. There's your frequency distribution.

Sometimes it is a good idea to graph your data first and then do whatever calculations or analysis is called for. By first looking at the data, you may gain insight into the relationship between variables, what kind of descriptive statistic is the right one to use to describe the data, and so on. This extra step might increase your insights and the value of what you are doing.

THE PLOT THICKENS: CREATING A HISTOGRAM

Now that we've got a tally of how many scores fall in which class intervals, we'll go to the next step and create what is called a **histogram**, which is a visual representation of the frequency distribution in which the frequencies are represented by bars.

Depending on the book you read and the software you use, visual representations of data are called graphs or charts. It really makes no difference. All you need to know is that a graph or a chart is the visual representation of data.

To create a histogram by hand, do the following:

1. Using a piece of graph paper, place values at equal distances along the x-axis, as shown in Figure 4.1. Now, identify the midpoint of the class intervals, which is the middle point in the class interval.

| **Figure 4.1** | Class Intervals Along the x-Axis |

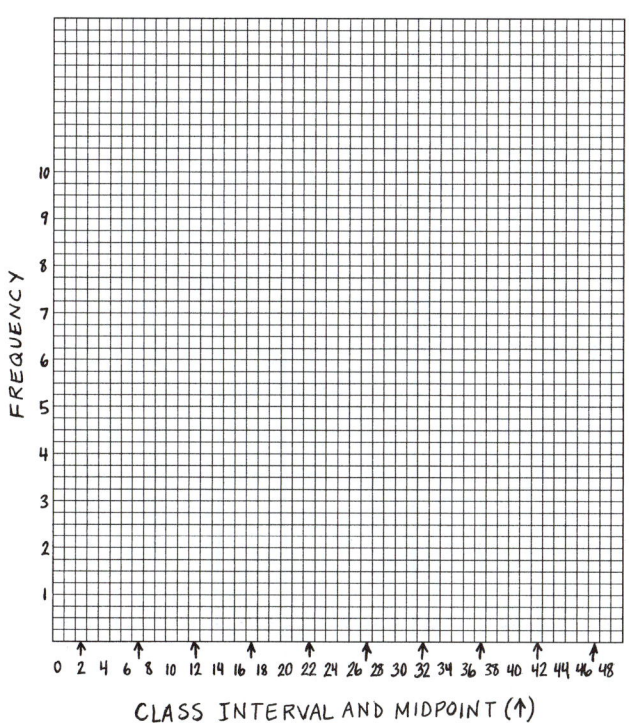

CLASS INTERVAL AND MIDPOINT (↑)

2. It's pretty easy to just eyeball, but you can also just add the top and bottom values of the class interval and divide by 2. For example, the midpoint of the class interval 0–4 is the average of 0 and 4, or (4 + 0) ÷ 2 = 2.

3. Draw a bar or column around each midpoint that represents the entire class interval and make its height represent the frequency of that class interval. For example, in Figure 4.2, you can see that in our first entry, the class interval of 0–4 is represented by the frequency of 1 (representing the one time a value between 0 and 4 occurs). Continue drawing bars (which use horizontal chart elements, as you will see) or columns (which use vertical chart elements, as you will see) until each of the frequencies for each of the class intervals is represented.

4. Figure 4.2 shows a nice hand-drawn (really!) histogram for the frequency distribution of the 50 scores with which we have been working so far. Notice that each class interval is represented by a range of scores along the *x*-axis and is the size of a class interval, in this case 5.

Figure 4.2   A Hand-Drawn Histogram

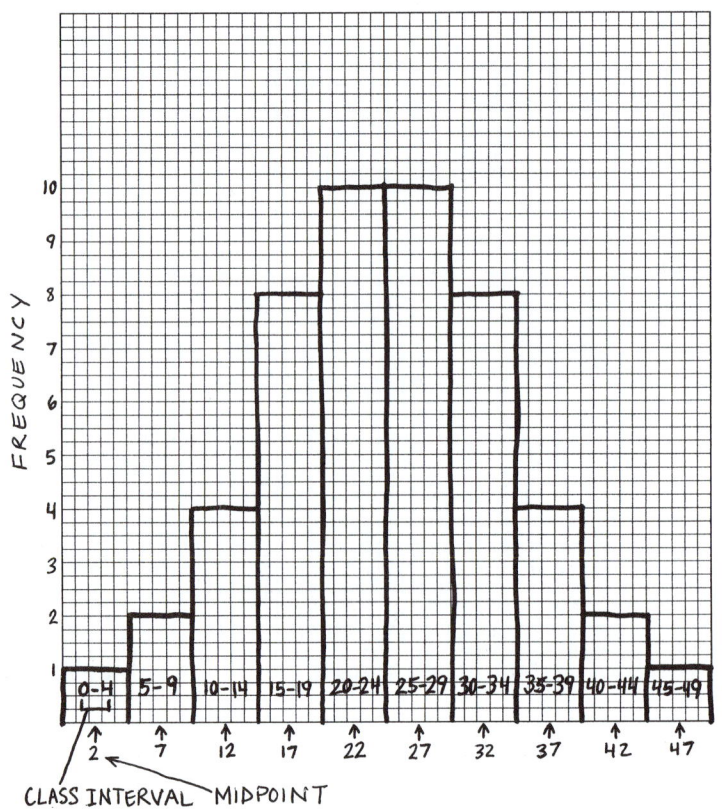

The Tally-Ho Method

From the simple frequency distribution in Figure 4.2, you already know more about the distribution of scores than you could tell from just a simple listing. You have a good idea what values occur with what frequency.

But another visual representation can be made by using tallies for each of the occurrences, as shown in Figure 4.3. We used tallies that correspond with the frequency of scores within each class, giving you an even better visual representation of how often certain scores occur relative to other scores.

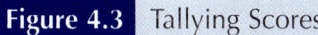

Figure 4.3 Tallying Scores

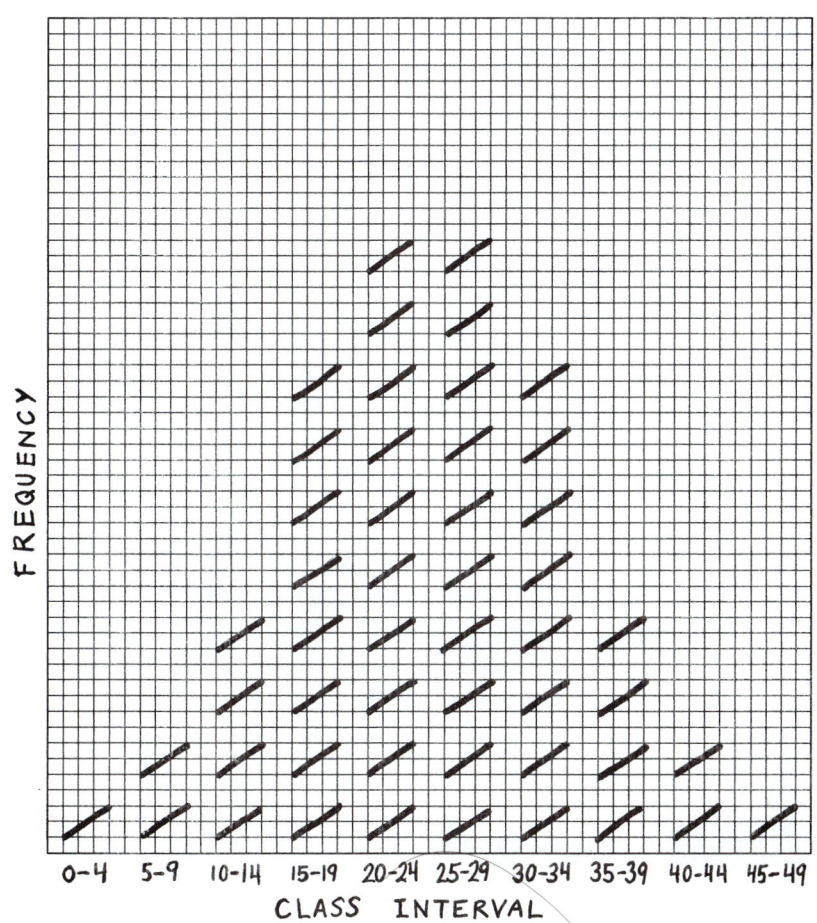

Using the Amazing Data Analysis Tools to Create a Histogram

Here's how Excel creates a histogram using the Histogram tool in the Data Analysis tools.

You will need to do three things:

1. Identify the cells that contain the data from which the histogram will be created.

2. Identify the "bins" or containers (we've been calling them class intervals) in which you want to put the data.

3. Select the Histogram tool from the Data Analysis tools.

You're in business. Try it yourself! Start by entering the data in a new worksheet (as you see in Figure 4.4).

| Figure 4.4 | Data That Will Be Used to Create a Histogram |

	A	B	C	D	E
1	Score				
2	47	10	31	25	20
3	2	11	31	25	21
4	44	14	15	26	21
5	41	14	16	26	21
6	7	30	17	27	24
7	6	30	16	29	224
8	35	32	15	29	23
9	38	33	19	28	20
10	35	34	18	29	21
11	36	32	16	27	20

1. Enter the bins you want to use (as in Figure 4.5). Instead of the range of a bin (or a class interval), you just enter the starting point (such as 4), and the next bin becomes the starting point for the next class interval (such as 9). You can see these bins in Cells G2 through G11 with a title, "Bins," that we entered as well.

| Figure 4.5 | Creating Bins for the Data Analysis Tools Histogram |

	A	B	C	D	E	F	G
1	Score						Bins
2	47	10	31	25	20		49
3	2	11	31	25	21		44
4	44	14	15	26	21		39
5	41	14	16	26	21		34
6	7	30	17	27	24		29
7	6	30	16	29	224		24
8	35	32	15	29	23		19
9	38	33	19	28	20		14
10	35	34	18	29	21		9
11	36	32	16	27	20		4

2. Highlight any blank cell in the worksheet. That's where the histogram will be placed.

3. Click Data → Data Analysis, and you will see the Data Analysis dialog box, as shown in Figure 4.6.

Figure 4.6 The Data Analysis Dialog Box

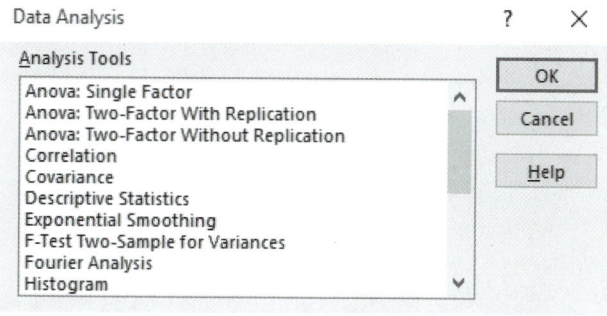

4. Scroll down until you see the Histogram tool and double-click on it. When you do this, you will see the Histogram dialog box, as shown in Figure 4.7.

Figure 4.7 The Histogram Dialog Box

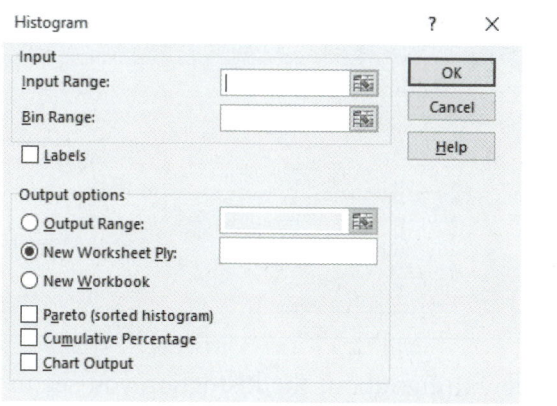

5. Click on the Input Range box and drag the mouse over the range that contains the data, which in this case is Cells A2 through E11.

6. Click on the Bin Range and drag the mouse over the range that contains the bins, which in this case is Cells G2 through G11.

7. Click the Output Range button. Enter the address where the histogram will be created. One cell will do. In our example, we entered H1.

8. Click the Cumulative Percentage and Chart Output options. The first gives you the cumulative values (adding up the frequencies) and the second a visual view. The completed dialog box for creating a histogram is shown in Figure 4.8.

Figure 4.8	The Completed Histogram Dialog Box

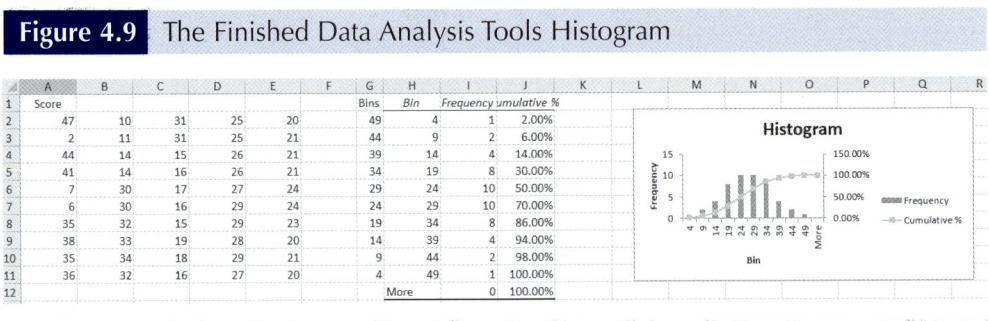

9. Click OK, and there you go as you see in Figure 4.9: a frequency distribution and a (cleaned up) pretty histogram.

Figure 4.9	The Finished Data Analysis Tools Histogram

	A	B	C	D	E	F	G	H	I	J
1	Score						Bins	Bin	Frequency	umulative %
2	47	10	31	25	20		49	4	1	2.00%
3	2	11	31	25	21		44	9	2	6.00%
4	44	14	15	26	21		39	14	4	14.00%
5	41	14	16	26	21		34	19	8	30.00%
6	7	30	17	27	24		29	24	10	50.00%
7	6	30	16	29	24		24	29	10	70.00%
8	35	32	15	29	23		19	34	8	86.00%
9	38	33	19	28	20		14	39	4	94.00%
10	35	34	18	29	21		9	44	2	98.00%
11	36	32	16	27	20		4	49	1	100.00%
12								More	0	100.00%

Notice a few things about the histogram you see in Figure 4.9.

- Excel always creates bins with the lowest bin value first.
- It creates two columns, one named Bin (where it creates the class intervals) and one named Frequency (where it enters the frequencies).
- It creates a category labeled More, where any values outside of the range that the bins can contain are placed. So, for example, if there were a value such as 87 in the data set, it would show up as 1 value in the More category.

The Next Step: A Frequency Polygon

Creating a histogram or a tally of scores wasn't so difficult, and the next step (and the next way of illustrating data) is even easier. We're going to use the same data—and, in fact, the histogram from

Figure 4.2—to create a frequency polygon. A **frequency polygon** is a continuous line that represents the frequencies of scores within a class interval, as shown in Figure 4.10.

Figure 4.10 A Hand-Drawn Frequency Polygon

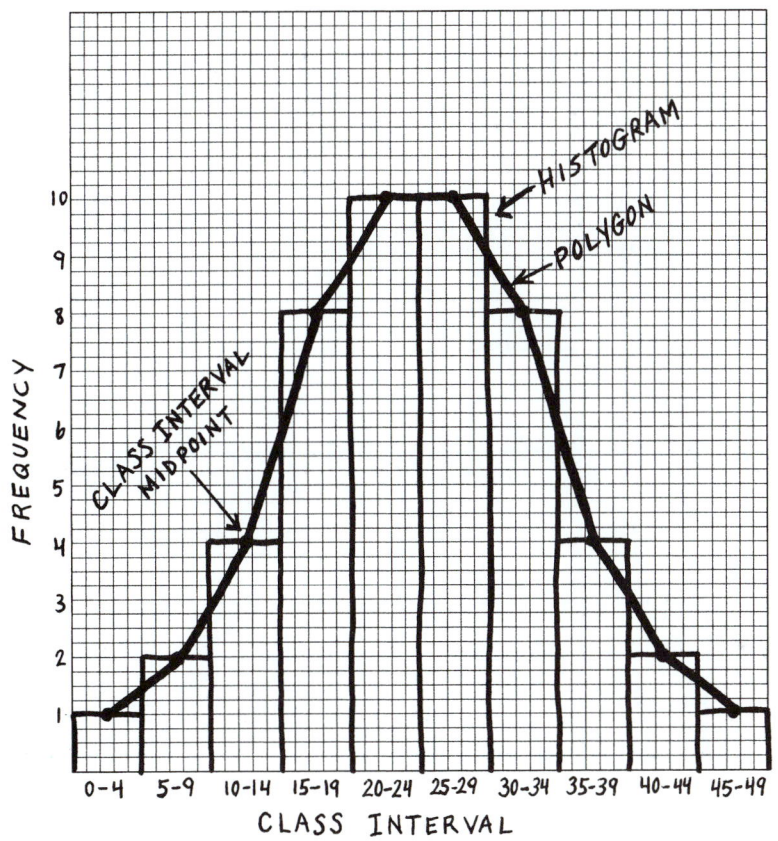

How did we draw this? Here's how.

1. Place a midpoint at the top of each bar or column in a histogram (see Figure 4.2).
2. Connect the lines, and you've got it—a frequency polygon!

Why use a frequency polygon rather than a histogram to represent data? It's more a matter of preference than anything else. A frequency polygon appears more dynamic than a histogram (a line that represents change in frequency always looks neat), but you are basically conveying the same information.

Cumulating Frequencies

Once you have created a frequency distribution and have visually represented those data using a histogram or a frequency polygon, another option is to create a visual representation of the cumulative frequency of occurrences by class intervals. This is called a **cumulative frequency distribution**.

A cumulative frequency distribution is based on the same data as a frequency distribution, but it has an added column (Cumulative Frequency), as shown below.

Class Interval	Frequency	Cumulative Frequency
45–49	1	50
40–44	2	49
35–39	4	47
30–34	8	43
25–29	10	35
20–24	10	25
15–19	8	15
10–14	4	7
5–9	2	3
0–4	1	1

The cumulative frequency distribution begins with the creation of a new column labeled Cumulative Frequency. Then, we add the frequency in a class interval to all the frequencies below it. For example, for the class interval of 0–4, there is 1 occurrence and none below it, so the cumulative frequency is 1. For the class interval of 5–9, there are 2 occurrences in that class interval and 1 below it for a total of 3 (2 + 1). The last class interval (45–49) contains 1 occurrence, and there is a total of 50 occurrences at or below that class interval.

Once we create the cumulative frequency distribution, the data can be plotted just as they were for a histogram or a frequency polygon. Only this time, we'll skip ahead and plot the midpoint of each class interval as a function of the cumulative frequency of that class interval. You can see the cumulative frequency distribution in Figure 4.11 based on the 50 scores from the beginning of this chapter.

But lo and behold! Don't overlook Figure 4.9 where there is a Cumulative % line which is (more or less) identical to the same line as the cumulative frequency. The most important point is that the shape remains very similar, regardless of whether you use frequencies or percentages.

Figure 4.11	A Hand-Drawn Cumulative Frequency Distribution

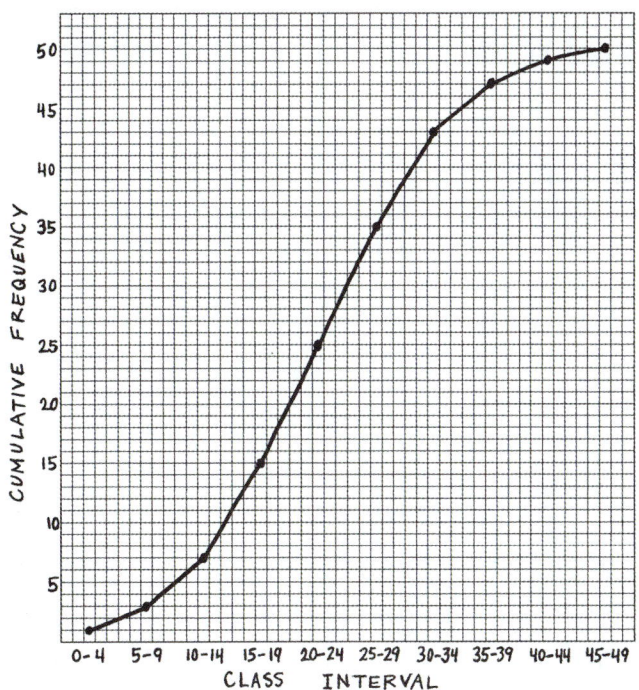

Another name for a cumulative frequency polygon is an **ogive**. And, if the distribution of the data is normal (see Chapter 8 for more on this), then the ogive is another way to illustrate what is popularly known as a bell curve or a normal distribution.

FAT AND SKINNY FREQUENCY DISTRIBUTIONS

You could certainly surmise by now that distributions can be very different from one another in a variety of ways. In fact, there are four ways in which they differ: average value, variability, skewness, and kurtosis. Those last two are new terms, and we'll define them as we show you what they look like. Let's describe each of the four characteristics and then illustrate them.

Average Value

We're back once again to measures of central tendency. You can see in Figure 4.12 how three distributions can differ in their average value. Notice that the average for Distribution C is more than the average for Distribution B, which, in turn, is more than the average for Distribution A.

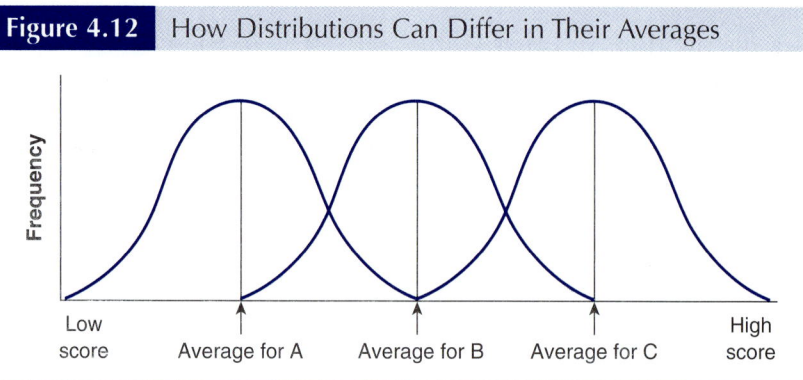

Figure 4.12   How Distributions Can Differ in Their Averages

Variability

In Figure 4.13, you can see three distributions that all have the same average value but differ in variability. The variability in

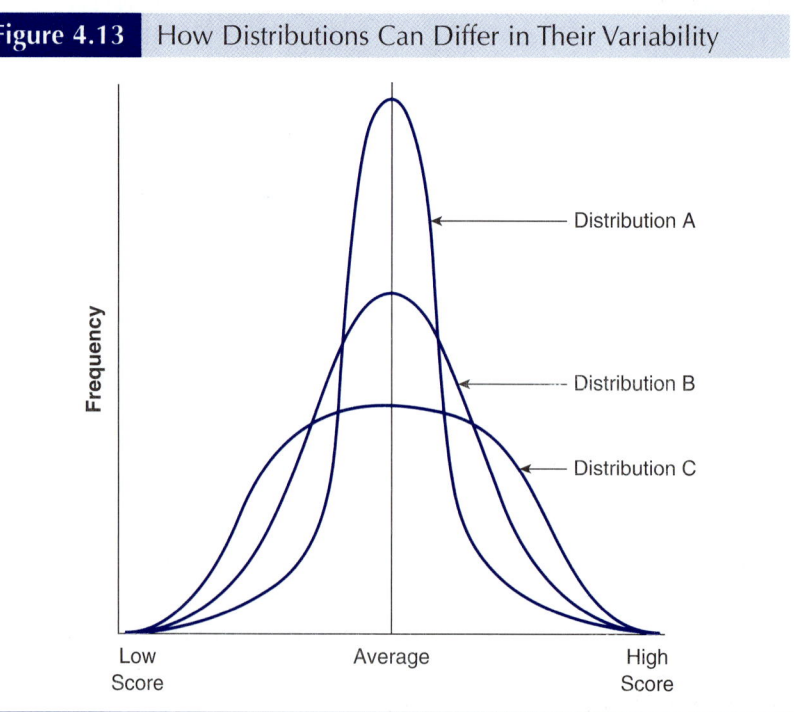

Figure 4.13   How Distributions Can Differ in Their Variability

Distribution A is less than that in Distribution B and, in turn, less than that found in C. Another way to say this is that Distribution C has the largest amount of variability of the three distributions and A has the least.

Skewness

Skewness is a measure of the lack of symmetry, or the lopsidedness, of a distribution. In other words, one "tail" of the distribution is longer than another. For example, in Figure 4.14, Distribution A's right tail is longer than its left tail, reflecting a smaller number of occurrences at the high end of the distribution. This is a *positively* skewed distribution. This might be the case when you have a test that is very difficult, on which a few people get scores that are relatively high and many more get scores that are relatively low.

In contrast, Distribution C's right tail is shorter than its left tail, reflecting a larger number of occurrences at the high end of the distribution. This is a *negatively* skewed distribution and would be the case for an easy test (lots of high scores and relatively few low scores).

And Distribution B—well, it's just right (Goldilocks would approve!), with equal lengths of tails and no skewness.

Figure 4.14	How Distributions Can Differ in Degree of Skewness

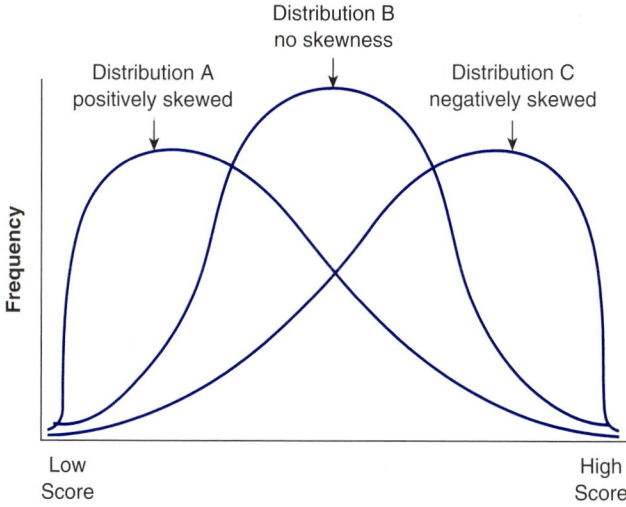

Note that if the mean is greater than the median, the distribution is positively skewed. If the median is greater than the mean, the distribution is negatively skewed.

Kurtosis

Even though this sounds like a medical condition, it's the last of the four ways that we can classify how distributions differ from one another. **Kurtosis** has to do with how flat or peaked a distribution appears, and the terms used to describe this characteristic are relative ones. For example, the term **platykurtic** refers to a distribution that is relatively flat compared with a normal, or bell-shaped, distribution. The term **leptokurtic** refers to a distribution that is relatively peaked compared with a normal, or bell-shaped, distribution. In Figure 4.15, Distribution A is platykurtic compared with Distribution B. Distribution C is leptokurtic compared with Distribution B.

Figure 4.15 looks similar to Figure 4.13 for a good reason: Distributions that are platykurtic, for example, are relatively more dispersed than those that are not. Similarly, a distribution that is leptokurtic is less variable or dispersed relative to others.

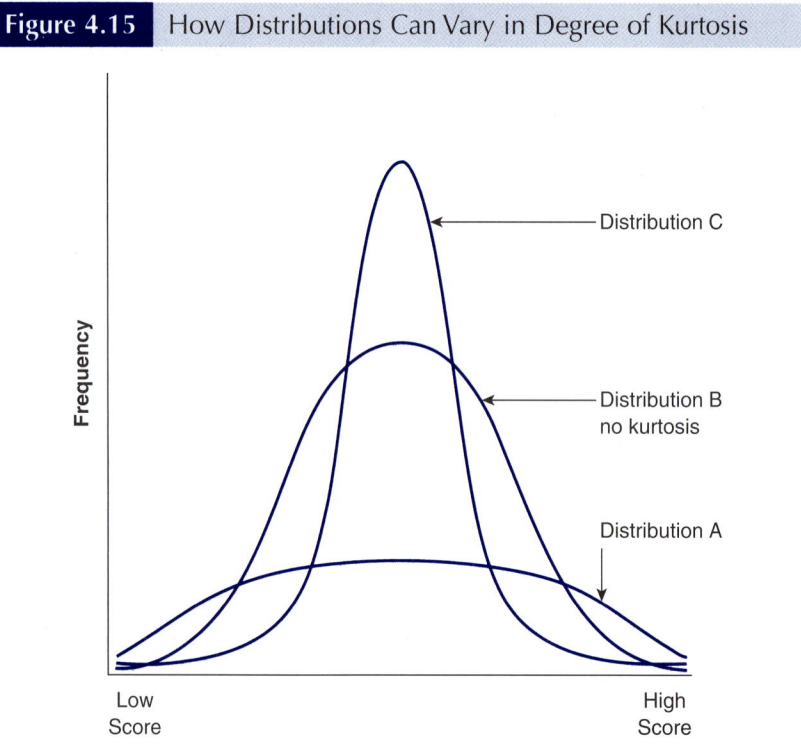

Figure 4.15   How Distributions Can Vary in Degree of Kurtosis

Excel can help you compute a value for kurtosis and skewness of a set of scores. You can use the **SKEW** and the **KURT** functions to compute

such values. For example, if you have 20 scores in Cells A1 through A20, then the functions would look like this:

=SKEW(A1:A20)

=KURT(A1:A20)

Just enter the function in the cell where you want the results returned.

While skewness and kurtosis are used mostly as descriptive terms (as in "That distribution is negatively skewed"), there are mathematical indicators of how skewed or kurtotic a distribution is (and indeed, the functions SKEW and KURT deliver values as measures of these distribution characteristics). Skewness is computed by subtracting the value of the median from the mean. For example, if the mean of a distribution is 100 and the median is 95, the skewness value is 100 − 95 = 5, and the distribution is positively skewed.

If the mean of a distribution is 85 and the median is 90, the skewness value is 85 − 90 = −5, and the distribution is negatively skewed. An even more sophisticated formula is not relative but takes the standard deviation of the distribution into account so that skewness indicators can be compared with one another:

$$sk = \frac{3(\overline{X} - M)}{s} \qquad (4.1)$$

where

sk   is Pearson's (he's the correlation guy you'll learn about in Chapter 5) measure of skewness;

$\overline{X}$ is the mean; and

M   is the median.

Using this formula, we can compare the skewness of one distribution with another in absolute, not relative, terms. For example, the mean of Distribution A is 100, the median is 105, and the standard deviation is 10. For Distribution B, the mean is 120, the median is 116, and the standard deviation is 10. Using Pearson's formula, the skewness of Distribution A is −1.5, and the skewness of Distribution B is 1.2. Distribution A is negatively skewed, and Distribution B is positively skewed. However, Distribution A is more skewed than Distribution B, regardless of the direction. One follow-up note: Formula 4.1 is not the one that Excel uses—we selected it since it is easier to understand and to use than the one that Excel uses.

EXCEL-LENT CHARTS

Now the fun begins.

In this section of this chapter on charts, we'll show you how Excel can be used to create a simple chart in a matter of minutes (actually seconds, and using just three—that's right, three—steps). We'll also show you how, once the chart is created, you can pretty it up and make it even more informative. We'll create the column chart you see in Figure 4.16 that shows the number of males and females who participated in a survey, and then show you how you can make some simple, but impressive, edits.

Why is the chart in Figure 4.16 called a column chart and not a bar chart? The folks who created Excel named charts with bars that are vertical *column charts* and charts with bars that are horizontal *bar charts*. That's just the way it is.

Figure 4.16   A Simple Column Chart

Just a few things to remember about creating Excel charts:

- Excel will chart the data that you highlight, but you may have to first compute the values you want charted. For example, if you have a list of values and want to chart the average value, you will have to compute the average value and then chart it.
- Excel creates a chart of the worksheet that contains the data used to create that chart in the first place, as you see in Figure 4.16. When you save a worksheet that contains a chart, you save both the data on which the chart is based and the chart itself.

- When the data that were used to create a chart change, the chart itself will change. These two elements (the data and the chart) are linked. This is sometimes called dynamic linking.
- Charts can easily be cut and pasted into other applications (as we will show you later). In addition, they can be linked so that changing the chart in Excel, for example, also changes the chart in a dynamically linked Word document.
- Excel offers a myriad (that means lots and lots) of different kinds of charts, all of which can be created with just a few clicks and then modified as you see fit.

Just one more note before the fun begins. Creating charts is easy. Creating good ones is not. Charts have to do everything that we've talked about since the beginning of this chapter. So do get excited and follow the rules and guidelines, but don't get so excited that you substitute a chart for understanding the data you are charting.

Your First Excel Chart:
A Moment to Remember (Sigh)

To create a chart in Excel, follow these steps:

1. Highlight the data you want to use to create the chart. In Figure 4.17, we would highlight Cells A1 through B2.

2. Click the Insert tab and in the Charts group, and select the type of chart you want to use. In Figure 4.17, we selected Column.

Figure 4.17 Selecting a Specific Type of Chart to Create

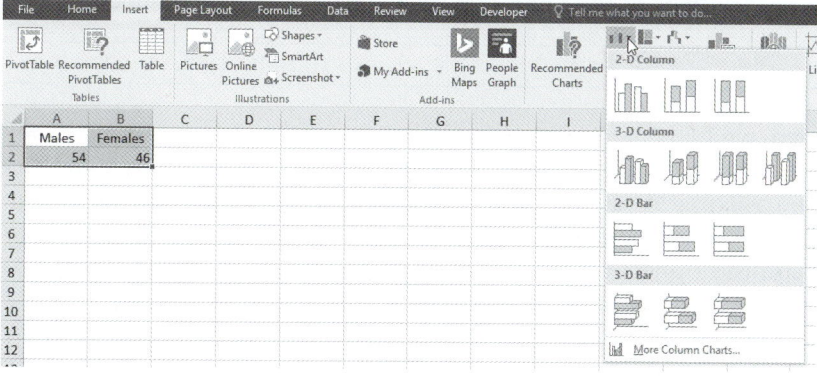

3. Click the first icon under 2-D Column (because Column will already be selected), and zingo—there you have it, just as you saw in Figure 4.16. A very nice and tidy column chart completed in very few clicks. It just does not get any easier.

You can easily increase or decrease the size of a chart on a worksheet by selecting the chart (just click on it) and dragging on any of the handles that appear. If you drag on one handle at the top or bottom, you will increase the height of the chart. If you drag on a handle located on the left or right, you will change the width. But in both these cases, only one dimension changes, and you're bound to get weird results. If you drag on a corner handle, on the other hand, then both dimensions change at the same time. Wonderful. You can also change the location of the chart on a worksheet by placing the cursor on the chart so that the pointer turns into a crosshair and then dragging the chart where you want it.

Now, that's pretty easy and all done in just a few clicks. And, as you can see in Figure 4.17, we could have selected any of the types of charts that are listed (or tried out the other chart options as well). Of course, a chart should be used only when the data are of the appropriate type, but there sure is a cool assortment of charts to create.

But what if you want to place a chart on its own worksheet? Here's how:

1. Select the chart by clicking anywhere in its boundaries.

2. Click Copy in the ribbon on the Home tab.

3. Create a new worksheet or open an established one by clicking on the + sign (it is within a circle) at the bottom of the current worksheet.

4. Click Paste in the ribbon on the Home tab.

Here we go with the dynamic linking stuff.

Once you create a chart, it is like any other Excel element and can be easily cut or copied from Excel and pasted into a new document (such as Word or any other Windows or Mac application). However, if you just do the straight cut/copy and paste, then changes in the data used to create the chart will not show up in the chart that is pasted into another application. To make this happen, you have to dynamically link the data used to create the chart to the chart in its new location.

This is very cool stuff, but be careful—remember that changes in your Excel worksheet will result in changes in the chart, if linked, no matter where the chart is pasted. Follow these steps:

1. Highlight the chart. Right-click and select the Copy option.

2. Switch to the Word document or any other Microsoft Office product such as PowerPoint (and often non-Microsoft products as well) into which you want to paste the chart.

3. On the Home tab, select the Use Destination Theme & Embed Workbook from the Paste Options menu on the ribbon. This way, whatever changes are made in the chart created in Excel will also be made in the chart in the new application.

EXCEL-LENT CHARTS PART DEUX: MAKING CHARTS PRETTY

There are a million ways to change the appearance of a chart, and every element in that chart—from the size and type of font, to the color of the lines, to the background—can be changed as well. Our advice—create a simple chart and then have some fun fooling around to see what you can do. But do try to avoid the feared land of Chart Junk. Also, always save your original chart as you work (just save your experiments under new names) so you can return to it when necessary (and if you fool around a lot, we guarantee it will be necessary).

Color is dandy if that's what you want to include in your charts to emphasize a particular visual point. However, color can be a mess unless you use it sparingly. Also, color sometimes prints pretty weirdly on black-and-white printers, and on color printers it's expensive to print. And it can make things even more confusing! So, keep it simple and use color only when you need to and when you can print in color as well.

There are several ways to modify the appearance of a chart such as the one you see in Figure 4.16.

- You can right-click on any element in the chart such as the vertical axis and make the changes you want.
- You can click once on the chart and then use the options under Chart Tools (with Design and Format options), which appears on the Excel ribbon.
- You can double-click on the chart and use the tools that show up to the right of the chart.

We'll review these approaches, with our main goal being ease of editing. We think a simple left-click with the mouse is the quickest and the easiest. Left-click on the chart to highlight it so that all the Chart Tools (which you see in Figure 4.18: the plus icon, the brush icon, and the funnel icon) are visible and available. We'll work only with Chart Elements and Chart Styles (the first two).

Figure 4.18   The Chart Tools

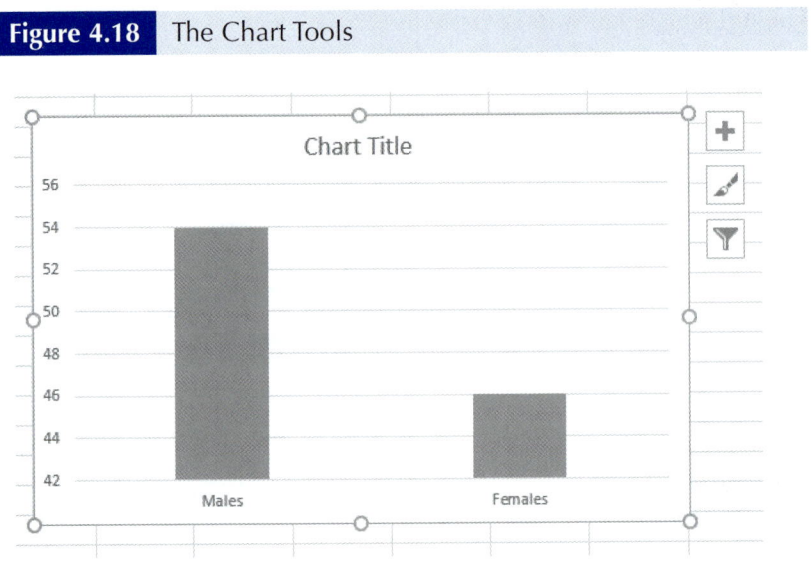

Working With Chart Elements

To work with a chart's elements, click on the "plus" icon as you see in Figure 4.19. Here you can select which elements will be visible in the chart. For example, in Figure 4.19 you can see that we have selected to view the Axes, Chart Title, and Gridlines.

Figure 4.19   Adding Elements to a Chart

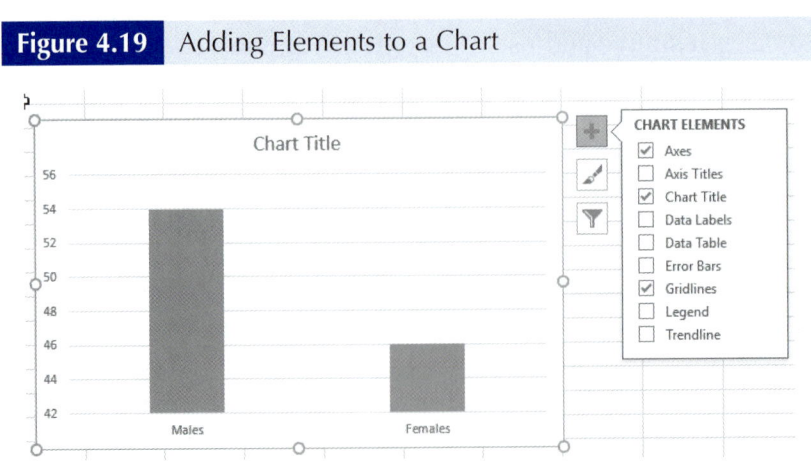

To make changes in what elements are available, just check or uncheck the appropriate box. For example, in Figure 4.20, we want to make visible just Axes and Chart Title, so we unclicked Gridlines so they would no longer appear in the chart. So far, our edited chart appears as shown in Figure 4.21.

Figure 4.20   Working With Chart Elements

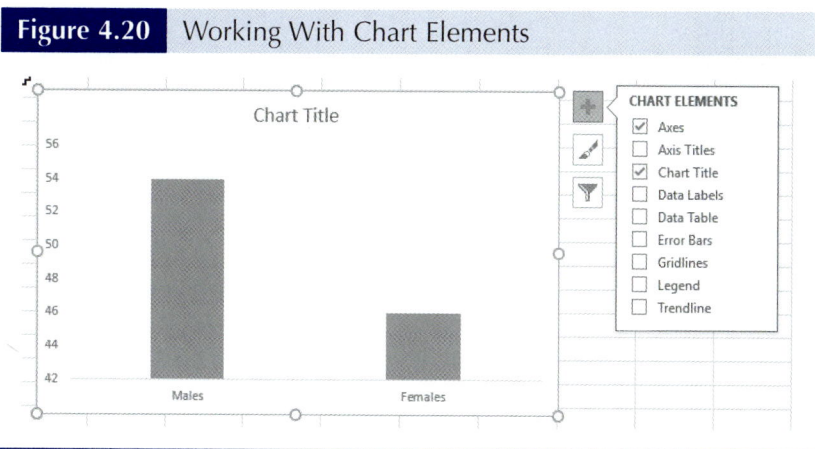

Figure 4.21   Changing Chart Elements

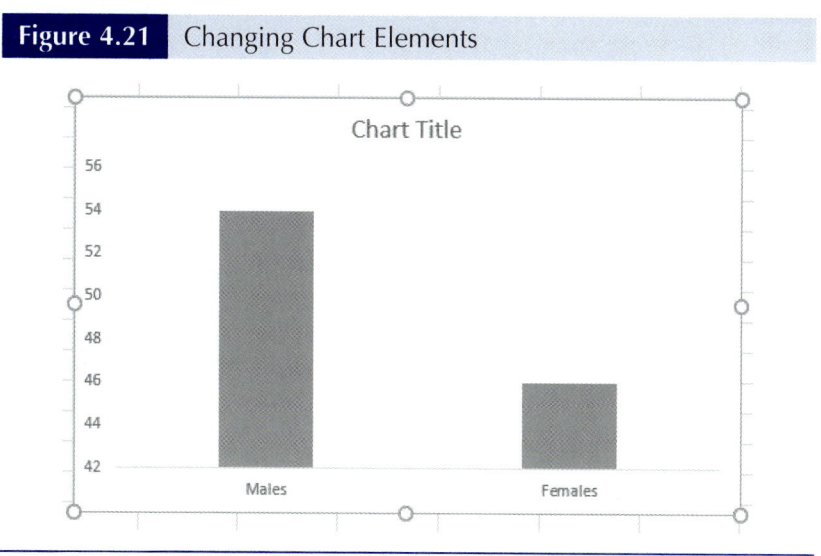

Working With Chart Styles

To work with a chart's styles, click on the "brush" icon as you see in Figure 4.22. Here you work with the Style and the Color(s) to change the appearance of the chart. For example, in Figure 4.23 we have selected Style 10 (of 16—and you have to scroll down to see it and it is not labeled 10 so just count) to accompany the other changes that we've made.

Figure 4.22   Working With Chart Styles

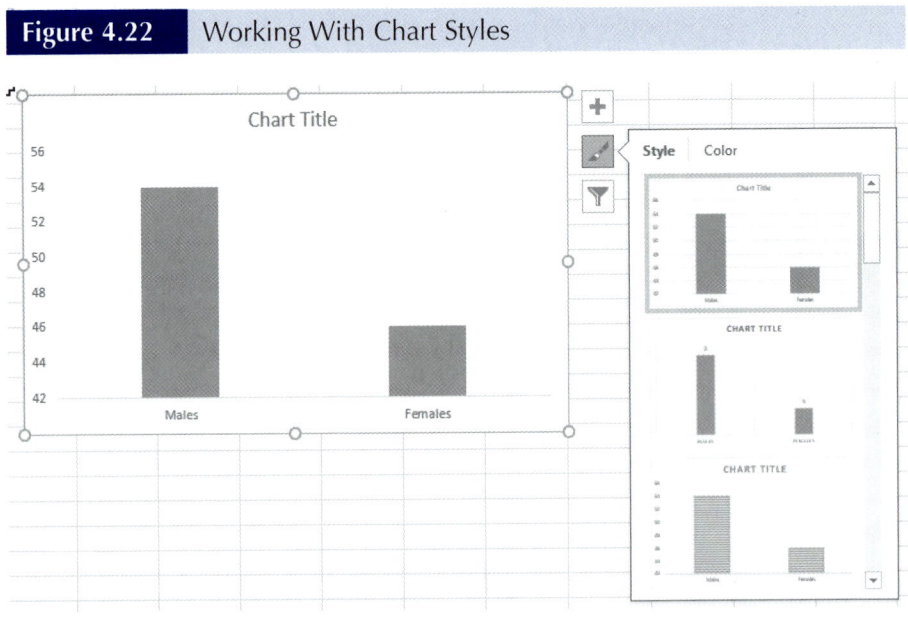

Figure 4.23   A Simple Chart, Simply Changed

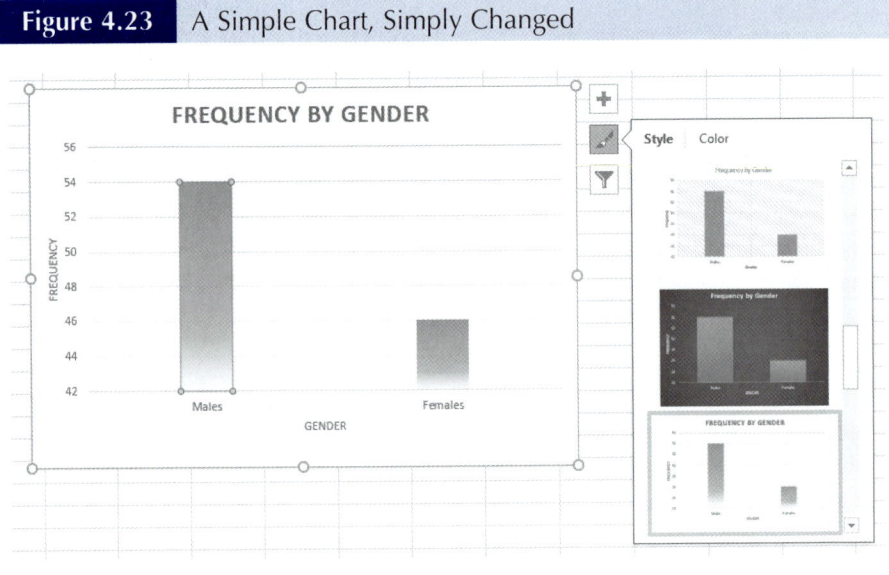

Here's the grand pooh-bah of editing charts. You can simply double-click (not single-click) on any area of the chart and you will get a host of options, such as you see in Figure 4.24. Here we just double-clicked on the Chart Title. Now, you can select from the smorgasbord of changes that can be made.

Figure 4.24 Clicking on a Chart Element and Making Changes

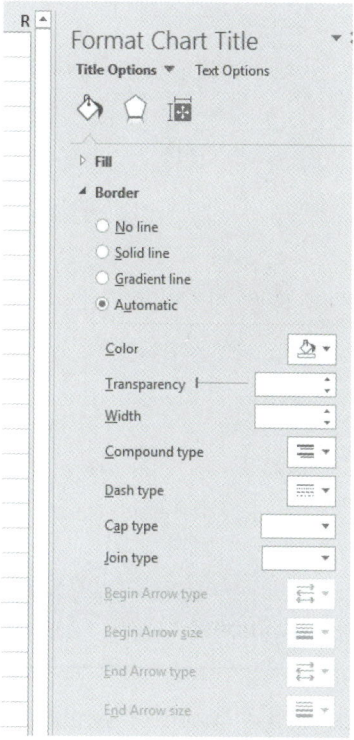

Here's something you may find very useful (and very cool)—using images as elements in a chart. For example, instead of having rectangles represent the number of males and females in the class in a bar chart, why not have little graphic icons? Much more visual and instantly informative. To use an image in a chart, follow these steps:

1. Create the chart.

2. Double-click on the element for which you want to substitute the image. In this case, we are selecting only one of the columns (since we want different graphics to be used for each column element). When you do this, you will see the Format Data Series panel on the right side of the window, as shown in Figure 4.25.

3. Click the Bucket icon. Click the Picture or texture fill option under the Fill drop-down menu. When you do this, you get a variety of options from where to select a picture including File. . ., Clipboard, or Online. . .

4. We selected Online, which took us to a collection of images (after we entered "male symbol" in the Search box).

Figure 4.25   The Format Data Series Options

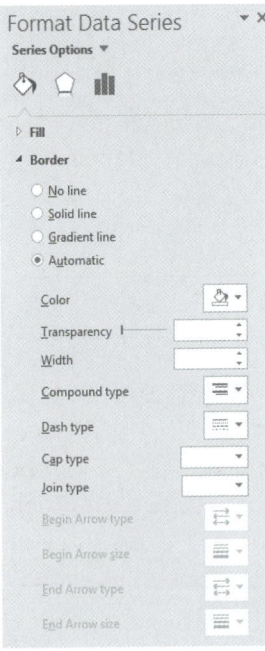

5. We then clicked on the image of symbol for males, and Excel replaced the Males column bar with that symbol. Then we repeated steps 3 and 4 above and found a symbol for a female. You can see the result in Figure 4.26.

Figure 4.26   Using Images as Chart Elements

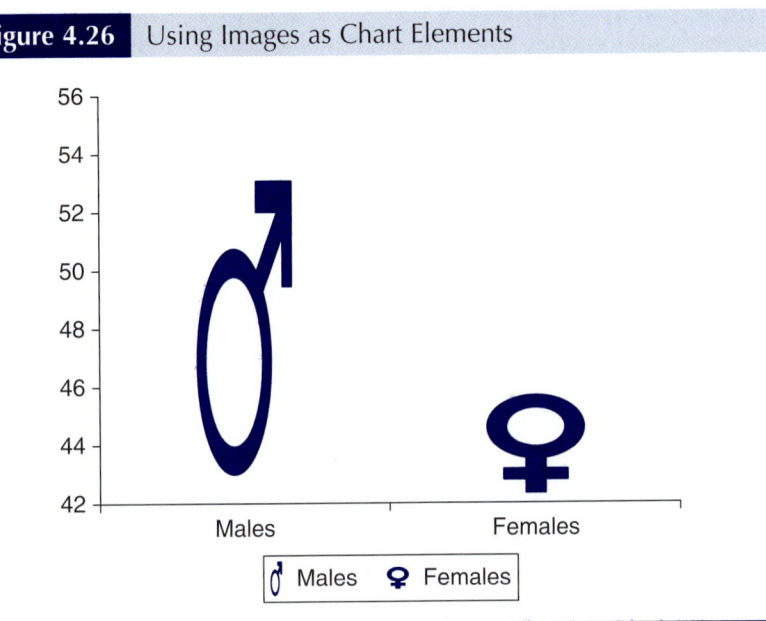

As you can see, you can pick a variety of fills, colors, styles, shadows, and more for the chart that you are modifying. And you can change titles, label axes, etc.—you can spend days on this stuff! But don't do that. That's the point—make it clear by making it simple.

Our advice: Fool around with all these options because that's the best way to get to know what they can do and when you should use them.

OTHER COOL CHARTS

What we've done so far in this chapter is show how charts such as histograms and polygons can be used to communicate data visually and how easily an Excel chart can be modified. But several other types of charts are used in the behavioral and social sciences, and although it's not necessary for you to know exactly how to create them, you should at least be familiar with their names and what they do. So, here are some popular charts and when to use them.

Bar Charts

A bar chart is identical to a column chart, but in this chart, categories are organized on the *y*-axis and values are shown horizontally on the *x*-axis.

Line Charts

A line chart should be used when you want to show a trend in the data at equal intervals. Here are some examples of when you might want to use a line chart:

- Number of cases of mononucleosis (mono) per season among college students at three state universities
- Change in student enrollment over the school year
- Number of travelers on two different airlines for each quarter

In Figure 4.27, you can see a chart of the number of complaints by month at a major retail chain.

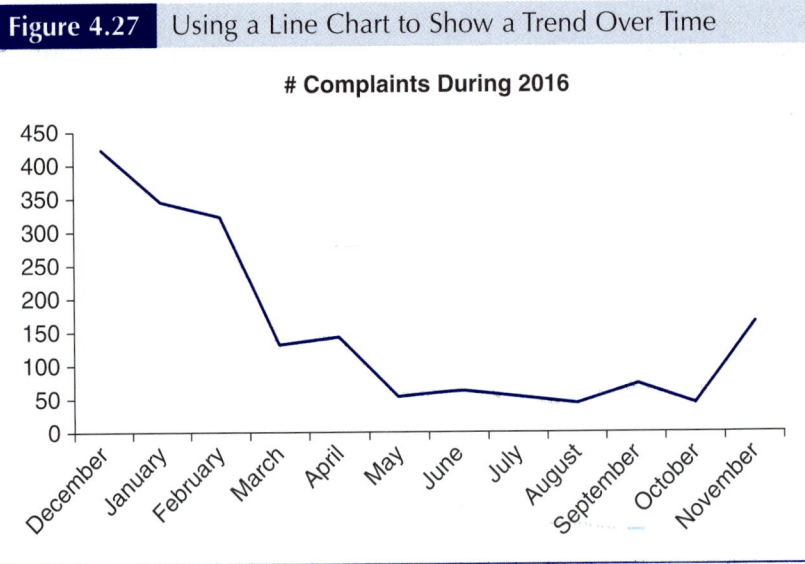

Figure 4.27   Using a Line Chart to Show a Trend Over Time

Pie Charts

A pie chart should be used when you want to show the proportion of an item that makes up a series of data points. Here are some examples of when you might want to use a pie chart:

- Percentage of children living in poverty by ethnicity
- Proportion of night students and day students enrolled
- Age of participants by gender

In Figure 4.28, you can see a pie chart of the number of volunteers by political party. We made it three-dimensional (sort of just for fun), but it doesn't look so bad in any case. You can also see in Figure 4.28 that resting the cursor on top of any segment of the chart gives you additional information about that segment of the chart. Pretty cool.

When creating charts in Excel, you have to learn when to single-click, when to double-click, and when to right-click. In the pie chart example, we would have right-clicked to select all the chart slices to change the fill pattern, but we would have left-clicked to select only one slice.

Figure 4.28	Using a Pie Chart to Show Proportions of Volunteers by Political Party

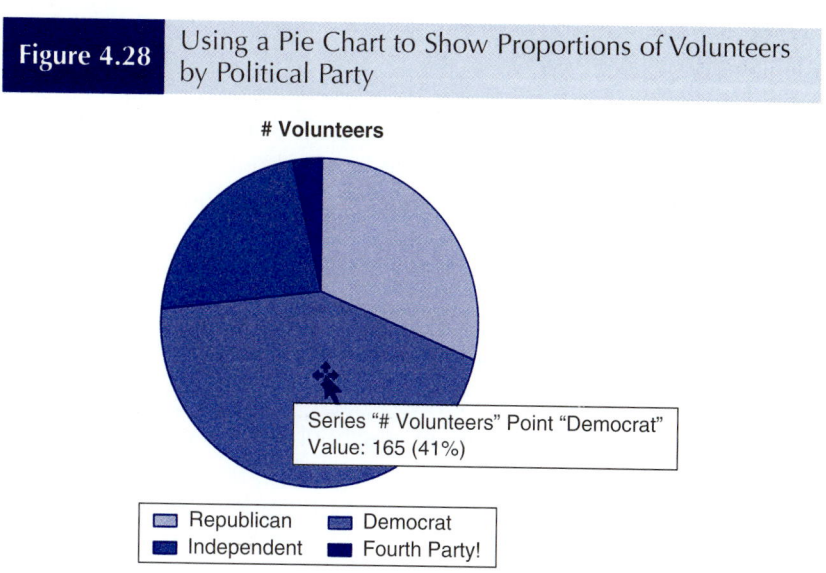

 # Volunteers

Series "# Volunteers" Point "Democrat"
Value: 165 (41%)

Republican　Democrat
Independent　Fourth Party!

REAL-WORLD STATS

A picture really is worth more than a thousand words. In this article, an oldie-but-goodie, the researchers examine how people perceive and process statistical graphs. Stephen Lewandowsky and Ian Spence review empirical studies designed to explore how suitable different types of graphs are and how what is known about human perception can impact the design and utility of these charts.

These authors focus on some of the theoretical explanations for why certain elements work and don't, the use of pictorial symbols (like a happy face symbol, which could make up the bar in a bar chart), and the use of multivariate displays to represent more than one set of data. And, as is very often the case with scholarly articles, they conclude that not enough data is available yet. Given the increasingly visual world in which we live (icons, anyone?), this is interesting and useful reading to gain a historical perspective on how information was (and still is) discussed as a scientific topic.

Want to know more? Go online or go to the library, and look for . . .

Lewandowsky, S., & Spence, I. (1989). The perception of statistical graphs. *Sociological Methods Research, 18,* 200–242.

SUMMARY

There's no question that charts are fun to create and can organize what at first appear to be disorganized data, greatly improving understanding. Follow our suggestions in this chapter and use charts well—only when they enhance, not just add to, what's already there.

TIME TO PRACTICE

1. A data set of 50 comprehension scores (Comp Score) named Chapter 4 Data Set 1 is available on the book's website at http://edge.sagepub.com/salkindexcel4e and in Appendix C. Complete the tasks and answer the questions below.

   a. Create a frequency distribution and a histogram for the set.

   b. Why did you select the class interval you used?

   c. Is this distribution skewed? How do you know?

2. What kind of chart would you use to illustrate the following data?

   a. The number of students in a school district over a period of 10 years

   b. The proportion of 9th, 10th, and 11th graders who participate in extracurricular activities

   c. The number of children who are fully immunized versus those who are not

3. For each of the following, indicate whether you would use a pie, line, or bar/column chart and explain why.

   a. The proportion of freshmen, sophomores, juniors, and seniors in a particular university

   b. Change in a student's GPA over four semesters

   c. Number of applicants for four different jobs

   d. Reaction times to a repeated stimulus

   e. Number of scores in each of 10 repeated categories for one participant

4. Go to the library and find a journal article in your area of interest that contains empirical data but does not contain any visual representation of them. Use the data to create a chart. Be sure to specify what type of chart you are creating and why you chose the one you did. You can create the chart manually or use Excel.

5. Create a simple column chart that graphs the sales of an ice cream shop over the summer, fall, winter, and spring seasons. If you can, use an ice cream cone for the column. Now, see if you can easily change the look of the chart by selecting the Chart Type.

6. Create the worst-looking chart that you can, crowded with chart and font junk. If it's worse than your study buddy's chart, you win.

7. Create a simple bar chart for number of faculty at different ranks (assistant, associate, and full professor) and label the data sets and include axes and chart titles, minor and major vertical grid lines, and data labels (outside of the bars).

5 Ice Cream and Crime

Computing Correlation Coefficients

Difficulty Scale ☺ ☺ (moderately hard)

How much Excel? 📊 📊 📊 📊 (lots and lots)

WHAT ARE CORRELATIONS ALL ABOUT?

Measures of central tendency and measures of variability are not the only descriptive statistics that we are interested in using to get a picture of what a set of scores looks like. You have already learned that knowing the value of the one most representative score (central tendency) and a measure of spread or dispersion (variability) is critical for describing the characteristics of a distribution.

However, sometimes we are as interested in the relationship between variables—or, to be more precise, how the value of one variable changes when the value of another variable changes. The way we express this interest is through the computation of a simple

127

correlation coefficient. For example, what's the relationship between age and strength? Income and education? Memory skills and drug use? Voting preferences and attitude toward regulation?

A **correlation coefficient** is a numerical index that reflects the relationship between two variables such as any of those we just listed. The value of this descriptive statistic ranges between −1 and +1. A correlation between two variables is sometimes referred to as a **bivariate** (for two variables) **correlation**. Even more specifically, the type of correlation that we talk about in the majority of this chapter is called the **Pearson product-moment correlation**, named for its inventor, Karl Pearson.

The Pearson correlation coefficient examines the relationship between two variables, when both of those variables are continuous in nature. In other words, they are variables that can assume any value along some underlying continuum, such as height, age, test score, or income. But a host of other variables are not continuous. These are called discrete or categorical variables, and examples include race (such as black and white), social class (such as high and low), and political affiliation (such as Democrat and Republican). You need to use other correlational techniques, such as the point-biserial correlation, in these cases. These topics are for a more advanced course, but you should know that such techniques exist and are very useful for certain analyses. We mention them briefly later in this chapter.

There are other types of correlation coefficients that measure the relationship between more than two variables, and we'll leave those for the next statistics course (which you are looking forward to already, right?).

Types of Correlation Coefficients: Flavor 1 and Flavor 2

A correlation reflects the dynamic quality of the relationship between variables. In doing so, it allows us to understand whether variables tend to move in the same or opposite directions when they change. If variables change in the same direction, the correlation is called a **direct correlation** or a positive correlation. If variables change in opposite directions, the correlation is called an **indirect correlation** or a negative correlation. Table 5.1 shows a summary of these relationships.

| Table 5.1 | Types of Correlations and the Corresponding Relationship Between Variables |

What Happens to Variable X	What Happens to Variable Y	Type of Correlation	Value	Example
X increases in value	Y increases in value	Direct or positive	Positive, ranging from 0 to +1	The more time you spend studying, the higher your test score will be.
X decreases in value	Y decreases in value	Direct or positive	Positive, ranging from 0 to +1	The less money you put in the bank, the less interest you will earn.
X increases in value	Y decreases in value	Indirect or negative	Negative, ranging from −1 to 0	The more you exercise, the less you will weigh.
X decreases in value	Y increases in value	Indirect or negative	Negative, ranging from −1 to 0	The less time you take to complete a test, the more you'll get wrong.

Now, keep in mind that the examples in the table reflect generalities. For example, *in general*, the less time someone takes to complete a test, the lower that person's score will be. Such a conclusion is not rocket science, because the faster one goes, the more likely one is to make careless mistakes, such as not reading instructions correctly. But, of course, there are people who can go very fast and do very well. And there are people who go very slowly and don't do well at all. The point is that we are talking about the performance of a *group* of people on two different variables. We are computing the correlation between the two variables for the group, not for any one particular person or observation.

There are several (easy but important) things to remember about the correlation coefficient:

- A correlation can range in value from −1 to +1.
- A correlation always reflects a situation in which there are at least two data points (or variables) per case.
- The absolute value of the coefficient reflects the strength of the correlation. So, a correlation of −.70 is stronger than a correlation of +.50. One of the frequently made mistakes regarding correlation coefficients occurs when students assume that a

direct or positive correlation is always stronger (i.e., "better") than an indirect or negative correlation because of the sign and nothing else. It ain't so.

- Another easy mistake is to assign a value judgment to the sign of the correlation. Many students assume that a negative relationship is not good and a positive one is good. That's why, instead of the terms *negative* and *positive*, the terms *indirect* and *direct* can communicate meaning more clearly.
- The Pearson product-moment correlation coefficient is represented by the small letter r with a subscript representing the variables that are being correlated. Here are some examples:

r_{XY} is the correlation between variable X and variable Y.

$r_{weight \cdot height}$ is the correlation between weight and height.

$r_{SAT \cdot GPA}$ is the correlation between SAT score and grade point average (GPA).

The correlation coefficient reflects the amount of variability that is shared between two variables and what they have in common. For example, you can expect an individual's height to be correlated with an individual's weight because (a) the two variables differ quite a bit across different people and (b) they are influenced by many of the same characteristics, such as the individual's nutritional and medical history, general health, and genetics.

However, if one variable does not change in value and therefore has nothing to share, then the correlation between the two variables is zero. For example, if you computed the correlation between age and number of years of school completed, and everyone in your study was 25 years old, there would be no correlation between the two variables because there would be literally nothing (any variability) about age available to share.

Likewise, if you constrain or restrict the range of one variable, the correlation between that variable and another variable is going to be less than if the range were not constrained. For example, if you correlated reading comprehension scores and grade in school for very high-achieving children, you'd find the correlation lower than if you computed the same correlation for children in general. That's because the reading comprehension score of very high-achieving students is quite high and much less variable than it would be for all children.

The moral? When you are interested in the relationship between two variables, try to collect sufficiently diverse data—that way, you'll get the truest and most representative result.

COMPUTING A SIMPLE CORRELATION COEFFICIENT

The computational formula for the simple Pearson product-moment correlation coefficient between a variable labeled X and a variable labeled Y is shown in Formula 5.1.

$$r_{XY} = \frac{n\Sigma XY - \Sigma X \Sigma Y}{\sqrt{\left[n\Sigma X^2 - (\Sigma X)^2\right]\left[n\Sigma Y^2 - (\Sigma Y)^2\right]}}, \qquad (5.1)$$

where

r_{XY} is the correlation coefficient between X and Y;

n is the size of the sample;

X is the individual's score on the X variable;

Y is the individual's score on the Y variable;

XY is the product of each X score times its corresponding Y score;

X^2 is the individual X score, squared; and

Y^2 is the individual Y score, squared.

Here are the data we will use in this example:

	X	Y	X²	Y²	XY
	2	3	4	9	6
	4	2	16	4	8
	5	6	25	36	30
	6	5	36	25	30
	4	3	16	9	12
	7	6	49	36	42
	8	5	64	25	40
	5	4	25	16	20
	6	4	36	16	24
	7	5	49	25	35
Total, Sum, or Σ	54	43	320	201	247

Before we plug the numbers in, let's make sure you understand what each one represents:

ΣX, or the sum of all the X values, is 54.

ΣY, or the sum of all the Y values, is 43.

ΣX^2, or the sum of each X value squared, is 320.

ΣY^2, or the sum of each Y value squared, is 201.

ΣXY, or the sum of the products of X and Y, is 247.

It's easy to confuse the *sum of a set of values squared* and the *sum of the squared values*. The sum of a set of values squared is taking values such as 2 and 3, summing them (to be 5), and then squaring that (which is 25). The sum of the squared values is taking values such as 2 and 3, squaring them (to get 4 and 9, respectively), and then adding those together (to get 13). Just look for the parentheses as you work.

Here are the steps in computing the correlation coefficient:

1. List the two values for each participant. You should do this in a column format so as not to get confused.

2. Compute the sum of all the X values. Then compute the sum of all the Y values.

3. Square each of the X values and square each of the Y values.

4. Find the sum of the XY products.

These values are plugged into the equation you see in Formula 5.2:

$$r_{XY} = \frac{(10 \times 247) - (54 - 43)}{\sqrt{\left[(10 \times 320) - 54^2\right]\left[(10 \times 201) - 43^2\right]}} \tag{5.2}$$

Ta-da! And you can see the answer in Formula 5.3:

$$r_{XY} = \frac{148}{213.83} = .692 \tag{5.3}$$

And Now . . . Using Excel's CORREL Function

To compute the correlation between two variable numbers using Excel, follow these steps:

1. Enter the individual scores into one column in a worksheet, such as you see in Figure 5.1.

Figure 5.1 Data for Computing the Correlation Coefficient

	A	B
	X	Y
1		
2	2	3
3	4	2
4	5	6
5	6	5
6	4	3
7	7	6
8	8	5
9	5	4
10	6	4
11	7	5

2. Select the cell into which you want to enter the **CORREL** function. In this example, we are going to place the function for the correlation in Cell B12.

3. Click on Cell B12 and type the CORREL function as follows:

   =CORREL(A2:A11,B2:B11)

   and press the Enter key,

   or

   use the Formulas → More Functions → Statistical → CORREL using the Inserting a Function technique we talked about in Little Chapter 1a to enter the CORREL function in Cell B12.

4. As you can see in Figure 5.2, the correlation coefficient was computed and the value returned to Cell B12. Notice that in the formula bar in Figure 5.2, you can see the CORREL function fully expressed and the value computed in Cell B12 as .692133.

Figure 5.2	Computing the Correlation Coefficient Using the CORREL Function

| B12 | ▼ | ⋮ | × | ✓ | f_x | =CORREL(A2:A11,B2:B11) |

	A	B	C	D	E	F
1	X	Y				
2	2	3				
3	4	2				
4	5	6				
5	6	5				
6	4	3				
7	7	6				
8	8	5				
9	5	4				
10	6	4				
11	7	5				
12		0.692133				

The **PEARSON** function is also a handy one to know. It returns the value of the Pearson product-moment correlation. And here's a good tip: the PEARSON function is synonymous with the CORREL function—they yield the same results.

It's really much more convenient to name a range of values rather than have to enter a particular set of cell references. So, instead of A2:A11, you can just as well name the range Correct X and Correct Y and then use those. You can review what you need to know about naming ranges in our discussion in Little Chapter 1a.

A Visual Picture of a Correlation: The Scatterplot

There's a very simple way to visually represent a correlation: Create what is called a **scatterplot**, or **scattergram**. This is simply a plot of each set of scores on separate axes.

Figure 5.3   A Simple Hand-Drawn Scatterplot

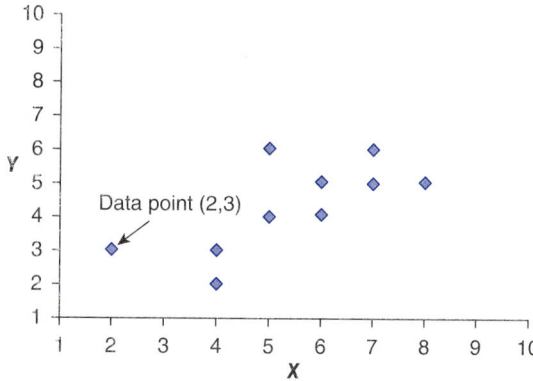

Here are the steps to complete a scattergram like you see in Figure 5.3 for the 10 pairs of two scores for which we computed the sample correlation above:

1. Draw the X-axis and the Y-axis. Usually, the X variable goes on the horizontal axis and the Y variable goes on the vertical axis. Working on graph paper always makes drawing a scatterplot easier.

2. Mark both axes with the range of values that you know to be the case for the data. For example, the value of the X variable in our example ranges from 2 to 8, so we marked the x-axis from 0 to 9. There's no harm in marking the axes a bit low or high—just as long as you allow room for the values to appear. The value of the Y variable ranges from 2 to 6, and we marked that axis from 0 to 9 as well. Having similarly labeled axes can sometimes make the finished scatterplot easier to understand.

3. Finally, for each pair of scores (such as 2 and 3, as shown in Figure 5.3), we entered a dot on the chart by marking the place where 2 falls on the X-axis and 3 falls on the Y-axis. The dot represents a **data point**, which is the intersection of the two values.

When all the data points are plotted, what does our illustration tell us about the relationship between the variables? To begin with, the general shape of the collection of data points indicates whether the correlation is direct (positive) or indirect (negative).

A positive slope occurs when the data points group themselves in a cluster from the lower left-hand corner on the X- and Y-axes through the upper right-hand corner. A negative slope occurs when the data points group themselves in a cluster from the upper left-hand corner on the X- and Y-axes through the lower right-hand corner.

Figures 5.4 to 5.6 provide some scatterplots showing very different correlations so you can see how the grouping of the data points reflects the sign and strength of the correlation coefficient. We used Excel to generate these figures, and we'll show you how to do that in a moment.

Figure 5.4 shows a perfect direct correlation where $r_{XY} = 1.00$ and all the data points are aligned along a straight line with a positive slope.

Figure 5.4 A Perfect Direct, or Positive, Correlation

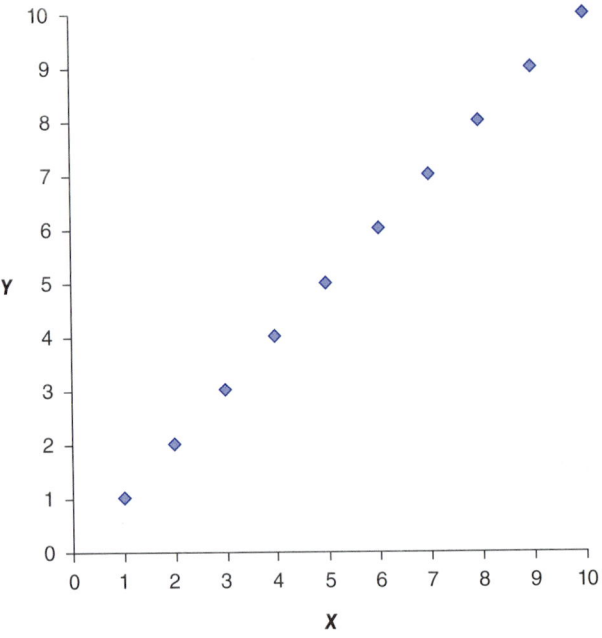

When creating a scatterplot, remember that the order in which the variables are listed in Excel will change the appearance of the plot. For example, if your X variable is in the first column and your Y variable is in the second column, you will get a different scatterplot than if the Y variable appears first in the array. The numerical relationship between the two variables does not change, but the appearance of the scatterplot does, and so can a reader's interpretation of it. Which order should you use? Actually, either variable (e.g., age and time to run a mile, level of education and income) can be called X or Y. Plot your pair of variables both ways and see which scatterplot is easier to interpret.

If the correlation were perfectly indirect, the value of the correlation coefficient would be −1.0, and the data points would again align themselves in a straight line, but from the upper left-hand corner of the chart to the lower right. In other words, the line that connects the data points would have a negative slope.

Don't ever expect to find a perfect correlation between any two variables in the behavioral or social sciences. It would say that two variables are so perfectly correlated, they share everything in common. In other words, knowing one is like knowing the other. Just think about your classmates. Do you think all these people share any one characteristic that is perfectly related to another of their characteristics across the group? Probably not. In fact, r values approaching .7 and .8 are just about the highest you'll see.

In Figure 5.5, you can see the scatterplot for a strong (but not perfect) direct relationship where $r_{XY} = .70$. Notice that the data points align themselves along a positive slope, although not perfectly.

Figure 5.5   A Strong Positive, but Not Perfect, Direct Relationship

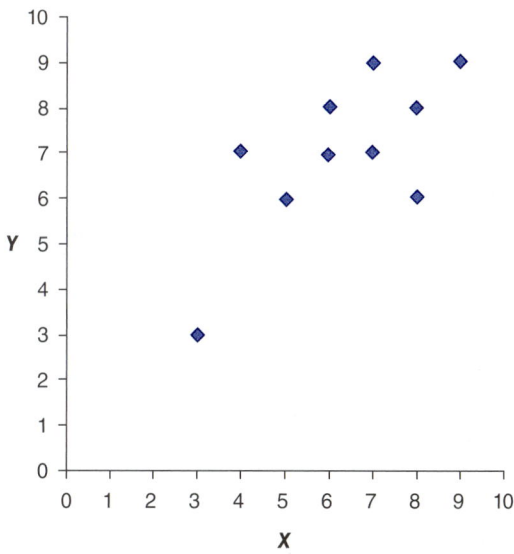

Now, we'll show you a strong indirect, or negative, relationship in Figure 5.6, where $r_{XY} = -.82$. Notice that the data points align themselves on a negative slope from the upper left-hand corner of the chart to the lower right-hand corner.

That's what different types of correlations look like as scatterplots. You can tell the general strength and direction of the correlation by examining the way the points are grouped.

Figure 5.6   A Strong Indirect Relationship

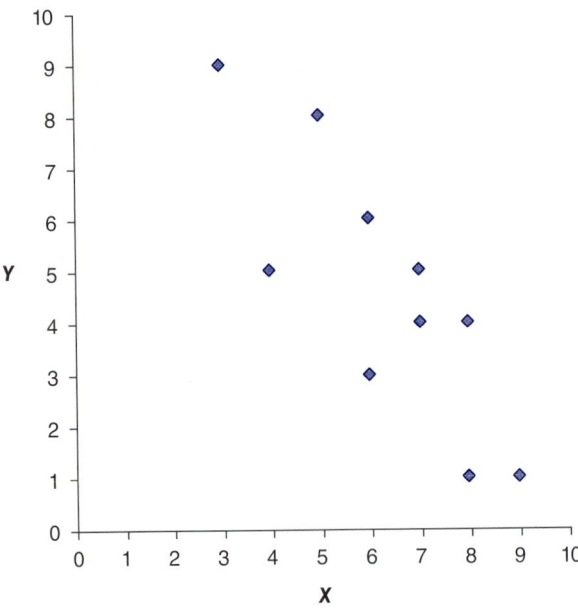

Using Excel to Create a Scatterplot

Now we're talking. We spent a considerable amount of time and energy in Chapter 4 creating charts and then modifying certain elements.

One type of chart we did not review is a scatterplot (we left it for this chapter).

You already know what a scatterplot is, and here's exactly how you create one. We're still working with the data you first saw in Figure 5.1. With just a few clicks . . . Amazing!

1. Highlight the entire range of values (do not include the column titles) from A2 through B11.

2. Click the Insert tab and under Charts, click the Scatter drop-down menu and select the type of scatterplot you want to create.

We clicked on the first one available, and in Figure 5.7 you see the finished scatterplot (with a little bit of fancy thrown in).

Very cool indeed.

Figure 5.7 shows the scatterplot after we modified the scales and the background and such, titled each axis (it turns out that X is a rating of attitude toward school and Y is a score on a test), and gave the entire chart a title. But this is absolutely a cinch to do—all it takes is some experimentation. Remember to save the worksheet as you work so you don't lose what you want and do lose what you don't!

Figure 5.7	Creating and Editing a Scatterplot With a Few Magic Clicks

	A	B	C	D	E	F	G	H	I
1	X	Y							
2	2	3							
3	4	2							
4	5	6							
5	6	5							
6	4	3							
7	7	6							
8	8	5							
9	5	4							
10	6	4							
11	7	5							
12		0.692133							
13									
14									
15									

Number Correct by Atttiude

Not all correlations are reflected by a straight line that represents a **linear relationship** between the X and the Y values. Let's take the correlation between age and memory. During the early years of life, the correlation is highly positive—the older children get, the better their memories. Then, into young and middle adulthood, there isn't much of a change or much of a correlation, because most young and middle adults maintain a good memory. But with old age, memory begins to suffer, and there is an indirect relationship between memory and aging in the later years. If you take these together, you find that the correlation between memory and age tends to look like a curve where memory increases, levels off, and then decreases. These variables have a curvilinear relationship, and sometimes the best description of the relationship is a curvilinear one.

Bunches of Correlations: The Correlation Matrix

What happens if you have more than two variables? How are the correlations illustrated? Use a **correlation matrix** like the one shown below—a simple and elegant solution.

	Income	Education	Attitude	Vote
Income	1.00	0.35	−0.19	0.51
Education		1.00	−0.21	0.43
Attitude			1.00	0.55
Vote				1.00

As you can see, there are four variables in the matrix: level of income (Income), level of education (Education), attitude toward voting (Attitude), and level of participation (from 1 through 5) in the election or vote (Vote).

For each pair of variables, there is a correlation coefficient. For example, the correlation between income level and education is .35 (meaning that as income increases, so does level of education). The correlation between income level and attitude is −.19, meaning that income level and attitude are indirectly related.

In such a matrix (where there are four variables), there are always $4!/(4 − 2)!2!$, or four things taken two at a time for a total of six correlation coefficients. Because variables correlate perfectly with themselves (those are the 1.00s down the diagonal), and because the correlation between Income and Vote is the same as the correlation between Vote and Income (for example), the matrix creates a mirror image of itself.

You will see such *matrices* (the plural of *matrix*) when you read journal articles that use correlations to describe the relationship among several variables. Next, we'll use the Data Analysis tools to generate a matrix as we deal with the correlation among more than two variables.

MORE EXCEL: BUNCHES OF CORRELATIONS À LA EXCEL

If you want to get ambitious and increase the bang you get out of Excel, you can create a matrix like the kind we showed above by placing the appropriate form of the CORREL function in the appropriate cell, as you see in Figure 5.8. Here, we used both the name range option on the Insert menu (remember about naming ranges from Little Chapter 1a) and the CORREL function.

But—and here's the big but—we are showing you the formulas in the cells rather than the results. How did we do this? Remember, you can see the formulas and functions, rather than the results that the formulas and functions return, by highlighting an individual cell or the entire spreadsheet (Ctrl+A), and then using the Ctrl+` key combination, which toggles between the results of the formulas and functions and the formulas and functions themselves. The data for the creation of the matrix appear in four columns, each representing one of four variables (Income, Education, Attitude, and Vote), and the functions for computing the correlations in the matrix appear below the columns.

Figure 5.8	Showing the Use of the Ctrl+` Key Combination to Reveal the CORREL Function in Various Cells to Create a Correlation Matrix

	A	B	C	D	E	F	G	H	I
1	Income	Education	Attitude	Vote					
2	57327	10	9	3		Income	Education	Attitude	Vote
3	93734	9	5	5	Income	=CORREL(A2:A21,A2:A21)	=CORREL(A2:A21,B2:B21)	=CORREL(A2:A21,C2:C21)	=CORREL(A2:A21,D2:D21)
4	39410	8	10	3	Education		1	=CORREL(B2:B21,C2:C21)	=CORREL(B2:B21,D2:D21)
5	94951	15	6	5	Attitude			1	=CORREL(C2:C21,D2:D21)
6	59090	15	10	3	Vote				1
7	34628	11	9	3					
8	31809	13	7	1					
9	46232	15	7	4					
10	78707	16	5	4					
11	37816	9	7	1					
12	47085	8	8	1					
13	58394	9	9	5					
14	77072	13	6	5					
15	97746	15	1	5					
16	50302	14	5	5					
17	61129	16	5	3					
18	83154	16	7	4					
19	42798	13	2	3					
20	83530	9	4	4					
21	84912	9	4	2					

USING THE AMAZING DATA ANALYSIS TOOLS TO COMPUTE CORRELATIONS

If you think that the CORREL function is amazing, you "ain't seen (actually heard) nothin' yet" (thanks to Al Jolson). Although the CORREL function is very useful, the Correlation tool in the Data Analysis tools is even easier to use.

Let's return to the data that we see in Figure 5.8 and follow these steps:

1. Click cell A22 where the analysis will appear.

2. Click the Data tab and then click Data Analysis. You will see the Data Analysis dialog box. Need a brush-up on how to use the tools? See Little Chapter 1b.

3. Click Correlation and then click OK, and you will see the Correlation dialog box as shown in Figure 5.9.

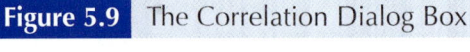

Figure 5.9   The Correlation Dialog Box

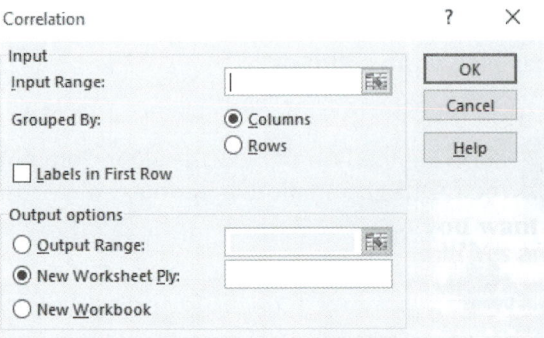

4. In the Input Range box, enter the range of data you want Excel to use in the computation of the correlations. Be sure to include the column headings (so the headings show up in the analysis). As you can see in Figure 5.10, the data we want to analyze are in Cells A1 through D21.

Figure 5.10   Entering the Input Range Information in the Correlation Dialog Box

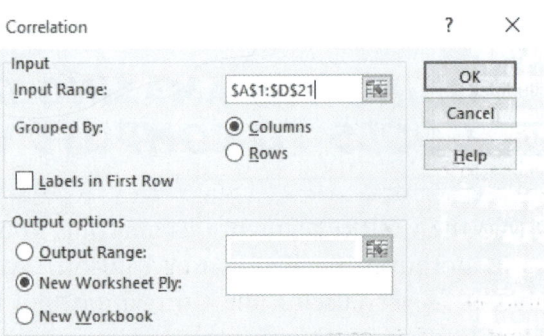

5. Click the Labels in First Row check box.

6. Now click the Output Range button in the Output options section of the dialog box and enter the location where you want Excel to return the results of the analysis. In this example, we checked E1.

7. Click OK, and there it is, folks, right out of the hopper as shown in Figure 5.11—and done with very little effort on your part. Truly a time to rejoice.

Figure 5.11	Using the Correlation Analysis Tool to Create a Matrix of Correlations

	A	B	C	D	E
1	Income	Education	Attitude	Vote	
2	57327	10	9	3	
3	93734	9	5	5	
4	39410	8	10	3	
5	94951	15	6	5	
6	59090	15	10	3	
7	34628	11	9	3	
8	31809	13	7	1	
9	46232	15	7	4	
10	78707	16	5	4	
11	37816	9	7	1	
12	47085	8	8	1	
13	58394	9	9	5	
14	77072	13	6	5	
15	97746	15	1	5	
16	50302	14	5	5	
17	61129	16	5	3	
18	83154	16	7	4	
19	42798	13	2	3	
20	83530	9	4	4	
21	84912	9	4	2	
22		*Income*	*Education*	*Attitude*	*Vote*
23	Income	1			
24	Education	0.222946649247945	1		
25	Attitude	-0.502605378880421	-0.279387309604115	1	
26	Vote	0.605915827243988	0.346282410856083	-0.267828819273384	1

Keep in mind that it is Excel's decision to create the matrix in the format you see with the number of decimal places in Figure 5.11 (far too many, in our opinion) and with that particular font. These entries are like any other data, and you can do with them what you want. Before we gave this our official stamp of approval, we changed the format to be a bit more intelligible, rounded off the decimals, and changed the general appearance using a variety of table options.

When a tool from the Data Analysis tools is used, it returns a value rather than the result of a formula; your cells contain numbers, not formulas or functions. You can do just about anything you want with the cell formatting.

UNDERSTANDING WHAT THE CORRELATION COEFFICIENT MEANS

Well, we have this numerical index of the relationship between two variables, and we know that the higher the value of the correlation (regardless of its sign), the stronger the relationship is. But because the correlation coefficient is a value that is not directly tied to the value of an outcome, just how can we interpret it and make it a more meaningful indicator of a relationship?

Here are different ways to look at the interpretation of that simple r_{XY}.

Some of you already know that the correlation coefficient can be checked for its *significance*, or how likely it is to have occurred by something other than chance, and we will get to that in Chapter 15. That's another valuable way to interpret correlation coefficients, but for now, let's stick with the simple, more descriptive way that follows. Once you have this under your belt, you'll be ready to move on to more sophisticated ideas.

Using-Your-Thumb Rule

Perhaps the easiest (but not the most informative) way to interpret the value of a correlation coefficient is by eyeballing it and using the information in Table 5.2.

Table 5.2   Interpreting a Correlation Coefficient

Size of the Correlation	Coefficient General Interpretation
.8 to 1.0	Very strong relationship
.6 to .8	Strong relationship
.4 to .6	Moderate relationship
.2 to .4	Weak relationship
.0 to .2	Very weak or no relationship

So, if the correlation between two variables is .5, you could safely conclude that the relationship is a moderate one—not strong, but certainly not weak enough to say that the variables in question don't share anything in common.

This eyeball method is perfectly acceptable for a quick assessment of the strength of the relationship between variables, such as a description in a research report. But because this rule of thumb does depend on a subjective judgment (of what's "strong" or "weak"), we would like a more precise method. That's what we'll look at now.

Also, note that there is some overlap in Table 5.2. For example, a correlation of .4 can fall into the weak or moderate relationship range. It's your call—further emphasizing that numbers don't tell the whole story—you do.

A Determined Effort: Squaring the Correlation Coefficient

Here's the much more precise way to interpret the correlation coefficient: compute the coefficient of determination. The **coefficient of determination** is the percentage of variance in one variable that is shared with the variance in the other variable. Quite a mouthful, huh?

Earlier in this chapter, we pointed out how variables that share something in common tend to be correlated with one another. If we correlated math and English grades for 100 fifth-grade students, we would find the correlation to be moderately strong, because many of the reasons why children do well (or poorly) in math tend to be the same reasons why they do well (or poorly) in English. The number of hours they study, how bright they are, how interested their parents are in their schoolwork, the number of books they have at home, and more are all related to both math and English performance and account for differences between children (and that's where the variability comes in).

The more these two variables share in common, the more they will be related. These two variables share the same influences on their variability—or the reason why children differ from one another. On the whole, the brighter child who studies more will do better. To determine exactly how much of the variance in one variable can be accounted for by the variance in another variable, the coefficient of determination is computed by squaring the correlation coefficient.

For example, if the correlation between GPA and number of hours of study time is .70 (or $r_{GPA \cdot time} = .70$), then the coefficient of determination, represented by r^2, is $.7^2$, or .49. This means that 49%

of the variance in GPA can be explained by the variance in studying time. And the stronger the correlation, the more variance can be explained (which only makes good sense). The more two variables share in common (such as good study habits, knowledge of what's expected in class, and lack of fatigue), the more information about performance on one score can be explained by the other score.

However, if 49% of the variance can be explained, this means that 51% cannot—so even for a strong correlation such as .70, many of the reasons why scores on these variables tend to be different from one another go unexplained. This amount of unexplained variance is called the **coefficient of alienation** (also called the **coefficient of nondetermination**). Don't worry. No aliens here. This isn't *X-Files* stuff; it's just the amount of variance in *Y* not explained by *X* (and, of course, vice versa).

How about a visual presentation of this sharing variance idea? Okay. In Figure 5.12, you'll find a correlation coefficient, the corresponding coefficient of alienation, and a diagram that represents how much variance is shared between the two variables. The larger the shaded area in each diagram (and the more variance the two variables share), the more highly the variables are correlated.

Figure 5.12	How Variables Share Variance and the Resulting Correlation

Correlation	Coefficient of Determination	Variable X	Variable Y
$r_{xy} = 0$	$r^2_{xy} = 0$		0% shared
$r_{xy} = .5$	$r^2_{xy} = .25$ or 25%		25% shared
$r_{xy} = .9$	$r^2_{xy} = .81$ or 81%		81% shared

The first diagram shows two circles that do not touch. They don't touch because they do not share anything in common. The correlation is 0.

The second diagram shows two circles that overlap. With a correlation of .5 (and $r^2_{XY} = .25$), they share about 25% of the variance between themselves.

Finally, the third diagram shows the two circles placed almost one on top of the other. With an almost perfect correlation of $r_{XY} = .90$ ($r^2_{XY} = .81$), they share about 81% of the variance between themselves.

AS MORE ICE CREAM IS EATEN, THE CRIME RATE GOES UP (OR ASSOCIATION VERSUS CAUSALITY)

Now, here's the really important thing to be careful about when computing, reading about, or interpreting correlation coefficients.

Imagine this. In a small Midwestern town, a phenomenon was discovered that defied any logic. The local police chief observed that as ice cream consumption increased, crime rates tended to increase as well. Quite simply, if you measured both, you would find the relationship was direct, which means that as people ate more ice cream, the crime rate increased. And as you might expect, as they ate less ice cream, the crime rate went down. The police chief was baffled until he recalled the Stat 1 class he took in college and still fondly remembered.

His wondering about how this could be true turned into an Aha! Moment: "Very easily," he thought. The two variables must share something or have something in common with one another. Remember that it must be something that relates to both level of ice cream consumption and level of crime rate. Can you guess what that is?

The outside temperature is what they both have in common. When it gets warm outside, such as in the summertime, more crimes are committed (it stays light longer, people leave the windows open, etc.). And because it is warmer, people enjoy the ancient treat and art of eating ice cream. And conversely, during the long and dark winter months, less ice cream is consumed and fewer crimes are committed as well.

Joe Bob, recently elected as a city commissioner, learns about these findings and has a great idea, or at least one that he thinks his constituents will love. (Keep in mind, he skipped the statistics offering in college.) Why not just limit the consumption of ice cream in the summer months, which will surely result in a decrease in the crime rate? Sounds good, right? Well, on closer inspection, it really makes no sense at all.

That's because of this simple principle: *Correlations express the association that exists between two or more variables; they have nothing to do with causality.* In other words, just because level of ice cream consumption and crime rate increase together (and decrease together as well) does not mean that a change in one necessarily results in a change in the other.

For example, if we took all the ice cream out of all the stores in town and no more was available, do you think the crime rate would decrease? Of course not, and it's preposterous to think so. But strangely enough, that's often how associations are interpreted—as being causal in nature—and complex issues in the social and behavioral sciences are reduced to trivialities because of this misunderstanding. Did long hair and hippiedom cause the Vietnam conflict? Of course not. Does the rise in the number of crimes committed have anything to do with more efficient and safer cars? Of course not. But they all happened (and happen) at the same time, which creates the illusion of being associated.

OTHER COOL CORRELATIONS

There are different ways in which variables can be assessed. For example, nominal-level variables are categorical in nature; examples are race (black or white) or political affiliation (independent or Republican). On the other hand, if you are measuring income and age, these are both interval-level variables because the underlying continuum on which they are based has equally appearing intervals. As you continue your studies, you're likely to come across correlations between data that occur at different levels of measurement. And to compute these correlations, you need some specialized techniques. Table 5.3 summarizes what these different techniques are and how they differ from one another.

Table 5.3   Correlation Coefficient Shopping, Anyone?

Level of Measurement and Examples			
Variable X	**Variable Y**	**Type of Correlation**	**Correlation Being Computed**
Nominal (voting preference, such as Republican or Democrat)	Nominal (sex, such as male or female)	Phi coefficient	The correlation between voting preference and sex
Nominal (social class, such as high, medium, or low)	Ordinal (rank in high school graduating class)	Rank biserial coefficient	The correlation between social class and rank in high school
Nominal (family configuration, such as intact or single parent)	Interval (grade point average)	Point biserial	The correlation between family configuration and grade point average

Level of Measurement and Examples			
Variable X	**Variable Y**	**Type of Correlation**	**Correlation Being Computed**
Ordinal (height converted to rank)	Ordinal (weight converted to rank)	Spearman rank coefficient	The correlation between height and weight
Interval (number of problems solved)	Interval (age in years)	Pearson correlation coefficient	The correlation between number of problems solved and age in years

REAL-WORLD STATS

This is a fun one and consistent with the increasing interest in how statistics is used in various sports in various ways. Informally, this discipline is called "sabermetrics," a term coined by Bill James (of *Moneyball* fame).

Stephen Hall and his colleagues examined the link between team payroll and how competitive teams are linked (for both professional baseball and soccer), and he was one of the first to look at this relationship from an empirical perspective. In other words, until these data were published, most people made decisions based on anecdotal evidence, rather than quantitative assessments. Hall used data on team payrolls in Major League Baseball and English soccer between 1980 and 2000 using a model that allows for the establishment of causality (and not just association). While in baseball both payroll and performance increased significantly in the 1990s, there is no evidence that causality runs in the direction from payroll to performance for this sport. In comparison, for English soccer, the researchers showed higher payrolls led to better performance. It's pretty cool how using special causal models lets us explore association.

Want to know more? Go online or go to the library, and look for . . .

Hall, S., Szymanski, S., & Zimbalist, A. S. (2002). Testing causality between team performance and payroll: The cases of Major League Baseball and English Soccer. *Journal of Sports Economics, 3,* 149–168.

SUMMARY

The idea of showing how things are related to one another and what they have in common is a very powerful idea, and correlation is a very useful descriptive statistic (one also used to make inferences about the relationship between variables in samples and how those inferences can then be applied to populations). Keep in mind that correlations express a relationship that is only associative and not causal, and you'll be able to understand how this statistic gives us valuable information about relationships and how variables change or remain the same in concert with others.

TIME TO PRACTICE

1. Use these data to answer Questions 1a and 1b. These data are saved as Chapter 5 Data Set 1.

Total No. of Problems Correct (out of a possible 20)	Attitude Toward Test Taking (out of a possible 100)
17	94
13	73
12	59
15	80
16	93
14	85
16	66
16	79
18	77
19	91

   a. Compute the Pearson product-moment correlation coefficient by hand and show all your work.
   b. Construct a scatterplot for these 10 values by hand. Based on the scatterplot, would you predict the correlation to be direct or indirect? Why?

2. Use these data to answer Questions 2a and 2b.

   a. Using either a calculator or Excel, compute the Pearson correlation coefficient.

Speed in Seconds (to complete a 50-yard swim)	Strength (no. of pounds bench-pressed)
21.6	135
23.4	213
26.5	243
25.5	167
20.8	120
19.5	134
20.9	209
18.7	176
29.8	156
28.7	177

b. Interpret the relationship between these variables using the descriptions in Table 5.2 ranging from "very weak" to "very strong." Then compute the coefficient of determination. How does your subjective analysis compare with the value of the r^2 you calculated?

3. Compute the correlation coefficient for the data below, saved as Chapter 5 Data Set 2, and interpret the coefficient. We are examining the relationship between the number of years of training that doctors have and their success using a certain procedure, with the doctors being evaluated on a scale from 1 to 10 where 1 is ☺☺☺☺☺ and 10 is ☺. In other words, the *lower* the score on the second variable, the *more* successful the doctor is using the procedure.

Years of Training	Successful Outcomes
1	9
9	1
1	8
4	7
3	6
3	7
7	9
9	5
7	5
6	6
6	7
1	4

4. Height and weight in humans tend to be correlated because they are the result of lots of similar experiences in an individual's life and the person's genetic traits. Name two variables that may not be correlated and explain why.

5. Use Chapter 5 Data Set 3 and the Data Analysis tools to compute the correlations between hand-washing efficiency scored on a scale of 1 to 5 with 1 being best (Wash), number of times hands are washed each day (Number), and number of hospital-wide infections (Infect). What can you tell us about the results?

6. The coefficient of determination between two variables is .64. Answer the following questions:

   a. What is the Pearson correlation coefficient?
   b. How strong is the relationship?
   c. How much of the variance in the relationship between these two variables is unaccounted for?

7. Look back at Table 5.3. What type of correlation coefficient would you use to examine the relationship between ethnicity (defined as different categories) and political affiliation (defined as Democrat, Republican, or unaffiliated)? How about club membership (yes or no) and high school GPA? Explain why you selected the answers you did.

8. When variables are related to each other, why might this be the case? And, when two variables are strongly related to one another, does it mean that a change in one causes a change in the other? Why or why not?

9. You're the director of the local health clinic, and you and the city's school district are conducting a study to examine the relationship between school dropout rate and teenage pregnancy. One of the local legislators has gotten a copy of the study and made the following statement to the press: "It's obvious that the longer children stay in school, the less likely they are to become pregnant." What's wrong with that statement?

10. For the following set of scores, calculate the Pearson correlation coefficient and interpret the outcome.

Budget Increase	Number of Clients Served
7%	11%
3%	14%
5%	13%
7%	26%
2%	8%

Budget Increase	Number of Clients Served
1%	3%
5%	6%
4%	12%
4%	11%

11. Rank the following correlation coefficients on strength of their relationship (list the weakest first):

+.71

+.36

−.45

+.47

−.62

12. How do you explain the observation that if parents wave garlic over an infant's crib, the child is likely to begin walking between 18 and 24 months of age? These two events are closely correlated!

6 Just the Truth

An Introduction to Understanding Reliability and Validity

Difficulty Scale ☺ ☺ ☺ (not so hard)

How Much Excel? 📊 (just a mention)

WHAT YOU'LL LEARN ABOUT IN THIS CHAPTER

✦ What reliability and validity are and why they are important

✦ This is a stats class! What's up with this measurement stuff?

✦ The basic measurement scales

✦ How to compute and interpret various types of reliability coefficients

✦ How to compute and interpret various types of validity coefficients

---

AN INTRODUCTION TO RELIABILITY AND VALIDITY

Professionals in the field of social welfare (and in other fields) recognize that the existence of more than a half million foster children in the United States is a serious concern. One of the major issues is how foster children adjust to their temporary adoptive families given that their biological families still play a very important role in their lives.

Sonya J. Leathers examined this question when she studied whether frequent parental visiting was associated with foster children's allegiances to foster families and biological parents. In a sample of 199 adolescents, she found that frequent visits with their family of origin did create conflicts, and she suggested interventions that might help minimize those conflicts.

To complete her study, she used a variety of different dependent variables (or variables representing the outcome being measured), and she collected data by way of the Children's Symptom Inventory as well as interviews. Among other things, what she really got right was a careful selection of measurement instruments that had established, and acceptable, levels of reliability and validity. This practice, which not every researcher undertakes, is our focus in this chapter.

Want to know more? Check out the original reference: Leathers, S. (2003). Parental visiting, conflicting allegiances, and emotional and behavioral problems among foster children. *Family Relations, 52,* 53–63.

What's Up With This Measurement Stuff?

A very good question. After all, you enrolled in a stats class, and up to now, this book has focused on statistics. Now it looks like you're faced with a topic that belongs in a tests and measurement class. So, what's this material doing in a stats book?

An excellent question, and one that you should be asking. Why? Well, most of what we have covered so far in *Statistics for People Who (Think They) Hate Statistics, Excel 2016 Edition* has to do with the collection, analysis, and interpretation of data. A very significant part of those activities is the collection part, and a significant part of collecting data is making sure that the data are what you think they are—that the data represent what you want to know about. In other words, if you're studying poverty, you want to make sure that the measure you use to assess poverty works. Or, if you are studying aggression in middle-aged males, you want to make sure that whatever tool you use to assess aggression does that.

More really good news: Should you continue in your education and want to take a class on tests and measurement, this introductory chapter will give you a real jump on understanding the scope of the area and the topics you'll be studying.

In order to make sure that the entire process of collecting data and making sense out of them works, you first have to make sure that what you use to collect data works as well. The fundamental questions that will be answered in this chapter are "How do I know that the test, scale, instrument, etc. I use works every time I use it?" (reliability) and "How do I know that the test, scale, instrument, etc. I use measures what it is supposed to?" (validity).

In Chapter 5, we did a pretty extensive job of introducing correlation coefficients and how they are used, and we'll also be talking about them later in this chapter (and more in Chapter 15 and some in Chapter 16). What you have already learned about using Excel is directly applicable here. Excel does not have tools named something like "reliability calculator" as such but instead uses the CORREL and the PEARSON functions and the Correlation tool from the Data Analysis tools.

Anyone who does research will tell you of the importance of establishing the reliability and validity of your test tool, whether it's a simple observational instrument of consumer behavior or one that measures a complex psychological construct such as attachment. Here's why this is important: If the tools that you use to collect data are unreliable or invalid, then the results of any test of any hypothesis you have put forth are inconclusive at best! If you are not sure that the test does what it is supposed to and that it does so consistently, how do you know whether the results you got are a function of the lousy test tools or fair and honest results of the hypothesis you are testing? Want a clean test of the hypothesis? Make reliability and validity one of your first orders of business.

ALL ABOUT MEASUREMENT SCALES

Before we can talk much about reliability and validity, we first have to talk about different **scales of measurement**. But first, what is **measurement**? It's the assignment of values to outcomes following a set of rules—simple enough. The rules are the different scales we'll define in a moment, and an outcome is anything we are interested in measuring, such as hair color, gender, test score, or height.

These scales of measurement, or rules, are particular levels at which outcomes are measured. Each level has a particular set of characteristics. And scales of measurement come in four flavors (there are four types): nominal, ordinal, interval, and ratio. Let's move on to a brief discussion and examples of the four scales of measurement.

A Rose by Any Other Name: The Nominal Level of Measurement

The **nominal level of measurement** is defined by the characteristics of an outcome that fits into one and only one class or category. For example, gender can be a nominal variable (female and male), as can ethnicity (Caucasian or African American), as can political affiliation (Republican, Democrat, or independent). Nominal-level variables are "names" (*nominal* in Latin), and this is the least precise level of measurement. Nominal levels of measurement have categories that are mutually exclusive; for example, political affiliation cannot be both Republican and Democrat. And a rose can't belong both to the Bourbon (no kidding) and polyantha classification.

Any Order Is Fine With Me: The Ordinal Level of Measurement

The *ord* in **ordinal level of measurement** stands for order, and the characteristic of things being measured here is that they are ordered. The perfect example is a rank of candidates for a job. If we know that Russ is ranked #1, Sheldon is ranked #2, and Hannah is ranked #3, then this is an ordinal arrangement. We have no idea how much higher on this scale Russ is relative to Sheldon than Sheldon is relative to Hannah. We just know that it's "better" to be #1 than #2 than #3, but not by how much.

1 + 1 = 2: The Interval Level of Measurement

Now we're getting somewhere. When we talk about the **interval level of measurement**, we're discussing a test or an assessment tool based on some underlying continuum such that we can talk about how much more a higher performance is than a lesser one. For example, 10 words correct on a vocabulary test is twice as many as 5 words correct. A distinguishing characteristic of interval-level scales is that the intervals along the scale are equal to one another. Ten words correct is 2 more than 8 correct, which is 3 more than 5 correct.

Can Anyone Have Nothing of Anything?
The Ratio Level of Measurement

Well, here's a little conundrum for you. An assessment tool at the **ratio level of measurement** is characterized by the presence of an absolute zero on the scale. What that means is the absence of any of the trait that is being measured. The conundrum? Do we ever measure outcomes where it is possible to have nothing of what is being measured? In some disciplines, that can be the case. For example, in the physical and biological sciences, you can have the absence of a characteristic, such as absolute zero (no molecular movement) or zero light. You can even be weightless in space, meaning that you don't weigh anything. In the social and behavioral sciences, it's a bit harder. Even if you score 0 on that spelling test or miss every item of an IQ test (in Russian), that result does not mean that you have no spelling ability or no intelligence, right? It just means that you didn't get any questions correct on the test.

In Sum . . .

These scales of measurement, or rules, represent particular levels at which outcomes are measured. And, in sum, we can say the following:

- Any outcome can be assigned to one of the four scales of measurement we discussed above.
- Scales of measurement have an order, from the least precise (nominal) to the most precise (ratio).
- The "higher up" the scale of measurement, the more precise the data being collected, and the more detailed and informative the data are. It may be enough to know that some people are rich and some poor (and that's a nominal or categorical distinction), but it's much better to know exactly how much money a subject makes (interval or ratio). We can always make the "rich"/"poor" distinction if we want to once we have all the information.
- Finally, the more precise scales contain all the qualities of the scales below them. For example, the interval scale has all the qualities of the ordinal and nominal scales. If you know that the Bears' batting average is .350, you know it is better than the Tigers' batting average of .250 by 100 points, but you also know that the Bears are better than the Tigers (without saying by how much) and that the Bears are different from the Tigers (without stating the direction of the difference).

And in sum again, take a look at this table, which shows what you need to determine the correct level of measurement.

	Characteristics			
Scale	Absolute Zero	Equidistant Points	Ranked Data	Data Are Categorical
Ratio	✓	✓	✓	✓
Interval		✓	✓	✓
Ordinal			✓	✓
Nominal				✓

RELIABILITY–DOING IT AGAIN UNTIL YOU GET IT RIGHT

Reliability is pretty easy to figure out. It's simply the degree to which a test, or whatever you use as a measurement tool, measures something consistently. If you administer a test of personality before a special treatment occurs, will the administration of that same test 4 months later be reliable? That, my friend, is one of the questions. And that is why there are different types of reliability, each of which we will get to after we define reliability just a bit more.

Test Scores—Truth or Dare

When you take a test in this class, you get a score, such as 89 (good for you) or 65 (back to the book!). That test score consists of several elements, including the **observed score** (or what you actually get on the test, such as 89 or 65) and a **true score** (the true, 100% accurate reflection of what you really know). We can't directly measure true score because it is a theoretical reflection of the actual amount of the trait or characteristic possessed by the individual.

Nothing about this tests and measurement stuff is clear-cut, and this true score stuff surely qualifies. Here's why. We just defined true score as the real, real, real value associated with some trait or attribute. So far, so good. But there's another point of view as well. Some psychometricians (the people who do tests and measurement for a living)

believe that true score has nothing to do with whether the construct of interest is really being reflected. Rather, true score is the *mean* score an individual would get if he or she took a test an infinite number of times, and it represents the theoretical typical level of performance on a given test. Now, one would hope that the typical level of performance would reflect the construct of interest, but that's another question (a validity one at that). The distinction here is that a test is reliable if it consistently produces whatever score a person would get on average, regardless of what the test is measuring. In fact, a perfectly reliable test might not produce a score that has anything to do with the construct of interest, such as "what you really know."

Why aren't true and observed scores the same? Well, they can be if the test (and the accompanying observed score) is a perfect (and we mean absolutely perfect) reflection of what's being measured.

But the Yankees don't always win, the bread sometimes falls on the buttered side, and Murphy's law tells us that the world is not perfect. So, what you see as an observed score may come close to the true score, but rarely are they the same. Rather, the difference as you see is in the amount of error that is introduced. What do we mean by error? Stay tuned.

Observed Score = True Score + Error Score

Error? Yes—in all its glory. For example, let's suppose for a moment that someone gets an 80 on a stats test but his or her true score (which we never really know but can only theorize) is 89. That 9-point difference is due to error (it's called the **error score**), and the presence of error is why individual test scores vary from being 100% true.

What might be the source of such error? Well, perhaps the room in which the test is taken is so warm that it causes you to fall asleep. That would certainly have an impact on your test score. Or perhaps you didn't study for the test as much as you should have. Ditto. Both of these examples would reflect testing situations or conditions rather than qualities of the trait being measured, right? Our job is to reduce those errors as much as possible by having, for example, good test-taking conditions and making sure you are encouraged to get enough sleep. Reduce the error and you increase the reliability, because the observed score more closely matches the true score.

The less error, the more reliable—it's that simple.

Different Types of Reliability

There are several different types of reliability, and we'll cover the four most important and most often used in this section. Table 6.1 summarizes all of them.

Table 6.1	Different Types of Reliability, When They Are Used, How They Are Computed, and What They Mean		
Type of Reliability	**When You Use It**	**How You Do It**	**An Example of What You Can Say When You're Done**
Test–retest reliability	When you want to know whether a test is reliable over time	Correlate the scores from a test given at Time 1 with the same test given at Time 2.	The Bonzo test of identity formation for adolescents is reliable over time.
Parallel forms reliability	When you want to know whether several forms of a test are reliable or equivalent	Correlate the scores from one form of the test with the scores from a second, different form of the same test of the same content.	The two forms of the Regular Guy test are equivalent to one another and have shown parallel forms reliability.
Internal consistency reliability	When you want to know whether the items on a test assess one, and only one, dimension	Correlate each individual item score with the total score.	All of the items on the SMART Test of Creativity assess the same construct.
Interrater reliability	When you want to know whether there is consistency in the rating of some outcome	Examine the percentage of agreement between raters.	The interrater reliability for the best-dressed Foosball player judging was .91, which indicates a high degree of agreement among judges.

Test–Retest Reliability

Test–retest reliability is used when you want to examine whether a test is reliable over time. For example, let's say that you are developing a test that will examine preferences for different types of vocational programs.

You may administer the test in September and then readminister the same test to the same people (and it's important that the test and the test takers be the same) again in June. Then, the two sets of scores are correlated, and you have a measure of reliability. Test–retest reliability is a must when you are examining differences or changes over time.

You must be very confident that you have measured your variable in a reliable way such that the results you are getting come as close as possible to the individual's score each and every time.

Computing Test–Retest Reliability. Here are some scores from a test at Time 1 and Time 2 for the MVE (Mastering Vocational Education Test) under development. Our goal is to compute the Pearson correlation coefficient as a measure of the test–retest reliability of the instrument.

ID	Score From Test 1	Score From Test 2
1	54	56
2	67	77
3	67	87
4	83	89
5	87	89
6	89	90
7	84	87
8	90	92
9	98	99
10	65	76

The first and last step in this process is to compute the Pearson product-moment correlation (see Chapter 5 for a refresher on using the CORREL function and the correlation tool in the Data Analysis tools), which is equal to

$$r_{\text{Time1·Time2}} = .90 \tag{6.1}$$

We'll get to the interpretation of this value shortly.

Parallel Forms Reliability

Parallel forms reliability is used when you want to examine the equivalence or similarity between two different forms of the same test.

For example, let's say that you are doing a study on memory and part of the task is to look at 10 words, memorize them as best

For a total of 12 periods (and 12 possible agreements), there are 10 where both Dave and Maureen agreed on whether a customer-friendly behavior took place or not (periods 1, 2, 3, 4, 5, 6, 7, 8, 9, and 12) and 2 where they did not agree (periods 10 and 11), for a total of 10 agreements and 2 disagreements.

Interrater reliability is computed using the following simple formula:

$$Interrater\ reliability = \frac{Number\ of\ agreements}{Number\ of\ possible\ agreements}, \quad (6.5)$$

and when we plug in the numbers as you see here,

$$Interrater\ reliability = \frac{10}{12} = .833, \quad\quad\quad (6.6)$$

the resulting interrater reliability coefficient is .833.

How Big Is Big? Interpreting Reliability Coefficients

Okay, now we get down to business, and guess what? Remember all you learned about interpreting the value of the correlation coefficient in Chapter 5? The process is almost the same when you interpret reliability coefficients, with a (little) bit of a difference. We want only two things, and here they are:

1. Reliability coefficients to be positive (or direct) and not to be negative (or indirect)

2. Reliability coefficients that are as large as possible (between .00 and ±1.00)

And If You Can't Establish Reliability . . . Then What?

The road to establishing the reliability of a test is not a smooth one at all, and it takes a good deal of work to travel it. What if the test is not reliable?

Here are a few things to keep in mind. Remember that reliability is a function of how much error contributes to the observed score. Lower that error, and you increase the reliability.

- Make sure that the instructions are standardized across all settings when the test is administered.

- Increase the number of items or observations, because the larger the sample from the universe of behaviors you are investigating, the more likely the sample is representative and reliable. This is especially true for achievement tests.
- Delete unclear items, because some people will respond in one way and others will respond in a different fashion regardless of their knowledge, ability level, or individual traits.
- For achievement tests especially (such as spelling or history tests), moderate the easiness and difficulty of tests, because any test that is too difficult or too easy does not reflect an accurate picture of performance.
- Minimize the effects of external events. If a particularly important event, such as Mardi Gras or graduation, occurs near the time of testing, you want to be able to postpone assessment.

Just One More Big Thing

The first step in creating an instrument that has sound psychometric (how's that for a big word?) properties is to establish its reliability (and we just spent some good time on that). Why? Well, if a test or measurement instrument is not reliable, is not consistent, and does not do the same thing time after time after time, it does not matter what it measures (and that's the validity question), right?

The first three items on the KACAS (Kids Are Cool at Spelling) test of introductory spelling could be these:

16 + 12 = ?

21 + 13 = ?

41 + 33 = ?

This is surely a highly reliable test, but just as surely not a valid one (spelling?). Now that we have reliability well understood, let's move on to an introduction to validity.

VALIDITY—WHOA! WHAT IS THE TRUTH?

Validity is, most simply, the property of an assessment tool that indicates that the tool does what it says it does. A valid test is a test that measures what it is supposed to. If a valid achievement test is supposed to measure knowledge of history, then that's what it does. If a valid intelligence test is supposed to measure whatever intelligence is defined as by the test's creators, then it does just that.

Different Types of Validity

Just as there are different types of reliability, so there are different types of validity, and we'll cover the three most important categories and most often used in this section. Table 6.2 summarizes them.

Table 6.2	Different Types of Validity, When They Are Used, How They Are Computed, and What They Mean		
Type of Validity	**When You Use It**	**How You Do It**	**An Example of What You Can Say When You're Done**
Content validity	When you want to know whether a sample of items truly reflects an entire universe of items in a certain topic	Ask Mr. or Ms. Expert to make a judgment that the test items reflect the universe of items in the topic being measured.	My weekly quiz in my stats class fairly assesses the chapter's content.
Criterion validity	When you want to know whether test scores are systematically related to other criteria that indicate the test taker is competent in a certain area	Correlate the scores from the test with some other measure that is already valid and assesses the same set of abilities.	Performance on the EATS test (of culinary skills) has been shown to be correlated with being a fine chef 2 years after culinary school (an example of predictive validity).
Construct validity	When you want to know whether a test measures some underlying psychological construct	Correlate the set of test scores with some theorized outcome that reflects the construct for which the test is being designed.	It's true—men who participate in body contact and physically dangerous sports score higher on the TEST(osterone) test of aggression.

Content Validity

Content validity is the property of a test such that the test items sample the universe of items for which the test is designed. Content validity is most often used with achievement tests (e.g., everything from your first-grade spelling test to the SATs).

Establishing Content Validity. Establishing content validity is actually very easy. All you need is to locate your local cooperative content expert. For example, if I were designing a test of introductory physics, I would go to the local physics expert (perhaps the teacher at the local high school or a professor at the university who teaches physics), and I would say, "Hey, Alberta (or Albert), do you think this set of 100 multiple-choice items accurately reflects all the possible topics and ideas that I would expect the students in my introductory class to understand?"

I would probably tell Alberta or Albert what the topics were, and then he or she would look at the items and basically provide a judgment as to whether the items meet the criterion I had established—a representation of the entire universe of all items that are introductory. If the answer is yes, I'm done (at least for now). If the answer is no, it's back to the drawing board and the creation of new items or refinement of existing ones.

Criterion Validity

Criterion validity assesses whether a test reflects a set of abilities in a current or future setting. If the criterion is taking place in the here and now, we talk about **concurrent validity**. If the criterion is taking place in the future, we talk about **predictive validity**. For criterion validity to be present, one need not establish both concurrent and predictive validity, only the one that works for the purposes of the test.

Establishing Concurrent Validity. For example, you've been hired by the Universal Culinary Institute to design an instrument that measures culinary skills. Some part of culinary training has to do with straight knowledge. (For example, what's a roux?) And that's left to the achievement test side of things.

So, you develop a test that you think does a good job of measuring culinary skills, and now you want to establish the level of concurrent validity. To do this, you design the COOK scale, a set of 5-point items across a set of criteria (presentation, cleanliness, etc.) that each judge will use. As a **criterion** (and that's the key here), you have another set of judges rank each student from 1 to 100 on overall ability. Then, you simply correlate the COOK scores with the judges' rankings. If the validity coefficient (a simple correlation) is high, you're in business—if not, it's back to the drawing board and the redesign of items that may work better.

Establishing Predictive Validity. Let's say that the cooking school has been percolating (heh-heh) along just fine for 10 years and you are interested not only in how well people cook (and that's the concurrent validity part of this exercise that you just established) but in how successful they will be as chefs in the future. Now we're talking predictive validity. The criterion changes from a here-and-now score (the one that judges give) to one from the future.

Here, we are interested in developing a test that predicts success as a chef 10 years down the line. To establish the predictive validity of the COOK test, you go back and locate graduates of the program who have been out cooking for 10 years and administer the test to them. The criterion that is used here is their level of success, and you use as measures (a) whether they own their own restaurant and (b) whether it has been in business for more than 1 year (given that the failure rate for new restaurants is more than 80% within the first year). The rationale here is that if a restaurant is in business for more than 1 year, then the chef must be doing something right.

To complete this exercise, you correlate the COOK score with a value of 1, meaning the restaurant has been in business for more than a year and is owned by the graduate, with the previous (10 years earlier) COOK score. A high coefficient indicates predictive validity, and a low correlation indicates the lack thereof.

Construct Validity

Construct validity is the most interesting and the most difficult of all the validities to develop because it is based on some underlying construct or idea behind a test or measurement tool.

You may remember from your studies in Psych 1 that a construct is a group of interrelated variables. For example, aggression is a construct (consisting of such variables as inappropriate touching, violence, lack of successful social interaction, etc.) as are intelligence, mother–infant attachment, and hope. And keep in mind that these constructs are generated from some theoretical position that the researcher assumes. For example, he or she might propose that aggressive men are more often in trouble with the authorities than nonaggressive men.

Establishing Construct Validity. So, you have the FIGHT test (of aggression), which is an observational tool that consists of a series of items that are an outgrowth of your theoretical view about what the construct of aggression consists of. You know from the criminology literature that males who are aggressive do certain types of things more than others—for example, they get into more arguments, they are more physically aggressive (pushing and such), they commit more crimes of violence against others, and they have fewer successful interpersonal relationships. The FIGHT scale includes items that describe different behaviors, some of them theoretically related to aggressive behaviors and some that are not. Once the FIGHT scale is completed, you examine the results to see whether positive scores on the FIGHT correlate with the presence of the kinds of behaviors you would predict (level of involvement in crime, quality of personal relationships, etc.) and don't correlate with the kinds of behaviors that should not be related (such as lack of domestic violence, completion of high school and college, etc.). And if the correlation is high for the items that you predict should correlate and low for the items that should not, then you can conclude that there is something about the FIGHT scale (and it is probably the items you designed that assess elements of aggression) that works. Congratulations.

And If You Can't Establish Validity . . . Then What?

Well, this is a tough one, especially because there are so many different types of validity.

In general, if you don't have the validity evidence you want, your test is not doing what it should. If it's an achievement test, and a satisfactory level of content validity is what you seek, then you probably have to redo the questions on your test to make sure they are more consistent with what they should be according to that expert.

If you are concerned with criterion validity, then you probably need to reexamine the nature of the items on the test and decide how well you would expect responses to these questions to relate to the criterion you selected.

And finally, if it is construct validity that you are seeking and can't seem to find—better take a close look at the theoretical rationale that underlies the test you developed. Perhaps your definition and model of aggression is wrong, for example, or perhaps intelligence needs some critical rethinking.

A LAST, FRIENDLY WORD

This measurement stuff is pretty cool. It's intellectually interesting, and, in these times of accountability, everyone wants to know about the progress of students, stockbrokers, social welfare agency programs, and more.

Because of this strong and growing interest, there's a great temptation for undergraduate students working on their honors thesis or semester project or graduate students working on their thesis or dissertation to design an instrument as their final project.

But beware that what sounds like a good idea might lead to a disaster. The process of establishing the reliability and validity of any instrument can take years of intensive work. And what can make matters even worse is when the naive or unsuspecting individual wants to create a new instrument to test a new hypothesis. That means that on top of everything else that comes with testing a new hypothesis, there is also the task of making sure the instrument works.

If you are doing original research of your own, such as for your thesis or dissertation requirement, be sure to find a measure that has already had reliability and validity evidence well established. That way, you can get on with the main task of testing your hypotheses and not fool with the huge task of instrument development—a career in and of itself. Want a good start? Try the Buros Center for Testing (formerly the Buros Institute of Mental Measurements), available online at www.unl .edu/buros/.

VALIDITY AND RELIABILITY: REALLY CLOSE COUSINS

Let's step back for a moment and recall one of the reasons that you're even reading this chapter.

It was assigned to you. No, really. This chapter is important because you need to know something about reliability and the validity of the instruments you are using to measure outcomes. Why? If these instruments are not reliable and valid, then the results of your experiment will always be in doubt.

As we mentioned earlier in this chapter, you can have a test that is reliable but not valid. However, you cannot have a valid test without it first being reliable. Why? Well, a test can do whatever it does over and over (that's reliability) but still not do what it is supposed to (that's validity). But, if a test does what it is supposed to, then it has to do it consistently to work.

You've read about the relationship between reliability and validity several places in this chapter, but there's a very cool relationship lurking out there. You may read about it later in your coursework, but you should also know about it now. This relationship says that the maximum level of validity is equal to the square root of the reliability coefficient. For example, if the reliability coefficient for a test of mechanical aptitude is .87, the validity coefficient can be no larger than .93 (which is the square root of .87). What this means in tech talk is that the validity of a test is constrained by how reliable it is. And that makes perfect sense if we stop to think that a test must do what it does consistently before we can be sure it does what it says it does.

REAL-WORLD STATS

Here's a classic example of why validity is such an important concept to understand and always to seek when doing any kind of research or using the results of research to inform actions by professionals. In this case, it has to do with the assessment of attention-deficit/hyperactivity disorder, or ADHD.

Often, this diagnosis is biased by the subjectivity of symptoms and reports of parents and teachers. The relatively new use of continuous performance tests (which measure sustained and selective attention) increased users' expectations that the diagnosis of ADHD would be standardized and accurate, both qualities of any reliable and valid test. In this study, Nathanel Zelnik and his colleagues looked at scores from the Test of Variables of Attention in 230 children who were referred to their ADHD clinic. Among the 179 children with diagnosed ADHD (the criterion group), the Test of Variables of Attention was suggestive of ADHD in 163 participants (91.1% sensitivity), but it was also suggestive for ADHD in 78.4% of the children without ADHD. The authors' conclusion? The instrument is just not a reliable enough measure to accurately discriminate between the two groups.

Want to know more? Go online or go to the library, and look for . . .

Zelnik, N., Bennett-Back, O., Miari, W., Geoz, H. R., and Fattal-Valevski, A. (2012). Is the Test of Variables of Attention reliable for the diagnosis of attention-deficit hyperactivity disorder (ADHD)? *Journal of Child Neurology, 27,* 703–707.

SUMMARY

Yep, this is a stats course, so what's the measurement stuff doing here? Once again, almost any use of statistics revolves around some outcome being measured. Just as you read basic stats to make sense out of lots of data, you need basic measurement information to make sense of how behaviors, test scores, rankings, and whatever else is measured are assessed.

TIME TO PRACTICE

1. Go to the library and find five journal articles in your area of interest in which reliability and validity data are reported. Discuss the outcome measures that are used. Identify the type of reliability that was established and the type of validity. Then comment on whether you think that the levels are acceptable. If not, how could they be improved?

2. Provide an example of when you would want to establish test–retest reliability and when you would want parallel forms reliability.

3. Here are the test scores for a group of 15 adults who were assessed on their long-term memory in June and again in August using the same instrument. What type of reliability measure would you use to establish reliability, and is this test reliable?

June Testing	August Testing
8	9
4	6
5	5
6	6
1	3
7	7
6	8

June Testing	August Testing
8	9
7	6
6	7
7	8
8	6
9	9
10	9

4. You are developing an instrument that measures vocational preferences (what someone wants to do for a living), and you need to administer the test several times during the year while students are attending a vocational program. You need to assess the test–retest reliability of the test and the data from two administrations (available as Chapter 6 Data Set 1)—one in the fall and one in the spring. Would you call this a reliable test? Why or why not?

5. Chapter 6 Data Set 2 includes the observational data between two judges across 50 days of rating. Would you substitute one judge for the other? Why or why not?

6. How can a test be reliable and not valid? And why is a test not valid unless it is reliable?

7. When you are testing any experimental hypothesis, why is it important that the test you use to measure the outcome be both reliable and valid?

8. Describe the difference between the two types of criterion validity and provide an example of each.

9. Why is construct validity often so difficult to establish?

PART III

Taking Chances for Fun and Profit

Snapshots

A scatterplot of student test scores.

What do you know so far, and what's next? To begin with, you've got a really solid basis for understanding how to describe the characteristics of a set of scores and how distributions can differ from one another. That's what you learned in Chapters 2, 3, and 4 of *Statistics for People Who (Think They) Hate Statistics, Excel 2016 Edition.* In Chapter 5, you also learned how to describe the relationships between variables using correlational tools, and in Chapter 6, you learned how to judge the usefulness of assessment tools.

Now it's time to bump up the ante a bit and start playing for real. In Part III of *Statistics for People Who (Think They) Hate Statistics, Excel 2016 Edition,* you will be introduced in Chapter 7 to the importance and nature of hypothesis testing, including an in-depth discussion of what a hypothesis is, what different types of hypotheses there are, the function of the hypothesis, and why and how hypotheses are tested.

Then in Chapter 8 we'll get to the all-important topic of probability, represented by our discussion of the normal curve and the basic principles underlying probability—the part of statistics that helps us define how likely it is that some event (such as a specific score on a test) will occur. We'll use the normal curve as a basis for these arguments, and you'll see that any score or occurrence within any distribution has a likelihood associated with it.

After some fun with probability and the normal curve, we'll be ready to start our extended discussion in Part IV of the application of hypothesis testing and probability theory to the testing of specific questions regarding relationships between variables. It only gets better from here!

7 Hypotheticals and You

Testing Your Questions

Difficulty Scale ☺ ☺ ☺ (don't plan on going out tonight)

How much Excel? None

WHAT YOU'LL LEARN ABOUT IN THIS CHAPTER

✦ The difference between a sample and a population (again)

✦ The importance of the null and research hypotheses

✦ The criteria for judging a good hypothesis

SO YOU WANT TO BE A SCIENTIST . . .

You might have heard the term *hypothesis* used in other classes. You may even have had to formulate one for a research project you did for another class, or you may have read one or two in a journal article. If so, then you probably have a good idea what a hypothesis is. For those of you who are unfamiliar with this often-used term, a **hypothesis** is basically "an educated guess." Its most important role is to reflect the general problem statement or question that was the motivation for asking the research question in the first place.

Chapter 7 is one of the few times in *Statistics for People . . .* when you will not be using Excel to actively learn about basic statistics. This chapter is pretty much full of ideas that are important to understand, and we will use Excel again in later chapters (beginning with the next one) to illustrate some of those ideas.

That's why taking the care and time to formulate a really precise and clear research question is so important. This research question will be your guide in the creation of a hypothesis, and in turn, the hypothesis will determine the techniques you will use to test the hypothesis and answer the question that was originally asked.

So, a good hypothesis translates a problem statement or a research question into a form that is more amenable to testing. We talk about what makes a good hypothesis later in this chapter. Before that, let's turn our attention to the difference between a sample and a population. This is an important distinction, because hypothesis testing deals with a sample and then the results are generalized to the larger population. We also address the two main types of hypotheses (the null hypothesis and the research hypothesis). But first, let's formally define some simple terms that we have used earlier in *Statistics for People* . . . .

Samples and Populations

As a good scientist, you would like to be able to say that if Method A is better than Method B, this is true forever and always and for all people in the universe, right? Indeed. And, if you do enough research on the relative merits of Methods A and B and test enough people, you may someday be able to say that. But don't get too excited, because it's unlikely that you will be able to speak with such confidence. It takes too much money ($$$) and too much time (assessing all those people!) to do all that research, and besides, it's not even necessary. Instead, you can just select a representative sample from the population and test your hypothesis about the relative merits of Methods A and B.

Given the constraints of never enough time and never enough research funds, under which almost all scientists work, the next best strategy is to take a portion of a larger group of participants and do the research with that smaller group. In this context, the larger group is referred to as a **population**, and the smaller group selected from that population is referred to as a **sample**.

A measure of how well a sample approximates the characteristics of a population is called **sampling error**. Sampling error is basically the difference between the values of the sample statistic and the population parameter. The higher the sampling error, the less precision one has in sampling, and the more difficult it will be to make the case that what you find in the sample indeed reflects what you expected to find in the population. And just as there are measures of variability regarding distributions, so there are measures of the variability of this difference between a sample measure and a population measure. This is often called the *standard error*—it's basically the standard deviation of the difference between scores.

Samples should be selected from populations in such a way that the sample matches as closely as possible the characteristics of the population. The goal is to have the sample be as much like the population as possible. The most important implication of ensuring similarity between the two is that the research results based on the sample can be generalized to the population. When the sample accurately represents the population, the results of the study are said to have a high degree of generalizability.

A high degree of generalizability is an important quality of good research because it means that the time and effort (and $$$) that went into the research may have implications for groups of people other than the original participants.

It's easy to equate "big" with "representative." Keep in mind that it is far more important to have an accurately representative sample than it is to have a big sample (people often think that big is better—only true on Thanksgiving, by the way). For example, having lots and lots of participants in a sample is very impressive, but if the participants do not represent the larger population, the research will have little value.

THE NULL HYPOTHESIS

So we have a sample of participants selected from a population, and to begin the test of our research hypothesis, we first formulate the **null hypothesis**.

The null hypothesis is an interesting little creature. If it could talk, it would say something like, "I represent no relationship between the variables that you are studying." In other words, null hypotheses are statements of equality demonstrated by the following real-life (brief) null hypotheses taken from a variety of popular social and behavioral science journals. Names have been changed to protect the innocent.

- There will be *no difference* in the average score of 9th graders and the average score of 12th graders on the ABC memory test.
- There is *no difference* between the effectiveness of community-based, long-term care and the effectiveness of in-home, long-term care in promoting the social activity of older adults when measured using the Margolis Scale of Social Activities.

- There is *no relationship* between reaction time and problem-solving ability.
- There is *no difference* between white and black families in the amount of assistance they offer to their children in school-related activities.

What these four null hypotheses have in common is that they all contain a statement that two or more things are equal, or unrelated, to each other.

The Purposes of the Null Hypothesis

What are the basic purposes of the null hypothesis? The null hypothesis acts as both a starting point and a benchmark against which the actual outcomes of a study can be measured. Let's examine each of these purposes in more detail.

First, the null hypothesis acts as a starting point because it is the state of affairs that is accepted as true in the absence of any other information. For example, let's look at the first null hypothesis we stated above:

There will be no difference in the average score of 9th graders and the average score of 12th graders on the ABC memory test.

Given absolutely no other knowledge of 9th and 12th graders' memory skills, you have no reason to believe that there will be differences between the two groups, right? If you know nothing about the relationship between these variables, the best you can do is guess. And that's taking a chance. You might speculate as to why one group might outperform another, but if you have no evidence a priori (before the fact), then what choice do you have but to assume that they are equal?

This lack of a relationship as a starting point is a hallmark of this method of answering questions. In other words, until you prove that there is a difference, you have to assume that there is no difference. And a statement of no difference or no relationship is exactly what the null hypothesis is all about.

Furthermore, if there are any differences between these two groups, you have to assume that these differences are due to the most attractive explanation for differences between any groups on any variable—chance! That's right: Given no other information, chance is always the most likely and attractive explanation for the observed differences between two groups or the relationship between variables. Chance explains what we cannot. You might have thought of chance as the odds of winning that $5,000 nickel jackpot at the slots, but we're talking about chance as all that other "stuff" that clouds the picture and makes it even more difficult to understand the "true" nature of relationships between variables.

For example, you could take a group of soccer players and a group of football players and compare their running speeds, thinking about whether playing soccer or playing football makes athletes faster. But look at all the factors we don't know about that could contribute to differences. Who is to know whether some soccer players practice more, or if some football players are stronger, or if both groups are receiving additional training? What's more, perhaps the way their speed is being measured leaves room for chance; a faulty stopwatch or a windy day can contribute to differences unrelated to true running speed. As good researchers, our job is to eliminate chance factors from explaining observed differences and to evaluate other factors that might contribute to group differences, such as intentional training or nutrition programs, and see how they affect speed. The point is, if we find differences between groups and the differences are not due to training, we have no choice but to attribute the difference to chance. And, by the way, you might find it useful to think of chance as being somewhat equivalent to the idea of error. When we can control sources of error, the likelihood that we can offer a clear explanation for some outcome increases.

The second purpose of the null hypothesis is to provide a benchmark against which observed outcomes can be compared to see if these differences are due to some other factor. The null hypothesis helps to define a range within which any observed differences between groups can be attributed to chance (which is the null hypothesis's contention and reason for being born). Outside this range, the differences may be due to something other than chance (perhaps the manipulation of some variable, such as training in the above example).

Most research studies have an implied null hypothesis, and you may not find it clearly stated in a research report or journal article. Instead, you'll find the research hypothesis clearly stated, which is now where we turn our attention.

THE RESEARCH HYPOTHESIS

Whereas a null hypothesis is a statement of no relationship between variables, a **research hypothesis** is a definite statement that there is a relationship between variables. For example, for each of the null hypotheses stated earlier, here is a corresponding research hypothesis. Notice that we said "a" and not "the" corresponding research hypothesis, because there certainly could be more than one research hypothesis for any one null hypothesis.

- The average score of 9th graders *is different* from the average score of 12th graders on the ABC memory test.
- The effectiveness of community-based, long-term care *is different* from the effectiveness of in-home, long-term care in promoting the social activity of older adults when measured using the Margolis Scale of Social Activities.
- Slower reaction time and problem-solving ability *are positively related.*
- There *is a difference* between white and black families in the amount of assistance families offer to their children in school-related activities.

Each of these four research hypotheses has one thing in common. They are all statements of *inequality.* They posit a relationship between variables such as a difference between two groups.

The nature of this inequality can take two forms—a directional or a nondirectional research hypothesis. If the research hypothesis posits no direction to the inequality (one such phrasing is "different from"), the hypothesis is a nondirectional research hypothesis. If the research hypothesis posits a direction to the inequality (it might be phrased as "more than" or "less than"), the research hypothesis is a directional research hypothesis.

The Nondirectional Research Hypothesis

A **nondirectional research hypothesis** reflects a difference between groups, but the direction of the difference is not specified.

For example, the research hypothesis

The average score of 9th graders is different from the average score of 12th graders on the ABC memory test

is nondirectional in that the direction of the difference between the two groups is not specified. The hypothesis is a research hypothesis because it states that there is a difference, but it says nothing about the direction of that difference.

A nondirectional research hypothesis such as the one described here would be represented by the following equation:

$$H_1: \overline{X}_9 \neq \overline{X}_{12},$$
(7.1)

where

  H_1 is the first of possibly several research hypotheses;

  $\overline{X}_9$ is the average memory score for the sample of 9th graders;

  $\overline{X}_{12}$ is the average memory score for the sample of 12th graders; and

  ≠ means "is not equal to."

The Directional Research Hypothesis

A **directional research hypothesis** reflects a difference between groups, and the direction of the difference is specified.

 For example, the research hypothesis

The average score of 12th graders is greater than the average score of 9th graders on the ABC memory test

is directional because the direction of the difference between the two groups is specified. One is hypothesized to be greater than (not just different from) the other.

 Examples of two other directional hypotheses are these:

1. A is greater than B (or A > B).

2. B is greater than A (or A < B).

These both represent inequalities, and the inequalities are of a specific nature (*greater than* or *less than*). A directional research hypothesis such as the one described above, where 12th graders are hypothesized to score better than 9th graders, would be represented by the following equation:

$$H_1: \overline{X}_{12} > \overline{X}_9, \qquad\qquad (7.2)$$

where

  H_1 is the first of possibly several research hypotheses;

  $\overline{X}_{12}$ is the average memory score for the sample of 12th graders;

  $\overline{X}_9$ is the average memory score for the sample of 9th graders; and

  > means "is greater than."

 Table 7.1 gives the four null hypotheses and accompanying directional and nondirectional research hypotheses.

Table 7.1 Null Hypotheses and Corresponding Research Hypotheses

Null Hypothesis	Nondirectional Research Hypothesis	Directional Research Hypothesis
There will be no difference in the average score of 9th graders and the average score of 12th graders on the ABC memory test.	Twelfth graders and 9th graders will differ on the ABC memory test.	Twelfth graders will have a higher average score on the ABC memory test than will 9th graders.
There is no difference between the effectiveness of community-based, long-term care and the effectiveness of in-home, long-term care in promoting the social activity of older adults when measured using the Margolis Scale of Social Activities.	The effect of community-based, long-term care is different from the effect of in-home, long-term care on the social activity of older adults when measured using the Margolis Scale of Social Activities.	Older adults exposed to community-based, long-term care score higher on the Margolis Scale of Social Activities than do older adults receiving in-home, long-term care.
There is no relationship between reaction time and problem-solving ability.	There is a relationship between reaction time and problem-solving ability.	There is a positive relationship between reaction time and problem-solving ability.
There is no difference between white and black families in the amount of assistance they offer to their children in school-related activities.	The amount of assistance offered by white families to their children is different from the amount of assistance offered by black families to their children in school-related activities.	The amount of assistance offered by white families to their children is more than the amount of assistance offered by black families to their children in school-related activities.

What is the purpose of the research hypothesis? It is this hypothesis that is directly tested as an important step in the research process. The results of this test are compared with what you expect by chance alone (reflecting the null hypothesis) to see which of the two is the more attractive explanation for any differences between groups you might observe.

 Another way to talk about directional and nondirectional hypotheses is to talk about one- and two-tailed tests. A **one-tailed test** (reflecting a directional hypothesis) posits a difference in a particular direction,

such as when we hypothesize that Group 1 will score higher than Group 2. A **two-tailed test** (reflecting a nondirectional hypothesis) posits a difference but in no particular direction. The importance of this distinction begins when you test different types of hypotheses (one- and two-tailed) and establish probability levels for rejecting or not rejecting the null hypothesis. More about this in Chapters 10 (Z-test) and 11 (t-test).

Some Differences Between the Null Hypothesis and the Research Hypothesis

Besides the null hypothesis representing an equality and the research hypothesis representing an inequality, the two types of hypotheses differ in several other important ways.

First, for a bit of review, the two types of hypotheses differ in that one (the null hypothesis) states that there is no relationship between variables (an equality), whereas the research hypothesis states that there is a relationship between the variables (an inequality). This is the primary difference.

Second, null hypotheses always refer to the population, whereas research hypotheses always refer to the sample. We select a sample of participants from a much larger population. We then try to generalize the results from the sample back to the population. If you remember your basic philosophy and logic (you did take these courses, right?), you'll remember that going from small (as in a sample) to large (as in a population) is a process of induction.

Third, because the entire population cannot be tested directly (again, it is impractical, uneconomical, and often impossible), you can't say with 100% certainty that there is no real difference between samples on some variable. Rather, you have to infer it (indirectly) from the results of the test of the research hypothesis, which is based on the sample. Hence, the null hypothesis is, by definition, indirectly tested, and the research hypothesis is directly tested.

The null hypothesis is written with an equal sign, while the research hypothesis is written with a not equal to, greater than, or less than sign. Also, by convention, the variables in the null hypothesis are represented with the Greek letter mu (μ), while those in the research hypothesis are represented by X-bar ($\bar{X}$). For example, the null hypothesis that the average score for 9th graders is equal to that of 12th graders is represented as you see here:

$$H_0: \mu_9 = \mu_{12}, \tag{7.3}$$

where

H_0 is the null hypothesis;

μ_9 is the theoretical average for the population of 9th graders; and

μ_{12} is the theoretical average for the population of 12th graders.

The research hypothesis that the average score for a sample of 12th graders is greater than the average score for a sample of 9th graders was shown in Formula 7.2.

Finally, because you cannot directly test the null hypothesis, it is an implied hypothesis. But the research hypothesis is explicit and is stated as such. This is another reason why you rarely see null hypotheses stated in research reports and will almost always see a statement (be it in symbols or words) of the research hypothesis.

WHAT MAKES A GOOD HYPOTHESIS?

You now know that hypotheses are educated guesses—a starting point for a lot more to come. As with any guess, some are better than others right from the start. We can't stress enough how important it is to ask the question you want answered and to keep in mind that any hypothesis you present is a direct extension of the original question you asked. This question will reflect your own personal interests and motivation and the research that has been done previously. With that in mind, here are criteria you might use to decide whether a hypothesis you read in a research report or one you formulate is acceptable.

To illustrate, let's use an example of a study that examines the effects of after-school child care for employees who work late on the parents' adjustment to work. Here is a well-written hypothesis:

Parents who enroll their children in after-school programs will miss fewer days of work in 1 year and will have a more positive attitude toward work, as measured by the Attitude Toward Work survey, than will parents who do not enroll their children in such programs.

Here are the criteria.

First, a good hypothesis is stated in declarative form and not as a question. In the above example, the question "Do you think parents and the companies they work for will be better . . . ?" was not posed because hypotheses are most effective when they make a clear and forceful statement.

Second, a good hypothesis posits an expected relationship between variables. The hypothesis that is being used as an example clearly describes the relationships among after-school child care, parents' attitude, and absentee rate. These variables are being tested to see if one (enrollment in the after-school program) has an effect upon the others (absentee rate and attitude).

Notice the word *expected* in the above criterion. Defining an expected relationship is intended to prevent a fishing trip to look for any relationships that may be found (sometimes called the "shotgun" approach), which may be tempting but is not very productive. You do get somewhere using the shotgun approach, but because you don't know where you started, you have no idea where you end up.

In the fishing-trip approach, you throw out your line and take anything that bites. You collect data on as many things as you can, regardless of your interest or even whether collecting the data is a reasonable part of a scientific investigation. Or, to use a shotgun analogy, you load up them guns and blast away at anything that moves, and you're bound to hit something. The problem is, you may not want what you hit, and worse, you may miss what you want to hit, and worst of all (if possible), you may not know what you hit! Big Data (see Chapter 20), anyone? Good researchers do not want just anything they can catch or shoot. They want specific results. To get them, researchers need their opening questions and hypotheses to be clear, forceful, and easily understood.

Third, hypotheses reflect the theory or literature on which they are based. As you read in Chapter 1, the accomplishments of scientists rarely can be attributed to just their own hard work. Their accomplishments are always due, in part, to those of many other researchers who came before them and laid the framework for later explorations. A good hypothesis reflects this, in that it has a substantive link to existing literature and theory. In the above example, let's assume there is literature indicating that parents are more comfortable knowing their children are being cared for in a structured environment and that parents can then be more productive at work. Knowing this would allow one to hypothesize that an after-school program would provide the security for which parents are looking. In turn, they feel free to concentrate on work rather than having to text the kids to find out whether they got home safely.

Fourth, a hypothesis should be brief and to the point. You want your hypothesis to describe the relationship between variables in a declarative form and to be as direct and explicit as possible. The more to the point it is, the easier it will be for others (such as your master's thesis or doctoral dissertation committee members!) to read your research and understand exactly what you are hypothesizing and what the important variables are. In fact, when people read and evaluate research (as you will learn more about later in this chapter), the first thing many of them do is find the hypotheses to get a good idea as to the general purpose of the research and how things will be done. A good hypothesis tells you both of these things.

Fifth, good hypotheses are testable hypotheses—and testable hypotheses contain variables that can be measured. This means that you can actually carry out the intent of the question reflected by the hypothesis. You can see from the sample hypothesis that the important comparison is between parents who have enrolled their child in an after-school program and those who have not. Then, such things as attitude and workdays missed will be measured. These are both reasonable objectives. Attitude is measured by the Attitude Toward Work survey (a fictitious title, but you get the idea), and absenteeism (the number of days away from work) is an easily recorded and unambiguous measure. Think how much harder things would be if the hypothesis were stated as *Parents who enroll their children in after-school care feel better about their jobs*. Although you might get the same message, the results might be more difficult to interpret given the ambiguous nature of words such as "feel better."

In sum, hypotheses should

- be stated in declarative form,
- posit a relationship between variables,
- reflect a theory or a body of literature on which they are based,
- be brief and to the point, and
- be testable.

When a hypothesis meets each of these five criteria, you know that it is good enough to continue with a study that will accurately test the general question from which the hypothesis was derived.

 # REAL-WORLD STATS

You might think that the scientific method and the use of null and research hypotheses is beyond question in the world of scientific research. Well, you would be wrong. Here's just a sampling of some of the articles published in professional journals over the past few years and the concerns they raise. No one is yet ready to throw out the scientific method as the best approach for testing hypotheses, but it's not a bad idea to every now and then question whether the method always and forever is the best model to use.

- Jeff Gill from California Polytechnic State University raises a variety of issues that call into question the use of the null hypothesis significance-testing model as the best way to evaluate hypotheses. He focuses on political science (his area) and how the use of the technique is widely misunderstood. Major problems are discussed and some solutions offered. You can find the article by looking for this reference: Gill, J. (1999). The insignificance of null hypothesis testing. *Politics Research Quarterly, 52,* 647–674.

- Howard Wainer and Daniel Robinson take these criticisms one step further and suggest that the historical use of such procedures was reasonable but that modifications to significance testing and the interpretations of outcomes would serve modern science well. Basically, they are saying that other tools should be used to evaluate outcomes (such as effect size, which we discuss in Chapter 11). Read all about it in Wainer, H., & Robinson, D. H. (2003). Shaping up the practice of null hypothesis significance testing. *Educational Researcher, 32,* 22–30.

- Finally, in the really interesting article "A Vast Graveyard of Undead Theories: Publication Bias and Psychological Science's Aversion to the Null," Christopher Ferguson and Moritz Heene raise the very real issue that many journals refuse to publish outcomes where a null result is found (such as no difference between groups). They believe that when such outcomes are not published, false theories are never taken to task and never tested for their truthfulness. Thus, the replicability of science (a very important aspect of the entire scientific process) is compromised. You can find more about this in Ferguson, C. J., & Heene, M. (2012). A vast graveyard of undead theories: Publication bias and psychological science's aversion to the null. *Perspectives on Psychological Science, 7,* 555–561.

We hope you get the idea from the above examples that science is not black-and-white, cut-and-dried, or any other metaphor indicating there is only a right way and only a wrong way of doing things. Science is an organic and dynamic process that is always changing in its focus, methods, and potential outcomes.

SUMMARY

A central component of any scientific study is the hypothesis, and the different types of hypotheses (null and research) help form a plan for answering the questions asked by the purpose of our research. The null hypothesis provides a starting point and benchmark for research, and we use it as a comparison as we evaluate the acceptability of the research hypothesis. Now let's move on to how null hypotheses are actually tested.

TIME TO PRACTICE

1. Go to the library and select five empirical research articles (those that contain actual data) from your area of interest. For each one, list the following:

    a. What is the null hypothesis (implied or explicitly stated)?

    b. What is the research hypothesis (implied or explicitly stated)?

    c. And what about those articles with no hypothesis clearly stated or implied? Identify those articles and see if you can write a research hypothesis for them.

2. While you're at the library, select two other articles from an area in which you are interested and write a brief description of the sample and how it was selected from the population. Be sure to include some words about whether the researchers did an adequate job of selecting the sample; be able to justify your answer.

3. For the following research questions, create one null hypothesis, one directional research hypothesis, and one nondirectional research hypothesis.

    a. What are the effects of attention span on out-of-seat classroom behavior?

    b. What is the relationship between the quality of a marriage and the quality of the spouses' relationships with their siblings?

    c. What's the best way to treat an eating disorder?

    d. How do early intervention programs before age 3 affect reading skills when the children are in sixth grade?

4. Go back to the five hypotheses that you found in question 1 above and evaluate each using the five criteria that were discussed at the end of the chapter.

5. What kinds of problems might using a poorly written or ambiguous research hypothesis introduce?

6. What is the null hypothesis, and what is one of its important purposes? How does it differ from the research hypothesis?

7. What is chance in the context of a research hypothesis? And what do we do about chance in our experiments?

8. Why does the null hypothesis presume no relationship between variables?

9. Time to be even more creative! Provide one null and one research hypothesis and an equation concerning each of the following:

   a. The amount of money spent on food by undergraduate student-athletes and other undergraduates

   b. The average amount of time taken by white and brown rats to get out of a maze

   c. The effects of Drug A and Drug B on a disease

   d. The time to complete a task using Method 1 and Method 2

8 Are Your Curves Normal?

Probability and Why It Counts

Difficulty Scale ☺ ☺ ☺ ☺ (not too easy and not too hard, but very important)

How much Excel? 📊 📊 📊 📊 (lots)

WHY PROBABILITY?

And here you thought this was a statistics class! Ha! Well, as you will learn in this chapter, the study of probability is the basis for the normal curve (much more on that later) and the foundation for inferential statistics.

Why? First, the normal curve provides us with a basis for understanding the probability associated with *any* possible outcome (such as the odds of getting a certain score on a test or the odds of getting a head on one flip of a coin).

Second, the study of probability is the basis for determining the degree of confidence we have in stating that a particular finding or outcome is "true." Or, better said, that an outcome (such as an average score) may not have occurred because of chance alone. For example, let's compare Group A (which participates in 3 hours of extra swim practice each week) and Group B (which has no extra swim practice each week). We find that Group A differs from Group B on a test of fitness, but can we say that the difference is due to the extra practice or due to something else? The tools that the study of probability provides allow us to determine the exact mathematical likelihood that the difference is due to practice versus something else (such as chance).

And, as you will see, all that time we spent on learning about hypotheses in the previous chapter was time well spent. Once we put our understanding of what a null hypothesis and a research hypothesis are together with the ideas that are the foundation of probability, we'll be in a position to discuss how likely certain outcomes (formulated by the research hypothesis) are.

THE NORMAL CURVE (AKA THE BELL-SHAPED CURVE)

What is a normal curve? Well, the **normal curve** (also called a **bell-shaped curve**, or bell curve) is a visual representation of a distribution of scores that has three characteristics. Each of these characteristics is illustrated in Figure 8.1.

| Figure 8.1 | The Normal, or Bell-Shaped, Curve |

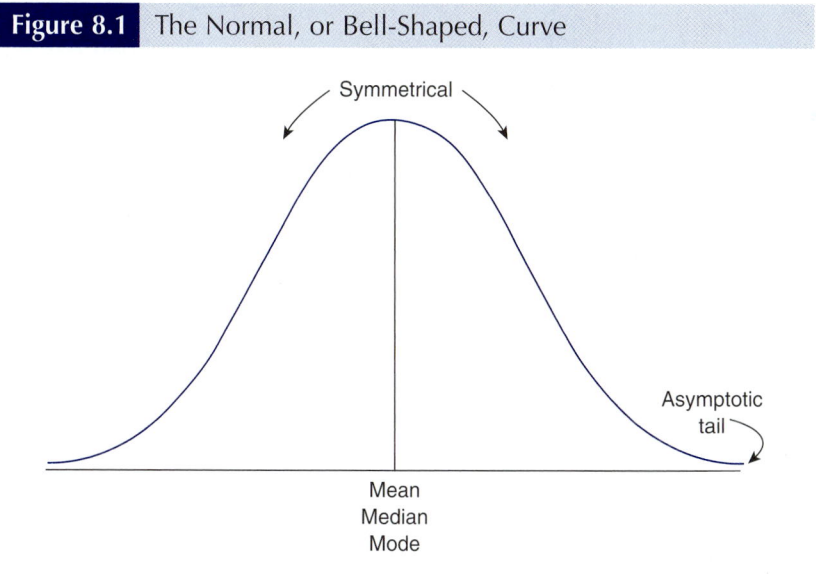

The normal curve represents a distribution of values in which *the mean, median, and mode are equal to one another.* You probably remember from Chapter 4 that if the median and the mean are different, then the distribution is skewed in one direction or the other.

The normal curve is not skewed. It's got a nice hump (only one), and that hump is right in the middle. The normal curve's bell-like shape also gives the graph its other name, the bell-shaped curve.

Second, the normal curve is *perfectly symmetrical about the mean.* If you folded one half of the curve along its center line, the two halves would fit perfectly on each other. They are identical. One half of the curve is a mirror image of the other.

Finally (and get ready for a mouthful), *the tails of the normal curve are* **asymptotic**—a big word. What it means is that they come closer and closer to the horizontal axis, but never touch the axis.

When your devoted author was knee-high, he always wondered how the tail of a normal curve could approach the horizontal or *x*-axis yet never touch it. Try this. Place two pencils 1 inch apart and then move them closer (by half) so they are one half inch apart, and then closer (one quarter inch apart), and closer (one eighth inch apart). They continually get closer, right? But they never (and never will) touch. Same thing with the tails of the curve. The tails slowly approach the axis on which the curve "rests," but they can never actually touch it. And that's why, no matter how unlikely any event, there is always a chance it will occur—no matter how small that chance is. Or, with thanks to Aristotle, "Probable impossibilities are to be preferred to improbable possibilities," or for the non-philosophy majors among us, the improbable is probable.

Why is this important? As you will learn later in this chapter, the fact that the tails never touch means that there is an infinitely small likelihood that a score can be obtained that is very extreme (way out in the left or right tail of the curve). If the tails did touch, then the likelihood that a very extreme score could be obtained would be nonexistent.

Hey, That's Not Normal!

We hope your next question is "But there are plenty of sets of scores where the distribution is not normal or bell shaped, right?" Yes—and here comes the big *but*—but when we deal with large sets of data (more than 30 observations), and as we take repeated samples of the data from a population, the values in the curve closely approximate the shape of a normal curve. This is very important (and more about it in the Tech Talk to follow), because much of what we do when we talk about inferring from a sample to a population is based on the assumption that the sample taken from a population is distributed normally.

And as it turns out, in nature in general, many things are distributed in the way we call normal. That is, there are lots of events or occurrences right in the middle of the distribution but relatively few on each end, as you can see in Figure 8.2, which shows the distribution of IQ and height in the general population.

Figure 8.2 How Scores Can Be Distributed

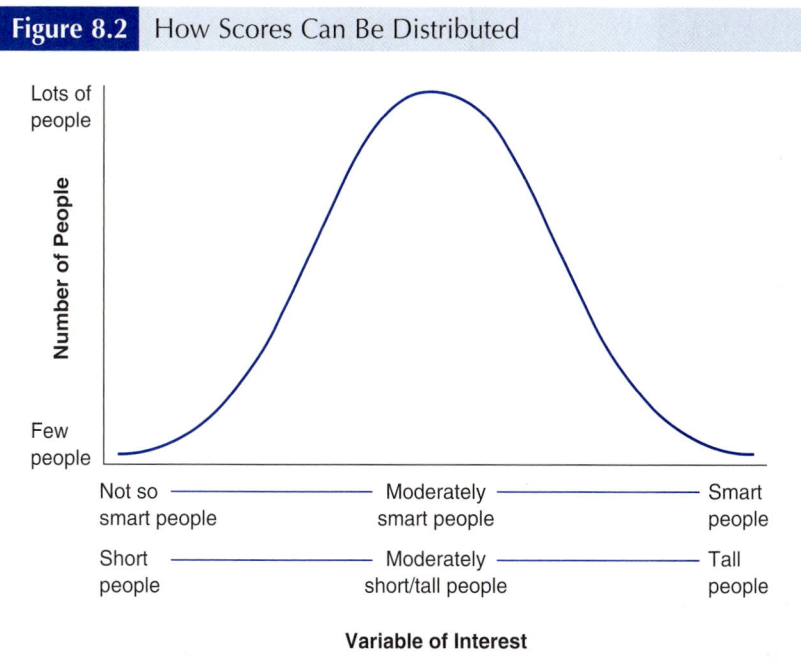

For example, there are very few people who are "smart people" (see the right end of the curve) and very few who are "not-so-smart people" (see the left end of the curve). There are lots who are right in the middle ("moderately smart people") and fewer as we move toward the tails of the curve.

As another example, consider that there are relatively few tall people and relatively few short people, but there are lots of people of moderate height right in the middle of the distribution of height.

In both of these examples, the distributions of intellectual skills and height approximate a normal distribution. Consequently, those events that tend to occur in the extremes of the normal curve have a smaller probability associated with each occurrence. We can say with a great deal of confidence that the odds of any one person (whose height we do not know beforehand) being very tall (or very short) are just not very great. But we know that the odds of any one person being average in height, or right around the middle, are pretty good (yikes—that's why it's called the average!). Those events that tend to occur in the middle of the normal curve have a higher probability of occurring than do those in the extremes.

The Central Limit Theorem

Here we are talking about curves, curves, and more curves, and you probably get by now the whole idea that an individual score can be assigned a probability. You also get that's part of the basis for how we can address the question of what may occur by chance and what may not.

But, just for a moment, let's take a step back and think about this notion of assigning probabilities to outcomes, especially as it applies to samples and populations.

A great deal of the inferential way of thinking about statistics is based on the normal distribution, which we discuss at some length throughout this chapter. All well and good. And, while we know that in theory and practice, many, many characteristics of humans (and other animals, and phenomena all over the physical and natural sciences) are distributed normally (such as height and weight and, supposedly, intelligence quotients), the population of scores may very well not be. So, what do we do when so much of what we study is based on normal distributions but the parent population, in fact, is not normal?

Have no fear. There is a very cool and practical idea called the **central limit theorem**. What the big boys and girls say this does is that in a world of somewhat random events (meaning somewhat random values), this theory explains the occurrence of somewhat normally distributed sample values (which form the basis for many of the inferential tools we will use as explained in the next chapter and in the later chapters in *Statistics for People . . .*).

There are two basic tenets of the central limit theorem.

First, the value (such as the sum or the mean) associated with a large number of independent observations will be distributed approximately in a normal fashion. Second, this "normality" gets more and more normal as the number of observations or samples increases. Here's a real live example.

Let's say that we have a population of 1,000 scores (from a distribution that is not normal) with values from 1 to 10. You can see what such a population distribution might look like in Figure 8.3. Not pretty . . . but surely random with no discernable pattern.

Now, we select 100 samples of size 5 and then compute the average of each sample. We end up with 100 averages that, when plotted as you see in Figure 8.4, begin to look kind of normal.

This observation is the critical link between obtaining the results from the sample and being able to generalize these results to the population. The key assumption is that repeated sampling from the population (even if that population distribution is a bit weird or clearly not normal) will result in a set of scores that approach normality. If this is not the case, then many parametric tests of inferential statistics (assuming a normal distribution) cannot be applied. Not the cowboy and cowgirl way.

| **Figure 8.3** | 1,000 Random Values |

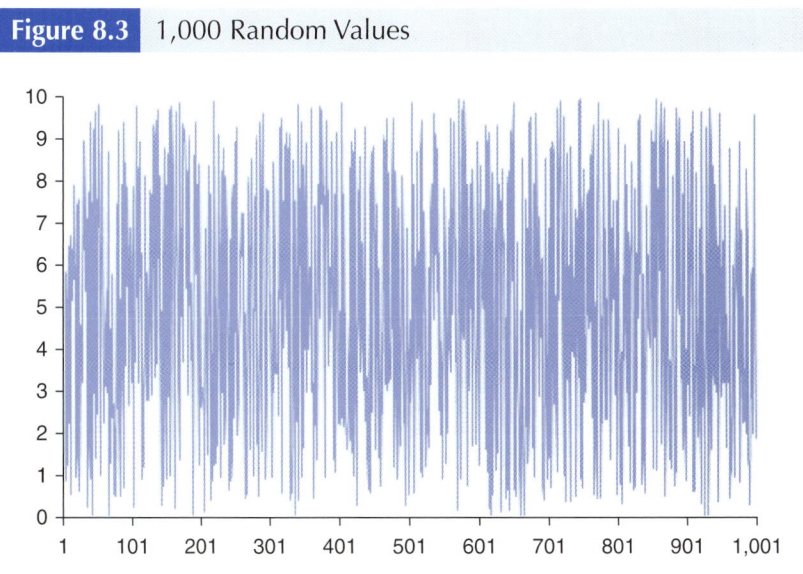

| **Figure 8.4** | 100 Averages Taken From the Population Shown in Figure 8.3 |

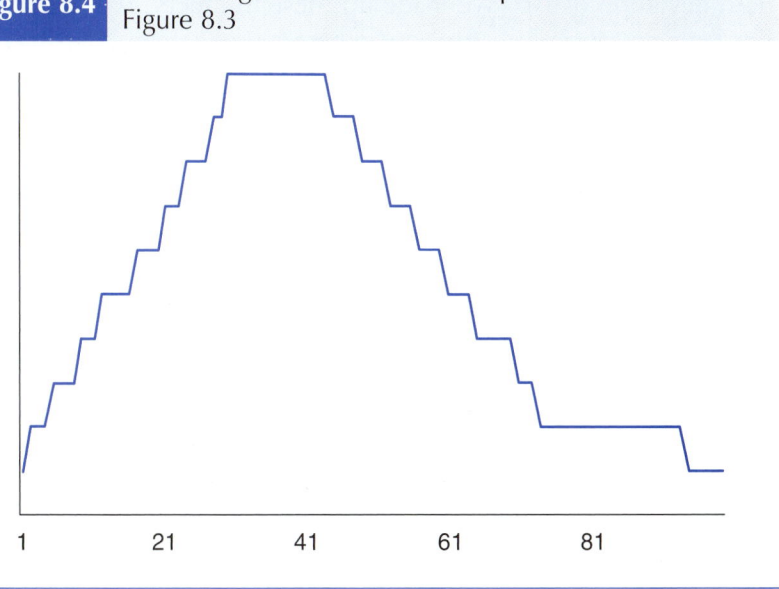

More Normal Curve 101

You already know the three main characteristics that make a curve normal or make it appear bell shaped, but there's more to it than that. Take a look at the curve in Figure 8.5.

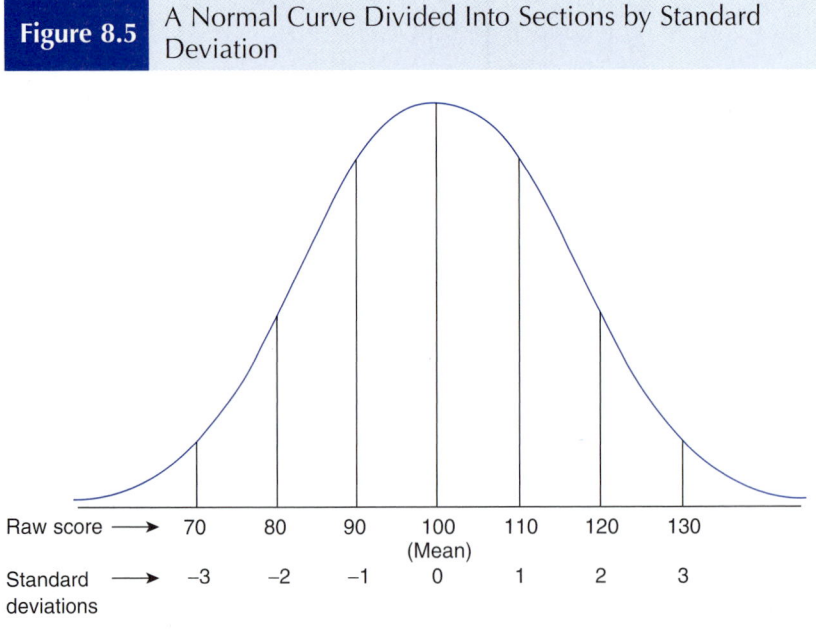

| **Figure 8.5** | A Normal Curve Divided Into Sections by Standard Deviation |

The distribution represented here has a mean of 100 and a standard deviation of 10. (We made up these numbers, 100 and 10, so don't go nuts trying to find out where we got them from.) We've added numbers across the *x*-axis that represent the distance in standard deviations from the mean for this distribution. You can see that the *x*-axis, representing the scores in the distribution, is marked from 70 through 130 in increments of 10, the value of 1 standard deviation.

Each vertical line within the curve separates the curve into a section, and each section is bounded by particular scores. For example, the first section to the right of the mean of 100 is bounded by the scores 100 and 110, representing 1 standard deviation from the mean.

And below each raw score (70, 80, 90, 100, 110, 120, and 130), you'll find a corresponding standard deviation (−3, −2, −1, 0, +1, +2, and +3). Recall that each standard deviation in our example is 10 points. So, 1 standard deviation from the mean of 100 is the mean plus 10 points (110) or the mean minus 10 points (90). Not so hard, is it?

By extending this argument, we see that the range of scores represented by a normal distribution with a mean of 100 and a standard deviation of 10 is 70 through 130 (which is −3 to +3 standard deviations).

Now, here's a big fact that is always true about normal distributions, means, and standard deviations: For any distribution of scores (regardless of the value of the mean and standard deviation), if the scores are distributed normally, almost 100% of the scores will fit between −3 and +3 standard deviations from the mean. This is very important, because it applies to all normal distributions. Because of this rule (once again, regardless of the value of the mean or standard deviation), distributions can be compared with one another. We'll get to that again later.

With all that said, we'll extend our argument a bit more. If the distribution of scores is normal, we can also say that a certain percentage of cases will fall between different points along the *x*-axis (such as between the mean and 1 standard deviation). In fact, between the mean (which in this case is 100—got that yet?) and 1 standard deviation above the mean (which is 110), you'll find about 34% (actually 34.13%) of all cases in the distribution of scores. This is a fact you can take to the bank because it will always be true.

Want to go further? Take a look at Figure 8.6. Here, you can see the same normal curve in all its glory (the mean again equals 100, and the standard deviation equals 10 in this example), and the percentage of cases that we would expect to fall within the boundaries are defined by the mean and standard deviation.

Figure 8.6 Distribution of Cases Under the Normal Curve

| Raw score ⟶ | 70 | 80 | 90 | 100 | 110 | 120 | 130 |

.13% 2.15% 13.59% 34.13% 34.13% 13.59% 2.15% .13%

| Standard deviations ⟶ | −3 | −2 | −1 | 0 | 1 | 2 | 3 |

Here's what we can conclude.

The distance between . . .	Contains . . .	And the scores that are included (if the mean = 100 and the standard deviation = 10) are . . .
the mean and 1 standard deviation	34.13% of all the cases under the curve	from 100 to 110
1 and 2 standard deviations	13.59% of all the cases under the curve	from 110 to 120
2 and 3 standard deviations	2.15% of all the cases under the curve	from 120 to 130
3 standard deviations and above	0.13% of all the cases under the curve	above 130

If you add up all the values in either half of the normal curve, guess what you get? That's right, 50%. Why? The distance between the mean and the largest score to the right of the mean underneath the normal curve contains 50% of all the scores.

And because the curve is symmetrical about its central axis (each half is a mirror image of the other), the two halves together represent 100% of all the scores. Not rocket science, but important to point out, nonetheless.

Now, let's extend the same logic to the scores to the left of the mean of 100.

The distance between . . .	Contains . . .	And the scores that are included (if the mean = 100 and the standard deviation = 10) are . . .
the mean and −1 standard deviation	34.13% of all the cases under the curve	from 90 to 100
−1 and −2 standard deviations	13.59% of all the cases under the curve	from 80 to 90
−2 and −3 standard deviations	2.15% of all the cases under the curve	from 70 to 80
−3 standard deviations and below	0.13% of all the cases under the curve	below 70

Now, be sure to keep in mind that we are using a mean of 100 and a standard deviation of 10 only as sample figures for a particular example. Obviously, not all distributions have a mean of 100 and a standard deviation of 10; in fact, most do not.

All of this is pretty neat, especially when you consider that the values of 34.13% and 13.59% and so on are absolutely independent of the actual values of the mean and the standard deviation. These values are due to the shape of the curve, not because of the value of any of the scores in the distribution or the value of the mean or standard deviation. In fact, if you actually drew a normal curve on a piece of cardboard and cut out the curve and then cut out the area between the mean and +1 standard deviation and then weighed it, it would tip the scale at exactly 34.13% of the weight of the entire cardboard curve. (Try it—it's true.)

In our example, this means that (roughly) 68% (34.13% doubled) of the scores fall between the raw score values of 90 and 110. What about the other 32%? Good question. One half (16%, or 13.59% + 2.15% + 0.13%) fall above (to the right of) 1 standard deviation above the mean, and one half fall below (to the left of) 1 standard deviation below the mean. And because the curve slopes, and the amount of area decreases as you move farther away from the mean, it is no surprise that the likelihood that a score will fall more toward the extremes of the distribution is less than the likelihood it will fall toward the middle. That's why the curve has a bump in the middle and is not skewed in either direction.

OUR FAVORITE STANDARD SCORE: THE Z SCORE

You have read more than once that distributions differ in measures of their central tendency and variability.

When conducting or reading about research, we will find ourselves working with distributions that are indeed different, yet we will be required to compare them with one another. And to do such a comparison, we need some kind of a standard.

Say hello to **standard scores**. These are scores that are comparable because they are standardized in units of standard deviations. For example, a standard score of 1 in a distribution with a mean of 50 and a standard deviation of 10 means the same thing as a standard score of 1 from a distribution with a mean of 100 and a standard deviation of 5; they both represent 1 standard score and are an equivalent distance from their respective means.

Standard scores are so powerful and useful because they can be compared with one another without regard to their mean or standard deviation values.

Also, we can use our knowledge of the normal curve and assign a probability to the occurrence of a value that is 1 standard deviation from the mean. This is a very powerful idea, and we'll do it later in the chapter.

Although there are other types of standard scores (such as *t* scores), the one that you will see most frequently in your study of statistics is called a **z score**. This is the result of dividing the amount that a raw score differs from the mean of the distribution by the standard deviation (see Formula 8.1).

$$z = \frac{(X - \bar{X})}{s},$$ (8.1)

where

z　　is the z score;

X　　is the individual score;

$\bar{X}$　　is the mean of the distribution; and

s　　is the distribution's standard deviation.

For example, in Formula 8.2, you can see how the z score is calculated if the mean is 100, the raw score is 110, and the standard deviation is 10:

$$z = \frac{(110 - 100)}{10} = +1.0$$ (8.2)

It's just as easy to compute a raw score given a z score as the other way around. You already know the formula for a z score given the raw score, mean, and standard deviation. But if you know only the z score and the mean and standard deviation, then what's the corresponding raw score? Easy. Just use the formula $X = (z \times s) + \bar{X}$. You can easily convert raw scores to z scores and back again if necessary. For example, a z score of –0.5 in a distribution with a mean of 50 and an *s* of 5 would equal a raw score of $X = (-0.5 \times 5) + 50$, or 47.5.

The following data show the original raw scores plus the z scores for a sample of 10 scores that has a mean of 12 and a standard deviation of 2. Any raw score above the mean will have a corresponding z score that is positive, and any raw score below the mean will have a corresponding z score that is negative. For example, a raw score of 15 has a corresponding z score of +1.5, and a raw score of 8 has a corresponding z score of −2. And of course, a raw score of 12 (or the mean) has a z score of 0 (because it is zero distance from the mean).

X	X − X̄	z Score
12	0	0.0
15	3	1.5
11	−1	−0.5
13	1	0.5
8	−4	−2.0
14	2	1.0
12	0	0.0
13	1	0.5
12	0	0.0
10	−2	−1.0

Below are just a few observations about these scores, as a little review.

First, those scores that fall below the mean (such as 8 and 10) have negative z scores, and those scores that fall above the mean (such as 13 and 14) have positive z scores.

Second, positive z scores always fall to the right of the mean and are in the upper half of the distribution. And negative z scores always fall to the left of the mean and are in the lower half of the distribution.

Third, when we talk about a score being located 1 standard deviation above the mean, it's the same as saying that the score is 1 z score above the mean. For our purposes, when comparing scores across distributions, z scores and standard deviations are equivalent. In other words, a z score is simply the number of standard deviations from the mean.

Finally (and this is very important), z scores across different distributions are comparable. Here's another table, similar to the one above, that illustrates this point. These 10 scores were selected from a set of 100 scores, with the scores having a mean of 58 and a standard deviation of 15.3.

Raw Score	$X - \bar{X}$	z Score
67	9	0.59
54	-4	-0.26
68	10	0.65
33	-25	-1.63
56	-2	-0.13
76	18	1.18
65	7	0.46
35	-23	-1.50
48	-10	-0.65
76	18	1.18

In the first distribution you saw earlier, with a mean of 12 and a standard deviation of 2, a raw score of 12.8 has a corresponding z score of +0.4, which means that a raw score of 12.8 is a distance of 0.4 standard deviations from the mean. In this second distribution, with a mean of 58 and a standard deviation of 15.3, a raw score of 64.2 has a corresponding z score of +0.4 as well.

Both raw scores of 12.8 and 64.2, *relative to one another,* are equal distances from the mean. A miracle? No—just a good idea.

When these raw scores are represented as standard scores, then they are directly comparable to one another in terms of their relative location in their respective distributions. That is a very cool way to compare outcomes and one that helps level the playing field in comparing performances from one group to another.

Using Excel to Compute z Scores

Using Excel to compute z scores (or any standard score for that matter) is a cinch and requires only the use of one simple formula. In Figure 8.7, you can see a worksheet of the same data you see in the table above with a mean of 12 and a standard deviation of 2. In the Formula Bar is the formula used to compute the z scores. That formula was then copied from Cell B2 through to Cell B11. Very easy and very quick.

Figure 8.7 Using Excel to Compute z Scores

	A	B	C	D	E	F	G	H
	X	z score						
1								
2	12	0						
3	15	1.5						
4	11	-0.5						
5	13	0.5						
6	8	-2						
7	14	1						
8	12	0						
9	13	0.5						
10	12	0						
11	10	-1						

(formula bar) B3 f_x =(A3-(AVERAGE($A$2:$A$11)))/STDEV($A$2:$A$11)

We did a few new and neat things here.

First, we used functions within a formula. Instead of using functions to compute the mean and the standard deviation and then using a formula to compute the z scores, we skipped right to using the functions. So, instead of the formula for a z score looking like

$$z = \frac{(X - \bar{X})}{s},$$ (8.3)

ours looks like this:

= (A3-(AVERAGE($A$2:$A$11)))/STDEV($A$2:$A$11)

Here, deviation from the mean was computed by taking the raw score (in Cell A3) and subtracting from it the average (computed using the AVERAGE function). That outcome was then divided by the standard deviation, which we computed using the STDEV function. The advantage of using the second formula is that it saved us the steps of creating separate values that then had to be plugged into a formula.

Second, what's with all those dollar signs $$$$? Simple. They just mean these cell references are *absolute* references rather than *relative* ones—the cells we are pointing to are in one place and don't change according to where we are calculating the z score. We entered the cell addresses as absolute references because the cells that are used to compute the mean and the standard deviation do not change, whereas the cell in which the computation of the z score occurs does. That's why, in Figure 8.7, you see the cell reference as A3 without dollar signs. This is a relative reference that will change as the formula is copied down the column.

Excel has a cute function (**STANDARDIZE** function) that computes the standard score for any raw score (or, as we show you, any set of raw scores). The function takes the form of

=STANDARDIZE(X,mean,standard deviation),

where

X	is the value for which you want to compute a z score;
mean	is the mean of the set of scores; and
standard deviation	is (guess what) the standard deviation of the set of scores.

For example, if you wanted to compute the z score for a raw score of 98, which is one data point from a set of data points with a mean of 95 and a standard deviation of 2.3 (whew), the function would look like this:

=STANDARDIZE(98,95,2.3)

Figure 8.8 shows it all. In Cell B1 is the raw score, in Cell B2 is the mean, in Cell B3 is the standard deviation, and in Cell B4 is the function that computes the z score of 1.30.

Figure 8.8	Using the STANDARDIZE Function to Compute a z Score

B4	▼	⋮	✕	✓	*fx*	=STANDARDIZE(B1,B2,B3)

◢	A	B	C	D
1	Raw Score	98		
2	Mean	95		
3	s	2.3		
4	z score for a raw score of 98	1.304348		

But this can be a lot of work for a simple z score. So, let's apply it to a group of z scores. Take a look at Figure 8.9. Look familiar? It contains the data we used for our first example of computing z scores (see Figure 8.7).

But here, we use the STANDARDIZE function for a set of scores, as well as the AVERAGE and STDEV functions, and copy the resulting formula down the column. Here's the formula we created from the STANDARDIZE, AVERAGE, and STDEV functions:

=STANDARDIZE(A3,AVERAGE($A$2:$A$11),STDEV($A$2:$A$11))

And as you can see in Figure 8.9, it works!

Figure 8.9	Using the STANDARDIZE Function in a Formula to Compute z Scores

B3	▼	:	×	✓	fx	=STANDARDIZE(A3,AVERAGE($A$2:$A$11),STDEV($A$2:$A$11))

	A	B	C	D	E	F	G	H	I
1	X	z score							
2	12	0							
3	15	1.5							
4	11	-0.5							
5	13	0.5							
6	8	-2							
7	14	1							
8	12	0							
9	13	0.5							
10	12	0							
11	10	-1							

What z Scores Represent

You already know that a particular z score represents both a raw score and a particular location along the x-axis of a distribution. And the more extreme the z score (such as +2 or −2.6), the further it is from the mean.

Because you already know the percentage of area that falls between certain points along the x-axis (such as 34% between the mean and a standard deviation of +1, and about 14% between a standard deviation of +1 and a standard deviation of +2), we can make, for example, the following statements that will be true as well:

- 84% of all the scores fall below a z score of +1 (the 50% that falls below the mean plus the 34% that falls between the mean and the +1 z score).
- 16% of all the scores fall above a z score of +1 (because the total area under the curve has to equal 100% and 84% of the scores fall below a score of +1.0).

Think about both of these statements for a moment. All we are saying is that, given the normal distribution, different areas of the curve are encompassed by different numbers of standard deviations or z scores. Okay—here it comes. These percentages or areas can also easily be seen as representing *probabilities* of a certain score occurring. For example, here's one of the big questions we can ask (drumroll, please):

In a distribution with a mean of 100 and a standard deviation of 10, what is the probability that any one score will be 110 or above?

The answer? It's 16% or 16 out of 100 or .16. How did we get this?

First, we computed the corresponding z score, which is +1 [(110 − 100)/10]. Then, given the knowledge we already have (see Figure 8.6), we know a z score of 1 represents a location on the x-axis below which 84% (50% plus 34%) of all the scores in the distribution fall. Above that is 16% of the scores or a probability of .16. Because we already know the areas between the mean and 1, 2, or 3 standard deviations above or below the mean, we can easily figure out the probability that the value of any one z score has of occurring.

The method we just went through is fine for z values of 1, 2, and 3. But what if the value of the z score is not a whole number like 2, but 1.23 or −2.01? We need to find a way to be more precise.

How do we do that? Simple—learn calculus and apply it to the curve to compute the area underneath it at almost every possible point along the x-axis, or (and we like this alternative much more) use Table B.1 found in Appendix B (the normal distribution table). This is a listing of all the values (except the most extreme extreme) for the area under a curve that corresponds to different z scores. This table has two columns. The first column, labeled z Score, is simply the z score that has been computed. The second column, Area Between the Mean and the z Score, is the exact area underneath the curve that is contained between the two points.

For example, if you want to know the area between the mean and a z score of +1, find the value 1.00 in the column labeled z score and read across to the second column, where you find the area between the mean and a z score of 1.00 to be 34.13. Seen that before?

Why aren't there any plus or minus signs in this table (such as +1.00)? Because the curve is symmetrical and it does not matter whether the value of the z score is positive or negative. The area between the mean and 1 standard deviation in any direction is always 34.13%.

Here's the next step. Let's say that for a particular z score of 1.38, you want to know the probability associated with that z score. If you want to know the percentage of the area between the mean and a z score of 1.38, you find the corresponding area for the z score in Table B.1 of 1.38, which is 41.62. This indicates that more than 41% of all the cases in the distribution fall within a z score of 0 and 1.38 and that about 92% (50% plus 41.62%) will fall at or below a z score of 1.38. Now, you should notice that we did this last example without any raw scores at all. Once you get to this table, they are just no longer needed.

But are we always interested only in the amount of area between the mean and some other z score? What about between two z scores, neither of which is the mean? For example, what if we were interested in knowing the amount of area between a z score of 1.5 and a z score of 2.5, which translates to a probability that a score falls between the two z scores? How can we use the table to compute these outcomes? It's easy. Just find the corresponding amount of area each z score encompasses and subtract one from the other.

Often, drawing a picture helps, as in Figure 8.10.

For example, let's say that we want to find the area between raw scores of 110 and 125 in a distribution with a mean of 100 and a standard deviation of 10. Here are the steps we would take:

1. Compute the z score for a raw score of 110, which is $(110 - 100)/10$, or +1.

2. Compute the z score for a raw score of 125, which is $(125 - 100)/10$, or +2.5.

3. Using Table B.1 in Appendix B, find the area between the mean and a z score of +1, which is 34.13%.

4. Using Table B.1 in Appendix B, find the area between the mean and a z score of +2.5, which is 49.38%.

5. Because you want to know the distance between the two, subtract the smaller from the larger: $49.38 - 34.13$, or 15.25%. Figure 8.10 gives you the picture that's worth a thousand words.

Figure 8.10	Using a Drawing to Figure Out the Difference in Area Between Two z Scores

z scores ⟶ 0 +1 +2.5

34.13% | 15.25%

49.38%

There's another way to compute the probability associated with a particular raw score, and that's through the use of the **NORM.S.DIST** function. This takes the form of

=NORM.S.DIST(z,cumulative),

where

z   is the z score for which you want to find the probability; and

cumulative   is a logical value. (In our case, it is almost always true.)

So, if you want to know the probability associated with a z score of 1, then the function would look like this:

=NORM.S.DIST(1,true)

And the result that would be returned to the cell would be .841345, which should look quite familiar to you. Try it—it's a very cool way to get the values you need when Table B.1 is missing!

Okay—so we can be pretty confident that the probability of a particular score occurring can be best understood by examining where that score falls in a distribution relative to other scores. In this example, the probability of a score occurring between a z score of +1 and a z score of +2.5 is about 15%.

Here's another example. In a set of scores with a mean of 100 and a standard deviation of 10, a raw score of 117 has a corresponding z score of 1.70. This z score corresponds to an area under the curve of 45.54%, which means that the probability of this score occurring between a score of 0 and a score of 1.70 is 95.54% (or 50% + 45.54%) or 95.5 out of 100 or .955.

First, even though we are focusing on z scores, there are other types of standard scores. For example, a t score is a type of standard score that is computed by multiplying the z score by 10 and adding 50. One advantage of this type of score is that you rarely have a negative t score. As with z scores, t scores allow you to compare standard scores from different distributions.

Second, a *standard score* is a whole different animal from a *standardized score*. A standardized score is one that comes from a distribution with a predefined mean and standard deviation. Standardized scores from tests such as the SAT and GRE (Graduate Record Exam) are used so that comparisons can be made easily between scores where the same mean and standard deviation are being used.

What z Scores Really Represent

The name of the statistics game is being able to estimate the probability of an outcome. If we take what we have talked about and done so far in this chapter one step further, statistics is about deciding the probability of some event occurring. Then we use some criterion to judge whether we think that event is as likely, more likely, or less likely than what we would expect by chance. The research hypothesis presents a statement of the expected event, and we use our statistical tools to evaluate how likely that event is.

That's the 20-second version of what statistics is, but that's a lot. So let's take everything from the previous paragraph and go through it again with an example.

Let's say that your lifelong friend, trusty Lew, gives you a coin and asks you to determine whether it is a "fair" one—that is, if you flip it 10 times, you should come up with 5 heads and 5 tails. We would expect 5 heads (or 5 tails) because the probability is .5 of either one head or one tail on any one flip. On 10 independent flips (meaning that one flip does not affect another), we should get 5 heads, and so on. Now the question is, how many heads would disqualify the coin as being fake or rigged?

Let's say the criterion for fairness that we will use is that if, in flipping the coin 10 times, we get heads less than 5% of the time, we'll say the coin is rigged and call the police on Lew (who, incidentally, is already on parole). This 5% is a standard that is used by statisticians. If the probability of the event (be it the number of heads or the score on a test or the difference between the average scores for two groups) occurs in the extreme (and we're saying the extreme is defined as less than 5% of all such occurrences), it's an unlikely or, in this case, an unfair outcome.

Here's the distribution of how many heads you can expect just by chance alone on 10 flips. All the possible combinations are 2^{10} or 1,024 possible outcomes, such as 9 heads and 1 tail, 7 heads and 3 tails, 10 heads and 0 tails, and on and on. For example, the probability associated with getting 6 heads in 10 flips is about 21%.

Number of Heads	Probability
0	0.00
1	0.01
2	0.04
3	0.12
4	0.21
5	0.25
6	0.21
7	0.12
8	0.04
9	0.01
10	0.00

So, the likelihood of any particular outcome, such as 6 heads on 10 tosses, is about .21, or 21%. Now it's decision time. Just how many heads would one have to get on 10 flips to conclude that the coin is fixed, biased, busted, broken, or loony?

Well, as all good statisticians, we'll define the criterion as 5%, which we noted earlier in this current discussion. If the probability of the observed outcome (the results of all our flips) is less than 5%, we'll conclude that it is so unlikely that something other than chance must be responsible—and our conclusion will be that the "something other than chance" is a bogus coin.

If you look at the table, you can see that 8, 9, or 10 heads all represent outcomes that have less than a 5% probability. So if the result of 10 coin flips was 8, 9, or 10 heads, the conclusion would be that the coin is not a fair one. (Yep, you're right: 0, 1, and 2 qualify for the same decision. Sort of the other side of the coin—groan.)

The same logic applies to our discussion of z scores earlier. Just how extreme a z score would we expect before we could proclaim that an outcome is due not just to chance but to some other factor? If you look at the normal curve table in Appendix B, you'll see that the cutoff point for a z score of 1.65 includes about 45% of the area under the curve. If you add that to the other 50% of the area on the other side of the curve, you come up with a total of 95%. That leaves just 5% above that point on the x-axis. Any score that represents a z score of 1.65 or above is then into pretty thin air—or at least in a location that has a much smaller chance of occurring than others. That's it!

Hypothesis Testing and z Scores: The First Step

What we just showed you is that any event can have a probability associated with it. And we use those probability values to make decisions as to how unlikely we think an event might be. For example, it's highly unlikely to get only 1 head and 9 tails in 10 tosses of a coin. And we also said that if an event seems to occur only 5 out of 100 times (5%), we will deem that event to be rather unlikely relative to all the other events that could occur. It's much the same with any outcome related to a research hypothesis. The null hypothesis, which you learned about in Chapter 7, claims that there is no difference between groups (or variables) and that the likelihood of no difference occurring is 100%. We try to test the armor of the null hypothesis for any chinks it might have. In fact, in Chapter 10 we will talk about a z-test, which uses a z score to test the hypothesis that any one score is, or is not, likely to be part of a distribution of scores. Can't wait, huh?

z scores are very cool and useful, as are the corresponding t scores and t-tests, which you will learn about in depth in Chapters 11 and 12. For now, though, it is important for you to know that z-tests are reserved for populations and t-tests are reserved for samples. This is why you so often see t-tests rather than z-tests reported in journal articles and other research reports.

In other words, if, through the test of the research hypothesis, we find that the likelihood of an event that occurred is somewhat extreme, then the research hypothesis is a more attractive explanation than is the null. So, if we find a z score that is extreme (How extreme? Having less than a 5% chance of occurring.), we like to say that the reason for the extreme score is something to do with treatments or relationships and not just chance. We'll go into much greater detail on this point in the following chapter.

REAL-WORLD STATS

You certainly have heard about all the concerns regarding childhood obesity. These researchers investigated the possible reduction of obesity in children by focusing on physical activity as an intervention. And what might this have to do with z scores? One of their primary outcome or dependent variables was mean body mass index, or BMI, and they determined that to be considered due to a treatment, the change in BMI had to have a z score of 3.24 or more.

The study participants were invited to attend a 1-week sports camp and be provided with a 6-month support system. After the camp, a coach from a local sports club supported the child during participation in a chosen sport for 6 months. Weight, height, body composition, and lifestyle were measured at baseline and after 12 months. The results? Children who participated in the intervention had a significant decrease in BMI z score. Why were z scores used and not just plain raw scores such as body weight or height? Most likely because the children who were being compared with one another come from different distributions of scores, and by using a standard score, those differences (at least in the variability of the scores) are eliminated.

Want to know more? Go online or go to the library, and look for . . .

Nowicka, P., Lanke, J., Pietrobelli, A., Apitzsch, E., & Flodmark, C. (2009). Sports camp with six months of support from a local sports club as a treatment for childhood obesity. *Scandinavian Journal of Public Health, 37,* 793–800.

SUMMARY

Being able to figure out a z score, and being able to estimate how likely it is to occur in a sample of data, is the first and most important skill in understanding the whole notion of inference. Once we know how likely a test score or a difference between groups is, we can compare that likelihood to what we would expect by chance and then make informed decisions. As we start Part IV of *Statistics for People Who (Think They) Hate Statistics, Excel 2016 Edition*, we'll apply this model to specific examples of testing questions about the difference.

TIME TO PRACTICE

1. Answer the following questions about normal curves:
   a. What are the characteristics of the normal curve?
   b. What human behavior, trait, or characteristic can you think of that is distributed normally?

2. Why is a z score a standard score, and why can z scores be used to compare scores from different distributions with one another?

3. What is the primary value of using z scores? Provide an example of how they might be used.

4. Compute the z scores for the following raw scores where $\bar{X} = 50$ and the standard deviation = 5.
   a. 55
   b. 50
   c. 60
   d. 58.5
   e. 46

5. Given a z score of 1.5, a mean of 40, and a standard deviation of 5, what is the corresponding raw score? What is the corresponding *t* score?

6. Questions 6a through 6d are based on a distribution of scores with $\bar{X} = 75$ and standard deviation = 6.38. Draw a small picture to help you see what's required.
   a. What is the probability of a score falling between a raw score of 70 and 80?
   b. What is the probability of a score falling above a raw score of 80?
   c. What is the probability of a score falling between a raw score of 81 and 83?
   d. What is the probability of a score falling below a raw score of 63?

7. Using the NORM.S.DIST function, compute the probability that a score would fall between +1 and +2 z scores. Remember, you don't need any raw score values because a z score of 1 is a z score of 1 is a z score of 1.

8. This exercise uses Chapter 8 Data Set 1. Using the NORM.S.DIST function, compute the probability for the first raw score in Cell A2 and then copy the function down to compute the probabilities for each corresponding z score.

9. Jake needs to score in the top 10% on a fitness test in order to earn a physical fitness certificate. The class mean is 78, and the standard deviation is 5.5. What raw score does he need to get that valuable piece of paper?

10. What is the value of understanding the central limit theorem?

11. Why doesn't it make sense to simply combine, for example, test grades across different courses—just take an average and call it a day?

12. Who is the better student, relative to his or her classmates? Here's all the information you ever wanted to know.

Math			
Class Mean	81		
Class Standard Deviation	2		
Reading			
Class Mean	87		
Class Standard Deviation	10		
Raw Scores			
	Math Score	Reading Score	Average
Noah	85	88	86.5
Talya	87	81	84
	z Scores		
	Math Score	Reading Score	Average
Noah			
Talya			

13. And, last but not least, our favorite fun questions: Why is there always a chance for rain (even if the sky is sunny and the forecast is clear)? And why is the only time there is a 100% chance of rain when it is actually raining?

PART IV

Significantly Different

Using Inferential Statistics

Snapshots

"I see that David here is already busy computing *z* scores..."

You've gotten this far and you're still alive and kicking, so congratulate yourself. By this point, you should have a good understanding of what descriptive statistics is all about, how chance figures as a factor in making decisions about outcomes, and how likely outcomes are to have occurred due to chance rather than some treatment.

You're an expert on creating and understanding the role that hypotheses play in social and behavioral science research. Now it's time for the rubber to meet the road. Let's see what you're made of in Part IV of *Statistics for People Who (Think They) Hate Statistics, Excel 2016 Edition*. Best of all, the hard work you've put in will shortly pay off with an understanding of applied problems!

This part of *Statistics for People . . .* deals exclusively with understanding and applying certain types of statistics to answer certain types of research questions. We'll cover the most common statistical tests and even some that are a bit more sophisticated. At the end of this section, we'll show you some of the more useful software packages that can be used to compute the same values that we'll compute using a good old-fashioned calculator.

Let's start with a brief discussion of the concept of significance and go through the steps for performing an inferential test. Then we'll go on to examples of specific tests. We'll have lots of hands-on work here, so let's get started.

9 Significantly Significant

What It Means for You and Me

Difficulty Scale ☺ ☺ (somewhat thought provoking and key to it all!)

How much Excel? 📊 (just a mention)

WHAT YOU'LL LEARN ABOUT IN THIS CHAPTER

◆ What the concept of significance is and why it is important

◆ The importance of and difference between Type I and Type II errors

◆ How inferential statistics works

◆ How to select the appropriate statistical test for your purpose

---

THE CONCEPT OF SIGNIFICANCE

Probably no term or concept causes the beginning statistics student more confusion than the concept of statistical significance. But it doesn't have to be that way for you. Although it's a powerful idea, it is also relatively straightforward and can be understood by anyone in a basic statistics class.

We need an example of a study to illustrate the points we want to make. Let's take E. Duckett and M. Richards's "Maternal Employment and Young Adolescents' Daily Experiences in Single Mother Families" (paper presented at the Society for Research in Child Development, Kansas City, MO, 1989—a long time ago in a galaxy far, far away . . .). These two authors examined the attitudes of 436 fifth- through ninth-grade adolescents toward maternal employment. Even though the presentation took place some years ago, as an example it's perfect for illustrating many of the important ideas at the heart of this chapter.

Specifically, the two researchers investigated whether differences are present between the attitudes of adolescents whose mothers work and the attitudes of adolescents whose mothers do not work. They also examined some other factors, but for this example, we'll stick with the mothers-who-work and mothers-who-don't-work groups. One more thing. Let's add the word *significant* to our discussion of differences, and we have a research hypothesis something like this:

> There is a significant difference in attitude toward maternal employment between adolescents whose mothers work and adolescents whose mothers do not work, as measured by a test of emotional state.

What we mean by the word *significant* is that any difference between the attitudes of the two groups is due to some systematic influence and not due to chance. In this example, that influence is whether or not mothers work. We assume that all of the other factors that might account for any differences between groups were controlled. Thus, the only thing left to account for the differences between adolescents' attitudes is whether or not their mothers work. Right? Yes. Finished? Not quite.

If Only We Were Perfect

Because our world is not a perfect one, we must allow for some leeway in how confident we are that only those factors we identify could cause any difference in our measure (or measures) of interest between groups. In other words, you need to be able to say that although you are pretty sure the difference between the two groups of adolescents is due to maternal employment, you cannot be absolutely, 100%, positively, unequivocally, indisputably (get the picture?) sure. There's always a chance, no matter how small, that you are wrong.

Why? Many reasons. For example, you could (horrors) just be plain ol' wrong. Maybe during this one experiment, differences between adolescents' attitudes were not due to whether mothers worked or didn't work but were due to some other factor that was inadvertently not accounted for, such as a speech given by the local Mothers Who Work Club that several students attended. How about if the people in one group were mostly adolescent males and the people in the other group were mostly adolescent females? That could be the source of a difference as well.

If you are a good researcher and do your homework, you can account for such differences, but it's always possible that you can't. And as a good researcher, you have to take that possibility into account.

So what do you do? In most scientific endeavors that involve testing hypotheses (such as the group differences example here), there is bound to be a certain amount of error that cannot be controlled—this is the chance factor that we have been talking about in the past few chapters. The level of chance or risk you are willing to take is expressed as a **significance level**, a term that unnecessarily strikes fear in the hearts of even strong men and women. Significance level (here's the quick-and-dirty definition) is the risk associated with not being 100% confident that what you observe in an experiment is due to the treatment or what was being tested—in our example, whether or not mothers worked. If you read that significant findings occurred at the .05 level (or $p < .05$ in the tech talk you regularly see in professional journals), the translation is that there is 1 chance in 20 (or .05 or 5%) that any differences found were not due to the hypothesized reason (whether mom works) but to some other, unknown reason or reasons. Your job is to reduce this likelihood as much as possible by removing all of the competing reasons for any differences that you observed. Because you cannot fully eliminate the likelihood (because no one can control every potential factor), you assign some level of probability and report your results with that caveat.

In sum (and in practice), the researcher defines a level of risk that he or she is willing to take. If the results fall within the region that says, "This could not have occurred by chance alone—something else is going on," the researcher knows that the null hypothesis (which states an equality) is not the most attractive explanation for the observed outcomes. Instead, the research hypothesis (that there is an inequality or a difference) is the favored explanation.

Let's take a look at another example, and this one is hypothetical.

A researcher is interested in whether there is a difference in the academic achievement of children who participated in a preschool program and children who did not participate. The null hypothesis is that the two groups are equal to each other on some measure of achievement.

The research hypothesis is that the mean score for the group of children who participated in the program is higher than the mean score for the group of children who did not participate in the program. As a good researcher, your job is to show (as best you can—and no one is so perfect that he or she can account for everything) that any difference that exists between the two groups is due only to the effects of the preschool experience and no other factor or combination of factors.

However, through a variety of techniques (that you'll learn about in your Stats II class!), you control or eliminate all the possible sources of difference, such as the influence of parents' education, number of children in the family, and so on. Once these other potential explanatory variables are removed, the only remaining alternative explanation for differences is the effect of the preschool experience itself.

But can you be absolutely (which is pretty darn) sure? No, you cannot. Why? First, because you can never be sure that you are testing a sample that reflects the profile of the population in every single respect. And even if the sample perfectly represents the population, there could always be other influences that might affect the outcome that you inadvertently missed when designing the experiment. There's always the possibility of error (sort of another word for chance).

By concluding that the differences in test scores are due to differences in treatment, you accept some risk. This degree of risk is, in effect (drumroll, please), the level of statistical significance at which you are willing to operate.

Statistical significance (here's the formal definition) is the degree of risk you are willing to take that you will reject a null hypothesis when it is actually true. For our example above, the null says that there is no difference between the two sample groups (remember, the null is always a statement of equality). In your data, however, you did find a difference. That is, given the evidence you have so far, group membership seems to have an effect on achievement scores. In reality, however, maybe there is no difference. If you reject the null you stated, you would be making an error. The risk you take in making this kind of error (or the level of significance) is also known as a Type I error.

The World's Most Important Table (for This Semester Only)

Here's what it all boils down to.

A null hypothesis can be true or false. Either there really is no difference between groups, or there really and truly is an inequality (such as the difference between two groups). But remember, you'll never know this true state because the null cannot be tested directly (remember that the null applies only to the population, and for a variety of reasons we have talked about, the population cannot be directly tested).

And, as a crackerjack statistician, you can choose to either ~~reject~~ or accept the null hypothesis. Right? These four different cond.~~itions~~ create the table you see here in Table 9.1.

Let's look at each cell.

More About Table 9.1

Table 9.1 has four important cells that describe the relationship between the nature of the null (whether it's true or not) and your action (fail to reject or reject the null hypothesis). As you can see, the null can be either true or false, and you can either reject or fail to reject it.

The most important thing about understanding this table is the fact that the researcher never really knows the true nature of the null hypothesis and whether there really is or is not a difference between groups. Why? Because the population (which the null

Table 9.1	Different Types of Errors	
	Action You Take	
	Accept the Null Hypothesis	**Reject the Null Hypothesis**
True nature of the null hypothesis — The null hypothesis is really true.	1 ☺ Bingo, you accepted a null when it is true and there is really no difference between groups.	2 ☹ Oops—you made a Type I error and rejected a null hypothesis when there really is no difference between groups. Type I errors are also represented by the Greek letter alpha, or α.
The null hypothesis is really false.	3 ☹ Uh-oh—you made a Type II error and accepted a false null hypothesis. Type II errors are also represented by the Greek letter beta, or β.	4 ☺ Good job—you rejected the null hypothesis when there really are differences between the two groups. This is also called **power**, or $1 - \beta$.

represents) is never tested directly. Why? Because it's impractical to do so. That's why we have inferential statistics.

- ☺ Cell 1 in Table 9.1 represents a situation in which the null hypothesis is really true (there's no difference between groups) and the researcher made the correct decision accepting it. No problem here. In our example, our results would show that there is no difference between the two groups of children, and we have acted correctly by accepting the null that there is no difference.

- ☹ Oops. Cell 2 represents a serious error. Here, we have rejected the null hypothesis (that there is no difference) when it is really true (and there is no difference). Even though there is no difference between the two groups of children, we will conclude there is, and that's an error—clearly a boo-boo called a **Type I error**, also known as the level of significance.

- ☹ Uh-oh, another type of error. Cell 3 represents a serious error as well. Here, we have accepted the null hypothesis (that there is no difference) when it is really false (and, indeed, there is a difference). We have said that even though there is a difference between the two groups of children, we will conclude there is not—also clearly a boo-boo, this time known as a **Type II error**.

- ☺ Cell 4 in Table 9.1 represents a situation where the null hypothesis is really false and the researcher made the correct decision in rejecting it. No problem here. In our example, our results show that there is a difference between the two groups of children, and we have acted correctly by rejecting the null that states there is no difference.

So, if .05 is good and .01 is even "better," why not set your Type I level of risk at .000001? For the very good reason that you would be so rigorous in your rejection of false null hypotheses that you might reject a null when it was actually true. Such a stringent Type I error rate allows for little leeway—indeed, the research hypothesis might be true but the associated probability might be .015—still quite rare and probably very useful information, but missed with the too-rigid Type I level of error.

Back to Type I Errors

Let's focus a bit more on Cell 2 in Table 9.1, where a Type I error was made, because this is the focus of our discussion.

This Type I error, or level of significance, has certain values associated with it that define the risk you are willing to take in any test of the null hypothesis. The conventional levels set are between .01 and .05.

For example, if the level of significance is .01, then on any one test of the null hypothesis, there is a 1% chance you will reject the null hypothesis when the null is true and conclude that there is a group difference when there really is no group difference at all.

If the level of significance is.05, it means that on any one test of the null hypothesis, there is a 5% chance you will reject it when the null is true (and conclude that there is a group difference) when there really is no group difference at all. Notice that the level of significance is associated with an independent test of the null. Therefore, it is not appropriate to say that "on 100 tests of the null hypothesis, I will make an error on only 5, or 5% of the time."

In a research report, statistical significance is usually represented as $p < .05$, read as "the probability of observing that outcome is less than .05," often expressed in a report or journal article simply as "significant at the .05 level."

With the introduction of fancy-schmancy software such as SPSS and Excel that can do statistical analysis, there's no longer the worry about the imprecision of such statements as "$p < .05$" or "$p < .01$." For example, $p < .05$ can mean anything from .000 to .049999, right? Instead, software such as Excel gives you the *exact* probability, such as .013 or .158, of the risk you are willing to take that you will commit a Type I error. So, when you see in a research article the statement that "$p < .05$," it means that the value of p is equal to anything from .00 to .049999999999 . . . (you get the picture). Likewise, when you see "$p > .05$" or "$p = $ n.s." (for nonsignificant), it means that the probability of rejecting a true null exceeds .05 and, in fact, can range from .0500001 to 1.00. So, it's actually terrific when we know the exact probability of an outcome because we can measure more precisely the risk we are willing to take.

But what to do if the p value is exactly .05? Well, given what you've already read, if you want to play by the rules, then the outcome is not significant. A result either is, or is not. So, .04999999999 is and .05 is not. Now, if Excel (or any other program) generates a value of .05, extend the number of decimal places—it may really be .04999999999.

There is another kind of error you can make, which, along with the Type I error, is shown in Table 9.1. A Type II error (Cell 3 in the chart) occurs when you inadvertently accept a false null hypothesis.

When talking about the significance of a finding, you might hear the word *power* used. Power is a construct that has to do with how well a statistical test can detect and reject a null hypothesis when it is false. The value is calculated by subtracting the value of the Type II error from 1, or $1 - \beta$. A more powerful test is always more desirable than a less powerful test, because the more powerful one lets you get to the heart of what's false and what's not.

For example, there may really be differences between the populations represented by the sample groups, but you mistakenly conclude there are not.

Ideally, you want to minimize both Type I and Type II errors, but doing so is not always easy or under your control. You have complete control over the Type I error level or the amount of risk that you are willing to take (because you actually set the level itself). Type II errors are not as directly controlled but, instead, are related to factors such as sample size. Type II errors are particularly sensitive to the number of subjects in a sample; as that number increases, Type II error decreases. In other words, as the sample characteristics more closely match those of the population (achieved by increasing the sample size), the likelihood that you will accept a false null hypothesis decreases. Just as you would expect, right?

SIGNIFICANCE VERSUS MEANINGFULNESS

What an interesting situation for the researcher when he or she discovers that the results of an experiment indeed are statistically significant. You know technically what statistical significance means—that the research was a technical success and the null hypothesis is not a reasonable explanation for what was observed. Now, if your experimental design and other considerations were well taken care of, statistically significant results are unquestionably the first step toward making a contribution to the literature in your field. However, the value of statistical significance and its importance or meaningfulness must be kept in perspective.

For example, let's take the case where a very large sample of illiterate adults (say, 10,000) is divided into two groups. One group receives intensive training to read using classroom teaching, and the other receives intensive training to read using computers. The average score for Group 1 (which learned in the classroom) is 75.6 on a reading test, the outcome variable. The average score on the reading test for Group 2 (which learned using the computer) is 75.7.

The amount of variance in both groups is about equal. As you can see, the difference in score is only one tenth of 1 point (75.6 vs. 75.7), but when a *t*-test for the significance between independent means is applied, the results are significant at the .01 level, indicating that computers do work better than classroom teaching on the variable of interest. (Chapters 11 and 12 discuss *t*-tests.)

The difference of 0.1 is indeed statistically significant, but is it meaningful? Does the improvement in test scores (by such a small margin) provide sufficient rationale for the $300,000 it costs to fund the program? Or is the difference negligible enough that it can be ignored, even if it is statistically significant?

Here are some conclusions about the importance of statistical significance that we can reach, given this and the countless other possible examples:

- Statistical significance, in and of itself, is not very meaningful unless the study has a sound conceptual base that lends some meaning to the significance of the outcome.
- Statistical significance cannot be interpreted independently of the context within which it occurs. For example, if you are the superintendent in a school system, are you willing to retain children in Grade 1 if the retention program significantly raises their standardized test scores by one half point?
- Although statistical significance is important as a concept, it is not the end-all and certainly should not be the only goal of scientific research. That is the reason why we set out to *test* hypotheses rather than *prove* them. If your study is designed correctly, then even null results tell you something very important. If a particular treatment does not work, that's important information that others need to know about. If your study is designed well, then you should know why the treatment does not work, and the next person down the line can design his or her study taking into account the valuable information you provided.

AN INTRODUCTION TO INFERENTIAL STATISTICS

Whereas descriptive statistics are used to describe a sample's characteristics, inferential statistics are used to infer something about the population based on the sample's characteristics.

At several points throughout the first half of *Statistics for People Who (Think They) Hate Statistics, Excel 2016 Edition*, we have emphasized that a hallmark of good scientific research is choosing a sample in such a way that it is representative of the population from which it was selected. The process then becomes an inferential one, in which you infer from the smaller sample to the larger population based on the results of tests (and experiments) conducted using the sample.

Before we start discussing individual inferential tests, let's go through the logic of how the inferential method works.

How Inference Works

Here are the general steps to see how the process of inference might work. We'll stay with adolescents' attitudes toward mothers working as an example.

Here's the sequence of events that might happen:

1. The researcher selects representative samples of adolescents who have mothers who work and adolescents who have mothers who do not work. These are selected in such a way that the samples represent the populations from which they are drawn.

2. Each adolescent is administered a test to assess his or her attitude. The mean scores for groups are computed and compared using some statistical test.

3. A conclusion is reached as to whether the difference between the scores is the result of chance (meaning some factor other than moms working is responsible for the difference) or the result of "true" and statistically significant differences between the two groups (meaning the results are due to moms working).

4. A conclusion is reached as to the relationship between maternal employment and adolescents' attitudes in the population from which the sample was originally drawn. In other words, an inference, based on the results of an analysis of the sample data, is made about the population of all adolescents.

How to Select What Test to Use

Step 3 above brings us to ask the question "How do I select the appropriate statistical test to determine whether a difference between groups exists?" Heaven knows, there are plenty of them (many hundreds), and you have to decide which one to use and when to use it. Well, the best way to learn which test to use is to be an experienced statistician who has taken lots of courses in this area and participated in lots of research. Experience is still the greatest teacher. In fact, there's no way you can really learn what to use and when to use it unless you've had the real-life, applied opportunity to use these tools. And as a result of taking this course, you are learning how to use these very tools.

So, for our purposes and to get started, we've created this nice little flowchart (aka cheat sheet) of sorts that you see in Figure 9.1. You have to have some idea of what you're doing so that selecting the correct statistical test is not done entirely on autopilot, but this flowchart certainly is a good place to start.

Don't think for a second that Figure 9.1 takes the place of your need to learn about when these different tests are appropriate. The flowchart is here only to help you get started.

This is really important. We just wrote that selecting the appropriate statistical test is not necessarily an easy thing to do. And the best way to learn how to do it is to do it, and that means practicing and even taking more statistics courses. The simple flowchart we present here works, but use it with caution. When you make a decision, check with your professor or some other person who has been through this stuff and feels more confident than you might (who also knows more!). You may also find the neat tool named Statistical Navigator at http://rimarcik.com/en/navigator/ to be interesting and of some help.

Here's How to Use the Chart

1. Assume that you're very new to this statistics stuff (which you are) and that you have some idea of what these tests of significance are, but you're pretty lost as far as deciding which one to use when.

2. Answer the questions at the top of the flowchart.

3. Proceed down the chart by answering each of the questions until you get to the end of the chart. That's the statistical test you should use. This is not rocket science, and with some practice (which you will get throughout this part of *Statistics for People . . .*), you'll be able to quickly and reliably select the appropriate test. Each of the chapters in this part of the book will begin with a chart like the one you see in Figure 9.1 and take you through the specific steps for the test statistic you should use.

Figure 9.1 A Quick (but Not Always Great) Approach to Determining What Statistical Test to Use

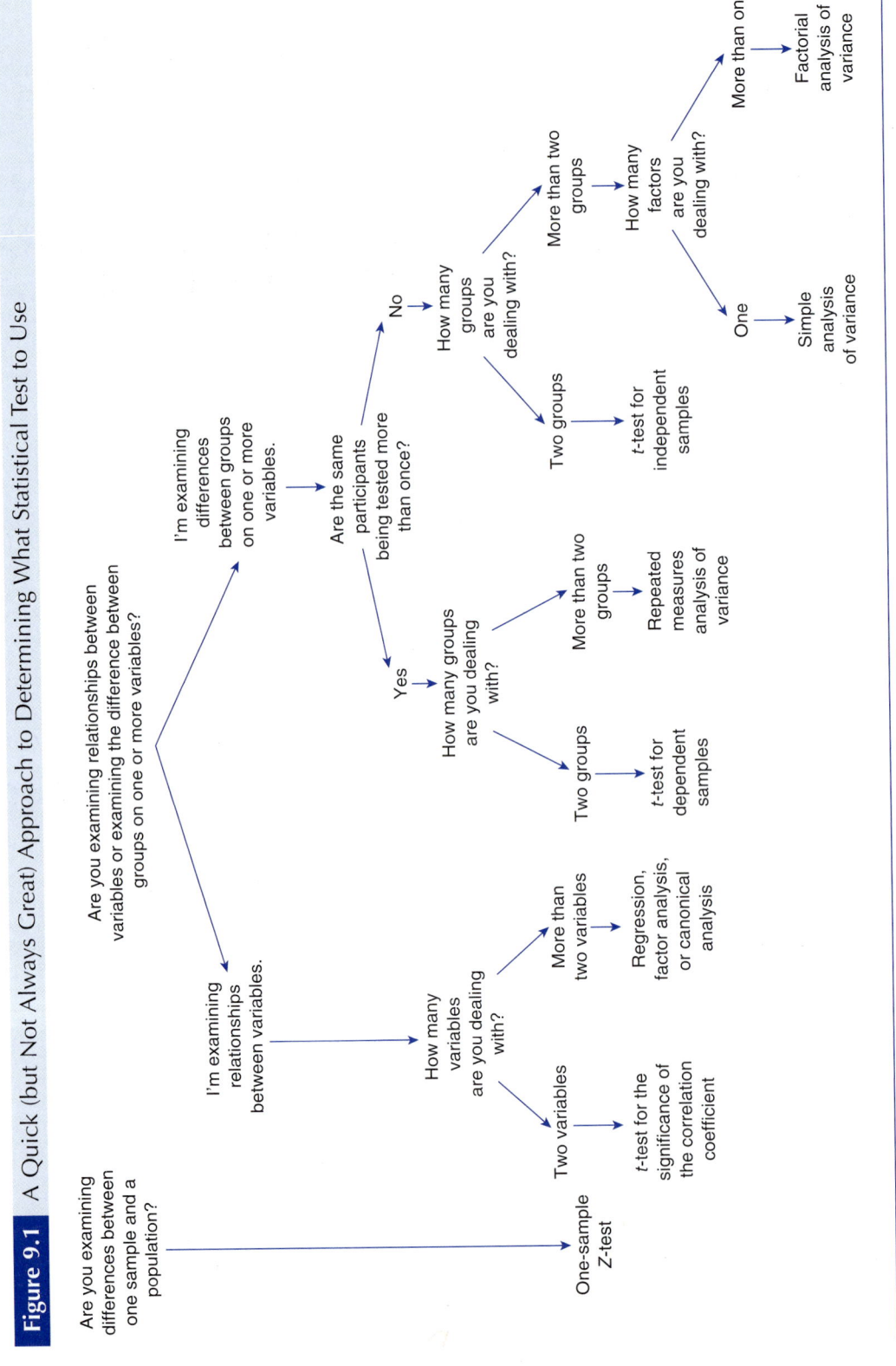

Does the cute flowchart in Figure 9.1 contain all the statistical tests there are? Not by a long shot. There are hundreds, but those in Figure 9.1 are the ones used most often (and we'll discuss most of them in coming chapters). And if you are going to become familiar with the research in your own field, you are bound to run into these.

AN INTRODUCTION TO TESTS OF SIGNIFICANCE

What inferential statistics does best is allow decisions to be made about populations based on information about samples. One of the most useful tools for doing this is a test of statistical significance that can be applied to different types of situations depending on the nature of the question being asked and the form of the null hypothesis.

For example, do you want to look at the difference between two groups, such as whether boys score significantly differently than girls on some test? Or the relationship between two variables, such as number of children in a family and average score on intelligence tests? The two cases call for different approaches, but both will result in a test of a null hypothesis using a specific test of statistical significance.

How a Test of Significance Works: The Plan

Tests of significance are based on the fact that each type of null hypothesis has associated with it a particular type of statistic. And each of the statistics has associated with it a special distribution that you compare with the data you obtain from a sample. A comparison between the characteristics of your sample and the characteristics of the test distribution allows you to conclude whether the sample characteristics are different from what you would expect by chance.

Here are the general steps to take in the application of a statistical test to any null hypothesis. These steps will serve as a model for each of the chapters that follow in Part IV.

1. *A statement of the null hypothesis.* Do you remember that the null hypothesis is a statement of equality? The null hypothesis is the "true" state of affairs given no other information on which to make a judgment.

2. *Setting the level of risk (or the level of significance or Type I error) associated with the null hypothesis.* With any research hypothesis comes a certain degree of risk that you are wrong. The smaller this error is (such as .01 compared with .05), the less risk you are willing to take. No test of a hypothesis is completely risk-free because you never really know the "true" relationship between variables. Remember that it is traditional to set the Type I error rate at .01 or .05; Excel and other programs specify the exact level.

3. *Selection of the appropriate test statistic.* Each null hypothesis has associated with it a particular test statistic. You can learn what test is related to what type of question in this part of *Statistics for People . . . .*

4. *Computation of the test statistic value.* The **test statistic value** (also called the **obtained value**) is the result or product of a specific statistical test. For example, there are test statistics for the significance of the difference between the averages of two groups, for the significance of the difference of a correlation coefficient from zero, and for the significance of the difference between two proportions. You'll actually compute the test statistic and come up with a numerical value.

5. *Determination of the value needed for rejection of the null hypothesis using the appropriate table of critical values for the particular statistic.* Each test statistic (along with group size and the risk you are willing to take) has a **critical value** associated with it. This is the value you would expect the test statistic to yield if the null hypothesis is indeed true.

6. *Comparison of the obtained value with the critical value.* This is the crucial step. Here, the value you obtained from the test statistic (the one you computed) is compared with the value (the critical value) you would expect to find by chance alone.

7. *If the obtained value is more extreme than the critical value, the null hypothesis cannot be accepted.* That is, the null hypothesis's statement of equality (reflecting chance) is not the most attractive explanation for differences that were found. Here is where the real beauty of the inferential method shines through. Only if your obtained value is more extreme than chance (meaning that the result of the test statistic is not a result of some chance fluctuation) can you say that any differences you obtained are not due to chance and that the equality stated by the null hypothesis is not the most attractive explanation for any differences you might have found.

Instead, the differences must be due to the treatment. What if the two values are equal (and you were about to ask your instructor that question, right?)? Nope—due to chance.

8. *If the obtained value does not exceed the critical value, the null hypothesis is the most attractive explanation.* If you cannot show that the difference you obtained is due to something other than chance (such as the treatment), then the difference must be due to chance or something you have no control over. In other words, the null is the best explanation.

Here's the Picture That's Worth a Thousand Words

What you see in Figure 9.2 represents the eight steps that we just went through. This is a visual representation of what happens when the obtained and critical values are compared. In this example, the significance level is set at .05, or 5%. It could have been set at .01, or 1%.

| **Figure 9.2** | Comparing Obtained Values With Critical Values and Making Decisions About Rejecting or Accepting the Null Hypothesis |

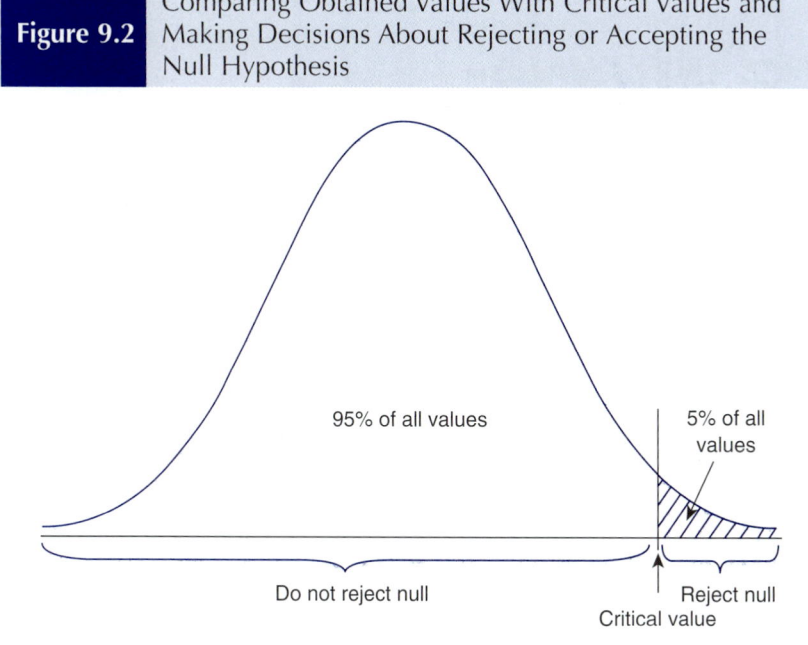

95% of all values

5% of all values

Do not reject null

Reject null

Critical value

In examining Figure 9.2, note the following:

1. The entire curve represents all the possible outcomes based on a specific null hypothesis, such as the difference between two groups or the significance of a correlation coefficient.

2. The critical value is the point beyond which the obtained outcomes are judged to be so rare that we conclude the obtained outcome is not due to chance but to some other factor. In this example, we define "rare" as having a less than 5% chance of occurring.

3. If the outcome representing the obtained value falls to the *left* of the critical value (it is less extreme), we conclude that the null hypothesis is the most attractive explanation for any differences that are observed. In other words, the obtained value falls in the region (95% of the area under the curve) where we expect only outcomes due to chance to occur.

4. If the obtained value falls to the *right* of the critical value (it is more extreme), the conclusion is that the research hypothesis is the most attractive explanation of any differences that are observed. In other words, the obtained value falls in the region (5% of the area under the curve) where we would expect only outcomes due to something other than chance to occur.

CONFIDENCE INTERVALS— BE EVEN MORE CONFIDENT

You now know that probabilities can be associated with outcomes— that's been an ongoing theme for this and the last chapter. Now we are going to say the same thing in a slightly different way and introduce a new idea called confidence intervals.

A **confidence interval** (or c.i.) is the best estimate of the range of a population value (or population parameter) that we can come up with given the sample value (or sample statistic representing the population parameter). Say we knew the mean spelling score for a sample of 20 third graders (of all the third graders in a school district). How much confidence could we have that the population mean will fall between two scores? A 95% confidence interval would be correct 95% of the time.

You already know that the probability of a raw score falling within ±1.96 z scores or standard deviations is 95%, right? (See page 204 in Chapter 8 if you need some review.) And you already know that the probability of a raw score falling within ±2.56 z scores or standard deviations is 99%. If we use the positive or negative raw scores equivalent to those z scores, we have ourselves a confidence interval.

While we are using the standard deviation to compute confidence intervals, many people choose to use the standard error of the mean, or SEM (see Chapter 10). The standard error of the mean is the standard deviation of all the sample means that could, in theory, be selected from the population. Remember that both the standard deviation and the standard error of the mean are "errors" in measurement that surround a certain "true" point (which in our case would be the true mean and the true amount of variability). The use of the SEM is a bit more complex, but it is an alternative way of computing, and understanding, confidence intervals.

Let's fool around with some real numbers.

Let's say that the mean spelling score for a random sample of 100 sixth graders is 64 (out of 75 words) and the standard deviation is 5. What confidence can we have in predicting the population mean for the average spelling score for the entire population of sixth graders?

The 95% confidence interval is equal to . . .

$$64 \pm 1.96(5)$$

In other words, it is a range from 54.2 to 73.8, so at the least you can say with 95% confidence that the population mean for the average spelling score for all sixth graders falls between those two scores.

Want to be more confident? The 99% confidence interval would be computed as . . .

$$64 \pm 2.56(5)$$

This is a range from 51.2 to 76.8, so you can conclude with 99% confidence that the population mean falls between those two scores.

Why does the confidence interval itself get larger as the probability of your being correct increases (from, say, 95% to 99%)? Because the larger range of the confidence interval (in this case from $73.8 - 54.2 = 19.6$ for a 95% confidence interval to $76.8 - 51.2 = 25.6$ for a 99% confidence interval) encompasses a larger number of possible outcomes. You can thereby be more confident. Ha! Isn't this stuff cool?

REAL-WORLD STATS

It's really interesting how different disciplines can learn from one another when they share. And it's a shame that this does not happen more often, which is one of the reasons why interdisciplinary studies are so vital to creating an environment where new and old ideas can be used in new and old settings.

One such discussion took place in a medical journal that devotes itself to articles on anesthesia. The focus was a discussion of the relative merits of statistical versus clinical significance. Drs. Timothy Houle and David Stump point out how many large clinical trials obtain a high level of statistical significance with minuscule differences between groups (just as we talked about earlier in the chapter in our hypothetical example of teaching adults to read). In this case, statistically significant results are clinically irrelevant. However, the authors point out that with proper marketing, billions can be made from results of dubious clinical importance. This is really a caveat emptor, or buyer beware, state of affairs. Clearly, there a few very good lessons here to learn about how the significance of an outcome may or may not be meaningful. How to know? Look at the context of the research and substance of the outcomes.

Want to know more? Go online or go to the library, and look for . . .

Houle, T. T., & Stump, D. A. (2008). Statistical significance versus clinical significance. *Seminars in Cardiothoracic and Vascular Anesthesia, 1*, 5–6.

SUMMARY

So, now you know exactly how the concept of significance works, and all that is left is applying it to a variety of research questions. That's what we'll start with in the next chapter and continue with through most of this part of the book.

TIME TO PRACTICE

1. Why is significance an important construct in the study and use of inferential statistics?

2. What's wrong with the following statements?

   a. A Type I error of .05 means that in 5 out of 100 tests of the research hypothesis, I will reject a true null hypothesis.

    b. It is possible to set the Type I error rate to zero.

    c. The smaller the Type I error rate, the better the results.

3. What does chance have to do with the testing of the research hypothesis for significance?

4. Given the following information, would your decision be to reject or fail to reject the null hypothesis? (Set the level of significance at .05 for decision making.) Provide an explanation for your conclusion.

    a. The null hypothesis that there is no relationship between the type of music a person listens to and the number of crimes he or she commits. $p < .05$.

    b. The null hypothesis that there is no relationship between the amount of coffee a student consumes and GPA. $p = .62$.

    c. The research hypothesis that there is a negative relationship between the number of hours worked and level of job satisfaction. $p = .51$.

5. Why is it "harder" to find a significant outcome (all other things being equal) when the research hypothesis is being tested at the .01 rather than the .05 level of significance?

6. Why should we think in terms of "failing to reject" the null rather than just accepting it?

7. What does the actual critical value represent?

8. What does the obtained value represent?

9. If you were to look at differences between two independent groups, what steps would you take using Figure 9.1?

10. In Figure 9.2, there is a striped area in the right-hand part of the curve.

    a. What does that area represent?

    b. If you tested the research hypothesis at a more rigorous level (say at .01 rather than .05), would that area get bigger or smaller, and why?

10 Only the Lonely

The One-Sample Z-Test

Difficulty Scale ☺ ☺ ☺ (not too hard—this is the first chapter of this kind, but you know more than enough to master it)

How much Excel? 📊 📊 📊 (lots)

WHAT YOU'LL LEARN ABOUT IN THIS CHAPTER

✦ When the Z-test for one sample is appropriate to use

✦ How to compute the observed z value

✦ How to interpret the z value and understand what it means

INTRODUCTION TO THE ONE-SAMPLE Z-TEST

Lack of sleep can cause all kinds of problems from grouchiness to fatigue and, in rare cases, even death. So, you can imagine health care professionals' interest in seeing that their patients get enough sleep. This is especially the case for those who are ill and have a real need for the healing and rejuvenating qualities that sleep brings. Dr. Joseph Cappelleri and his colleagues looked at the sleep difficulties of patients with a particular illness, fibromyalgia, to evaluate the usefulness of the Medical Outcomes Study (MOS) Sleep Scale as a measure of sleep problems. While other analyses were completed, including one that compared a treatment group and control group with one another, the important analysis (for our discussion) is the comparison of participants' MOS scores with national MOS norms. Such a comparison between a sample's score (the value of the MOS score for participants in this study) and a population's score (the norms) necessitates the use of a one-sample Z-test. And the researchers' findings? MOS Sleep Scale scores were statistically ($p < .001$) lower, meaning the study participants did not sleep as well. This means that the sample being tested did not have the same characteristics (at least on this measure of sleep) as did the general population. In other words, the null hypothesis that the sample average and the population average were equal could not be accepted.

So why use the one-sample Z-test? Cappelleri and his colleagues wanted to know if the *sample* values were different from *population* (national) values collected using the same measure. They were, in effect, comparing a sample statistic to a population parameter and seeing if they could conclude that the sample was (or was not) representative of the population.

Want to know more? Check out Cappelleri, J. C., Bushmakin, A. G., McDermott, A. M., Sadosky, A. B., Petrie, C. D., & Martin, S. (2009). Psychometric properties of a single-item scale to assess sleep quality among individuals with fibromyalgia. *Health and Quality of Life Outcomes*, 7, 766–770.

The Path to Wisdom and Knowledge

Here's how you can use Figure 10.1, the flowchart introduced in Chapter 9, to select the appropriate test statistic, the *one-sample Z-test*. Follow along the highlighted sequence of steps in Figure 10.1. Now this is pretty easy (and they are not all this easy) because this is the only inferential procedure in all of Part IV of *Statistics for People* . . . where we have only one group. And there's lots of stuff here that will take you back to Chapter 8 and standard scores. And, since you're an expert on those . . .

1. We are examining differences between one sample and a population.

2. The appropriate test statistic is a one-sample Z-test.

As in sooooo many statistical procedures, different symbols and words are used to represent the same thing (remember mean, $\bar{X}$, and average?). So it is with one-sample Z-tests. Sometimes you'll see the lowercase z used and sometimes the uppercase Z. We're sticking with the uppercase Z because we like it and that's the way that Excel does it in its **Z.TEST** function. So, z scores and z values and Z-tests.

Figure 10.1   Determining That a One-Sample Z-Test Is the Correct Statistic

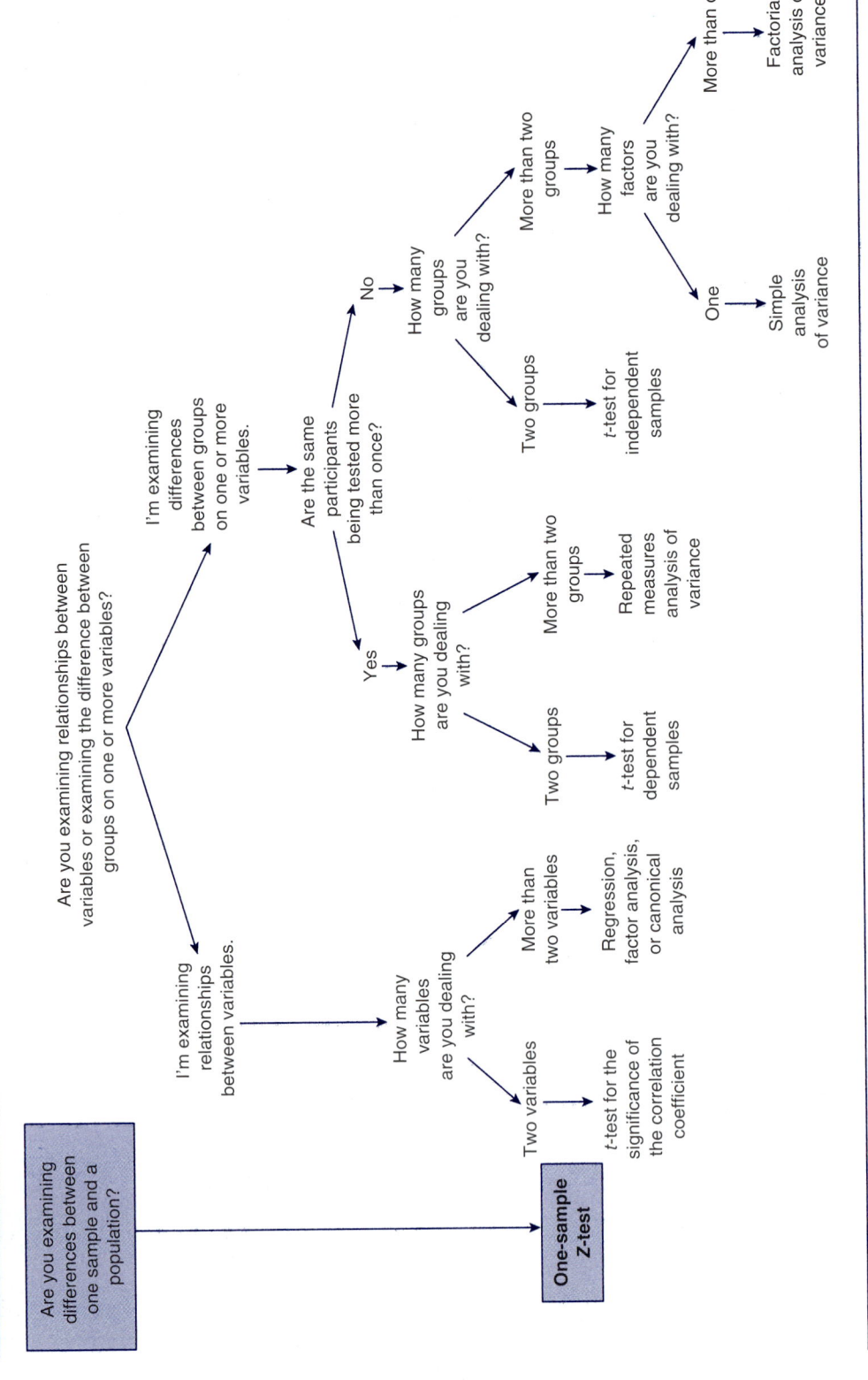

COMPUTING THE TEST STATISTIC

The formula used for computing the value for the one-sample Z-test is shown in Formula 10.1. Remember that we are testing whether a sample mean belongs to or represents a population mean. The difference between the sample mean ($\bar{X}$) and the population (μ) mean makes up the numerator for the z value. The denominator, an error term, is called the standard error of the mean (SEM), and it is the value we would expect by chance given all the variability that surrounds the selection of all possible sample means from a population. Using this standard error of the mean (and the key term here is *standard*) allows us once again (as we showed in Chapter 9) to use the table of z scores to reach a decision as to the probability of an outcome.

$$Z = \frac{\bar{X} - \mu}{SEM}, \qquad\qquad (10.1)$$

where

$\bar{X}$ is the mean of the sample;

μ   is the population average; and

SEM   is the standard error of the mean.

Now, to compute the standard error of the mean that you need in Formula 10.1, use the following formula . . .

$$SEM = \frac{\sigma}{\sqrt{n}}, \qquad\qquad (10.2)$$

where

σ   is the standard deviation for the population; and

n is the size of the sample.

The standard error of the mean is the standard deviation of all the possible means selected from the population. It's the best *estimate* we can come up with given that it is impossible to compute *all* the possible means. If our sample selection were perfect, the difference between the sample and the population averages would be zero, right? Right.

On the other hand, if the sampling from a population were not done correctly (randomly and representatively), then the standard deviation of all these samples could be huge, right? Right. So we do try, but nonetheless we just can't seem to select the perfect sample—there's always some error, and the standard error of the mean reflects what that value would be for the entire population of all mean values. And yes, Virginia, this is the standard error of the mean. There can be (and are) standard errors for other measures as well.

Time for an Example

Dr. McDonald thinks that his group of earth science students are particularly special (in a good way), and he is interested in knowing whether their class average falls within the boundaries of the average score for the larger group of students who have taken earth science over the last 20 years. Since he's kept good records, McDonald knows the means and standard deviations for both his current group of 36 students and the larger group of 1,000 enrollees past and present. Here are the data he has. The values that we will need to compute the z score are italicized.

	Size	Mean	Standard Deviation
Sample	36	100	5
Population	1,000	99	2.5

Here are the famous eight steps and the computation of the Z-test statistic:

1. *State the null and research hypotheses.* The null hypothesis states that sample average is equal to the population average. If the null is not rejected, then the sample is representative of the population. If the null is rejected in favor of the research hypothesis, then the sample average is different from the population average.

The null hypothesis is this:

$$H_0: \overline{X} = \mu \tag{10.3}$$

The research hypothesis in this example is this:

$$H_0: \overline{X} \neq \mu \tag{10.4}$$

2. *Set the level of risk (or the level of significance or Type I error) associated with the null hypothesis.* The level of risk or Type I error or level of significance (any other names?) is .05. This value is decided by the researcher.

3. *Select the appropriate test statistic.* Using the flowchart shown in Figure 10.1, we determined that the appropriate test is a one-sample Z-test.

4. *Compute the test statistic value (called the obtained value).* Now's your chance to plug in values and do some computation. The formula for the z value was shown in Formula 10.1. The specific values are plugged in, first for the SEM in Formula 10.5 and then for z in Formula 10.6. (We got all this data from the table at the start of these steps.) With the values plugged in, we get the following results:

$$SEM = \frac{2.5}{\sqrt{36}} = .42 \qquad (10.5)$$

$$z = \frac{100 - 99}{.42} = 2.38 \qquad (10.6)$$

The z value for a comparison of the sample mean with this population mean is 2.38.

5. *Determine the value needed for rejection of the null hypothesis using the appropriate table of critical values for the particular statistic.* Here's where we go to Table B.1 in Appendix B, which lists the probabilities associated with specific z values. These are the critical values for the rejection of the null hypothesis in this example. We can use the values in Table B.1 to see if two means "belong" to one another by comparing what we would expect by chance (the tabled or critical value) with what we observe (the obtained value).

   This is just what we did in Chapter 9 with several examples. From our work in Chapter 9, we know that a z value of +1.96 has associated with it a probability of .025. And if we consider that the sample mean could be bigger, or smaller, than the population mean, we need to consider both ends of the distribution (and a range of ±1.96) and a total Type I error rate of .05.

6. *Compare the obtained value and the critical value.* The obtained z value is 2.38. So, for a test of this null hypothesis at the .05 level with 36 participants, the critical value is ±1.96. This value

is the cutoff at which chance is the most attractive explanation as to why the sample mean and the population mean differ. A value beyond this critical value in either direction (remember that our research hypothesis is nondirectional and this is a two-tailed test) means that we need to provide an explanation as to why the sample and the population means differ.

7. and 8.   *Decision time!* If the obtained value is more extreme than the critical value (remember Figure 9.2), the null hypothesis cannot be accepted. If the obtained value does not exceed the critical value, the null hypothesis is the most attractive explanation. In this case, the obtained value (2.38) does exceed the critical value (1.96), and it is absolutely extreme enough for us to say that the class average of the sample of 36 students in Dr. McDonald's class is different from that of the previous 1,000 students who have also taken the course. If the obtained value were less than 1.96, then we would have concluded that there was no difference between the test performance of the sample and the 1,000 students who have taken the test over the past 20 years. In this case, the 36 students would have performed at essentially the same level as the previous 1,000.

And the final step? Why, of course. *Why does this group of students differ?* Perhaps Professor McDonald is right in that they are smarter, but they may also be better users of technology, more motivated, or more diligent. All questions to be tested some other time.

So How Do I Interpret z = 2.38, p < .05?

- z represents the test statistic that was used.
- 2.38 is the obtained value, calculated using the formulas we showed you earlier in the chapter.
- $p < .05$ (the really important part of this little phrase) indicates that the probability is less than 5% that on any one test of the null hypothesis, the sample and the population averages differ.

USING THE EXCEL Z.TEST FUNCTION TO COMPUTE THE Z VALUE

Here's our first opportunity to use Excel to perform a Z-test to see if a particular sample average belongs to a population of scores. However, like many Excel Data Analysis tools, this one requires just a few changes and uses different information. Also, you won't be using the probability table (Appendix B.1) and interpreting the results in the same way as for the usual z score you learned about earlier.

It's important to note that the Z.TEST function does not provide a score that you test or evaluate for significance, as we just did manually. Instead, Z.TEST provides the probability of that sample value occurring and, in our example above, being greater than the average of the population. In other words, in Excel, Z.TEST is a one-tailed test. So, unlike the manual method, the Z.TEST function returns the exact probability that a score is a member of a population and not the actual z score associated with that raw score. The higher the value of Z.TEST, the more unlikely it is that the sample value is not representative of the population.

The data we use for Z.TEST are much like those in the example above, only Excel requires the entire population. So we entered 100 scores, the mean of the population being X. The data are available as Chapter 10 Data Set 1, and the sample value we are testing is 76. In other words, how likely is it that the sample value of 76 represents the population?

1. Click Formulas → More Functions → Statistical → Z.TEST. This brings up the Z.TEST dialog box, as shown in Figure 10.2. For our purposes here, we placed the function in Cell C1.

Figure 10.2 The Z.TEST Function Dialog Box

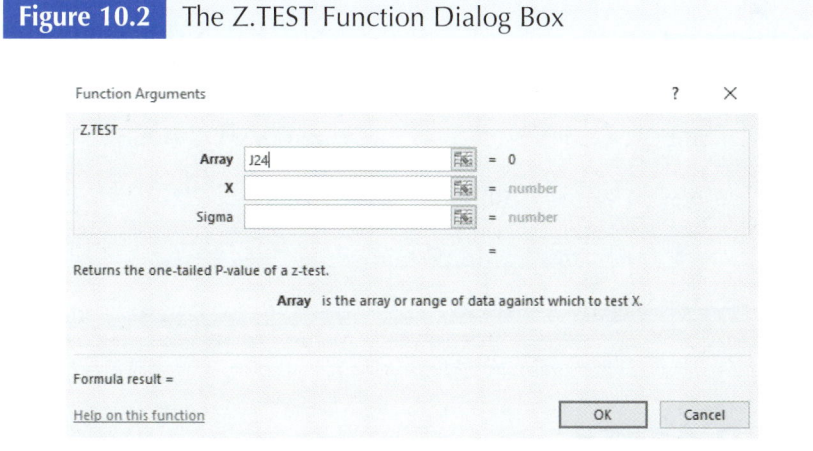

2. Select the array containing the data (Cells A1 through A101).

3. Enter the value that is being tested (X = 76) to determine whether it belongs to the population. You can see the completed dialog box in Figure 10.3. (There's no need to specify sigma.)

Figure 10.3 The Completed Z.TEST Dialog Box

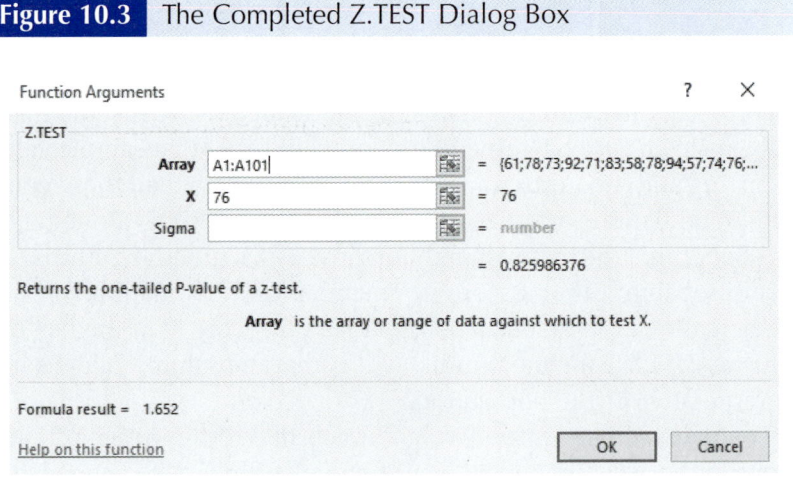

4. Click OK, and as you see in Figure 10.4, the returned value is .826. This means the likelihood (that is, the probability) that the value specified (76) does not belong to the population of values (in Chapter 10 Data Set 1) is pretty high, but it's not at the level that we would generally accept as "significant," which would be .95. Or, in other words, the value specified (76) is not significantly different from the values (the population) from which it was selected. In practical terms, this student's score is nothing "special."

Figure 10.4 Result of Z.TEST on Value 76 and Chapter 10 Data Set 1

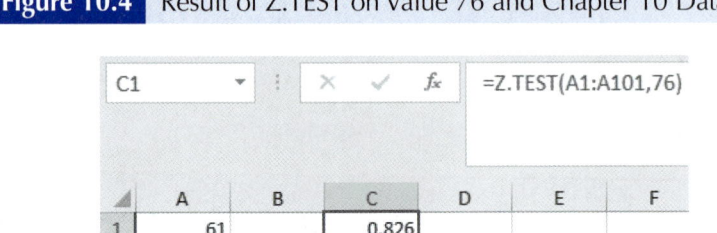

 **REAL-WORLD STATS**

Been to the doctor lately? Had your test results explained to you? Know anything about the trend toward electronic medical records? In many doctors' offices, clinics, and hospitals, patient information is already all on the computer. In the study that's described here, Noel Brewer and his colleagues compared the usefulness of tables versus bar graphs for reporting the results of medical tests.

Using a Z-test, the researchers found that participants required less viewing time to understand information when looking at bar graphs than when reading tables. The researchers attribute this difference to bar graphs' superior performance in communicating essential information. (Of course, you remember Chapter 4 where we stressed that a picture, such as a bar graph, is well worth a thousand words, such as a table.) And not very surprisingly, when participants viewed their information in both formats, those with experience with bar graphs preferred bar graphs, and those with experience with tables found bar graphs equally easy to use. Next time you get to your doc and he or she shows you a table, say you want to see the results as a bar graph. Now that's statistics applied to real-world, everyday occurrences.

Want to know more? Go online or go to the library, and look for . . .

Brewer, N. T., Gilkey, M. B., Lillie, S. E., Hesse, B. W., & Sheridan, S. L. (2012). Tables or bar graphs? Presenting test results in electronic medical records. *Medical Decision Making, 32,* 545–553.

SUMMARY

The one-sample Z-test is the simplest example of an inferential test, and that's why we started off with an explanation of what this test does and how it is applied. The (very) good news is that most, if not all, of the steps we take as we move to more complex analytic tools are exactly the same as the ones we read about here. Let's move on to a very common inferential test (and an extension of the Z-test we covered here), the simple *t*-test between the means of two different groups.

TIME TO PRACTICE

1. When is it appropriate to use the one-sample Z-test?

2. What's with the Z in Z-test? In what way is it similar to a simple z or standard score?

3. For the following situations, write out a research hypothesis:

   a. Bob wants to know if the weight loss for his group on the chocolate-only diet is representative of weight loss in a large population of middle-aged men who are on a chocolate-only diet.

   b. The health department is charged with finding out whether the rate of flu per thousand citizens for this past flu season is comparable to the rate of the last 50 seasons.

    c. Blair is the landlord of several apartment buildings. He is almost sure that his monthly costs over the last year for his current group of apartments are not representative of his monthly costs over the past 20 years.

4. Flu cases this past flu season (4 months or 20 weeks) in the Butterfield, Kansas, school system were about 15 per week. For the entire state, the weekly average was 16 and the standard deviation 2.35. Are the kids in Butterfield as sick as the kids throughout the state? Do this one manually.

5. Mark's class just took the admission test for business school and averaged 83.4. Chapter 10 Data Set 2 contains the population of scores for the 10 other classes in Mark's university. How did Mark's class do?

6. Sales at Joe's BBQ in Salina, Kansas, were $35,676 for the first week of June 2015. How did Joe do compared with the rest of the barbecue restaurants in the county association? Sales are shown in Chapter 10 Data Set 3.

11 t(ea) for Two

Tests Between the Means of Different Groups

Difficulty Scale ☺ ☺ ☺ Here we continue with more inferential tests, but they're just as straightforward as the one-sample Z-test we did in Chapter 10.

How much Excel? 📊 📊 📊 (lots)

WHAT YOU'LL LEARN ABOUT IN THIS CHAPTER

✦ When the *t*-test for independent means is appropriate to use

✦ How to compute the observed *t* value

✦ How to use the T.TEST function

✦ How to use the *t*-Test Data Analysis tools to compute the *t* value

✦ How to interpret the *t* value and understand what it means

---

INTRODUCTION TO THE *T*-TEST FOR INDEPENDENT SAMPLES

Even though eating disorders are recognized for their seriousness, little research has been done that compares the prevalence and intensity of symptoms across different cultures. John P. Sjostedt, John F. Schumaker, and S. S. Nathawat undertook this comparison with groups of 297 Australian and 249 Indian university students. Each student was tested on the Eating Attitudes Test and the

Goldfarb Fear of Fat Scale. The groups' scores were compared with one another. On a comparison of means between the Indian and the Australian participants, Indian students scored higher on both of the tests. The results for the Eating Attitudes Test were $t_{(544)} = -4.19$, $p < .0001$, and the results for the Goldfarb Fear of Fat Scale were $t_{(544)} = -7.64$, $p < .0001$.

Now just what does all this mean? Read on.

Why was the t-test for independent means used? Sjostedt and his colleagues were interested in finding out whether there was a difference in the average scores of one (or more) variable(s) between the two groups, which were independent of one another. By independent, we mean that the two groups were not related in any way. Each participant in the study was tested only once. Using the t-test for independent means, the researchers concluded that for each of the outcome variables, the differences between the two groups were significant at or beyond the .0001 level. Such a small Type I error means that there is very little chance that the difference in scores between the two groups is due to something other than group membership, in this case representing nationality, culture, or ethnicity.

Want to know more? Check out Sjostedt, J. P., Schumaker, J. F., & Nathawat, S. S. (1998). Eating disorders among Indian and Australian university students. *Journal of Social Psychology, 138,* 351–357.

The Path to Wisdom and Knowledge

To use Figure 11.1, the flowchart first introduced in Chapter 9, to select the appropriate test statistic, follow the highlighted sequence of steps. They take you to the t-test for independent means.

1. The differences between the groups of Australian and Indian students are being explored.

2. Participants are being tested only once.

3. There are two groups.

4. The appropriate test statistic is t-test for independent samples.

Figure 11.1 Determining That a *t*-Test Is the Correct Statistic

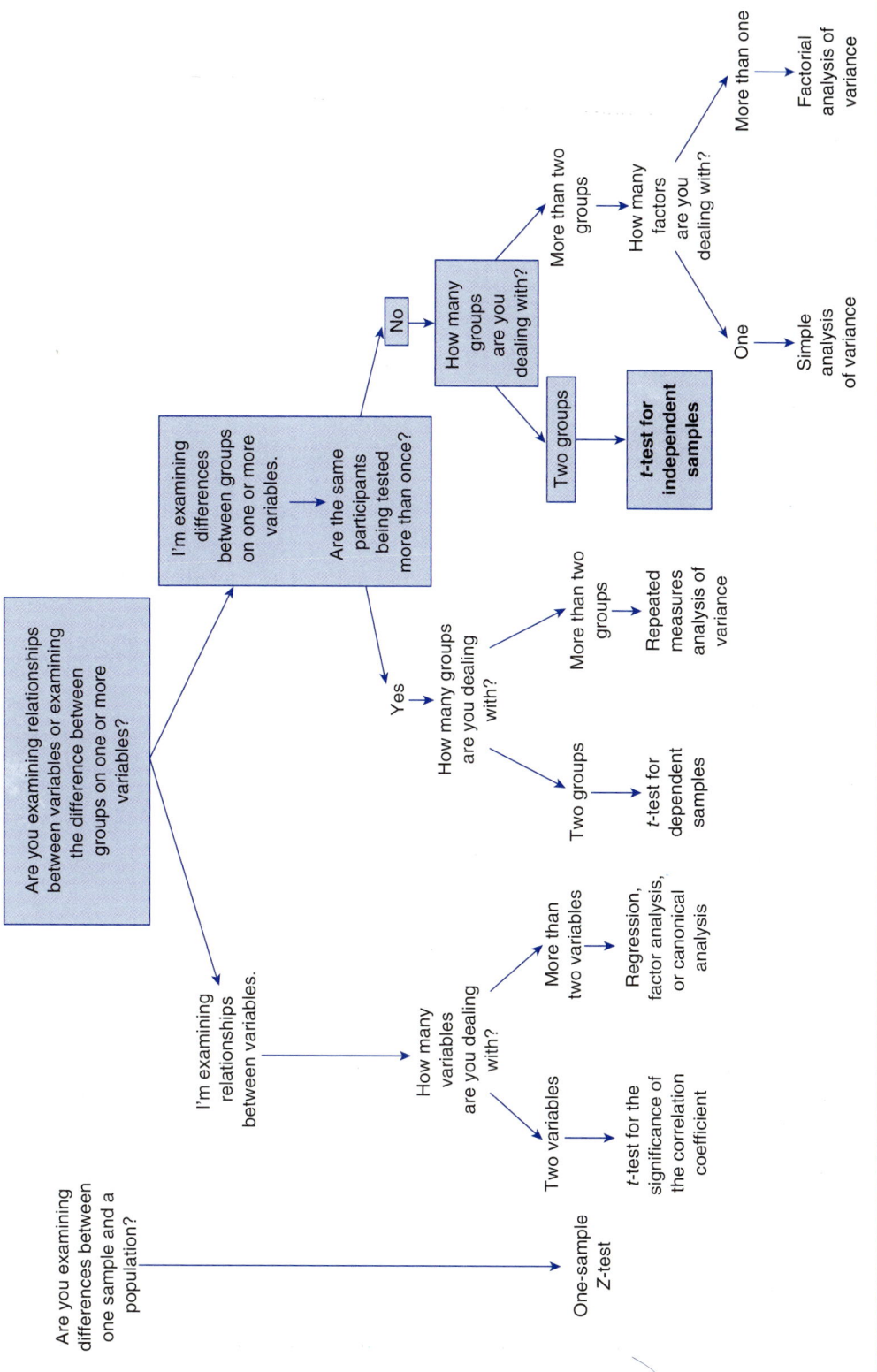

Almost every statistical test makes certain assumptions that underlie the use of the test. For example, the *t*-test assumes that the amount of variability in each of the two groups is equal. The name of this assumption is the "homogeneity of variance assumption." Although this assumption can be safely violated if the sample size is big enough, small samples and a violation of this assumption can lead to ambiguous results and conclusions. Although such assumptions are rarely violated, it is worth knowing that they exist.

COMPUTING THE TEST STATISTIC

The formula for computing the *t* value for the *t*-test for independent means is shown in Formula 11.1. The difference between the means makes up the numerator, and the amount of variation within and between each of the two groups makes up the denominator.

$$t = \frac{\overline{X}_1 - \overline{X}_2}{\sqrt{\left[\dfrac{(n_1-1)s_1^2 + (n_2-1)s_2^2}{n_1+n_2-2}\right]\left[\dfrac{n_1+n_2}{n_1 n_2}\right]}}, \qquad (11.1)$$

where

$\overline{X}_1$ is the mean for Group 1;

$\overline{X}_2$ is the mean for Group 2;

n_1 is the number of participants in Group 1;

n_2 is the number of participants in Group 2;

s_1^2 is the variance for Group 1; and

s_2^2 is the variance for Group 2.

Nothing new here at all. It's just a matter of plugging in the correct values.

Time for an Example

Here are some data reflecting the number of words remembered following a program designed to help Alzheimer's patients remember the order of daily tasks. Study participants in Group 1 were

taught using visuals, and those in Group 2 were taught using visuals
and intense verbal rehearsal. We'll use the data to compute the test
statistic step-by-step.

Group 1			Group 2		
7	5	5	5	3	4
3	4	7	4	2	3
3	6	1	4	5	2
2	10	9	5	4	7
3	10	2	5	4	6
8	5	5	7	6	2
8	1	2	8	7	8
5	1	12	8	7	9
8	4	15	9	5	7
5	3	4	8	6	6

Here are the famous eight steps in the computation of the *t*-test
statistic:

1. *State the null and research hypotheses.* As represented by
   Formula 11.2 below, the null hypothesis states that there is
   no difference between the means for Group 1 and Group 2.
   For our purposes, the research hypothesis, shown in Formula
   11.3, states that there is a difference between the means of the
   two groups. The research hypothesis is a two-tailed, nondirectional research hypothesis because it posits a difference,
   but in no particular direction.

   The null hypothesis is as follows:

   $$H_0: \mu_1 = \mu_2 \qquad (11.2)$$

   And the research hypothesis is this:

   $$H_1: \overline{X}_1 \, \pi \, \overline{X}_2 \qquad (11.3)$$

2. *Set the level of risk (or the level of significance or Type I error)
   associated with the null hypothesis.* The level of risk or Type I
   error or level of significance (any other names?) is .05. This
   number is completely up to the researcher.

3. *Select the appropriate test statistic.* Using the flowchart shown in Figure 11.1, we determined that the appropriate test is a *t*-test for independent samples (or means). It is not a *t*-test for dependent means (a common mistake beginning students make) because the groups are independent of one another.

4. *Compute the test statistic value (called the obtained value).* Now's your chance to plug in values and do some computation. The formula for the *t* value was shown in Formula 11.1. When the values in our example are plugged in, we get the equation shown in Formula 11.4. (We already computed the mean and standard deviation.)

$$t = \frac{5.43 - 5.53}{\sqrt{\left[\frac{(30-1)3.42^2 + (30-1)2.06^2}{30+30-2}\right]\left[\frac{30+30}{30 \times 30}\right]}} \quad (11.4)$$

With the numbers plugged in, Formula 11.5 shows how we get the final value of −0.1371, which we can round to −0.14. The value is negative because a larger value (the mean of Group 2, which is 5.53) is being subtracted from a smaller number (the mean of Group 1, which is 5.43).

Remember, though, that because the test is nondirectional and any difference is hypothesized, the *sign* of the difference is meaningless. In other words, you can ignore it!

$$t = \frac{-0.1}{\sqrt{\left[\frac{339.20 + 123.06}{58}\right]\left[\frac{60}{90}\right]}} = -0.14 \quad (11.5)$$

When a nondirectional test is discussed, you may find that the *t* value is represented as an absolute value looking like this, |*t*|, which ignores the sign of the value altogether. Your teacher may even express the *t* value as such to emphasize that the sign is relevant for a one-directional test but surely not for a nondirectional one (and don't call me Shirley).

5. *Determine the value needed for rejection of the null hypothesis using the appropriate table of critical values for the particular statistic.* Here's where we go to Table B.2 in Appendix B,

which lists the critical values for the *t*-test. We can use this distribution to see whether two independent means differ from one another by comparing what we would expect by chance (the tabled or critical value) with what we observe (the obtained value). Our first task is to determine the **degrees of freedom** (df), which approximates the sample size. For this particular test statistic, the degrees of freedom is $n_1 - 1 + n_2 - 1$, or $n_1 + n_2 - 2$. So for each group, add the size of the two samples and subtract 2. In this example, 30 + 30 − 2 = 58. This is the degrees of freedom value for this test statistic, not necessarily for any other.

The idea of degrees of freedom means pretty much the same thing no matter what statistical test you use. But the way that the degrees of freedom is computed for specific tests can differ from teacher to teacher and from book to book. We tell you that the correct degrees of freedom for the above test is computed as $n_1 - 1 + n_2 - 1$. However, some teachers believe that you should use the smaller of the two *n*'s (a more conservative alternative you may want to consider).

Using this number (58), the level of risk you are willing to take (earlier defined as .05), and a two-tailed test (because there is no direction to the research hypothesis), you can use the *t*-test table to look up the critical value. At the .05 level, with 58 degrees of freedom for a two-tailed test, the value needed for rejection of the null hypothesis is . . . oops! There's no 58 degrees of freedom in the table! What do you do? Well, if you select the value that corresponds to 55, you're being conservative in that you are using a value for a sample smaller than what you have (and the tabled or critical *t* value will be larger).

If you go for 60 degrees of freedom (the closest to your value of 58), you will be closer to the size of the population but a bit liberal in that 60 is larger than 58. Although statisticians have different opinions about what to do in this situation, let's go with the value that's closest to the actual sample size (which is 60). So, the value needed to reject the null hypothesis with 58 degrees of freedom at the .05 level of significance is 2.001.

6. *Compare the obtained value and the critical value.* The obtained value is −0.14, and the critical value for rejection of the null hypothesis, that Group 1 and Group 2 performed the same,

is 2.001. The critical value of 2.001 represents the value at which chance is the most attractive explanation for any of the observed differences between the two groups, given 30 participants in each group and the willingness to take a .05 level of risk.

7. and **8.** *Decision time!* If the obtained value is more extreme than the critical value (remember Figure 9.2?), the null hypothesis cannot be accepted. If the obtained value does not exceed the critical value, the null hypothesis is the most attractive explanation.

In this case, the obtained value (−0.14) does not exceed the critical value (2.001)—it is not extreme enough for us to say that the difference between Groups 1 and 2 occurred by anything other than chance. If the value were greater than 2.001, it would represent a value that is just like getting 8, 9, or 10 heads in a coin toss—so extreme that we believe something other than chance is going on. In the case of the coin, it would be an unfair coin; in this example, it would be that one way of teaching memory skills to people with Alzheimer's is better than the other.

So, to what can we attribute the small difference between the two groups? If we stick with our current argument, then we could say the difference is due to anything from sampling error to rounding error to simple variability in participants' scores. Most important, we're pretty sure (but, of course, not [and never can we be] 100% sure) that the difference is not due to anything in particular that one group or the other experienced during the treatment.

So How Do I Interpret $t_{(58)}$ = −.14, p > .05?

- t represents the test statistic that was used.
- 58 is the number of degrees of freedom.
- −0.14 is the obtained value, calculated using the formula we showed you earlier in the chapter.
- $p > .05$ (the really important part of this little phrase) indicates that the probability is greater than 5% that on any one test of the null hypothesis, the two groups do not differ because of the way they were taught. Also note that $p > .05$ can also appear as p = n.s. for *nonsignificant*.

And Now . . . Using Excel's T.TEST Function

Interestingly, Excel does not have a function that computes the *t* value for the difference between two independent groups. Rather, **T.TEST** returns the probability of that value occurring. Very useful, but if you need the *t* value for a report, you know the manual method for computing it. Here are the steps for using the T.TEST function:

1. Enter the individual scores into columns in a worksheet (available as Chapter 11 Data Set 1). Label one column as Group 1 and one as Group 2, as you see (partially) in Figure 11.2.

Figure 11.2 Partial Data for Using the T.TEST Function

	A	B
1	Group 1	Group 2
2	7	5
3	3	4
4	3	4
5	2	5
6	3	5
7	8	7
8	8	8
9	5	8
10	8	9
11	5	8
12	5	3
13	4	2
14	6	5

2. Select the cell into which you want to enter the T.TEST function. In this example, we are going to have the T.TEST value returned to Cell D1 (and that location was not chosen for any particular reason).

3. Now click Formulas → More Functions → Statistical menu option and scroll down to select T.TEST. The function looks like this:

$$=T.TEST(array1,array2,tails,type),$$

where

    array1   is the cell addresses for the first set of data (in this case A2:A31);

    array2   is the cell addresses for the second set of data (in this case B2:B31);

tails   is 1 or 2 depending on whether this is a one-tailed (directional, which is a 1) or two-tailed (nondirectional, which is a 2) test; and

type   is 1 if it is a paired *t*-test, 2 if it is a two-sample test (independent with equal variances), and 3 if it is a two-sample test with unequal variances.

4. For this example, shown in Figure 11.3, the finished function T.TEST looks like this:

$$=T.TEST(A2:A31,B2:B31,2,1)$$

Click OK, and you see the value returned: 0.877992.

Figure 11.3   Using T.TEST to Compute the Probability of a *t* Value

| D1 | ▼ | ⋮ | ✕ | ✓ | *fx* | =T.TEST(A2:A31,B2:B31,2,1) |

◢	A	B	C	D	E	F
1	Group 1	Group 2		0.877992		
2	7	5				

Notice two important things about T.TEST.

First, it does not compute the *t* value, but . . . (second), it returns the *likelihood* that the resulting *t* value is due to chance (given that the null hypothesis is true, of course). As we said earlier, the interpretation of a *t* value with an associated probability of .88 (and remember, it can only go to 1 or 100%) is that it is pretty darn high.

Believe it or not, way back in the olden days, when your author and perhaps your instructor were graduate students, there were only huge mainframe computers and not a hint of such marvels as we have today on our desktops. In other words, everything that was done in our statistics class was done only by hand. The great benefit of that is, first, it helps you to better understand the process. Second, should you be without a computer, you can still do the analysis. So, if the computer does not spit out all of what you need, use some creativity. As long as you know the basic formula for the obtained value and have the appropriate tables, you'll do fine.

Oops. If the first set of data (in array 1) and the second set of data (in array 2) have a different number of data points and you enter 1 (as the type of data), then the T.TEST function returns the #N/A error message. Why? Because you can't have unequal numbers of values in your groups but have paired (or dependent) scores. You'll see how to deal with this situation in Chapter 12.

There is a pretty dramatic difference between what you get when you compute the *t* value using the formula and when you use one of the functions. Remember that when you did it manually, you had to use a table to locate the critical value and then compare the observed value with that? Well, with T.TEST and the Data Analysis tools discussion that follows later in this chapter, there's no more "$p <$." That's because Excel computes the exact, exactamento, precise, one-of-a-kind probability. No need for tables—just get that number, which is the probability associated with the outcome.

USING THE AMAZING DATA ANALYSIS TOOLS TO COMPUTE THE *T* VALUE

Once again, we'll find that the Data Analysis tools give us all the information we need to make a very informed judgment about the value of *t* and its significance. The tools also provide us with other information that, as you will see, is very helpful and saves us the effort of extra analyses as well.

1. Click Data → Data Analysis, and you will see the Data Analysis dialog box shown in Figure 11.4.

Figure 11.4	The Dialog Box That Gets Us Started With the Data Analysis Tools

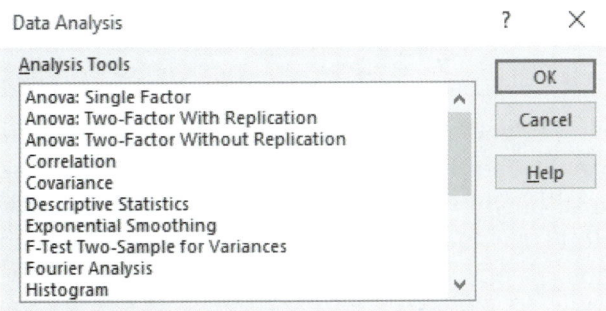

2. Click t-Test: Two-Sample Assuming Equal Variances and then click OK, and you will see the Descriptive Statistics dialog box, as shown in Figure 11.5.

Figure 11.5   The *t*-Test Dialog Box

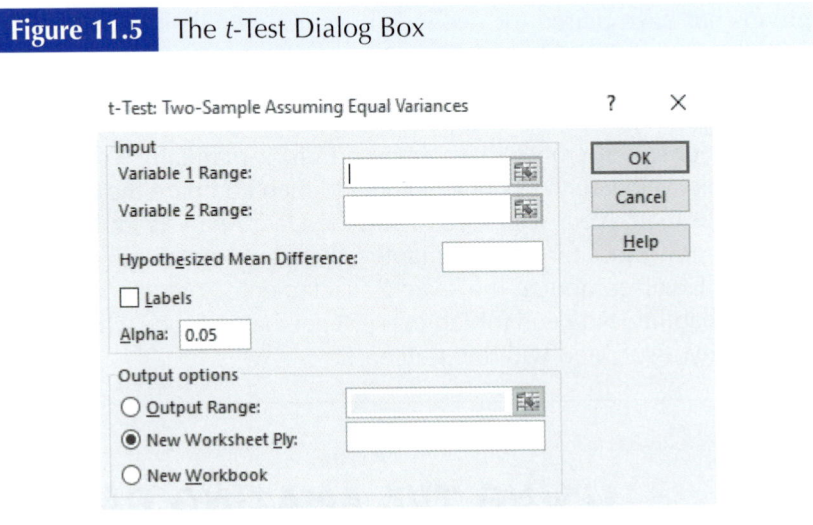

3. In the Variable 1 Range, enter the cell addresses for the first group of data. In our sample spreadsheet that you saw in Figure 11.2, the cell addresses are A1:A31 (this includes the label Group 1).

4. In the Variable 2 Range, enter the cell addresses for the second group of data. In our sample spreadsheet that you saw in Figure 11.2, the cell addresses are B1:B31 (this includes the label Group 2).

5. Click the Labels box so that labels are included in the output that Excel generates.

6. Click the Output Range button and enter an address on the same worksheet as the data where you want the output located. In this example, we are placing the output beginning in Cell D1.

7. Click OK, and as you can see in Figure 11.6, you get a summary of important data relating to this analysis (we cleaned it up a bit by reformatting so it fits nicely). Below that is Table 11.1, which lists the descriptions of what each statistic means.

Figure 11.6	Data Summary

	A	B	C	D	E	F
1	Group 1	Group 2		t-Test: Two-Sample Assuming Equal Variances		
2	7	5				
3	3	4			Group 1	Group 2
4	3	4		Mean	5.43	5.53
5	2	5		Variance	11.70	4.26
6	3	5		Observations	30	30
7	8	7		Pooled Variance	7.98	
8	8	8		Hypothesized Mean Difference	0	
9	5	8		df	58	
10	8	9		t Stat	-0.137	
11	5	8		P(T<=t) one-tail	0.446	
12	5	3		t Critical one-tail	1.672	
13	4	2		P(T<=t) two-tail	0.891	
14	6	5		t Critical two-tail	2.002	
15	10	4				

Table 11.1	Guide to Output of *t*-Test: Two-Sample Assuming Equal Variances

Statistic	Description
Mean	The average score for each variable
Variance	The variance for each variable
Observations	The number of observations in each group
Pooled Variance	The variance for both groups
Hypothesized Mean Difference	What you may have indicated to be the difference you expect (back in the dialog box)
df	The degrees of freedom
t Stat	The value of the *t* statistic
P(T<=t) one-tail	The probability of *t* occurring by chance for a one-tailed test
t Critical one-tail	The critical value one needs to exceed for a one-tailed test (Remember those critical values from Chapter 9?)
P(T<=t) two-tail	The probability of *t* occurring by chance for a two-tailed test
t Critical two-tail	The critical value one needs to exceed for a two-tailed test (Remember those critical values from Chapter 9?)

Remember that it takes only a moment to pretty up the Data Analysis tools output, copy it from Excel, and paste it (or whatever you need from it) into another document.

Results

The results of the analysis show that although Group 2 did have a higher score than Group 1, that score was not significantly different. The *t* value for a two-tailed test was –0.14, with an associated *p* value of .89. Here's a summary:

	Group 1	Group 2
Mean	5.43	5.53
Variance	11.70	4.26
Observations	30	30
Degrees of freedom	58	
t statistic	–0.14	
p value	.89	

SPECIAL EFFECTS: ARE THOSE DIFFERENCES FOR REAL?

Okay, now you have some idea how to test for the difference between the averages of two separate or independent groups. Good job. But that's not the whole story.

You may have a significant difference between groups, but the $64,000 question is not only whether that difference is (statistically) significant but also whether it is *meaningful*. We mean, is there enough separation between the distributions that represent each group that the difference you observe and the difference you test is really a difference? Hmm . . . Welcome to the world of effect size.

Effect size (ES) is a measure of how different two groups are from one another, and it's not just about how big the difference is—it's a measure of the magnitude of the treatment. It's kind of like asking, "How big is big?" And what's especially interesting about computing effect size is that sample size is not (directly) taken into account.

Calculating effect size, and making a judgment about it, adds a whole new dimension to understanding significant outcomes.

Let's take the following example. A researcher tests the question of whether participation in community-sponsored services (such as card games, field trips, etc.) increases the quality of life (as rated from 1 to 10, with 1 being a higher quality of life than 10) for older Americans. The researcher implements the treatment over a 6-month period and then, at the end of the treatment period, measures quality of life in the two groups. Each group consists of 50 participants over the age of 80, and one group got the services and the other group did not. And, yes, the participants were randomly assigned to groups, etc. Here are the results:

	No Community Services	Community Services
Mean	7.46	6.90
Standard deviation	1.03	1.53

And the verdict is that the difference is significant at the .034 level (which is $p < .05$, right?).

So there's a significant difference. But what about the magnitude of the difference?

The great Pooh-Bah of effect size was Jacob Cohen, who wrote some of the most influential and important articles on this topic. He authored a very important and influential book (your stats teacher has it on his or her shelf) that instructs researchers how to figure out the effect size for a variety of different questions that are asked about differences and relationships between variables. Here's how you do it.

Computing and Understanding Effect Size

Just as with many other statistical techniques, there are many different ways to compute effect size. We are going to show you the simplest and most straightforward. You can learn more about effect sizes by consulting some of the references we'll be giving you in a minute.

By far, the most direct and simple way to compute effect size is to simply divide the difference between the means by any one of the standard deviations. Danger, Will Robinson—this does assume that the standard deviations (and the amount of variance) between groups are equal to one another. For our example above, we'll do this:

$$ES = \frac{\overline{X}_1 - \overline{X}_2}{s}, \tag{11.6}$$

where

ES is effect size;

$\bar{X}_1$ is the mean for Group 1;

$\bar{X}_2$ is the mean for Group 2; and

s is the standard deviation from either group.

So, in our example . . .

$$ES = \frac{7.46 - 6.90}{1.53} = .366 \qquad (11.7)$$

So, the effect size for this example is .37.

What does it mean? One of the very cool things that Cohen (and others) figured out was just what a small, medium, or large effect size is. They used the following guidelines:

A small effect size ranges from 0 to .2.

A medium effect size ranges from .2 to .5.

A large effect size is any value above .5.

Our example, with an effect size of .37, is categorized as medium. But what does it really mean?

Effect size gives us an idea about the relative positions of one group to another. For example, if the effect size is zero, that means that both groups tend to be very similar and overlap entirely—there is no difference between the two distributions of scores. On the other hand, an effect size of 1 means that the two groups overlap about 45% (having that much in common). And, as you might expect, as the effect size gets larger, it reflects the increasing lack of overlap between the two groups.

Jacob Cohen's book *Statistical Power Analysis for the Behavioral Sciences*, first published in 1967 with the latest edition (1988) published by Routledge, is a must for anyone who wants to go beyond the very general information that is presented here. It is full of tables and techniques for allowing you to understand why a statistically significant finding is only half the story—the other half is the magnitude of that effect.

So, you really want to be cool about this effect size thing. You can do it the simple way, as we just showed you (by subtracting means from one another and dividing by either standard deviation), or you can really wow that good-looking classmate who sits next to you. The grown-up formula for the effect size uses the pooled variance in the denominator of the ES equation that you saw above. The pooled standard deviation is sort of an average of the standard deviation from Group 1 and the standard deviation from Group 2. Here's the formula:

$$ES = \frac{\bar{X}_1 - \bar{X}_2}{\sqrt{\dfrac{\sigma_1^2 + \sigma_2^2}{2}}},$$

(11.8)

where

ES is effect size;

$\bar{X}_1$ is the mean for group 1;

$\bar{X}_2$ is the mean for group 2;

σ_1^2 is the variance for group 1; and

σ_2^2 is the variablce for group 2.

If we applied this formula to the same numbers we showed you above, you'd get a whopping effect size of .43—not very different from .37, which we got using the more direct method shown earlier. Both results are in the medium-size category, but this formula is a more precise method and one that is well worth knowing about.

A Very Cool Effect Size Calculator

Why not take the A train and go right to www.uccs.edu/~faculty/lbecker/, where statistician Lee Becker from the University of Colorado–Colorado Springs has developed an effect size calculator? With this calculator, you just plug in the values, click Compute, and the program does the rest, as you see in Figure 11.7. Thanks, Dr. Becker!

Figure 11.7   The Very Cool Effect Size Calculator

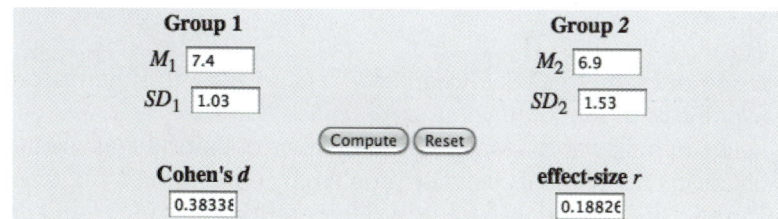

REAL-WORLD STATS

There's nothing like being prepared, so say the Boy Scouts and Girl Scouts. But what's the best way to teach preparedness?

In this study by Serkan Celik from Kirikkale University in Turkey, online versus face-to-face first aid instruction were compared with one another to test the effectiveness of mode of delivery. Interestingly, with the same instructor teaching in both modes, the online forum resulted in higher achievement scores at the end of the course. What did the researcher do for his analysis? Independent *t*-tests, of course, and the resulting *t* values showed a difference between pre- and posttest scores.

Want to know more? Go online or go to the library, and look for . . .

Celik, S. (2013). A media comparison study on first aid instruction. *Health Education Journal, 72,* 95–101.

SUMMARY

Learning about the *t*-test is your first introduction to performing a real statistical test and trying to understand the whole matter of significance from an applied point of view. Be sure that you understand what's in this chapter before you move on. And be sure you can do by hand the few calculations that were asked for. Next, we move on to using another form of the same test; only this time, there are two measures taken from one group of participants rather than one measure taken from two separate groups.

TIME TO PRACTICE

1. Using the data in the file named Chapter 11 Data Set 2, test the research hypothesis at the .05 level of significance that males raise their hands in class more often than females. Do this practice problem by hand using a calculator. What is your conclusion regarding the research hypothesis? Remember to first decide whether this is a one- or two-tailed test.

2. Using the same data set (Chapter 11 Data Set 2), test the research hypothesis at the .01 level of significance that there is a difference between males and females in the number of times they raise their hands in class. Do this practice problem by hand using a calculator. You use the same data for this problem as for Question 1, but you

have a different hypothesis (one is directional and the other is non-directional). What is your conclusion regarding this research hypothesis? How do the results differ, and why?

3. Using the data in the file named Chapter 11 Data Set 3, test the null hypothesis that urban and rural residents have the same attitudes toward gun control. Use the T.TEST function to test the hypothesis. Assume that the variance from each group is equal.

4. For your Friday afternoon report to the boss, you need to let her know if the two stores in Newark, New Jersey (your author's fair city of origin), are selling the same amount of merchandise each week on average or a different amount. Use the data in the file named Chapter 11 Data Set 4 and the Data Analysis tools to let her know. Better hurry.

5. During the last football season, the Brutes managed to gain an average of 203 yards per game while their opponents averaged 288 yards per game. Fire the coach? Use the data in Chapter 11 Data Set 5 to make that decision.

6. What would it mean if a difference were statistically significant but the effect size were not meaningful?

12 *t*(ea) for Two (Again)

Tests Between the Means of Related Groups

Difficulty Scale ☺ ☺ ☺ (hard—just like the one in Chapter 11, but answering a different question)

How much Excel? 📊 📊 (some)

WHAT YOU'LL LEARN ABOUT IN THIS CHAPTER

✦ When the *t*-test for dependent means is appropriate to use

✦ How to compute the observed *t* value

✦ How to interpret the *t* value and understand what it means

✦ How to use the T.TEST function and the T.DIST function

✦ How to use the *t*-Test Data Analysis tools for computing the *t* value

---

INTRODUCTION TO THE T-TEST FOR DEPENDENT SAMPLES

How best to educate children is clearly one of the most vexing questions that faces any society. Because children are so different from one another, a balance needs to be found between meeting the basic needs of all while ensuring that special children (on either end of the continuum) get the opportunities they need. An obvious and important part of education is reading, and three professors at the University of Alabama studied the effects of resource and regular classrooms on the reading achievement of children with learning disabilities. Renitta Goldman, Gary L. Sapp, and Ann Shumate Foster found that, in general, 1 year of daily instruction in both settings resulted in no difference in overall reading achievement scores. On one specific comparison between the pretest and the posttest scores of the resource group, they found that $t_{(34)} = 1.23$, $p > .05$. At the beginning of the program, average reading achievement scores for children in the resource room were 85.8. At the end of the program, average reading achievement scores for children in the resource room were 88.5—a difference, but not a significant one.

So why a test for dependent means? A *t*-test for dependent means indicates that a single group of the same subjects is being studied under two conditions. In this example, the conditions are before the start of the experiment and after its conclusion. Primarily, it is because the same children were tested at two times, before the start of the 1-year program and at the end of the 1-year program, that the researchers used the *t*-test for dependent means. As you can see from the above result, there was no difference in scores at the beginning and the end of the program. The very small *t* value (1.23) is not nearly extreme enough to fall outside the region where we would reject the null hypothesis. In other words, we cannot say that this difference occurred due to something other than chance. The small difference of 2.7 (88.5 − 85.8) is probably due to sampling error or variability within the groups.

Want to know more? Check out Goldman, R., Sapp, G. L., & Foster, A. S. (1998). Reading achievement by learning disabled students in resource and regular classes. *Perceptual and Motor Skills, 86,* 192–194.

The Path to Wisdom and Knowledge

To use the flowchart to select the appropriate test statistic, follow the highlighted sequence of steps in Figure 12.1. You'll arrive at the *t*-test for dependent means.

1. The difference between the students' scores on the pretest and on the posttest is the focus.

2. Participants are being tested more than once.

3. There are two groups.

4. The appropriate test statistic is *t*-test for dependent means.

Figure 12.1 Determining That a *t*-Test for Dependent Means Is the Correct Test Statistic

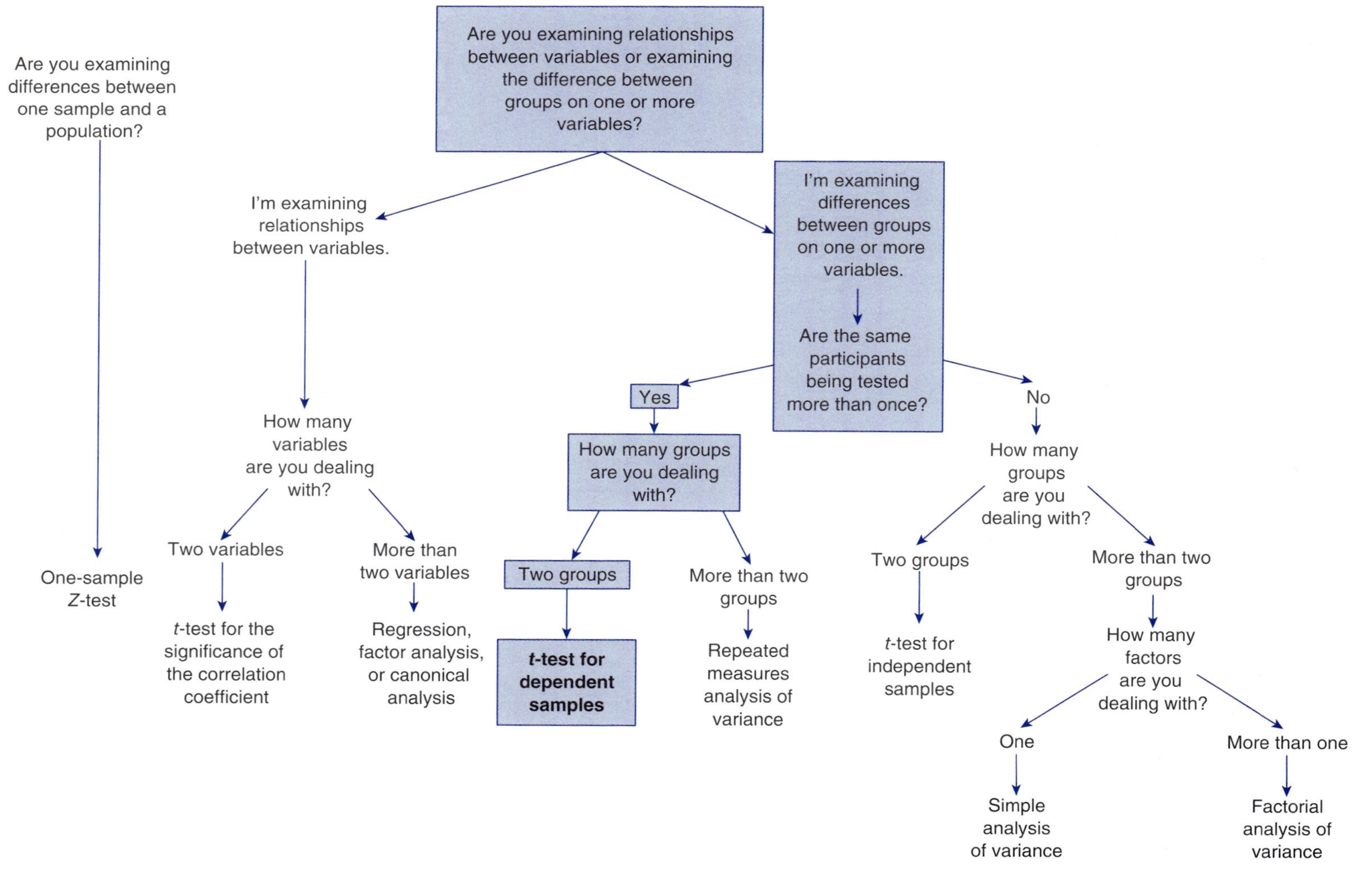

There's another way that statisticians sometimes talk about dependent tests—as repeated measures. Dependent tests are often called "repeated measures" both because the measures are repeated across time or conditions or some factor and because they are repeated across the same cases, be each case a person, place, or thing.

COMPUTING THE TEST STATISTIC

The *t*-test for dependent means involves a comparison of means from each group and focuses on the differences between the scores. As you can see in Formula 12.1, the sum of the differences between the two tests forms the numerator and reflects the difference between groups.

$$t = \frac{\Sigma D}{\sqrt{\dfrac{n\Sigma D^2 - (\Sigma D)^2}{n-1}}}, \tag{12.1}$$

where

  D   is the difference between each individual's score from point 1 to point 2;

  ΣD is the sum of all the differences between groups;

  ΣD^2 is the sum of the differences squared between groups; and

  n   is the number of pairs of observations.

Here are some data to illustrate how the *t* value is computed. Just as in the above example, there is a pretest and a posttest, and for illustration's sake, assume that these numbers are children's scores before and after a reading program.

Pretest (Before)	Posttest (After)	Difference	D²
3	7	4	16
5	8	3	9
4	6	2	4
6	7	1	1
5	8	3	9
5	9	4	16
4	6	2	4

Pretest (Before)	Posttest (After)	Difference	D²
5	6	1	1
3	7	4	16
6	8	2	4
7	8	1	1
8	7	−1	1
7	9	2	4
6	10	4	16
7	9	2	4
8	9	1	1
8	8	0	0
9	8	−1	1
9	4	−5	25
8	4	−4	16
7	5	−2	4
7	6	−1	1
6	9	3	9
7	8	1	1
8	12	4	16
Sum 158	188	30	180
Mean 6.32	7.52	1.2	7.2

Here are the famous eight steps in the computation of the t-test statistic:

1. *State the null and research hypotheses.* The null hypothesis states that there is no difference between the means for the pretest and the posttest scores on reading achievement. The research hypothesis is a one-tailed, nondirectional research hypothesis because it posits that the posttest score will be higher than the pretest score.

   The null hypothesis is as follows:

   $$H_0: \mu_{posttest} = \mu_{pretest} \qquad (12.2)$$

   The research hypothesis is this:

   $$H_1: \overline{X}_{postest} > \overline{X}_{pretest} \qquad (12.3)$$

2. *Set the level of risk (or the level of significance or Type I error)*
   associated with the null hypothesis. The level of risk or Type I
   error or level of significance is .05. This number is entirely up
   to the researcher.

3. *Select the appropriate test statistic.* Using the flowchart shown
   in Figure 12.1, we determined that the appropriate test is a
   t-test for dependent means. It is not a *t*-test for independent
   means because the groups are not independent of each other.
   In fact, they're not groups of participants but rather groups of
   scores for the same participants. The groups (and the scores)
   are dependent on one another. Other names for the *t*-test for
   dependent means are the *t*-test for paired samples or the *t*-test
   for correlated samples. You'll see in Chapter 15 that there is a
   very close relationship between a test of the significance of
   the correlation between these two sets of scores (pre- and
   posttreatment) and the *t* value we are computing here.

4. *Compute the test statistic value (called the obtained value).*
   Now's your chance to plug in values and do some computation. The formula for the *t* value was shown above. When the
   values from this example are plugged in, we get the equation
   shown in Formula 12.4. (We already computed the means
   and standard deviations for the pretest and posttest scores.)

$$t = \frac{30}{\sqrt{\dfrac{(25 \times 180) - 30^2}{25 - 1}}} \tag{12.4}$$

With the numbers plugged in, we have the following equation with a final obtained *t* value of 2.45. The mean score for
pretest performance was 6.32, and the mean score for posttest
performance was 7.52.

$$t = \frac{30}{\sqrt{150}} = 2.45 \tag{12.5}$$

5. *Determine the value needed for rejection of the null hypothesis*
   using the appropriate table of critical values for the particular
   statistic. Here's where we go once again to Table B.2, which
   lists the critical values for the *t*-test, to find out the critical
   value for rejection of the null hypothesis.

   Our first task is to determine the degrees of freedom (*df*),
   which approximate the sample size. For this particular test
   statistic, the degrees of freedom are *n* − 1, where *n* equals the

number of pairs of observations, or 25 − 1 = 24. These are the degrees of freedom for this test statistic only and not necessarily for any other.

Using this number (24), the level of risk you are willing to take (earlier defined as .05), and a one-tailed test (because there is a direction to the research hypothesis, that the posttest score will be larger than the pretest score), we find that the value needed for rejection of the null hypothesis is 1.711.

6. *Compare the obtained value and the critical value.* The obtained value is 2.45, larger than the critical value needed for rejection of the null hypothesis.

7. and 8. *Time for a decision!* If the obtained value is more extreme than the critical value, the null hypothesis cannot be accepted. If the obtained value does not exceed the critical value, the null hypothesis is the most attractive explanation. In this case, the obtained value does exceed the critical value—it is extreme enough for us to say that the difference between the pretest and the posttest occurred due to something other than chance. And if we did our experiment correctly, then what could the factor be that affected the outcome? Easy—the introduction of the daily reading program. We know the difference is due to a particular factor. The difference between the pretest and the posttest groups could not have occurred by chance but instead is due to the treatment.

So How Do I Interpret $t_{(24)} = 2.45$, $p < .05$?

- *t* represents the test statistic that was used.
- 24 is the number of degrees of freedom.
- 2.45 is the obtained value using the formula we showed you earlier in the chapter.
- $p < .05$ (the really important part of this little phrase) indicates that the probability is less than 5% on any one test of the null hypothesis that the average of posttest scores is greater than the average of pretest scores due to chance alone—there's something else going on. Because we defined .05 as our criterion for the research hypothesis being more attractive than the null hypothesis, our conclusion is that there is a significant difference between the two sets of scores. That's the something else.

And Now . . . Using Excel's T.TEST Function

Interestingly, Excel uses the same function that computes the *t* value for the difference between two dependent groups (as it does for the independent test we covered in Chapter 11). The T.TEST function returns the probability of that value occurring, and you use it almost the same way as we showed you in Chapter 11 (only you change one of the options, as you will see).

In addition to the T.TEST function, there's the **T.DIST** function. Here you enter the value of *t*, the degrees of freedom, and the number of tails (1 or 2) at which the hypothesis is being tested, and Excel returns the probability of the outcome. So, for example, remember your normal curve learnings in Chapter 8? A *t* of 1.96 with *df* = 10,000 (virtually identical to a *z* score with a sample that large) will have a probability of about .05. Aren't you smart!

Figure 12.2	Data for Using the T.TEST Function With a Set of Dependent Means

	A	B
1	Pretest	Postest
2	3	7
3	5	8
4	4	6
5	6	7
6	5	8
7	5	9
8	4	6
9	5	6
10	3	7
11	6	8
12	7	8
13	8	7
14	7	9
15	6	10
16	7	9
17	8	9
18	8	8
19	9	8
20	9	4
21	8	4
22	7	5
23	7	6
24	6	9
25	7	8
26	8	12

Enter the individual scores into two columns in a worksheet and label one as Pretest and one as Posttest, as you see in Figure 12.2. (We're using the same data we used in the earlier example.)

Select the cell into which you want to enter the T.TEST function. In this example, we are going to have the T.TEST value returned to Cell D1 (and that location was not chosen for any particular reason).

Now use the Formulas → More Functions → Statistical → T.TEST menu options and the "Inserting a Function" technique we talked about in Little Chapter 1a to enter the T.TEST function in Cell D1. The function looks like this:

$$=T.TEST(array1,array2,tails,type),$$

where

array1   is the cell addresses for the first set of data (in this case A2:A26);

array2   is the cell addresses for the second set of data (in this case B2:B26);

tails   is 1 or 2 depending on whether this is a one-tailed (directional, which is a 1, as in our current example) or two-tailed (nondirectional, which is a 2) test; and

type   is 1 or 2 depending on whether the variances are equal (1, as in our current example) or not equal (2).

For this example, the finished function T.TEST looks like this, and you can also see this in Figure 12.3. (Note that the type is equal to 1 because the observations are paired or dependent.)

$$=T.TEST(A2:A26,B2:B26,1,1)$$

Click OK, and you see the value returned: 0.010991.

As we concluded earlier, the treatment did have a significant effect because the probability of the difference (and a more-than difference at that, right?) between the pretest and posttest being due to chance was less than .010991, or about 1%. Pretty unlikely.

Once again, remember two important things about the T.TEST function.

- It does not, does not, does *not* compute the *t* value. (Thinking it does is an easy mistake to make.)

- It returns the likelihood that the resulting *t* value is due to chance. For example, the interpretation of a *t* value with an associated probability of .88 (and remember, the probability maxes out at 1.00, or 100% likely) is that it is pretty darn high.

Figure 12.3 Using T.TEST to Compute the Probability of a *t* Value

D1		⋮	✕	✓	*fx*	=T.TEST(A2:A26,B2:B26,1,1)

	A	B	C	D	E	F
1	Pretest	Posttest		0.010991		
2	3	7				
3	5	8				

USING THE AMAZING DATA ANALYSIS TOOLS TO COMPUTE THE T VALUE

Once again, as with the *t*-test for the difference between independent means, the Data Analysis tools give us the equipment and all the information we need to make a very informed judgment about the value of *t* and its significance. Here we go, with a very similar procedure to what we did in Chapter 11, only this time, we are using the same data and selecting the *t*-Test: Paired Two Sample for Means option.

1. Click Data → Data Analysis, and you will see the Data Analysis dialog box shown in Figure 12.4.

Figure 12.4 The Data Analysis Tools Dialog Box That Gets Us Started

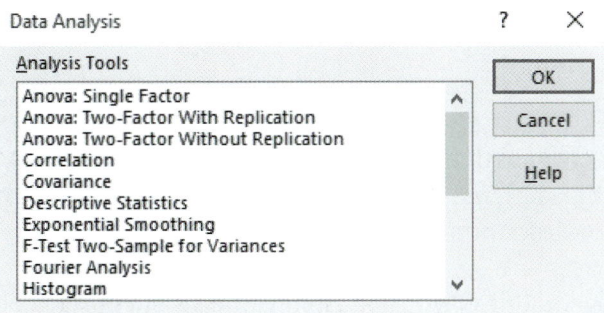

2. Double-click the t-Test: Paired Two Sample for Means (Excel's way of describing dependent means) option and then click OK. You will see the Descriptive Statistics dialog box, as shown in Figure 12.5.

Figure 12.5	The *t*-Test for Dependent Means or Paired Samples Dialog Box

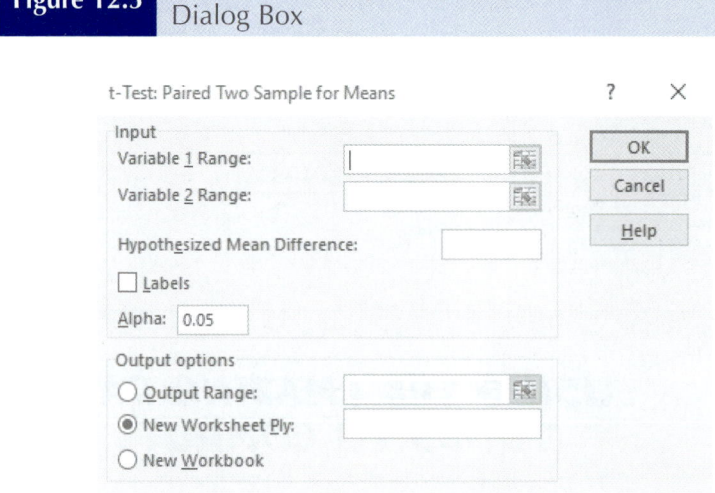

3. In the Variable 1 Range, enter the cell addresses for the pretest. In our sample spreadsheet that you saw in Figure 12.2, the cell addresses are A1:A26 (and these cells include the label Pretest).

4. In the Variable 2 Range, enter the cell addresses for the posttest. In our sample spreadsheet that you saw in Figure 12.2, the cell addresses are B1:B26 (and these cells include the label Posttest).

5. Click the Labels box so that labels are included.

6. Click the Output Range button and enter an address where you want the output located. In this example, we are placing the output beginning in Cell D1.

7. Click OK, and as you can see in Figure 12.6, you get a tidy (we cleaned this up a bit) summary of important data relating to this analysis. Below that is Table 12.1 listing each statistic and a description of what it means.

Once again, our conclusion from earlier is supported. The probability of a one-tailed *t* value of −2.45 occurring by chance alone is .01, which is pretty tiny. Our conclusion? Must be something else going on, and that something else is the implementation of a treatment.

When you select a range of cells when using a dialog box like the one shown in Figure 12.5, you can select by highlighting from the cell at the topmost part of the worksheet and then dragging to the bottom, or you can start at the bottom and drag up. Excel knows what you want, regardless of direction. And, for data that take up more than one screen, it's nice to be able to start where you want—at the top or bottom.

Figure 12.6 Data Summary

	A	B	C	D	E	F
1	Pretest	Postest		t-Test: Paired Two Sample for Means		
2	3	7				
3	5	8			Pretest	Postest
4	4	6		Mean	6.32	7.52
5	6	7		Variance	2.98	3.34
6	5	8		Observations	25	25
7	5	9		Pearson Correlation	0.05	
8	4	6		Hypothesized Mean Difference	0	
9	5	6		df	24	
10	3	7		t Stat	-2.45	
11	6	8		P(T<=t) one-tail	0.01	
12	7	8		t Critical one-tail	1.71	
13	8	7		P(T<=t) two-tail	0.02	
14	7	9		t Critical two-tail	2.06	
15	6	10				

Table 12.1 Guide to Output of t-Test: Two-Sample Assuming Equal Variances

Statistic	Description
Mean	The average score for each variable
Variance	The variance for each variable
Observations	The number of observations in each group
Pooled Variance	The variance for both groups
Hypothesized Mean Difference	What you may have indicated to be the difference you expect (back in the dialog box)
df	The degrees of freedom
t Stat	The value of the *t* statistic

(Continued)

Statistic	Description
P(T<=t) one-tail	The probability of *t* occurring by chance for a one-tailed test
t Critical one-tail	The critical value one needs to exceed for a one-tailed test (Remember those critical values from Chapter 9?)
P(T<=t) two-tail	The probability of *t* occurring by chance for a two-tailed test
t Critical two-tail	The critical value one needs to exceed for a two-tailed test (Remember those critical values from Chapter 9?)

Table 12.1 (Continued)

So what's with the minus sign for the *t* value in Figure 12.6? The only reason it's there is the way that the Data Analysis tools compute the *t* value. Excel always subtracts the second value from the first, and because the second value is larger, the result has a negative sign. If you identified the Posttest as the first array, the value of −2.45 would have appeared as 2.45, but other values would not have changed. What's important is the significance of the *t* value (which in this case, for a one-tailed test, is about .01).

REAL-WORLD STATS

You may be part of the "sandwich" generation, so-called because adults are taking care of their elderly parents at the same time as they are raising their own children. This situation (and the aging of a population, such as is taking place in the United States) speaks to the importance of evaluating the elderly (however this stage of life is defined) and the use of statistical evaluation tools to do so.

The purpose of this study was to determine whether the life satisfaction of a sample of elderly Thai participants depends on their daily living practices. Elderly people were tested to see who perceived themselves as life satisfied or life dissatisfied, and scores of 85% and above on the life satisfaction instrument were used as a criterion to identify life satisfaction. Then the participants were matched on other characteristics, and a two-tailed *dependent* t-test (because the samples were matched—in effect, the researchers considered them the same participants) was used to examine differences in mean scores both overall and for each domain of daily living practices. The group of elderly participants with high life satisfaction scores had significantly higher scores on daily living practices than their dissatisfied counter-parts. One of the most interesting questions is how these results might apply to other samples or elderly participants in different cultures.

Go online or go to the library and look for the following if you want to know more . . .

Othaganont, P., Sinthuvorakan, C., & Jensupakarn, P. (2002). Daily living practice of the life-satisfied Thai elderly. *Journal of Transcultural Nursing, 13*, 24–29.

SUMMARY

That's it for two group designs that use means. You've just learned how to compare data from independent (Chapter 11) and dependent (Chapter 12) groups, and now it's time to move on to another class of significance tests that deals with more than two groups (be they independent or dependent). This class of techniques, called analysis of variance, is very powerful and popular and will be a valuable tool in your war chest!

TIME TO PRACTICE

1. What is the difference between a test of independent means and a test of dependent means, and when is each appropriate?

2. For Chapter 12 Data Set 1, compute the *t* value using the Data Analysis tools and write a conclusion as to whether there was a change in tons of paper used as a function of the recycling program in 25 districts. (Hint: *Before* and *after* become the two levels of treatment.) Test the hypothesis at the .01 level.

3. In the following examples, indicate whether you would perform a *t*-test of independent means or dependent means.

   a. Two groups were exposed to different levels of treatment for ankle sprains. Which treatment was more effective?

   b. A researcher in nursing wanted to know whether patients who received additional in-home care recovered more quickly than others who received the standard amount of in-home care.

   c. A group of adolescent boys was offered interpersonal skills counseling and then tested in September and May to see if there was any impact on family harmony.

   d. One group of adult men was given instructions for reducing their high blood pressure whereas another group was not given any instructions, and the blood pressure of men in both groups was measured before and after.

   e. One group of men was provided access to an exercise program and tested two times over a 6-month period for heart health.

4. For Chapter 12 Data Set 2, compute the t value (do it manually, argh!) and write a conclusion as to whether there was a change in a group of families' satisfaction level (the higher the score, the more satisfied) with their use of service centers following a social service intervention. Then do this exercise using Excel and report the exact probability of the outcome.

5. Here's a tough one. For the same data where two groups are being compared, the critical value for rejection of the null hypothesis is higher for a set of dependent groups than for a set of independent groups. Why?

6. Ace used-car sales manager Jack has no idea whether the $100,000 he pays for training for his used-car salespeople works. He asks Dave, the leading salesperson, and Dave says he thinks it works but can't really tell. So, Jack has hired your local helpful stats star and asked whether the training makes a difference. Here are the data—you tell Jack whether the training worked.

Month	Before Training	After Training
December	$58,676	$87,890
January	$46,567	$87,876
February	$87,656	$56,768
March	$65,431	$98,980
April	$56,543	$98,784
May	$45,456	$65,414
June	$67,656	$99,878
July	$78,887	$67,578
August	$65,454	$76,599
September	$56,554	$88,767
October	$58,876	$78,778
November	$54,433	$98,898

7. Use the data from Chapter 12 Data Set 3 to see whether counseling adolescents at the beginning of the school year had a positive impact on their tolerance for other adolescents who are ethnically different from them. Assessments were made right before the treatment and then 6 months later. Did the program work? The outcome variable is score on a test of attitudes toward others, with possible scores ranging from 0 to 50; the higher the score, the more tolerance. Perform the analysis any way you want!

8. In the data set named Chapter 12 Data Set 4, a comparison is shown between yards rushing for the first and last games of the season for 10 different football teams. Which team is best? And, yes, this is a trick question—can you find the trick?

13

Two Groups Too Many?

Try Analysis of Variance

Difficulty Scale ☺ ☺ ☺ (longer and harder than the others, but a very interesting and useful procedure—worth the work!)

How much Excel? 📊 📊 📊 📊 (lots and lots)

WHAT YOU'LL LEARN ABOUT IN THIS CHAPTER

✦ What analysis of variance is and when it is appropriate to use

✦ How to compute and interpret the F statistic

✦ How to use the F.TEST and F.DIST function

✦ How to use the ANOVA: Single Factor Data Analysis tool for computing the F value

INTRODUCTION TO ANALYSIS OF VARIANCE

One of the upcoming fields in the area of psychology is the psychology of sports. Although the field focuses mostly on enhancing performance, many aspects of sports receive special attention. One aspect focuses on what psychological skills are necessary to be a successful athlete. With this question in mind, Marious Goudas, Yiannis Theodorakis, and Georgios Karamousalidis have tested the usefulness of the Athletic Coping Skills Inventory.

As part of their research, they used a simple **analysis of variance** (or ANOVA—practice saying this; it sounds very cool) to test the hypothesis that number of years of experience in sports is related to coping skill (or an athlete's score on the Athletic Coping Skills Inventory). ANOVA was used because more than two groups were being tested and these groups were compared on their average performance. In particular, Group 1 included athletes with 6 years of experience or less, Group 2 included athletes with 7 to 10 years of experience, and Group 3 included athletes with more than 10 years of experience.

The test statistic for ANOVA is the *F*-test (named for R. A. Fisher, the creator of the statistic), and the results showed that $F_{(2,\ 110)} = 13.08$, $p < .01$. The means of the three groups' score on the Peaking Under Pressure subscale of the test did differ from one another. In other words, any difference in test score was due to number of years of experience in athletics rather than some chance occurrence of scores.

Want to know more? Check out the original reference: Goudas, M., Theodorakis, Y., & Karamousalidis, G. (1998). Psychological skills in basketball: Preliminary study for development of a Greek form of the Athletic Coping Skills Inventory–28. *Perceptual and Motor Skills, 86*, 59–65.

The Path to Wisdom and Knowledge

Follow the highlighted sequence of steps in the flowchart shown in Figure 13.1 to select ANOVA as the appropriate test statistic.

1. We are testing for differences among scores of the different groups, in this case, the differences among the peaking scores of athletes.

2. The athletes are not being tested more than once.

3. There are three groups (6 years or less, 7–10 years, and more than 10 years of experience). We are concerned with different levels of one factor.

4. The appropriate test statistic is simple analysis of variance (ANOVA).

Different Flavors of ANOVA

ANOVA comes in many flavors. The simplest kind, and the focus of this chapter, is the **simple analysis of variance**, where there is one factor or one treatment variable (such as group membership) being explored and there are more than two levels within this factor. Simple ANOVA is also called **one-way analysis of variance** or **single-factor analysis of variance** because there is only one grouping dimension. The technique is called analysis of variance because the variance due to differences in performance is separated

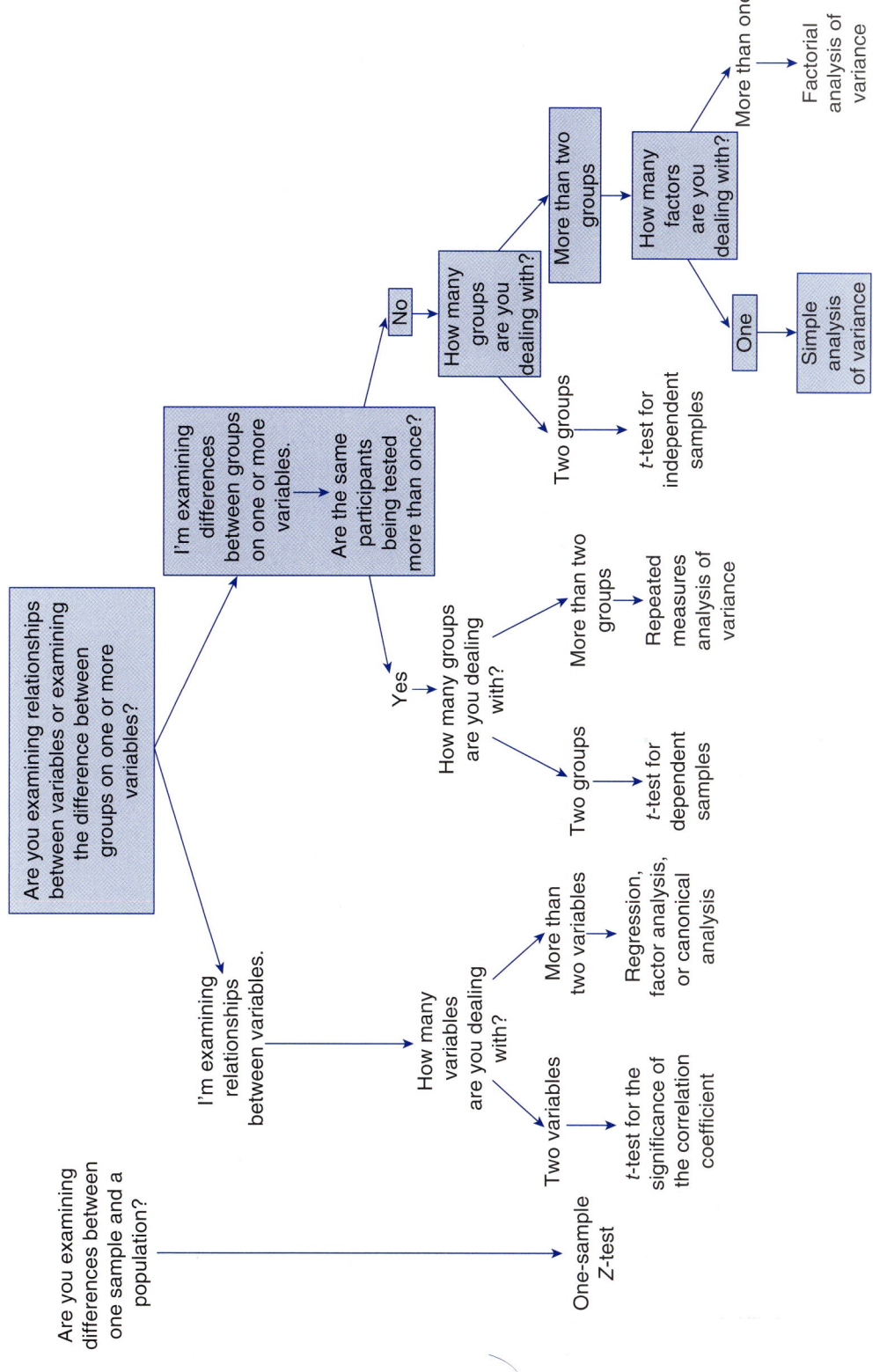

into variance that's due to differences between individuals within groups and variance due to differences between groups. Then, the two types of variance are compared with one another. Once you learn more about what the previous two sentences mean as you read through the chapter, you'll find how really logical and cool an idea partitioning differences in variability is.

In fact, ANOVA is, in many ways, similar to a *t*-test (which you learned about in Chapters 11 and 12). In both procedures, differences between means are computed. But with ANOVA, there are more than two means.

For example, let's say we were investigating the effects on language development of being in preschool for 5, 10, or 20 hours per week. The group to which the children belong is the treatment variable, or the grouping factor. Language development is the **dependent variable**, or the outcome. The experimental design—a single-factor or one-way ANOVA design as we mentioned earlier—looks something like this:

Group 1 (5 hours per week)	Group 2 (10 hours per week)	Group 3 (20 hours per week)
Language development test score	Language development test score	Language development test score

Another, more complex type of ANOVA, called a **factorial design**, is used to explore more than one treatment factor. Here's an example where the effect of number of hours of preschool participation is being examined, but the effects of gender differences are being examined as well. The experimental design can look something like this:

		Number of Hours of Participation		
		Group 1 (5 hours per week)	Group 2 (10 hours per week)	Group 3 (20 hours per week)
Gender	Male	Language development test score	Language development test score	Language development test score
	Female	Language development test score	Language development test score	Language development test score

This factorial design is described as a 3 × 2 factorial design. The 3 indicates that there are three levels (Group 1, Group 2, and Group 3) of one grouping factor (Number of Hours of Participation). The 2 indicates that there are two levels (Male and Female) of the other grouping factor (Gender). In combination, there are six possibilities (males who spend 5 hours per week in preschool, females who spend 5 hours per week in preschool, males who spend 10 hours per week in preschool, etc.).

These factorial designs follow the same basic logic and principles of simple ANOVA, but they are more ambitious in that they can test the influence of more than one factor at a time as well as a combination of factors. Don't worry—you'll learn all about factorial designs in the next chapter.

COMPUTING THE F-TEST STATISTIC

Simple ANOVA involves testing the difference between the means of more than two groups on one factor or dimension. For example, you might want to know whether four groups of people (20, 25, 30, and 35 years of age) differ in their attitude toward public support of private schools. Or you might be interested in determining whether five groups of children from different grades (2nd, 4th, 6th, 8th, and 10th) differ in the level of parental participation in school activities.

Any analysis where . . .

- there is only one dimension or treatment,
- there are more than two levels of the grouping factor, and
- one is looking at differences across groups in average scores

. . . requires that simple ANOVA be used.

The formula for the computation of the F value, which is the test statistic needed to evaluate the hypothesis that there are overall differences between groups, is shown in Formula 13.1. It is simple at this level, but it takes a bit more effort to compute than some of the other test statistics you worked with in earlier chapters.

$$F = \frac{\text{MeanSquares}_{\text{Between}}}{\text{MeanSquares}_{\text{Within}}} \qquad (13.1)$$

The logic behind this ratio goes something like this. If there were absolutely no variability within each group (all the scores were the same), then any difference between groups would be meaningful, right? Probably so. The ANOVA formula (which is a ratio) compares the amount of variability between groups (which is due to the grouping factor) with the amount of variability within groups (which is due to chance or error). If that ratio is 1, then the amount of variability due to within-group differences is equal to the amount of variability due to between-group differences, and any difference between groups is not significant. As the average difference between groups gets larger (and the numerator of the ratio increases in value), the *F* value increases as well. As the *F* value increases, it becomes more extreme in relation to the distribution of all *F* values and is more likely due to something other than chance. Whew!

Here are some data and some preliminary calculations to illustrate how the *F* value is computed. For our example, let's assume these are three groups of preschoolers, each having attended a different number of hours of preschool. Here are their language scores.

Group 1	Group 2	Group 3
87	87	89
86	85	91
76	99	96
56	85	87
78	79	89
98	81	90
77	82	89
66	78	96
75	85	96
67	91	93

Here are the famous eight steps and the computation of the *F*-test statistic:

1. *State the null and research hypotheses.* The null hypothesis, shown in Formula 13.2, states that there is no difference among the means of the three different groups. ANOVA, also

called the F-test (because it produces an F statistic or an F ratio or an F value [remember R. A. Fisher?]), looks for an overall difference among groups.

$$H_0: \mu_1 = \mu_2 = \mu_3 \qquad (13.2)$$

Note that ANOVA does not look at pairwise differences, such as the difference between Group 1 and Group 2. For that, we have to use another technique, which we discuss later in the chapter.

The research hypothesis, shown in Formula 13.3, states that there is an overall difference among the means of the three groups. Note that there is no direction to the difference because all F-tests are nondirectional.

$$H_1: \overline{X}_1 \neq \overline{X}_2 \neq \overline{X}_3 \qquad (13.3)$$

Up to now, we've talked about one- and two-tailed tests. No such thing when talking about ANOVA. Because more than two levels of a treatment factor are being tested, and because the F-test is an *omnibus* (how's that for a word?) test (meaning that it tests for an overall difference among means), talking about the direction of specific differences would not make any sense.

---

2. *Set the level of risk (or the level of significance or Type I error) associated with the null hypothesis.* The level of risk or Type I error or level of significance (any other names?) is .05. Once again, the level of significance is at the discretion of the researcher.

3. *Select the appropriate test statistic.* Using the flowchart shown in Figure 13.1, we determined that the appropriate test is a simple ANOVA.

4. *Compute the test statistic value (called the obtained value).* Now's your chance to plug in values and do some computation. There's a good deal of computation to do.

   a. The F ratio is a ratio of variability between groups to variability within groups. To compute these values, we first have to compute what is called the sum of squares for each source of variability—between groups, within groups, and the total.

b. The *between-group sum of squares* is equal to the sum of the differences between the mean of all scores and the mean of each group's score, which is then squared. This gives us an idea of how different each group's mean is from the overall mean.

c. The *within-group sum of squares* is equal to the sum of the differences between each individual score in a group and the mean of each group, which is then squared. This gives us an idea of how different each score in a group is from the mean of that group.

d. The *total sum of squares* is equal to the sum of the between-group and within-group sum of squares.

Okay, let's calculate these values. Figure 13.2 shows the hours in preschool data you saw above with all the values you need to compute the between-group, within-group, and total sum of squares.

Figure 13.2   Computing the Important Values for a One-Way ANOVA

Group	Test Score	X^2	Group	Test Score	X^2	Group	Test Score	X^2	
1	87	7,569	2	87	7,569	3	89	7,921	
1	86	7,396	2	85	7,225	3	91	8,281	
1	76	5,776	2	99	9,801	3	96	9,216	
1	56	3,136	2	85	7,225	3	87	7,569	
1	78	6,084	2	79	6,241	3	89	7,921	
1	98	9,604	2	81	6,561	3	90	8,100	
1	77	5,929	2	82	6,724	3	89	7,921	
1	66	4,356	2	78	6,084	3	96	9,216	
1	75	5,625	2	85	7,225	3	96	9,216	
1	67	4,489	2	91	8,281	3	93	8,649	
10			10			10			$N = 30.00$
n									$\Sigma\Sigma X = 2{,}534.00$
ΣX	766			852			916		$(\Sigma\Sigma X)^2/N = 214{,}038.53$
$\bar{X}$	76.60			85.20			91.60		$\Sigma\Sigma(X^2) = 216{,}910$
$\Sigma(X^2)$	59,964			72,936			84,010		$\Sigma(\Sigma X)^2/n = 215{,}171.6$
$(\Sigma X)^2/n$	58,675.60			72,590.40			83,905.60		

First, let's look at what we have in this expanded table. Starting down the left column . . .

n is the number of participants in each group (such as 10);

ΣX is the sum of the scores in each group (such as 766);

$\bar{X}$ is the mean of each group (such as 76.60);

$\Sigma(X^2)$ is the sum of each score squared (such as 59,964); and

$(\Sigma X)^2/n$ is the sum of the scores in each group squared and then divided by the size of the group (such as 58,675.60).

Now looking down the right-most column . . .

N is the total number of participants (such as 30);

$\Sigma\Sigma X$ is the sum of all the scores across groups (such as 2,534.00);

$(\Sigma\Sigma X)^2/N$ is the sum of all the scores across groups squared and divided by N (such as 214,038.53);

$\Sigma\Sigma(X^2)$ is the sum of all the sums of squared scores (such as 216,910); and

$\Sigma(\Sigma X)^2/n$ is the sum of the sum of each group's scores squared and divided by n (215,171.60).

That is a load of computation to carry out, but we are almost finished.

First, we compute the sum of squares for each source of variability. Here are the calculations:

Between sum of squares	$\Sigma(\Sigma X)^2/n - (\Sigma\Sigma X)^2/N$, or 215,171.60 − 214,038.53	1,133.07
Within sum of squares	$\Sigma\Sigma(X^2) - \Sigma(\Sigma X)^2/n$, or 216,910 − 215,171.60	1,738.40
Total sum of squares	$\Sigma\Sigma(X^2) - (\Sigma\Sigma X)^2/N$, or 216,910 − 214,038.53	2,871.47

Second, we need to compute the mean sum of squares, which is simply an average sum of squares. These are the variance estimates that we need to eventually compute the all-important F ratio.

We do that by dividing each sum of squares by the appropriate number of degrees of freedom (df). Remember, degrees of freedom is an approximation of the sample or group size.

We need two sets of degrees of freedom for ANOVA. For the between-group estimate, it is $k - 1$, where k equals the number of groups (in this case, there are 3 groups, so there are 2 degrees of freedom); for the within-group estimate, we need

N − k, where N equals the total sample size (which means that the number of degrees of freedom is 30 − 3, or 27). And the F ratio is simply a ratio of the mean sums of squares due to between-group differences to the mean sums of squares due to within-group differences, or 566.54/64.39 = 8.799. This is the obtained F value.

Here's a summary table of the variance estimates used to compute the F ratio. This is how most F tables appear in professional journals and manuscripts.

Source	Sums of Squares	df	Mean Sums of Squares	F
Between groups	1,133.07	2	566.54	8.799
Within groups	1,738.40	27	64.39	
Total	2,871.47	29		

All that trouble for one little F ratio! But as we have said earlier, it's essential to do these procedures at least once by hand. It gives you an important appreciation of where the numbers come from and some insight into what they mean.

Because you already know about t-tests, you might be wondering how a t value (which is always used for the test between the difference of the means for two groups) and an F value (which is always used to test for differences among more than two groups) might be related. Interestingly enough, an F value for two groups is equal to a t value for two groups squared:

$$t^2 = F, \text{ or } t = \sqrt{F}$$

Handy trivia question, right? But also useful if you know the value of one statistic and need to know the value of the other.

5. *Determine the value needed for rejection of the null hypothesis using the appropriate table of critical values for the particular statistic.* As we have done before, we have to compare the obtained and critical values. We now need to turn to the table that lists the critical values for the F-test, Table B.3 in Appendix B. Our first task is to determine the degrees of freedom for the numerator, which is k − 1, or 3 − 1 = 2. Then, determine the

degrees of freedom for the denominator, which is $N - k$, or 30 $- 3 = 27$. Together, they are represented as $F_{(2, 27)}$.

The obtained value is 8.80, or $F_{(2, 27)} = 8.80$. The critical value at the .05 level with 2 degrees of freedom in the numerator (represented by columns in Table B.3) and 27 degrees of freedom in the denominator (represented by rows in Table B.3) is 3.36. So, at the .05 level, with 2 and 27 degrees of freedom for an omnibus test among the means of the three groups, the value needed for rejection of the null hypothesis is 3.36.

6. *Compare the obtained value and the critical value.* The obtained value is 8.80, and the critical value for rejection of the null hypothesis at the .05 level that the three groups are different from one another (without concern for where the difference lies) is 3.36.

7. and 8. *Decision time!* If the obtained value is more extreme than the critical value, the null hypothesis cannot be accepted. If the obtained value does not exceed the critical value, the null hypothesis is the most attractive explanation. In this case, the obtained value does exceed the critical value—it is extreme enough for us to say that the difference between the three groups is not due to chance. And if we did our experiment correctly, then what could the factor be that affected the outcome? Easy—the number of hours of preschool. We know the difference is due to a particular factor because the difference between the groups could not have occurred (just) by chance but instead is due to the treatment.

So How Do I Interpret $F_{(2, 27)} = 8.80$, $p < .05$?

- *F* represents the test statistic that was used.
- 2 and 27 are the numbers of degrees of freedom for the between-group and within-group estimates, respectively.
- 8.80 is the obtained *F* value using Formula 13.1.
- $p < .05$ (the really important part of this little phrase) indicates that the probability is less than 5% on any one test of the null hypothesis that the average scores of each group's language skills differ due to chance alone rather than the effect of the treatment. Because we defined .05 as our criterion for the research hypothesis being more attractive than the null hypothesis, our conclusion is that there is a significant difference among the three sets of scores.

Imagine this scenario. You're a high-powered researcher at an advertising company, and you want to see whether packaging color makes
a difference in sales. You've decided you'll test this at the .05 level.
So, you put together a brochure that is all black-and-white, one that
is 25% color, the next 50% color, then 75%, and, finally, 100%
color, for five different levels. You do an ANOVA and find out that
there is a difference in sales. But because ANOVA is an omnibus test,
you don't know where the source of the significant difference lies.
So, you take two groups at time (such as 25% color and 75% color)
and test them against each other. In fact, you test every combination
of two brochures against each other. Kosher? No way. This is performing multiple *t*-tests, and it is actually against the law in some
jurisdictions. When you do this, the Type I error rate (which you set
at .05) balloons depending on the number of tests you conduct.
There are 10 possible comparisons (no color vs. 25%, no color vs.
50%, no color vs. 75%, etc.), and the real Type I error rate is equal
to $1 - (1 - a)^k$, where

α is the Type I error rate, which is .05 in this example; and

k is the number of comparisons.

So, instead of .05, the actual error rate that each comparison is being
tested at is

$$1 - (1 - .05)^{10} = .40 \text{ (!!!!!)}$$

Surely not .05. Quite a difference, no?

And Now . . . Using Excel's F.DIST and F.TEST Functions

Interestingly, just as with the T.TEST, Excel does not have a function
that computes the specific value of the *F*-test statistic. Also, **F.DIST**
and **F.TEST** calculate values for only two groups of data (which is
what we used the T.TEST and T.DIST functions and the Data
Analysis tools for in the previous chapter). So, we'll just move on to
the Data Analysis tools and the powerful ANOVA tools that it offers.

USING THE AMAZING DATA ANALYSIS TOOLS TO COMPUTE THE F VALUE

ANOVA is more sophisticated than any of the other inferential tools
that we have covered so far in *Statistics for People . . .* , and it's the
ANOVA tools that really shine, bringing out the value of learning
statistics through the use of Excel.

There are three ANOVA options within the Data Analysis tools, as follows:

- Anova: Single Factor
- Anova: Two-Factor With Replication
- Anova: Two-Factor Without Replication

We'll cover the first of these in the following section and the other two in the next chapter when we cover factorial analysis of variance. Hold on tight! We're using the data shown to you earlier in the chapter; these appear in Figure 13.3 as three columns, each column representing a different level of treatment (5, 10, and 20 hours per week). (Because some of you can't wait until that next chapter . . . the *replication* part of analysis of variance means that the same subjects are tested more than once—kind of like *dependent* means in a *t*-test but with more than two groups.)

Figure 13.3	Data for a Single-Factor Analysis of Variance

	A	B	C
1	Group 1 (5 hours)	Group 2 (10 Hours)	Group 3 (20 Hours)
2	87	87	89
3	86	85	91
4	76	99	96
5	56	85	87
6	78	79	89
7	98	81	90
8	77	82	89
9	66	78	96
10	75	85	96
11	67	91	93

1. Click Data → Data Analysis, and you will see the Data Analysis dialog box shown in Figure 13.4.

2. Click Anova: Single Factor and then click OK. You will see the Anova: Single Factor dialog box, as shown in Figure 13.5.

Figure 13.4	The Dialog Box That Gets Us Started With the Data Analysis Tools

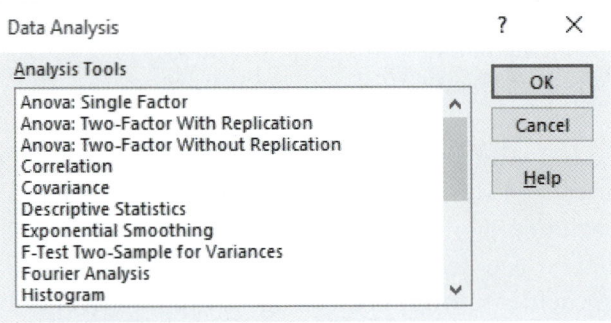

Figure 13.5	The Anova: Single Factor Dialog Box

3. In the Input Range, enter the cell addresses for the three groups of data. In the sample spreadsheet that you saw in Figure 13.3, the cell addresses are A1:C11 (and these include the labels for each group).

4. Click whether the data are Grouped By: Columns or Rows. (They will almost always be grouped by columns, as they are here.)

5. Click the Labels box so that labels are included.

6. Click the Output Range button and enter an address where you want the output located. In this example, we are placing the output beginning in cell E1.

7. Click OK, and as you can see in Figure 13.6, you get a tidy (and we did a bit of housecleaning) summary of important data relating to this analysis. Following that is Table 13.1, listing each statistic and describing what it means.

Figure 13.6   The Output for the Anova: Single Factor

	A	B	C	D	E	F	G	H	I	J	K
	Group 1 (5 hours)	Group 2 (10 Hours)	Group 3 (20 Hours)								
1					Anova: Single Factor						
2	87	87	89								
3	86	85	91		SUMMARY						
4	76	99	96		Groups	Count	Sum	Average	Variance		
5	56	85	87		Group 1 (5 hours)	10	766	76.6	143.1555556		
6	78	79	89		Group 2 (10 Hours)	10	852	85.2	38.4		
7	98	81	90		Group 3 (20 Hours)	10	916	91.6	11.6		
8	77	82	89								
9	66	78	96								
10	75	85	96		ANOVA						
11	67	91	93		Source of Variation	SS	df	MS	F	P-value	F crit
12					Between Groups	1133.07	2	566.53	8.80	0.001	3.35
13					Within Groups	1738.40	27	64.39			
14											
15					Total	2871.466667	29				

Table 13.1   Your Official Decoder Chart

Statistic	Description
Groups	The listing of each of the groups
Count	The number of observations in each group
Sum	The sum of the values
Average	The mean for each group
Variance	The variance for each group
Source of Variation	The source of error
SS	The sums of squares
df	Degrees of freedom associated with each source of error
MS	The mean square
F	The F value (the obtained value)
P-value	The level of significance of the F value
F crit	The value needed to reject the null hypothesis

As we showed you before, the F value is large enough that we would not expect it to be due to chance alone. So, our conclusion is that there is a difference in language development as a function of the number of hours spent in preschool.

REAL-WORLD STATS

How interesting it is when different disciplines combine to answer different questions! Just take a look at the journal in which this appeared—*Music and Medicine*. In this study, where the authors examined anxiety among performing musicians, they tested five professional singers' and four flute players' arousal levels. In addition, they used a 5-point Likert-type scale to assess the subjects' nervousness.

Every musician performed an easy and a challenging piece with an audience (like a concert) and without an audience (like a rehearsal). Then the researchers used a one-way analysis of variance measuring heart rate (HR) and heart rate variability (HRV), which showed a significant difference across the four different conditions (easy/rehearsal, strenuous/rehearsal, easy/concert, and strenuous/concert) within subjects. There were no differences in age, sex, or instrument (voice/flute) when those factors were examined.

Want to know more? Go online or go to the library, and look for . . .

Harmat, L., & Theorell, T. (2010). Heart rate variability during singing and flute playing. *Music and Medicine, 2,* 10–17.

SUMMARY

Analysis of variance (either single or factorial) is the most complex of all the inferential tests you will learn in *Statistics for People Who (Think They) Hate Statistics, Excel 2016 Edition*. It takes a good deal of concentration to perform the manual calculations, and even when you use Excel, you have to be on your toes to understand that this is an overall test; the test statistic does not give you information about differences between specific pairs of treatments. We have one more test among averages, a factorial ANOVA—the Holy Grail of ANOVAs—which can involve two or more factors. It's coming up in Chapter 14.

TIME TO PRACTICE

1. Using the following table, provide three examples of a simple one-way ANOVA, two examples of a two-factor ANOVA, and one example of a three-factor ANOVA. We show you some examples. Be sure to identify the grouping and the test variable as we have done here.

Design	Grouping Variable(s)	Test Variable
Simple ANOVA	Four levels of hours of training—2, 4, 6, and 8 hours	Typing accuracy
	Enter your example here.	Enter your example here.
	Enter your example here.	Enter your example here.
Two-factor ANOVA	Two levels of training and gender (2 × 2 design)	Typing accuracy
	Enter your example here.	Enter your example here.
	Enter your example here.	Enter your example here.
Three-factor ANOVA	Two levels of training, two of gender, and three of income	Voting attitudes
	Enter your example here.	Enter your example here.

2. Using the data in Chapter 13 Data Set 1 and Excel, compute the F value for a comparison among the three levels representing the average amount of time that swimmers practice weekly (<15 hours, 15–25 hours, and >25 hours), with the dependent or outcome variable being their time for the 100-yard freestyle. Answer the question of whether practice time makes a difference. Either use the Data Analysis tools or do the calculations manually.

3. Stephen recognizes that there are different techniques for attracting attention to advertisements, and he wants to test three of these for the sample product: all color, all black-and-white, and a combination. Here are the data on the attractiveness of each product on a scale from 1 to 10. Now he wants to know whether the three formats differ in their attractiveness. Do they?

Color	Black-and-White	Combination
10	4	9
8	5	8
7	4	8
8	3	9
9	3	8
6	4	7
7	5	8

Color	Black-and-White	Combination
6	6	9
6	5	9
7	7	10
8	6	10
7	5	9
6	4	8
5	5	9
6	4	10
7	4	10
7	3	8

4. Using Chapter 13 Data Set 2, the researchers want to find out whether there is a difference among the graduation rates (and these are percentages) of five high schools over a 10-year period. Is there? (Hint: Are the years a factor?)

5. Chapter 13 Data Set 3 contains the average sales for five stores across four seasons. Which season was the best of all for sales?

14

Two Too Many Factors

Factorial Analysis of Variance—A Brief Introduction

Difficulty Scale ☺ (some challenging ideas—but we're only touching on the main concepts here)

How much Excel? 📊 📊 (some)

✦ When to use analysis of variance with more than one factor

✦ All about main and interaction effects

✦ How to use the amazing Data Analysis tools to perform a factorial analysis of variance

INTRODUCTION TO FACTORIAL ANALYSIS OF VARIANCE

How people make decisions has fascinated psychologists for decades. The data that have resulted from their studies have been applied to such broad fields as advertising, business, planning, and even theology. Miltiadis Proios and George Doganis investigated how the experience of being actively involved in the decision-making process (in a variety of settings) and age can have an impact on moral reasoning. The sample consisted of a total of 148 sports referees—56 who refereed soccer, 55 who refereed basketball, and 37 who refereed handball. Their ages ranged from 17 to 50 years, and gender was not considered an important variable. Within the entire sample, about 8% had not had any experience in social, political, or athletic settings where they fully participated in the decision-making process; about 53% were active but did not fully participate; and about 39% were both active and did participate in the decisions made within that organization. A two-way (multivariate—see the discussion of MANOVA in Chapter 18 for more about this statistical method) analysis of variance showed an interaction between the effects of experience and age on the moral reasoning and goal orientation of referees.

Why a two-way analysis of variance? Easy—there were two independent factors, with the first being level of experience and the second being age. Here, just as with any analysis of variance procedure, there is

- a test of the main effect for age,
- a test of the main effect for experience, and
- a test for the interaction between experience and age (which turned out to be significant in this study).

The very cool thing about analysis of variance when more than one factor or **independent variable** is tested is that the researcher can look at the individual effects of each factor as well as the simultaneous effects of both, through what is called an interaction. We talk more about this interaction effect later in this chapter.

Want to know more? See Proios, M., & Doganis, G. (2003). Experiences from active membership and participation in decision-making processes and age in moral reasoning and goal orientation of referees. *Perceptual and Motor Skills, 96,* 113–126.

Two Flavors of Factorial ANOVA

There are two types of factorial ANOVAs. Excel calls one "Anova: Two-Factor With Replication" and the other "Anova: Two-Factor Without Replication." Both involve two factors, but the difference is in how many times one factor is tested across the same individuals.

For example, in an analysis of variance *without replication*, we could test the effects of two factors: location of residence (urban or rural) and voting preference (Green Party or not Green Party). As an outcome, we'll use attitude toward environmental waste. In this design (shown below), there are separate and independent observations in each of the four cells. No one can have his or her primary residence in both an urban and a rural area, nor can he or she belong to both a Green and a non-Green voting bloc. There's no replication.

		Primary Residence	
		Urban	Rural
Political Affiliation	Green		
	Not Green		

In an analysis of variance *with replication,* we could test the effects of two factors such as change over time (from September to July) and subject matter (math or spelling). As an outcome, we'll use achievement. In this example, the replication is over the variable named Time, because the same (here's where the replication comes in) subjects are being tested twice. Here's the design.

		Time	
		September	June
Achievement	Math		
	Spelling		

Guess what? Excel is about the coolest personal computer application ever invented. But it, like others, has its shortcomings. One is that the ANOVA tools, the ones with and without replication, don't provide equally clear output. Because the option without replication does not provide a clear example of how this technique works, we will avoid going into excruciating detail (after all, that's why you are using *this* book) by only dealing with the replication option. Take a look at the software sampler in Chapter 19 to find out about other programs that you might want to use.

The Path to Wisdom and Knowledge

Follow the highlighted sequence of steps in the flowchart shown in Figure 14.1. You will arrive at ANOVA (but this time with more than one factor) as the appropriate test statistic. As in Chapter 13, we decide that ANOVA is the correct procedure (to examine differences in more than two levels of the independent variable), but because we have more than one factor, factorial ANOVA is the right choice.

Figure 14.1 Determining That Factorial Analysis of Variance (Factorial ANOVA) Is the Correct Test Statistic

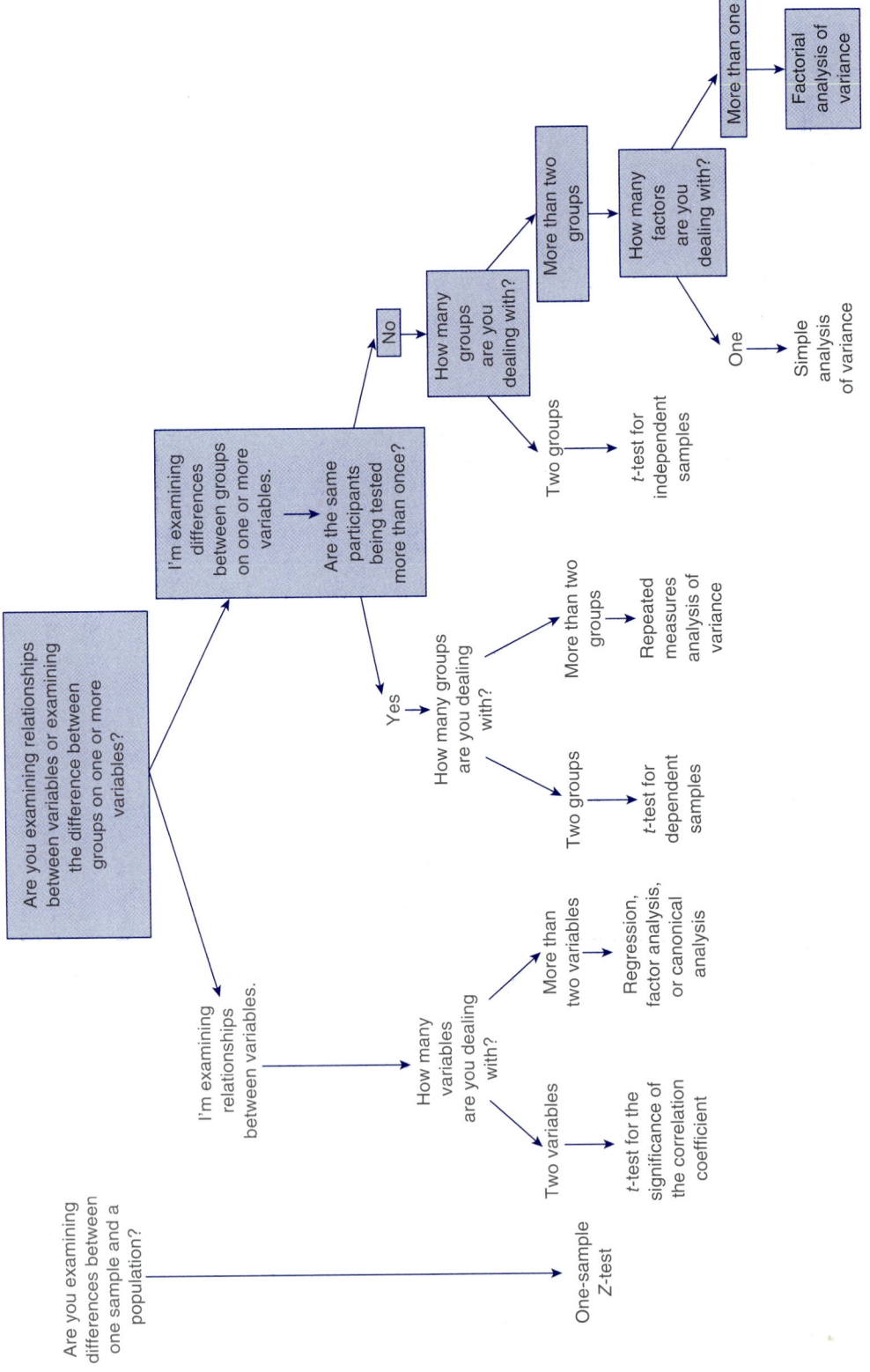

1. We are testing for differences between scores of the same participants.
2. The participants are not being tested more than once.
3. We are dealing with two or more groups.
4. We are dealing with more than one factor or independent variable.
5. The appropriate test statistic is factorial analysis of variance (factorial ANOVA), with replication or repeated across conditions.

ANOVA with replication is also referred to as repeated-measures ANOVA or within-measures ANOVA, because the measure is repeated across participants (or other objects of study!).

A New Flavor of ANOVA

You've already tasted one flavor of ANOVA, the simple analysis of variance we discussed in Chapter 13. In this case, one factor or one treatment variable (such as group membership) was being explored, and there were more than two groups or levels within this factor or treatment variable.

Now, we bump up the entire technique a notch to include the exploration of more than one factor simultaneously, and we call this a **factorial analysis of variance**.

Let's look at a simple example that includes two factors, gender (male or female) and treatment (high- or low-impact exercise), and an outcome—a weight loss score. The treatment is a weight loss program that has two levels of involvement—high impact and low impact—and the loss is measured in pounds. The same people experience both the high- and the low-impact conditions in a counterbalanced order (one half gets low first, then high; the other half, vice versa). Here's what the experimental design would look like. And keep in mind (again) that this analysis is with replication, where the impact treatment is the repeated measure.

		Impact	
		High	Low
Gender	Male		
	Female		

ANOVA designs that contain a factor where there is repetition and a factor where there is not are sometimes called *mixed designs*.

Then, we will look at what the main effects and an interaction look like. Not a lot of data analysis here until a bit later on in the chapter—it's mostly just look and learn for now.

There are three questions that you can ask and answer from this type of analysis:

1. Is there a difference between the levels of impact? Remember that each person participates at both the high and low level.

2. Is there a difference between the two levels of gender, male and female?

3. What is the effect of different levels of impact for males or females (and this is the famous interaction effect you will learn about shortly)?

Questions 1 and 2 deal with the presence of main effects, whereas question 3 deals with the interaction between the two factors.

THE MAIN EVENT: MAIN EFFECTS IN FACTORIAL ANOVA

You might remember that the primary task of analysis of variance is to test for the difference between two or more groups. When an analysis of the data reveals a difference between the levels of any factor, we talk about there being a **main effect**. Let's continue with our example and say there are 10 participants in each of the four groups, for a total of 40 participants. Here's what the results of the analysis look like. This is called a **source table**.

Source	Sum of Squares	df	Mean Square	F	Sig.
Impact	429.025	1	429.025	3.011	**.091**
Gender	3,222.025	1	3,222.025	22.612	**.000**
Impact × Gender	27.225	1	27.225	0.191	**.665**
Error	5,129.700	36	142.492		

Pay special attention to only the *Source* and the *Sig.* columns (whose contents are in boldface). The conclusion we can reach is that at the $p < .05$ level of significance, there is a main effect for gender ($p = .000$), no main effect for impact ($p = .091$), and no interaction between the two main factors ($p = .665$). So, as far as weight loss, it didn't matter whether one was in the high- or low-impact group, but it did matter if one were male or female. And because there was no interaction between the treatment factor and gender, there were no differential effects for treatment across gender. If you plotted the means of these values, you would get something that looks like Figure 14.2.

| **Figure 14.2** | Mean Scores Across Treatments for Males and Females |

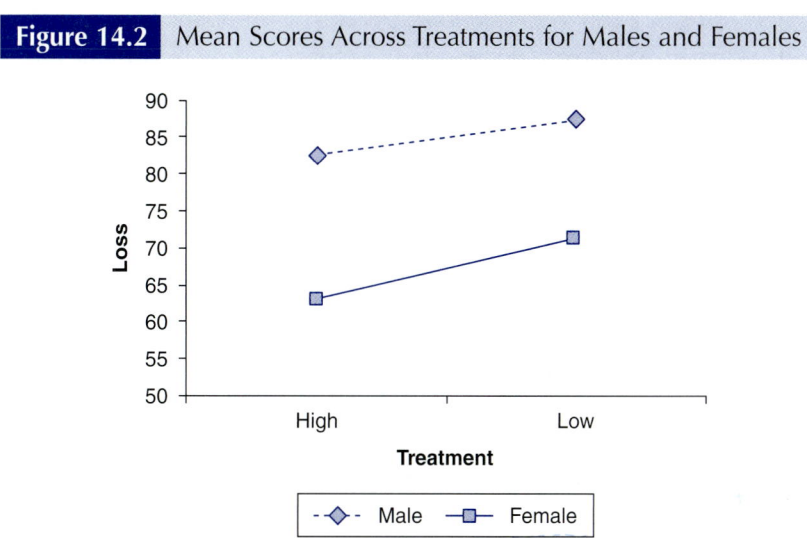

You can see a big difference in distance on the loss axis between males and females (mean score for all males is 85.25 and for females is 67.30), but for each treatment (if you computed the means), you would find there to be little difference (with the mean score across all highs being 73.00 and across all lows being 79.55). Now, of course, this is an analysis of variance, and the variability in the groups does matter, but in this example, you can see the differences between groups (such as males and females) within each factor (such as the treatment) and how they are reflected in the results of the analysis.

EVEN MORE INTERESTING: INTERACTION EFFECTS

Okay—now let's move to the interaction. Let's look at a new source table that indicates men and women are affected differentially across treatments, indicating the presence of an **interaction effect**. And, indeed, you will see some very cool outcomes.

Source	Sums of Squares	df	Mean Square	F	Significance
Treatment	265.225	1	265.225	2.444	**.127**
Gender	207.025	1	207.025	1.908	**.176**
Treatment × Gender	1,050.625	1	1,050.625	9.683	**.004**
Error	3,906.100	36	108.503		
Total	224,321.000	39			

Here, at the $p < .05$ level of significance, there is no main effect for treatment or gender ($p = .127$ and $.176$, respectively), but yikes, there is one for the interaction ($p = .004$), which makes this a very interesting outcome. In effect, weight loss is not affected by whether one is in the high- or low-impact treatment group or whether one is male or female, but the treatment does have an impact differentially on the weight loss of males and females.

Here's what a chart of the mean for each of the four groups looks like.

	Male	Female
High Impact	73.70	79.40
Low Impact	78.80	64.00

And Figure 14.3 shows what the actual means look like (all compliments of the Excel AVERAGE function).

Figure 14.3 Averages Across Treatments for Males and Females

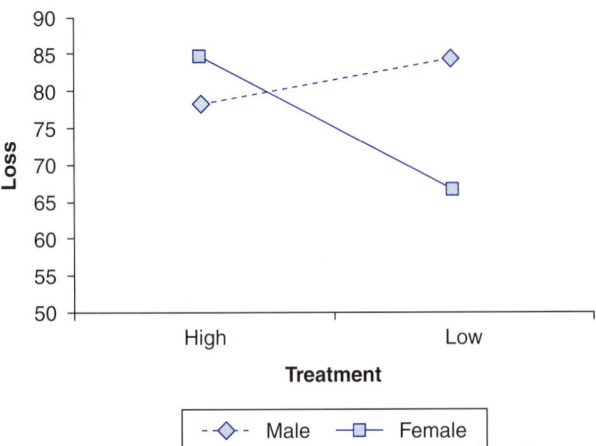

What to make of this? Well, the interpretation here is pretty straightforward, and being as smart as you are, you can recognize that these are the answers to the three questions we listed earlier.

- There is no main effect for type of exercise.
- There is no main effect for gender.
- There is a clear interaction between treatment and gender, which means females lose more weight than males under the high-impact treatment condition, and males lose more weight than females under the low-impact condition.

This is all pretty remarkable stuff. If you didn't know any better (and never read this chapter), you would think that all you have to do is a simple *t*-test between the averages for males and females, and then another simple *t*-test for the averages between those who participated in the high-impact and those who participated in the low-impact treatment. If you did this analysis, you would find nothing (well, not exactly nothing—only no main effects, which is surely a finding of importance). But using the idea of an interaction between main factors, you find out that there is a differential effect—an outcome that would have gone unnoticed otherwise. Indeed, if you can bear the admission, interactions really are the most interesting outcomes in any factorial analysis of variance.

USING THE AMAZING DATA ANALYSIS TOOLS TO COMPUTE THE ANOVA F STATISTIC

Here's a change for you. Throughout *Statistics for People Who (Think They) Hate Statistics, Excel 2016 Edition*, we have provided you with examples of how to perform particular techniques the old-fashioned way (by hand using a calculator) as well as with tools such as Excel.

With the introduction of factorial ANOVA, we are illustrating the analysis using only Excel—nothing manual. Completing a factorial ANOVA using a calculator is no more of an intellectual challenge than using Excel, and it certainly is more laborious. Here are the data we'll use for this example.

High-Impact Male	High-Impact Female	Low-Impact Male	Low-Impact Female
76	65	88	65
78	90	76	67
76	65	76	67
76	90	76	87
76	65	56	78
74	90	76	56
74	90	76	54
76	79	98	56
76	70	88	54
55	90	78	56

Before we get into using the Data Analysis tool for a factorial or two-way ANOVA tool (so don't enter any data yet), first let's state the null and research hypotheses.

There are actually three null hypotheses, shown in Formulas 14.1a, 14.1b, and 14.1c. These state that there is no difference between the means for the two factors and there is no interaction. Here we go.

First for the treatment:

$$H_0: \mu_{high} = \mu_{low} \tag{14.1a}$$

And now for gender:

$$H_0: \mu_{male} = \mu_{female} \tag{14.1b}$$

And now for the interaction between treatment and gender:

$$H_0: \mu_{high \bullet male} = \mu_{high \bullet female} = \mu_{low \bullet female} \neq \mu_{low \bullet male} \tag{14.1c}$$

The research hypotheses, shown in Formulas 14.2a, 14.2b, and 14.2c, state that there is a difference between the means of the groups and there is an interaction. Here they are.

First for the treatment:

$$H_1: \overline{X}_{high} \neq \overline{X}_{low} \tag{14.2a}$$

And now for gender:

$$H_1: \overline{X}_{male} \neq \overline{X}_{female} \qquad (14.2b)$$

And now for the interaction between treatment and gender:

$$H_1: \overline{X}_{high \bullet male} \neq \overline{X}_{high \bullet female} \neq \overline{X}_{low \bullet female} \neq \overline{X}_{low \bullet male} \quad (14.2c)$$

We'll use the Anova: Two-Factor With Replication option, and here are the steps. The above data are available on the book's website (http://edge.sagepub.com/salkindexcel4e) as Chapter 14 Data Set 1, in Appendix C, and in Figure 14.4. If you want to actually follow along using the Data Analysis tools, then be sure that this data file is open, or you can enter the data and save the file.

Figure 14.4 Chapter 14 Data Set 1 for the ANOVA Example

	A	B	C
1		High	Low
2	Male	76	88
3		78	76
4		76	76
5		76	76
6		76	56
7		74	76
8		74	76
9		76	98
10		76	88
11		55	78
12	Female	65	65
13		90	67
14		65	67
15		90	87
16		65	78
17		90	56
18		90	54
19		79	56
20		70	54
21		90	56

1. Click Data → Data Analysis, and you will see the Data Analysis dialog box. Need a brush-up on how to use the Data Analysis tools? See Little Chapter 1b: All You Need to Know About Using the Amazing Data Analysis Tools.

2. Click Anova: Two-Factor With Replication and then click OK, and you will see the Anova: Two-Factor With Replication dialog box, as shown in Figure 14.5.

3. In the Input Range box, enter the range of data you want Excel to use in the computation of the ANOVA. As you can see in Figure 14.4, the data we want to analyze along with the column and row headings are in Cells A1 through C21.

Figure 14.5　The Anova: Two-Factor With Replication Dialog Box

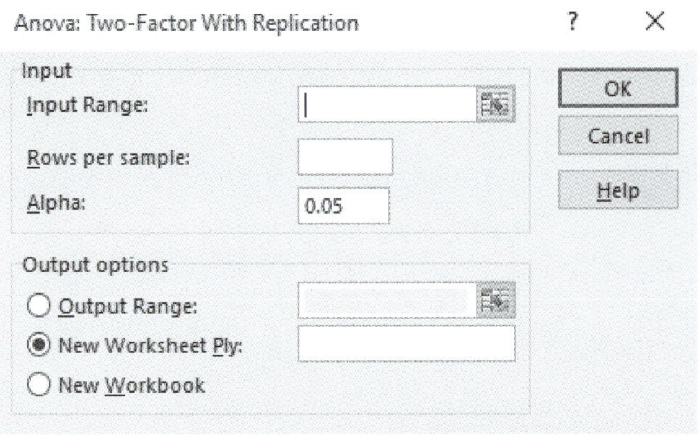

4. Enter the number of rows per sample. This is the same as the number of observations that you have in each cell, which is 10.

5. Enter the level of significance at which you would like the *F* value tested. In this example, we are going to use the $p < .05$ level.

6. Now click the Output Range button in the Output options section of the dialog box and enter the location where you want Excel to return the results of the analysis. In this example, we checked E1. The completed dialog box should appear as shown in Figure 14.6.

7. Click OK, and there it is, folks, the output you see in Figure 14.7. Truly a time to rejoice. (P.S. We did a bit of editing to produce Figure 14.7 by rounding cell contents and such to make the output a bit more attractive and easier to understand.)

And, as you can see, none of the main effects are significant, but the interaction is.

Figure 14.6	The Completed ANOVA Dialog Box

Figure 14.7	A Completed (and Tidied Up) Two-Way ANOVA Using Excel's Data Analysis Tools

	A	B	C	D	E	F	G	H	I	J	K
1		High	Low		Anova: Two-Factor With Replication						
2	Male	76	88								
3		78	76		SUMMARY	High	Low	Total			
4		76	76		*Male*						
5		76	76		Count	10	10	20			
6		76	56		Sum	737	788	1525			
7		74	76		Average	73.7	78.8	76.25			
8		74	76		Variance	44.46	121.96	85.67			
9		76	98								
10		76	88		*Female*						
11		55	78		Count	10	10	20			
12	Female	65	65		Sum	794	640	1434			
13		90	67		Average	79.40	64	71.70			
14		65	67		Variance	141.38	126.22	189.17			
15		90	87								
16		65	78		*Total*						
17		90	56		Count	20	20				
18		90	54		Sum	1531	1428				
19		79	56		Average	76.55	71.40				
20		70	54		Variance	96.58	175.20				
21		90	56								
22											
23					ANOVA						
24					*Source of Variation*	SS	df	MS	F	P-value	F crit
25					Sample	207.03	1	207.03	1.91	0.18	4.11
26					Columns	265.22	1	265.22	2.44	0.13	4.11
27					Interaction	1050.63	1	1050.63	9.68	0.00	4.11
28					Within	3906.10	36	108.50			
29											
30					Total	5428.98	39				

In this tool in the Data Analysis tools, Excel does not label the sources of variance but instead uses general terms. So, in this example, "Sample" represents gender, "Columns" represents level of impact, and "Interaction" represents the interaction between level of impact and gender.

The analysis that you are learning here is a *univariate* analysis of variance. This is an analysis that looks at only one dependent or outcome variable—in this case, weight loss score. If we had more than one dependent variable as part of the research question (such as attitude toward eating), then the analysis would be a multivariate analysis of variance, which not only looks at group differences but also controls for the relationship between the dependent variables. More about these types of experiments in Chapter 18.

REAL-WORLD STATS

You've seen the news: Certain disorders, such as autism spectrum disorders and attention deficit hyperactivity disorder, have been increasing in frequency. This trend may be because of changing diagnostic criteria, or the occurrence of these disorders may actually be increasing. In any case, certain behaviors and outcomes need to be accurately measured as a first step in considering such diagnoses.

That's what this study is all about. Researchers used measures of behavioral inhibition to investigate the factorial validity, ecological validity, and reliability of five performance-based measures of behavioral inhibition in a sample of seventy 3-, 4-, and 5-year-old children. A 2 × 3 factorial analysis of variance using sex and age-group (two factors) as independent variables showed significant main effects for sex and age and a nonsignificant interaction. Some of the measures correlated with teacher rating while others did not, leading the researchers to conclude that some of the measures of behavioral inhibition might be useful but others need further exploration.

Want to know more? Go online or go to the library, and look for . . .

Floyd, R. G., & Kirby, E. A. (2001). Psychometric properties of measures of behavioral inhibition with preschool-age children: Implications for assessment of children at risk for ADHD. *Journal of Attention Disorders, 5,* 79–91.

You've successfully completed Chapters 9 through 14, which deal with differences between means in a variety of scenarios. Congratulations! To tell the truth, these are tools that are used in many, many analyses in the social and behavioral sciences. So, you are very well equipped to go out into the world and call yourself a novice statistician. But there's more! Now that we are done, done, done with testing differences between means, we'll move on to examine the significance of correlations, or the relationship between two variables.

TIME TO PRACTICE

1. When would you use a factorial ANOVA rather than a simple ANOVA to test the significance of the difference between the averages of two or more groups?

2. Create a 2 × 3 experimental design that would lend itself to a factorial ANOVA.

3. Using Excel and the data in Chapter 14 Data Set 2, complete the analysis and interpret the results. It is a 2 × 3 experiment: There are two levels of severity, where Level 1 is severe and Level 2 is mild, and there are three levels of treatment, where Level 1 is Drug #1, Level 2 is Drug #2, and Level 3 is Placebo. This is an ANOVA with replication because each participant received all three levels of treatment, which are represented by the columns of data; severity is represented by the rows (or "Sample" as the Excel Data Analysis tools feature likes to call it).

4. The data in Chapter 14 Data Set 3 show the results of an experiment in which three levels of nutrition education and two levels of dietary intervention were tested to see their effects on a 10-point scale, with 10 indicating the highest level of healthy eating. Answer these questions.

   a. Did the intervention work? That is, did the intervention affect healthy eating scores?

   b. Does level of nutrition education matter?

   c. Is there an interaction between the main factors?

   d. And your genius conclusion is . . . ? (One sentence should do it.)

5. In Chapter 14, Data Set 4, you can find a 3 × 4 design with three levels of participation in after-school activities and four levels of GPA (1st, 2nd, 3rd, or 4th quartile). The outcome is success (as measured by peer rating) 4 years after graduation, with a score of 4 indicating the greatest success. What's more important to postgraduate success: participation in after-school activities or one's GPA?

15

Cousins or Just Good Friends?

Testing Relationships and the Significance of the Correlation Coefficient

Difficulty Scale ☺ ☺ ☺ ☺ (easy—you don't even have to figure anything out!)

How much Excel? 📊 📊 (some)

INTRODUCTION TO TESTING THE SIGNIFICANCE OF THE CORRELATION COEFFICIENT

In his article on his investigation of the relationship between the quality of a marriage and the quality of the relationship between a parent and a child, Daniel Shek tells us that there are at least two possibilities. First, a poor marriage might enhance parent–child relationships. This is because parents who are dissatisfied with their marriage might substitute their relationship with their children for emotional gratification. Or, according to the *spillover hypothesis*, a poor marriage might damage the parent–child relationship by setting the stage for increased difficulty in parenting children.

Shek examined the link between marital quality and parent–child relationships in 378 Chinese married couples over a 2-year period. He found that higher levels of marital quality were related to higher levels of parent–child relationships; this was found for concurrent measures (at the present time) as well as longitudinal measures (over time). He also found that the strength of the relationship between parents and children was the same for both mothers and fathers. This is an obvious example of how using the correlation coefficient gives us the information we need to make a decision about whether sets of variables are related to one another. Shek computed a whole bunch of different correlations across mothers and fathers at both Time 1 and Time 2, but all with the same purpose: to see if there was a significant correlation between the variables. Remember that this does not say anything about the causal nature of the relationship, only that the variables are associated with one another.

Want to know more? Check out Shek, D. T. L. (1998). Linkage between marital quality and parent–child relationship: A longitudinal study in the Chinese culture. *Journal of Family Issues, 19,* 687–704.

The Path to Wisdom and Knowledge

In the flowchart shown in Figure 15.1, follow the highlighted sequence of steps to select the appropriate test statistic: the *t*-test for the correlation coefficient.

1. The relationship between variables, and not the difference between groups, is being examined.
2. Only two variables are involved.
3. The appropriate test statistic to use is the *t*-test for the correlation coefficient.

COMPUTING THE TEST STATISTIC

Here's something you'll probably be pleased to learn: The correlation coefficient can act as its own test statistic. This makes things much easier because you don't have to compute any test statistics,

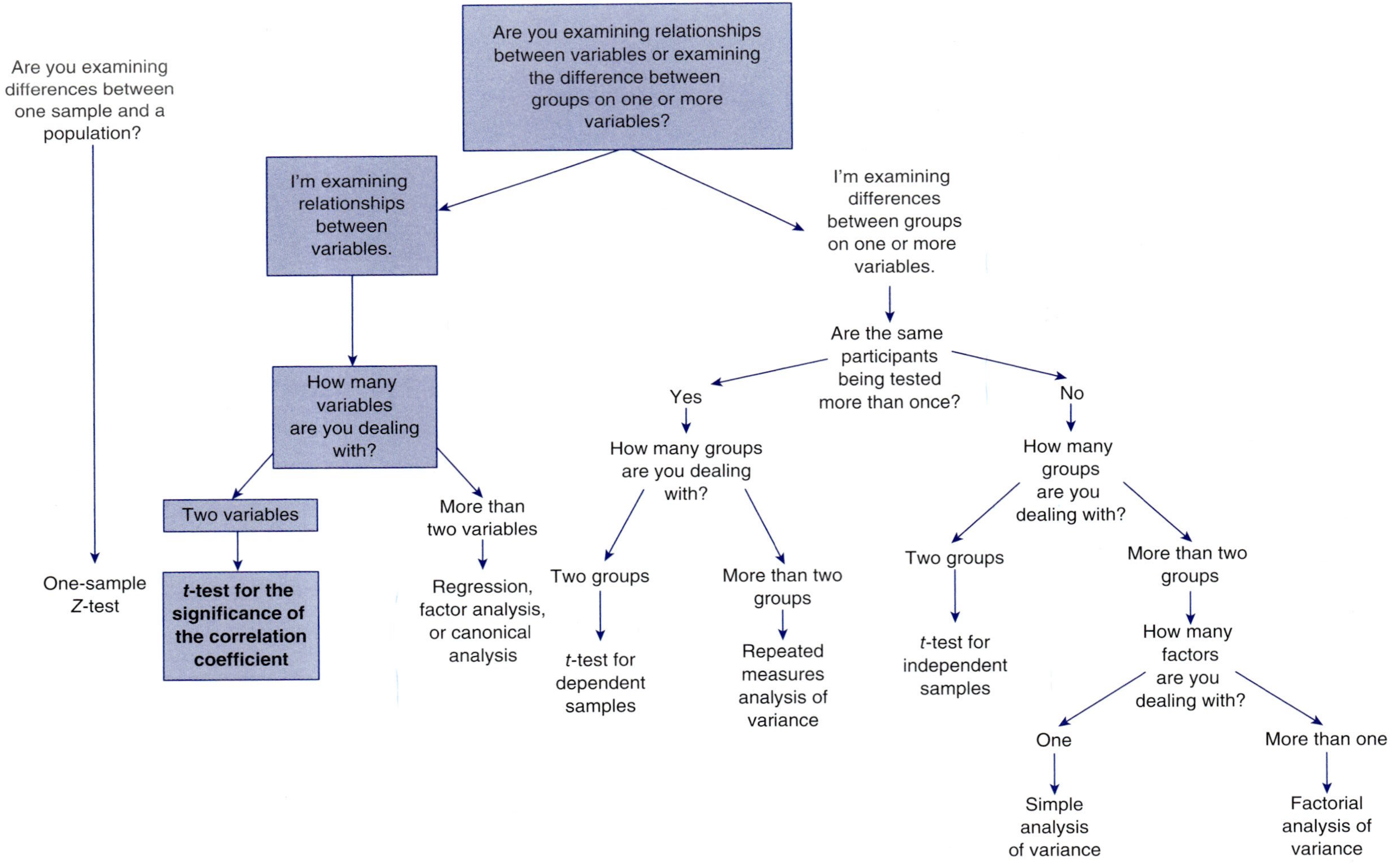

Figure 15.1 Determining That a *t*-Test for the Correlation Coefficient Is the Correct Test Statistic

and examining the significance is very easy indeed. Let's use, as an example, the following data that examine the relationship between two variables, the quality of marriage (the higher the score, the higher the quality) and the quality of parent–child relationships (the higher the score, the higher the quality).

Quality of Marriage	Quality of Parent–Child Relationship
76	43
81	33
78	23
76	34
76	31
78	51
76	56
78	43
98	44
88	45
76	32
66	33
44	28
67	39
65	31
59	38
87	21
77	27
79	43
85	46
68	41
76	41
77	48
98	56
99	55
98	45
87	68
67	54
78	33

You can use Formula 5.1 from Chapter 5 to compute the Pearson correlation coefficient. When you do, you will find that $r = .393$. Now let's go through the steps of testing the value for significance and making a decision as to what the value means.

You already know about the use of the CORREL function, as well as the Correlation tool in the Data Analysis tools, and how easy they are to use to compute the correlation coefficient. Excel offers one other correlation tool that you should know about, and that's the **PEARSON** function, which calculates the correlation coefficient much as do the CORREL function and the Correlation tool. For your purposes, all three of these compute the same value and are interchangeable. When you take Stats II, you may want to begin worrying about how CORREL and PEARSON are different (and the answer is, in no significant way).

Here are the famous eight steps in the computation of the t-test statistic:

1. *State the null and research hypotheses.* The null hypothesis states that there is no relationship between the quality of the marriage and the quality of the relationship between parents and children. The research hypothesis is a two-tailed, nondirectional research hypothesis because it posits that there is a relationship between the two variables but the direction is not important for the purposes of testing the hypothesis. Remember that correlations can be positive (direct) or negative (indirect) and the most important characteristic of a correlation coefficient is its absolute value or size and not its sign (positive or negative).

   The null hypothesis is shown in Formula 15.1:

   $$H_0: \rho_{xy} = 0 \tag{15.1}$$

   The Greek letter ρ, or rho, represents the population estimate of the correlation coefficient.

   The research hypothesis (shown in Formula 15.2) states that there is a relationship between the two values and that the relationship differs from a value of 0.

   $$H_1: r_{xy} \neq 0 \tag{15.2}$$

One tail or two? It's pretty easy to conceptualize what a one-tailed versus a two-tailed test is when it comes to differences between means (remember, we discussed this in Chapter 7). And it may even be easy for you to understand a two-tailed test of the correlation coefficient (where any difference from zero is what's tested). But what about a one-tailed test? It's really just as easy. A directional test of the research hypothesis that there is a relationship posits that relationship as being either direct (positive) or indirect (negative). So, if you think that there is a positive correlation between two variables, then the test is one-tailed. Similarly, if you hypothesize that there is a negative correlation between two variables, the test is one-tailed as well. It's only when you don't predict the direction of the relationship that the test is two-tailed. Got it?

2. *Set the level of risk (or the level of significance or Type I error) associated with the null hypothesis.* We'll use a level of risk or Type I error or level of significance of .05. This is up to us (meaning you!).

3. and 4. *Select the appropriate test statistic.* Using the flow-chart shown in Figure 15.1, we determined that the appropriate test is for the correlation coefficient. In this instance, we do not need to compute a test statistic because the sample r value ($r_{xy} = .393$) is, for our purposes, the test statistic.

5. *Determine the value needed for rejection of the null hypothesis using the appropriate table of critical values for the particular statistic.* Table B.4 in Appendix B lists the critical values for the correlation coefficient. Our first task is to determine the degrees of freedom (df), which approximates the sample size. For this particular test statistic, the degrees of freedom are $n - 2$, or $29 - 2 = 27$, where n is equal to the number of pairs used to compute the correlation coefficient. This is the degrees of freedom only for this test statistic and not necessarily for any other.

Using this number (27), the level of risk you are willing to take (.05), and a two-tailed test (because there is no direction to the research hypothesis), we calculate that the critical value is .381 (using $df = 25$ because it is more conservative [and closer]). So, at the .05 level and with 27 degrees of freedom for a two-tailed test, the value needed for rejection of the null hypothesis is .381.

 Okay, we cheated a little. Actually, you can compute a *t* value (just as for the test of the difference between means) for the significance of the correlation coefficient. The formula is not any more difficult than any other you have dealt with up to now, but you won't see it here. The point is that some smart statisticians have computed the critical *r* value for different sample sizes (and, likewise, degrees of freedom) for one- and two-tailed tests at different levels of risk (.01, .05), as you see in Table B.4. But, if you are reading a journal article and see that a correlation was tested using a *t* value, you'll know why.

6. *Compare the obtained value and the critical value.* The obtained value is .393, and the critical value for rejection of the null hypothesis that the two variables are not related is .381.

7. and 8. *Make a decision!* Now comes our decision. If the obtained value (or the value of the test statistic) is more extreme than the critical value (or the tabled value), the null hypothesis cannot be accepted. If the obtained value does not exceed the critical value, the null hypothesis is the most attractive explanation.

In this case, the obtained value (.393) does exceed the critical value (.381)—it is extreme enough for us to say that the relationship between the two variables (quality of marriage and quality of parent–child relationships) is due to something other than chance.

So How Do I Interpret $r_{(28)}$ = .393, p < .05?

- *r* represents the test statistic that was used.
- 28 is the number of degrees of freedom.
- .393 is the obtained value using the formula we showed you in Chapter 5. You can also use the CORREL function, the PEARSON function, or the Correlation tool in the Data Analysis tools.
- *p* < .05 (the really important part of this little phrase) indicates that the probability is less than 5% on any one test of the null hypothesis that the relationship between the two variables is due to chance alone. Because we defined .05 as our criterion for deciding the research hypothesis is more attractive than the null hypothesis, our conclusion is that there is a significant relationship between the two variables. This means that as the

level of marital quality increases, so does the level of quality of the parent–child relationship. Similarly, as the level of marital quality decreases, so does the level of quality of the parent–child relationship.

Remember way back in Chapter 6 that we used correlations to assess the reliability and the validity of different types of measurement tools? Correlations are also used in a variety of more sophisticated statistical techniques that fall under the general category of data reduction (such as factor analysis). So, if you don't get it already, correlations (even if they can sometimes be overinterpreted—remember the ice cream and crime thing?) are very useful and often used.

Causes and Associations (Again!)

You'd have thought that you heard enough of this already, but this is so important that we really can't emphasize it enough. So, we'll emphasize it again. Just because two variables are related to one another (as in the above example), that does not mean one causes the other. In other words, having a terrific marriage of the highest quality in no way ensures that the parent–child relationship will be of a high quality as well. These two variables may be correlated because they both reflect some traits that might make a person a good spouse and also a good parent (patience, understanding, willingness to sacrifice), but it's certainly possible to see how someone could be a good spouse and have a terrible relationship with his or her children.

Remember the crime and ice cream example from Chapter 5? It's the same here. Just because things are related and share something in common has no bearing on whether a causal relationship exists between the two.

Significance Versus Meaningfulness (Again, Again!)

In Chapter 5, we reviewed the importance of the use of the coefficient of determination for understanding the meaningfulness of the correlation coefficient. You may remember that you square the correlation coefficient to determine the amount of variance in one variable accounted for by another variable. In Chapter 9, we also went over the general issue of significance versus meaningfulness, and in Chapter 11, we went over it again with respect to effect size.

But we should discuss this topic again. Even if a correlation coefficient is significant (as was the case in the example in this chapter), it does not mean that the amount of variance accounted for is meaningful. For example, in this case, the coefficient of determination for a simple Pearson correlation value of .393 is equal to .154, indicating that 15.4% of the variance is accounted for and a whopping 84.6% of the variance is not. It leaves lots of room for further explanation, doesn't it?

So, even though we know that there is a positive relationship between the quality of a marriage and the quality of a parent–child relationship and they tend to "go" together, the *relatively* weak correlation of .393 indicates that lots of other things going on in that relationship may be important as well. So, we can apply a popular saying to statistics: "What you see is not always what you get."

 # REAL-WORLD STATS

With all the attention given to social media (in the social media, of course), it's interesting to look at how researchers evaluate "social" well-being in college students and even more so when the students live in a different cultural context.

This study investigated the relationship (yes, correlations) between five personality domains and social well-being among 236 Iranian students. Correlations showed some relationship between personality factors and dimensions of social well-being. For example, neuroticism was negatively related to social acceptance, social contribution, and social coherence. Conscientiousness was positively related to social contribution. Openness was positively related to social contribution and social coherence, and agreeableness was related to social acceptance and social contribution. Male students scored significantly higher than female students on social well-being. The researchers discuss these findings in light of cultural differences between countries and the general relationship between personality traits and well-being. Interesting stuff!

Want to know more? Go online or go to the library, and look for . . .

Joshanloo, M., Rastegar, P., & Bakhshi, A. (2012). The Big Five personality domains as predictors of social well-being in Iranian university students. *Journal of Social and Personal Relationships, 29,* 639–660.

SUMMARY

Correlations are powerful tools that point out the direction of a relationship and help us to understand what two different outcomes share with one another. Remember that correlations only help you talk about associations and never help you talk about causality.

TIME TO PRACTICE

1. Given the following information, use Table B.4 in Appendix B to determine whether the correlations are significant and how you would interpret the results.

   a. The correlation between speed and strength for 20 women is .567. Test these results at the .01 level using a one-tailed test.

   b. The correlation between the number correct on a math test and the time it takes to complete the test is −.45. Test whether this correlation is significant for 80 children at the .05 level of significance. Choose either a one- or two-tailed test and justify your choice.

   c. The correlation between number of friends and grade point average (GPA) for 50 adolescents is .37. Is this significant at the .05 level for a two-tailed test?

2. Use the data in Chapter 15 Data Set 1 to answer the questions below. Do the analysis manually or using the Data Analysis tools.

   a. Compute the correlation between motivation and GPA.

   b. Test for the significance of the correlation coefficient at the .05 level using a two-tailed test.

   c. The more highly you are motivated, the more you will study—true or false? Which did you select and why?

3. Discuss the general idea that just because two things are correlated, one does not necessarily cause the other. Provide an example (other than ice cream and crime!).

4. For review, go to Chapter 15 Data Set 2 and use the CORREL or PEARSON functions to calculate the correlation between number of books in the home and general educational level (or years of school completed, with 12 years being equal to graduating from high school). So, it's true that if you want people to attend graduate school and get a PhD, you should just deliver thousands of books to their doorstep, right?

5. Chapter 15 Data Set 3 includes data about level of risk for juvenile detention (from 1 to 5 with 5 being high risk), number of at-risk factors (such as poverty, truancy from school), and progress for 25 juveniles, measured on a scale from 1 through 100, 10 years after the introduction of a program. What conclusion might you draw?

16 Predicting Who'll Win the Super Bowl

Using Linear Regression

Difficulty Scale ☺ (as hard as they get!)

How much Excel? 📊 📊 📊 📊 📊 (a ton)

WHAT YOU'LL LEARN ABOUT IN THIS CHAPTER

✦ How prediction works and how it can be used in the social and behavioral sciences

✦ How and why linear regression works when predicting one variable from another

✦ How to judge the accuracy of predictions

✦ How to use the INTERCEPT and SLOPE functions

✦ How to use the always cool Data Analysis Regression tool

✦ What multiple regression is and why it is useful

WHAT IS PREDICTION ALL ABOUT?

Here's the scoop. Not only can you compute the degree to which two variables are related to one another (by computing a correlation coefficient, as we did in Chapter 5 and also just talked about when we dealt with significance and correlations in Chapter 15), but you can also use these correlations as the basis for the prediction of the value of one variable from the value of another. This is a very special case of how correlations can be used, and it is a very powerful tool for social and behavioral sciences researchers.

The basic idea is to use a set of previously collected data (such as data on variables *X* and *Y*), calculate the degree to which these variables are correlated with one another, and then use that correlation and the knowledge of X to predict Y. Sound difficult? It's not really, especially once you see it illustrated.

For example, a researcher collects data on final high school grade point average (GPA) and first-year college GPA for 400 students in their freshman year at the state university. He computes the correlation between the two variables. Then, he uses the techniques you'll learn about later in this chapter to take a *different* set of high school GPAs and (knowing the relationship between high school GPA and first-year college GPA from the previous set of students) predict what first-year GPA should be for a new sample of 400 students. Pretty nifty, huh?

Here's another example. A group of teachers is interested in finding out how well retention works. That is, do children who are retained in kindergarten (and not passed on to first grade) eventually do better in first grade once they get there? Once again, if these teachers know the correlation between being retained and first-grade performance for one set of students, they can apply this correlation to a new set of students and predict first-grade performance based on kindergarten performance. How does this work? Easy. Data are collected on past events (such as the existing relationship between two variables) and then applied to a future event given knowledge of only one variable. It's easier than you think.

The higher the absolute value of the correlation coefficient, the more accurately we are predicting one variable from the other based on the correlation between the two. This makes sense, because the more two variables share in common, the more you know about the second variable from your knowledge of the first variable. And you may already surmise that when the correlation is perfect (+1.0 or −1.0), the prediction is perfect as well. If $r_{XY} = -1.0$ or +1.0 and you know the value of X, then you also know the exact value of Y. Likewise, if $r_{YX} = -1.0$ or +1.0 and you know the value of Y, then you also know the exact value of X. Either way works just fine.

What we'll do in this chapter is go through the process of using linear regression to predict a Y score from an X score. We'll begin by discussing the general logic that underlies prediction, then go to a review of some simple line-drawing skills, and, finally, discuss the prediction process using specific examples.

THE LOGIC OF PREDICTION

Before we dig into the calculations and show you how correlations are used for prediction, let's create the argument for why and how prediction works. Then, we will continue with the example of predicting college GPA from high school GPA.

Prediction is an activity that computes future outcomes from present ones. When we want to predict one variable from another, we need to first compute the correlation between the two variables. Table 16.1 shows the data we will be using in this example. Figure 16.1 shows the scatterplot (see Chapter 5) of the two variables that are being computed.

| Table 16.1 | Data Set of Final High School GPA and First-Year College GPA |

High School GPA	First-Year College GPA
3.5	3.3
2.5	2.2
4.0	3.5
3.8	2.7
2.8	3.5
1.9	2.0
3.2	3.1
3.7	3.4
2.7	1.9
3.3	3.7

To predict college GPA from high school GPA, we have to create a **regression equation** and use that to plot what is called a **regression line**. A regression line reflects our best guess as to what score on the Y variable (college GPA) would be predicted by a score on the X variable (high school GPA). You'll learn shortly how to draw this line, shown in Figure 16.2.

What does this regression line represent?

First, it's the regression of the Y variable on the X variable. In other words, Y (college GPA) is being predicted from X (high school GPA). This regression line is also called the **line of best fit**. The line best fits these data because it minimizes the distance between each individual predicted point and the regression line. For example, if you took all of these points and tried to find the line that best fits them all at once, the line you would arrive at is the one you see in Figure 16.2.

Figure 16.1 Scatterplot of High School GPA and College GPA

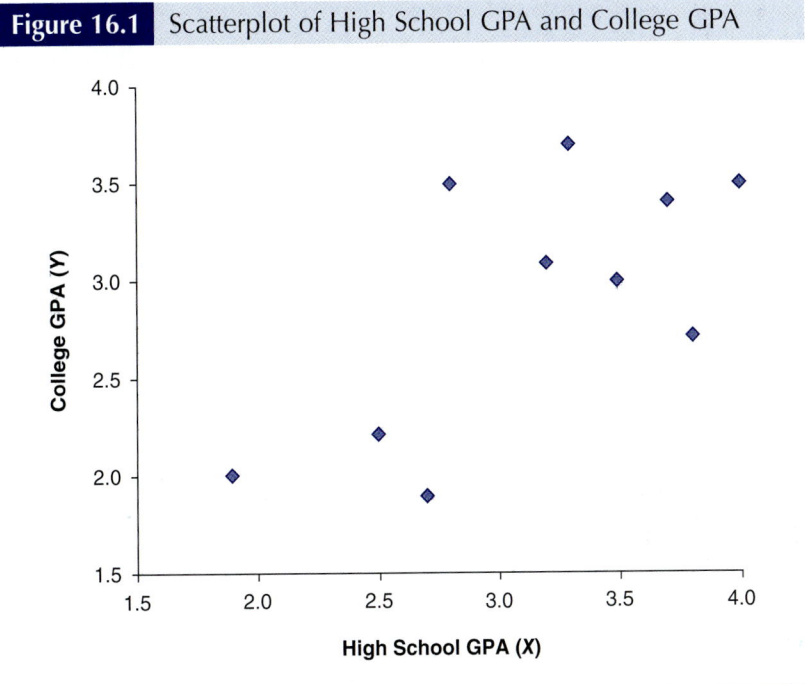

Figure 16.2 Regression Line of College GPA (*Y*) on High School GPA (*X*)

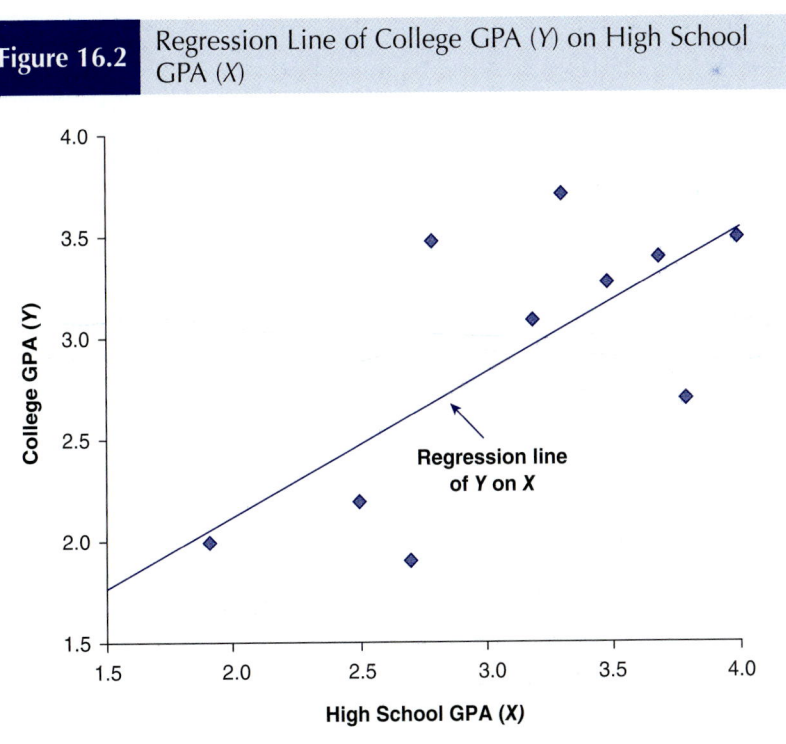

Second, it's the line that represents our best guess at, in this case, estimating what college GPA would be given each student's high school GPA. For example, if high school GPA is 3.0, then college GPA should be around (remember, this is only an eyeball prediction) 2.8. Take a look at Figure 16.3 to see how we did this. We located the predictor value (3.0) on the *x*-axis, then drew a perpendicular line from the *x*-axis to the regression line, and then drew a horizontal line to the *y*-axis and *estimated* what the value would be.

Figure 16.3　Estimating College GPA Given High School GPA

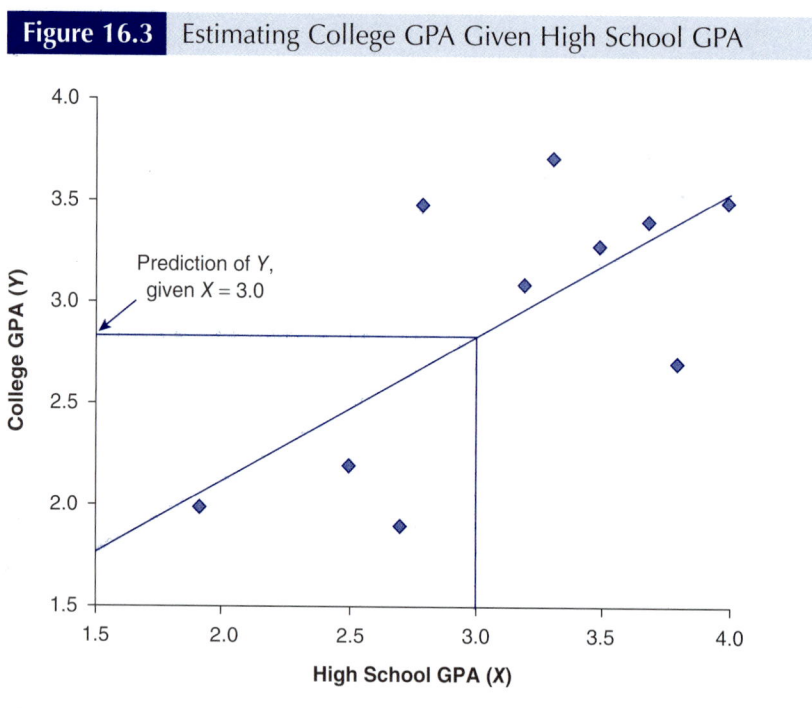

Third, the distance between each individual data point and the regression line is the **error in prediction**—a direct reflection of the correlation between the two variables. For example, if you look at data point (3.3, 3.7), marked in Figure 16.4, you can see that this (*X*, *Y*) data point is above the regression line. The distance between that point and the line is the error in prediction, because if the prediction were perfect, then all the predicted points would fall where? Right on the regression or prediction line. You might think, at first glance, that the line should be drawn *perpendicular* to the regression line. Although that seems to make sense, it actually would not give you a true reading of the amount of error because the error can be computed based only on the distance of the data point from the *axes*, not the line.

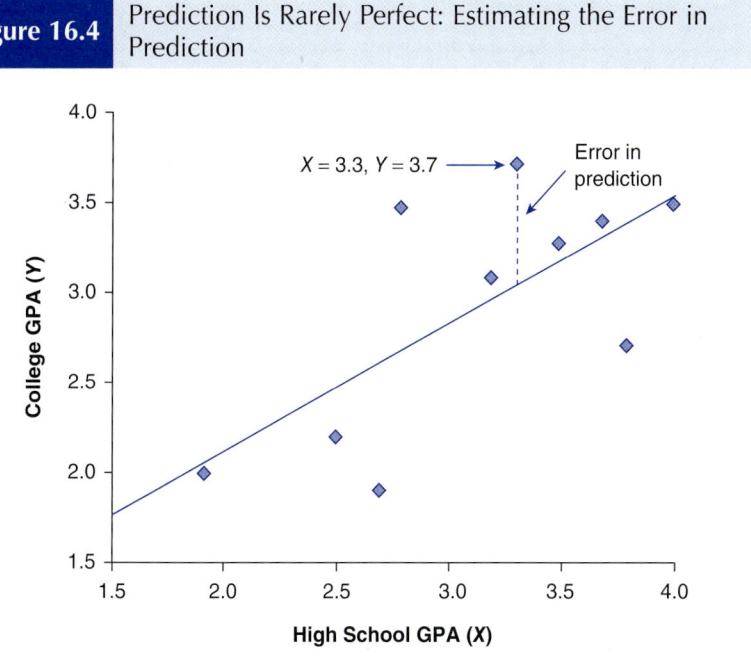

| Figure 16.4 | Prediction Is Rarely Perfect: Estimating the Error in Prediction |

Fourth, if the correlation were perfect (and the scale for the *x*- and *y*-axes were the same), all the data points would align themselves along a 45° angle, and the regression line would pass through each point (just as we said above).

Given the regression line, we can use it to predict any future score. That's what we'll do right now—create the line and then make some predictions.

DRAWING THE WORLD'S BEST LINE (FOR YOUR DATA)

The simplest way to think of a prediction is that it determines the score on one variable (which we'll call *Y*—the **criterion** or **dependent variable**) from the value of another score (which we'll call *X*—the **predictor** or **independent variable**).

The way that we find out how well *X* can predict *Y* is through the creation of the regression line. This line is created from data that have already been collected. The equations are then used to predict scores using a new value for *X*, the predictor variable.

Formula 16.1 shows the general formula for the regression line, which may look familiar because you probably used it in your high school and college math courses. It's the same as the formula for any straight line.

$$Y' = bX + a, \qquad\qquad (16.1)$$

where

Y'   is the predicted score of Y based on a known value of X;

b   is the slope, or direction, of the line;

a   is the point at which the line crosses the y-axis (also called the intercept); and

X   is the score being used as the predictor.

Let's use the same data shown in Table 16.1 and throw in a few more calculations that we will need.

	X	Y	X²	Y²	XY
	3.5	3.3	12.25	10.89	11.55
	2.5	2.2	6.25	4.84	5.50
	4.0	3.5	16.00	12.25	14.00
	3.8	2.7	15.44	7.29	10.26
	2.8	3.5	7.84	12.25	9.80
	1.9	2.0	3.61	4.00	3.80
	3.2	3.1	10.24	9.61	9.92
	3.7	3.4	13.69	11.56	12.58
	2.7	1.9	7.29	3.61	5.13
	3.3	3.7	10.89	13.69	12.21
Total	31.4	29.3	102.50	89.99	94.75

Here's what the totals in the bottom row mean:

ΣX, or the sum of all the X values, is 31.4.

ΣY, or the sum of all the Y values, is 29.3.

ΣX^2, or the sum of each X value squared, is 102.50.

ΣY^2, or the sum of each Y value squared, is 89.99.

ΣXY, or the sum of the products of X and Y, is 94.75.

Formula 16.2 is used to compute the slope of the regression line (*b* in the equation for a straight line):

$$b = \frac{\Sigma XY - (\Sigma X \Sigma Y / n)}{\Sigma X^2 - [(\Sigma X)^2 / n]} \qquad (16.2)$$

Using this formula, you can compute the value for *b*, the slope of the line, in our example (Formula 16.3).

$$b = \frac{94.75 - \left(31.4 \times \dfrac{29.3}{10}\right)}{102.5 - \left(\dfrac{31.4^2}{10}\right)} \qquad (16.3)$$

$$b = \frac{2.75}{3.904} = 0.705$$

Formula 16.4 is used to compute the point at which the line crosses the *y*-axis (*a* is the *y*-intercept in the equation for a straight line):

$$a = \frac{\Sigma Y - b\Sigma X}{n}, \qquad (16.4)$$

where

n is the number of subjects.

In Formula 16.5, you can see the computed value for *a* for our data.

$$a = \frac{29.3 - (0.705 \times 31.4)}{10} \qquad (16.5)$$

$$a = \frac{7.163}{10} = 0.716$$

Now, if we go back and substitute *b* and *a* into the equation for a straight line (*Y'* = *bX* + *a*), we come up with the final regression line in Formula 16.6:

$$Y' = 0.705X + 0.7163 \qquad (16.6)$$

Why the *Y'* and not just a plain *Y*? Remember, we are using *X* to predict *Y*, with the predicted value of *Y* noted as *Y'* (read: **Y prime**) being the predicted and not the actual value of *Y*. So, now that we have this equation, what can we do with it? Predict *Y*, what else?

For example, let's say that a recent high school graduate's GPA equals 2.8 (or *X* = 2.8). If we substitute the value of 2.8 into the equation, we get Formula 16.7:

$$Y' = 0.705(2.8) + 0.7163 = 2.69 \qquad (16.7)$$

So, 2.69 is the predicted value of *Y* (or *Y'*) given *X* is equal to 2.8. Now, for any *X* score, we can easily and quickly compute a predicted *Y* score.

You can use this formula and the known values to compute predicted values. That's most of what we just talked about. But you can also plot a regression line to show how well the scores (what you are trying to predict) actually fit the data from which you are predicting. Take a look at Figure 16.2, which is a plot of the High School–College GPA data we showed you earlier and includes a trend line (which is another name for the regression line). How did we get this line? Easy. We used the same charting skills you learned in Chapter 5 to create a scatterplot; then we selected Trend Line from the Chart option and selected Linear. Poof! Done!

You can see the trend is positive (in that the line has a positive slope) and that the correlation is .6835—very positive. And you can see that the data points do not align directly on the line, but they are pretty close, which indicates that there is a relatively small amount of error.

Not all lines that are the best fit for a bunch of data points are straight. Rather, they could be curvilinear, reflecting the curvilinear relationship we discussed in Chapter 5. For example, the relationship between anxiety and performance is such that when people are not at all anxious or very anxious, they don't perform very well. But if they're moderately anxious, then performance can be maximized. The relationship between these two variables is curvilinear, and the prediction of *Y* from *X* takes that into account. But having data that are curvilinear calls for a bump up in the complexity of the explanation and use of different analytic tools, all of which is best left for your next course.

A lot of functions deal with linear regression of some sort, such as **TREND, LINEST, FREQUENCY, STEYX,** and **FORECAST** (you can use Excel Help [press the F1 key] to find out what they do and how to use them). We're going to deal only with the two that best reflect what we have discussed throughout this chapter. The first is **SLOPE,** which computes the slope of the line or what was named b in the equation $Y' = bX + a$, and the second is **INTERCEPT,** which will compute a in the same equation or the point where the line crosses the y-axis.

And Now . . . Using Excel's SLOPE Function

The SLOPE function computes the slope of the line, or what we called b in the linear regression equation we discussed earlier. To compute SLOPE, follow these steps:

1. We're using the data you see in Figure 16.5, which represent two sets of scores.

Figure 16.5 Data for the Regression Example

	A High School GPA	B First Year College GPA
1		
2	3.5	3.3
3	2.5	2.2
4	4.0	3.5
5	3.8	2.7
6	2.8	3.5
7	1.9	2.0
8	3.2	3.1
9	3.7	3.4
10	2.7	1.9
11	3.3	3.7

2. Select the cell into which you want to enter the SLOPE function. In this example, we are going to place the value in Cell B13. We also placed a label in Cell A13 to keep everything clear and understandable.

3. Click Formulas → More Functions → Statistical → SLOPE, and you will see the Function Arguments dialog box, as shown in Figure 16.6.

Figure 16.6	The SLOPE Function Arguments Dialog Box

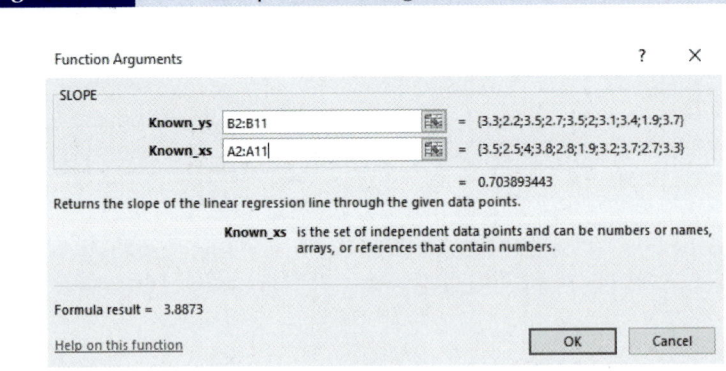

4. Enter the range of cells for the Known_ys (the variable you want to predict), which is college GPA or the *Y* variable. Here this range is Cells B2 through B11, as you saw in Figure 16.5.

5. Enter the range of cells for the Known_xs (the variable from which you are predicting), which is high school GPA or the *X* variable. Here this range is Cells A2 through A11. The completed dialog box should look like the one in Figure 16.7.

Figure 16.7	The Completed Dialog Box for the SLOPE Function

6. Click OK, and you will see the slope of the best-fitting regression line in Cell B13, as shown in Figure 16.8. Take note of the entire function, which appears in the formula bar.

Figure 16.8	The Completed SLOPE Function

| B13 | ▼ | ⋮ | × | ✓ | *fx* | =SLOPE(B2:B11,A2:A11) |

	A	B	C	D	E
1	High School GPA	First Year College GPA			
2	3.5	3.3			
3	2.5	2.2			
4	4.0	3.5			
5	3.8	2.7			
6	2.8	3.5			
7	1.9	2.0			
8	3.2	3.1			
9	3.7	3.4			
10	2.7	1.9			
11	3.3	3.7			
12					
13	Slope(b)	0.7039			

We are sure that you have noticed that there is a difference between the values that Excel provides for the slope and the intercept and the values worked manually earlier in this chapter. The simple (and advanced) answer is that Excel uses many more decimal spaces and is, perhaps (and only perhaps), more precise. The values shown are very close together and negligible when it comes to making decisions as to what the values substantively represent.

And Now . . . Using Excel's INTERCEPT Function

The INTERCEPT function computes the location where the regression line crosses the y-axis, or the *a* in the regression equation we discussed earlier.

To compute INTERCEPT, follow these steps:

1. We're using the same data as we used to illustrate the calculation of SLOPE (see Figure 16.5).

2. Select the cell into which you want to enter the INTERCEPT function. In this example, we are going to place the value in Cell B14. We also placed a label in Cell A14 to keep everything clear and understandable.

3. Click Formulas → More Functions → Statistical → INTERCEPT, and you will see the Function Arguments dialog box, as shown in Figure 16.9.

Figure 16.9   The INTERCEPT Function Arguments Dialog Box

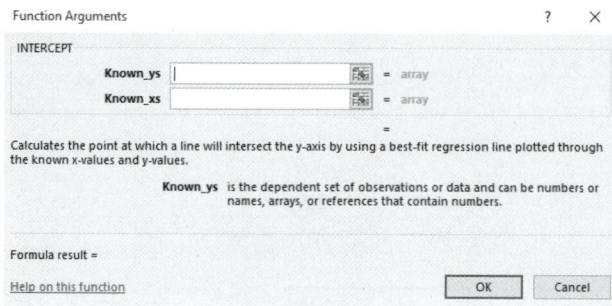

4. Enter the range of cells for the Known_ys (the variable you want to predict), which is college GPA or the *Y* variable. Here that range is again Cells B2 through B11.

5. Enter the range of cells for the Known_xs (the variable from which you are predicting), which is high school GPA or the *X* variable. Again, that range is Cells A2 through A11. The completed dialog box should appear as shown in Figure 16.10.

6. Click OK, and you will see the intercept of the best-fitting regression line in Cell B13, as shown in Figure 16.11. Be sure to look at the entire function, too, shown in the formula bar in Figure 16.11. And we cleaned up both the slope and the intercept values.

Figure 16.10   The Completed Dialog Box for the INTERCEPT Function

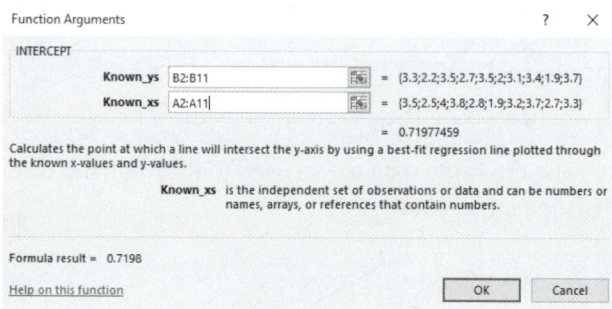

Figure 16.11 The Completed INTERCEPT Function

Figure 16.11	The Completed INTERCEPT Function

B14 ▾ : ✕ ✓ *fx* =INTERCEPT(B2:B11,A2:A11)

	A	B	C	D	E	F
1	High School GPA	First Year College GPA				
2	3.5	3.3				
3	2.5	2.2				
4	4.0	3.5				
5	3.8	2.7				
6	2.8	3.5				
7	1.9	2.0				
8	3.2	3.1				
9	3.7	3.4				
10	2.7	1.9				
11	3.3	3.7				
12						
13	Slope(b)	0.7039				
14	Intercept(a)	0.7198				

So, just as we manually calculated the values for the slope (*b*) and the intercept (*a*) of the regression line, we used SLOPE and INTERCEPT to do the same in Excel. Now, if we want to be especially cute (and efficient), we can construct a worksheet like the one you see in Figure 16.12, which in Cell B18 contains a

Figure 16.12	Predicting a Score Based on the INTERCEPT and SLOPE Functions

B18 ▾ : ✕ ✓ *fx* =(B13*A18)+B14

	A	B	C	D
1	High School GPA	First Year College GPA		
2	3.5	3.3		
3	2.5	2.2		
4	4.0	3.5		
5	3.8	2.7		
6	2.8	3.5		
7	1.9	2.0		
8	3.2	3.1		
9	3.7	3.4		
10	2.7	1.9		
11	3.3	3.7		
12				
13	Slope(b)	0.7039		
14	Intercept(a)	0.7198		
15				
16				
17	Actual Score	Predicted Score		
18	3.5	3.1834		

formula that incorporates both functions to compute an estimated or predicted score from an actual *X* score (in this example, the actual *X* score is 3.5 from Cell A2). Be sure to look at the
formula in the formula bar to see how we incorporated the calculations that Excel did for us. Magic!

USING THE AMAZING DATA ANALYSIS TOOLS TO COMPUTE THE REGRESSION EQUATION

There are lots of computations involved in computing the slope and
intercept and, finally, the regression equation (as you well know by
now). But Excel does excel in providing us with a tool that makes
computing these kinds of solutions a snap. We'll use the Data Analysis
Regression tool and the data that you already saw in Figure 16.5.

1. Click Data → Data Analysis → Regression, and you will see
   the Data Analysis dialog box for Regression, as shown in
   Figure 16.13.

2. In the Input Y Range box, enter the range of data for the
   dependent variable you want Excel to use in the computation
   of the regression values. As you can see in Figure 16.5, the
   data we want to analyze and their label are in Cells B1
   through B11. Include the column heading.

Figure 16.13	The Regression Dialog Box From the Data Analysis Tools

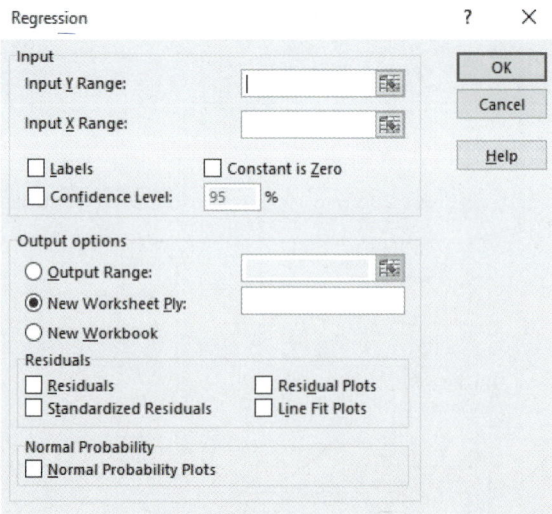

3. In the Input X Range box, enter the range of data for the independent variable you want Excel to use. As you can see in Figure 16.5, the data we want to analyze are in Cells A1 through A11. Include the column heading.

4. Click the Labels box.

5. Now click the Output Range button in the Output options section of the dialog box and enter the location where you want Excel to return the results of the analysis. In this example, we checked D1. The completed dialog box should appear as shown in Figure 16.14.

Figure 16.14 The Completed Regression Dialog Box

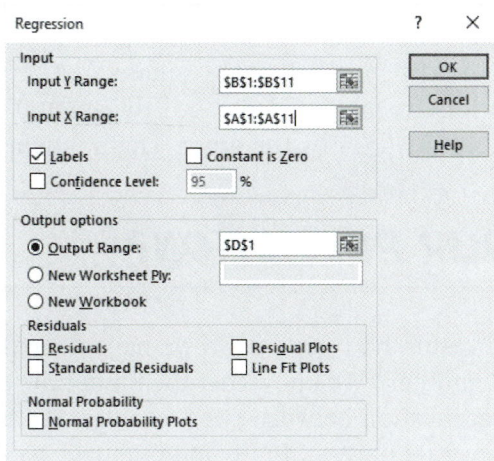

6. Click OK, and there it is, folks, the output you see in Figure 16.15 (we cleaned it up a bit). Easy and fast!

Figure 16.15 A Completed Regression Using Excel's Data Analysis Tools

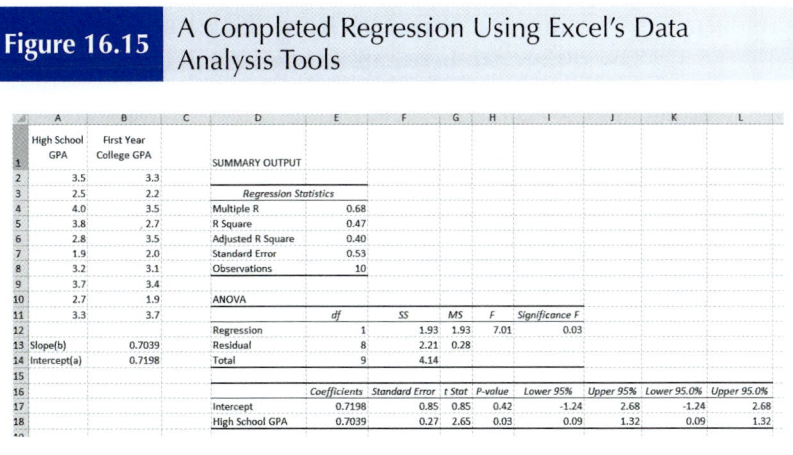

And there it is. So, what do we have? Some output goes beyond what we have discussed in this chapter, but let's stretch a bit and see what makes sense to talk about at this point.

At the bottom of the output, you can see the value for Intercept is 0.7198 (the same value that we obtained using the INTERCEPT function), and the value for High School GPA is 0.7039 (the same value we obtained using the SLOPE function). And, a bit to the right of these values, there's "P-value" (we have used a lowercase p up to now, but so what—you know that "p" = "P"). This is a measure of how significant the contribution of any one independent variable (High School GPA) is to understanding the outcome or dependent variable (First-Year College GPA). In this case, the p value is .03, so we can rest assured that the predictor is doing a pretty good job.

At the top of the output is the multiple R value (.68), which in the case of only one predictor is the simple Pearson correlation value. We also find here the R value squared (.47), which as you know from our discussion in Chapter 5 is the amount of variance in one variable accounted for by the other. That's the important stuff.

HOW GOOD IS OUR PREDICTION?

How can we measure how good a job we have done predicting one outcome from another? We know that the higher the absolute magnitude of the correlation between two variables, the better the prediction. In theory, that's great. But being practical, we can also look at the difference between the predicted value (Y') and the actual value (Y) when we first compute the formula of the regression line.

For example, if the formula for the regression line is $Y' = 0.705X + 0.7163$, the predicted Y (or Y') for an X value of 2.8 is $0.705(2.8) + 0.7163$, or 2.69. We know that the actual Y value that corresponds to an X value of 2.8 is 3.5 (from the data set shown in Table 16.1). The difference between 3.5 and 2.69, 0.81, is known as an **error of estimate**.

If we take all of these differences, we can compute a measure of how much each data point (on the average) differs from the predicted data point, or the **standard error of estimate**. It's like a standard deviation of all the error scores. This value tells us how much imprecision there is in our estimate. As you might expect, the higher the correlation between the two values (and the better the prediction), the lower this error will be. In fact, if the correlation between the two variables is perfect (either +1 or −1), then the standard error of estimate is 0. Why? Because when prediction is perfect, all of the actual data points fall on the regression line, and there's no error in estimating Y from X.

And guess what? (Wait for it . . .) Excel already has done it. If you are extra attentive, you'll find the standard error of estimate shown in Figure 16.15 as the result of the Data Analysis tools analysis. It's .5252, interpreted as any other type of standard deviation.

We're sure that it's no surprise to you, but Excel contains a function, STEYX, that computes the standard error of prediction (a very close cousin if not an identical twin to the standard error of estimate). To use this function, you simply enter the known Ys and known Xs, as we have done several times throughout this chapter, and you end up with a standard deviation of the predicted Y scores (which gives you a very accurate measure of how good your prediction is).

Another measure of error that you could use is the coefficient of determination (see Chapter 5), which is the percentage of error that is reduced in the relationship between variables. For example, if the correlation between two variables is .4 and the coefficient of determination is 16% or $.4^2$, the reduction in error is 16% (since initially we suspect the relationship between the two variables starts at 0 or 100% error (no predictive value at all).

The predicted Y', or dependent variable, need not always be a continuous one, such as height, test score, or problem-solving skills. It can be a categorical variable, such as admit/don't admit, Level A/Level B, or Social Class 1/Social Class 2. The score that's used in the prediction is "dummy coded" to be a 1 or a 2 and then used in the same equation.

THE MORE PREDICTORS, THE BETTER? MAYBE

All of the examples that we have used so far in the chapter have been for one criterion or outcome measure and one predictor variable. Regression can also be applied when more than one predictor or independent variable is used to predict a particular outcome. If one variable can predict an outcome with some degree of accuracy, then why couldn't two do a better job?

For example, if high school GPA is a pretty good indicator of college GPA, then how about high school GPA plus number of hours of extracurricular activities? So, instead of

$$Y' = bX + a, \tag{16.8}$$

the model for the regression equation becomes

$$Y' = b_1X_1 + b_2X_2 + a, \tag{16.9}$$

where

Y' is the value of the predicted score;

X_1 is the value of the first independent variable;

X_2 is the value of the second independent variable; and

b is the regression weight for that particular variable.

a is the intercept.

As you may have guessed, this model is called **multiple regression**. So, in theory anyway, you are predicting an outcome from two (and of course, even more) independent variables, rather than one. But you want to add additional independent variables only under certain conditions. First, any variable you add has to make a unique contribution to understanding the dependent variable. Otherwise, why use it? Now what do we mean by *unique*? The additional variable needs to explain differences in the predicted variable that the first predictor does not. That is, the two variables in combination would have to predict Y better than either one of the variables would do alone.

In our example, level of participation in extracurricular activities could make a unique contribution. But should we add a variable such as the number of hours each student studied in high school as a third independent variable or predictor? Because number of hours of study is probably highly related to high school GPA (another of our predictor variables, remember?), study time probably would not add much to the overall prediction of college GPA. We might be better off looking for another variable (such as ratings on letters of recommendation) rather than spending our time collecting the data on study time.

The Big Rule When It Comes to Using Multiple Predictor Variables

If you are going to use more than one predictor variable, try to keep the following two important guidelines in mind:

1. When selecting an independent variable to predict an outcome, select a predictor variable (X) that is related to the
   predicted variable (Y). That way, the two share something in
   common (remember, they should be correlated).

2. When selecting more than one independent variable (such as
   X_1 and X_2), try to select variables that are independent or
   uncorrelated with one another but are both related to the
   outcome or predicted (Y) variable.

In effect, you want only independent or predictor variables that
are related to the dependent variable and are unrelated to each
other. That way, each one makes as unique a contribution as possible to predicting the dependent or predicted variable.

How many predictor variables are too many? Well, if one variable
predicts some outcome, and two are even more accurate, then why
not three, four, or five predictor variables? In practical terms, every
time you add a variable, an expense is incurred. Someone has to go
collect the data, it takes time (which is $$$ when it comes to research
budgets), and so on. From a theoretical perspective, there is a fixed
limit on how many variables can contribute to an understanding of
what we are trying to predict. Remember, too, that it is best when the
predictor or independent variables are independent or unrelated to
each other. The problem is that once you get to three or four variables,
few of them will be unrelated. Better to be accurate and conservative
than to include too many variables and waste money and the power
of prediction.

REAL-WORLD STATS

How children feel about what they do is often very closely related
to how well they do what they do. The aim of this study was to
analyze the consequences of emotion during a writing exercise.
In the model that this research follows, motivation and affect play
an important role during the writing process. Here, fourth and
fifth graders were instructed to write autobiographical narratives
with neutral emotional content, positive emotional content, and
negative emotional content. The results showed no effect regard-
ing emotional instructions on the proportion of spelling errors,
but they did reveal an effect on the number of words children
wrote.

A simple regression analysis (just like the ones we did and discussed in this chapter) showed a correlation and some predictive value between working memory capacity and the number of spelling errors in the neutral condition only. Since the model on which the researchers based much of their preliminary thinking talks about how emotions can increase the cognitive load or the amount of "work" necessary while writing, that becomes the focus of the discussion.

Want to know more? Go online or go to the library, and look for . . .

Fartoukh, M., Chanquoy, L., & Piolat, A. (2012). Effects of emotion on writing processes in children. *Written Communication, 29,* 391–411.

SUMMARY

Prediction is a special case of simple correlation, and it is a very powerful tool for examining complex relationships. This chapter might have been a little more difficult than others, but you'll be well served by what you have learned, especially if you can apply it to the research reports and journal articles that you have to read. Now, after a bunch of chapters about inference, we're going to move on to using statistics when the sample size is very small or when the assumption that the scores are distributed in a normal way is violated.

TIME TO PRACTICE

1. Chapter 16 Data Set 1 contains the data for a group of participants who took a timed test. The data are the average amount of time the participants took on each item (Response Time) and the number of guesses it took to get each item correct (Number Correct).

   a. What is the regression equation for predicting Response Time from Number Correct? Use the SLOPE and INTERCEPT functions to create the equation.

   b. What is the predicted Response Time if the Number Correct is 8?

   c. What is the difference between the predicted and the actual Response Time for each of the Number Correct scores, and what is the standard error of estimate or prediction?

2. Betsy is interested in predicting how many 75-year-olds will develop Alzheimer's disease and is using as predictors level of education and general physical health graded on a scale from 1 to 10. But she is interested in using other predictor variables as well. Answer the following questions.

a. What criteria should she use in the selection of other predictors? Why?

b. Name two other predictors that you think might be related to the development of Alzheimer's disease.

c. With the four predictor variables (level of education, general physical health, and the two new ones that you name), write out the model of the regression equation.

3. You're interested in predicting success in business. You're a stats star! Why not go out and collect 15 different variables and combine them to see which combination best predicts success (however you want to measure it)?

4. Go to the library and locate three examples of research studies in your area of interest in which linear regression was used. It's okay if a study contains more than one predictor variable. Answer the following questions for each study.

a. What is one independent variable? What is the dependent variable?

b. If there is more than one independent variable, what argument does the researcher make that these variables are independent from one another?

c. Which of the three studies seems to present the least convincing evidence that the dependent variable is predicted by the independent variable, and why?

5. Here's where you can apply the information in one of this chapter's tips and get a chance to predict a Super Bowl winner! Coach Kent is curious to know whether the average number of games won in a year predicts Super Bowl performance (win or lose). The X variable is the average number of games won during the past 10 seasons. The Y variable is whether the team has won the Super Bowl during the past 10 seasons. Here are the data:

Team	Average Number of Wins Over 10 Years	Won a Super Bowl in Past 10 Years? (1 = yes and 0 = no)
Savannah Sharks	12	1
Pittsburgh Pelicans	11	0
Williamstown Warriors	15	0
Bennington Bruisers	12	1
Atlanta Angels	13	1
Trenton Terrors	16	0
Virginia Vipers	15	1
Charleston Crooners	9	0
Harrisburg Heathens	8	0
Eaton Energizers	12	1

    a. How would you assess the usefulness of the average number of wins as a predictor of whether a team ever won a Super Bowl?

    b. What's the advantage of being able to use a categorical variable (such as 1 or 0) as a dependent variable?

    c. What other variables might you use to predict the dependent variable, and why would you choose them?

6. Why is the standard error of estimate or prediction higher when the predictive quality of variables is lower?

7. In Chapter 16 Data Set 2, you will find scores on three variables. The outcome variable is overall health (Health)—the higher the score, the healthier the person is. The predictor variables are preference for sweets (Sweets), with a higher number indicating "I love 'em"; Gender, with 1 indicating male and 2 indicating female; and body mass index (BMI), a measure of obesity with higher numbers indicating greater obesity. Use the Data Analysis Regression tool to find out how well these predictor variables predict overall health.

8. Take a look at Chapter 16 Data Set 3 and reach a conclusion as to whether number of years of training makes a good chef (and the higher the better on the Chef's Score).

17

What to Do When You're Not Normal

Chi-Square and Some Other Nonparametric Tests

Difficulty Scale ☺ ☺ ☺ ☺ (easy)

How much Excel? 📊 📊 📊 📊 lots

WHAT YOU'LL LEARN ABOUT IN THIS CHAPTER

✦ What chi-square is and how it can be used

✦ A bit about the CHISQ.TEST function

✦ A brief survey of nonparametric statistics and when and how they should be used

INTRODUCTION TO NONPARAMETRIC STATISTICS

Almost every statistical test that we've covered so far in *Statistics for People Who (Think They) Hate Statistics, Excel 2016 Edition* assumes that the data set with which you are working has certain characteristics. For example, one assumption underlying a *t*-test between means (whether the means are independent or dependent) is that the variances of each group are homogeneous, or similar. Another assumption of many **parametric statistics** is that the sample is large enough to represent the entire population. Statisticians have found that it takes a sample size of about 30 to fulfill this assumption. Many of the statistical tests we've covered so far are also robust, or powerful, enough that even if one of these assumptions is violated, the test is still valid.

But what do you do when the assumptions may be violated? The original research questions are certainly still worth asking and answering. That's when we use **nonparametric statistics** (also called distribution-free statistics). These tests don't follow the same "rules" (meaning they don't require the same assumptions as the parametric tests we've reviewed), but they are just as valuable. The use of nonparametric tests also allows us to analyze data that come as frequencies, such as the number of children in different grades or the percentage of people receiving Social Security.

For example, if we wanted to know whether the number of people who voted for school vouchers in the most recent election is what we would expect by chance, or if there was really a pattern of preference, we would then use a nonparametric technique called **chi-square**.

In this chapter, we cover chi-square, one of the most commonly used nonparametric tests, and provide a brief review of some others just so you can become familiar with some other nonparametric tests that are available. There's an entire course waiting at your school on this material, a set of very powerful tools well worth exploring.

INTRODUCTION TO ONE-SAMPLE CHI-SQUARE

Chi-square is an interesting nonparametric test that allows you to determine whether what you observe in a distribution of frequencies is what you would expect to occur by chance. A **one-sample chi-square** or **goodness-of-fit test** includes only one dimension, such as the example you'll see here. A **two-sample chi-square** (also called **test of independence**) includes two dimensions, such as whether preference for school vouchers is independent of political party affiliation and gender. That's left for the next course (or the next edition of this book).

For example, here are data from a sample selected at random from the 1990 census data collected in Sonoma County, California. As you can see, the table organizes information about level of education.

Level of Education			
No College	Some College	College Degree	Total
25	42	17	84

The question of interest here is whether the number of respondents is equally distributed across all levels of education. To answer this question, the chi-square value (chi-square, the symbol, looks like this: χ^2) was computed and then tested for significance. In this example, the chi-square value is equal to 11.643, which is significant beyond the .05 level. The conclusion is that the number of respondents at the various levels of education for this sample is not equally distributed. In other words, it's not what we would expect by chance, and this sample is unequally distributed among levels of education.

The rationale behind the one-sample chi-square test is that in any set of occurrences, you can easily compute what you would expect by chance. You do this by dividing the total number of occurrences by the number of classes or categories. In the results from the sample of census data example above, the observed total number of occurrences was 84. We would expect that, by chance, the total of all frequencies divided by the total number of categories, or 84 ÷ 3 = 28, respondents would fall into each of the three categories of level of education.

Then, we look at how different what we expect by chance is from what we observe. If there is no difference between what we expect and what we observe, the chi-square value is equal to zero.

Let's look more closely at how the chi-square value is computed.

COMPUTING THE CHI–SQUARE TEST STATISTIC

The chi-square test involves a comparison between what is observed and what would be expected by chance. The formula for computing the chi-square value for a one-sample chi-square test is shown in Formula 17.1.

$$\chi^2 = \Sigma \frac{(O - E)^2}{E},$$ (17.1)

where

χ^2 is the chi-square value;

Σ is the summation sign;

O is the observed frequency; and

E is the expected frequency.

Here are some data we'll use to compute the chi-square value.

Preference for School Vouchers			
For	**Maybe**	**Against**	**Total**
23	17	50	90

Here are the famous eight steps to test this statistic:

1. *State the null and research hypotheses.* The null hypothesis shown in Formula 17.2 states that there is no difference in the frequency or the proportion of occurrences in each category.

$$H_0: P_1 = P_2 = P_3 \qquad (17.2)$$

The *P* in the null hypothesis represents the percentage of occurrences in any one category. This null hypothesis states that the proportion of cases in Category 1 (For), Category 2 (Maybe), and Category 3 (Against) is equal. We are using only three categories, but the number could be extended to fit the situation as long as each of the categories is *mutually exclusive,* which means that any one observation cannot be in more than one category. For example, you can't be both for and against—your tally has to go into one of the three categories and only one.

The research hypothesis shown in Formula 17.3 states that there is a difference in the frequency or proposition of occurrences in each category.

$$H_0: P_1 \neq P_2 \neq P_3 \qquad (17.3)$$

2. *Set the level of risk (or the level of significance or Type I error) associated with the null hypothesis.* The Type I error rate is set at .05. This is entirely at the researcher's discretion.

3. *Select the appropriate test statistic.* Any test between frequencies or proportions of mutually exclusive categories (such as For, Maybe, and Against) requires the use of chi-square. The flowchart we have used until now to select the type of statistical test to use is not applicable to nonparametric procedures.

4. *Compute the test statistic value (called the obtained value).* Let's go back to our voucher data from our earlier example and construct a worksheet that will help us compute the chi-square value. Then we'll continue the next of the eight steps.

Category	O (observed frequency)	E (expected frequency)	D (difference)	$(O - E)^2$	$(O - E)^2/E$
For	23	30	7	49	1.63
Maybe	17	30	13	169	5.63
Against	50	30	20	400	13.33
Total	90	90			20.59

Here are the steps we took to prepare this worksheet:

A. Enter the categories (Category) of For, Maybe, and Against. Remember that these three categories are mutually exclusive. Any data point can be in only one category at a time.

B. Enter the observed frequency (O), which reflects the data that were collected.

C. Enter the expected frequency (E), which is the total of the observed frequency (90) divided by the number of categories (3), or 90/3 = 30.

D. For each cell, subtract the expected frequency from the observed frequency (D). It does not matter which is subtracted from the other because these values are squared in the next step.

E. Square the observed minus the expected value. You can see these values in the column named $(O - E)^2$. This could also be expressed as D^2.

F. Divide the squared difference between the observed and the expected frequencies by the expected frequency. You can see these values in the column marked $(O - E)^2/E$.

G. Sum this last column, and you have the total chi-square value of 20.59.

Now back to step 5 of the famous eight steps . . .

5. *Determine the value needed for rejection of the null hypothesis using the appropriate table of critical values for the particular statistic.* Here's where we go to Table B.5 (in Appendix B) for the list of critical values for the chi-square test.

Our first task is to determine the degrees of freedom (*df*), which approximates the number of categories in which data have been organized. For this particular test statistic, the degrees of freedom is $c - 1$, where c equals categories, or $3 - 1$ $= 2$. In other books, or in class, you may see $c - 1$ represented as $r - 1$, for rows minus 1.

Using this number (2) and the level of risk you are willing to take (earlier defined as .05), you can use the chi-square table to look up the critical value. It is 5.99. So, at the .05 level, with 2 degrees of freedom, the value needed for rejection of the null hypothesis is 5.99.

6. *Compare the obtained value and the critical value.* The obtained value is 20.6, and the critical value for rejection of the null hypothesis that the frequency of occurrences in Groups 1, 2, and 3 is equal is 5.99.

7. and 8. *Decision time!* Now comes our decision. If the obtained value is more extreme than the critical value, the null hypothesis cannot be accepted. If the obtained value does not exceed the critical value, the null hypothesis is the most attractive explanation. In this case, the obtained value exceeds the critical value—it is extreme enough for us to say that the distribution of respondents across the three groups is not equal. Indeed, there is a difference in the frequency of people voting for, maybe, or against when it comes to preference for school vouchers.

A commonly used name for the one-sample chi-square test is *goodness of fit.* This name suggests the question of how well a set of data "fits" an existing set. The "set" of data is, of course, what you observe. The "fit" part suggests that there is another set of data to which the observed set can be matched. This standard is the set of expected frequencies that is calculated in the course of computing the c^2 value. If the observed data fit, the match is too close to what you would expect by chance and does not differ significantly. If the observed data do not fit, then what you observed is different from what you would expect.

So How Do I Interpret $\chi^2 = 20.6$, p < .05?

- χ^2 represents the test statistic.
- 20.6 is the obtained value using Formula 17.1.
- $p < .05$ (the really important part of this little phrase) indicates that the probability is less than 5% on any one test of the null hypothesis that the frequency of votes is equally distributed across all categories by chance alone. Because we defined .05

as our criterion for the research hypothesis being more attractive than the null hypothesis, our conclusion is that there is a significant difference between the two sets of scores.

And Now . . . Using Excel's CHISQ.TEST Function

Excel doesn't offer any functions that mirror exactly what we did above. There's no function (or Data Analysis tool) that computes the value of chi-square for a one-sample test. However, a function named **CHISQ.TEST** will compute the probability of a particular chi-square value if you enter the degrees of freedom and the value of chi-square. In our earlier example, the completed function would look like what you see above, and the value that would be returned would be 3.36331E-05, which is .0000336331 (which is pretty darn small).

And **CHISQ.DIST** provides the probability of an outcome given the degrees of freedom and the value of the statistic χ^2. Keep in mind that you need no raw data to use this function if you already have the chi-square value. Just plug in the value and the degrees of freedom, and you're home free.

Here's how to do it using the data entered as you see in Figure 17.1:

| Figure 17.1 | Data for a Chi-Square Analysis |

	A	B	C
1	Category	Observed Frequency	Expected Frequency
2	For	23	30
3	Maybe	17	30
4	Against	50	30

1. Select the cell into which you want to enter the CHISQ.TEST function. In this example, we are going to have the CHISQ. TEST value returned to Cell B6 (and that location was not chosen for any particular reason).

2. Now click Formulas → More Functions → Statistical menu option and scroll down to select the CHISQ.TEST function. You will see that dialog box, as shown in Figure 17.2.

3. Enter the range of actual values (those from Cells B2 to B4) into the Actual_range box in the dialog box.

Figure 17.2   The CHISQ.TEST Function Dialog Box

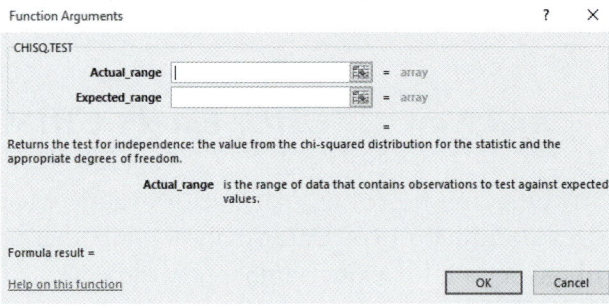

4. Enter the range of expected values (those from Cells C2 to C4) into the Expected_range box in the dialog box. You can see the completed dialog box in Figure 17.3.

5. Click OK, and the probability of the categories being equally distributed is returned to Cell B6, where in Figure 17.4 you can see the value of 3.36331E-05 (or .0000336331). This is very, very small. Our conclusion? The patterning of voting was very much not-random. Be sure to take a look also at the formula argument or syntax, shown in the formula bar.

Figure 17.3   The Completed CHISQ.TEST Dialog Box

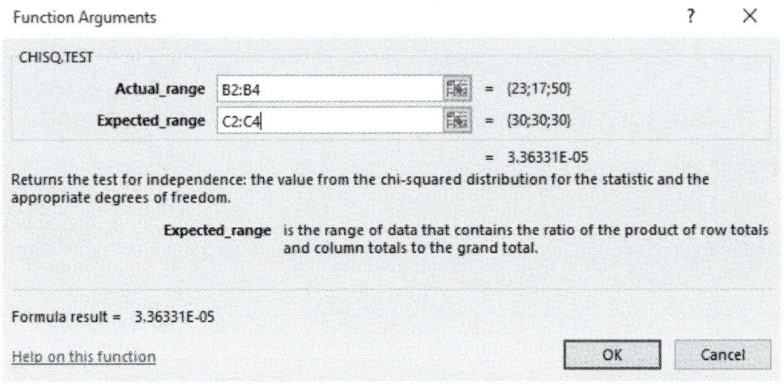

It's also really easy to create your very own formula to compute the actual chi-square value, as you see in Figure 17.5. Here we entered preference data, and you can see the correct formula in the formula bar and the resulting chi-square value of 20.6 in cell C6. But, of course, this formula is restricted to three levels of one variable, so if you have more levels, you will have to do a bit of tweaking.

Figure 17.4 The CHISQ.TEST Value

| B6 | ▼ | ⋮ | × | ✓ | f_x | =CHISQ.TEST(B2:B4,C2:C4) |

	A	B	C	D	E
1	Category	Observed Frequency	Expected Frequency		
2	For	23	30		
3	Maybe	17	30		
4	Against	50	30		
5					
6		3.36331E-05			

Figure 17.5 Creating a Formula That Will Compute the Chi-Square Value

| C7 | ▼ | | f_x | =((B3-C3)^2/C3)+((B4-C4)^2/C4)+((B5-C5)^2/C5) |

	A	B	C	D	E	F
2						
3	Republican	23	30			
4	Democrat	17	30			
5	Independent	50	30			
6						
7		Chi Square	20.6			

The chi-square procedure you just learned about is called a simple chi-square or a goodness-of-fit test. The other kind that can be very useful is called a test of independence. Here two factors are compared to see whether their frequencies of occurrence in categories are independent of one another. So for example, you might have the following data . . .

	Pass Course	Fail Course
Participation in Extracurricular Activities	22	18
No Participation in Extracurricular Activities	18	22

. . . which allow us to see whether participation in extracurricular activities is independent of course performance. Just as with a simple chi-square test, the actual and expected values are obtained and then used to compute a chi-square value, and a probability is assigned to that outcome. Then, a conclusion is reached as to whether these two factors are independent of one another given the likelihood that the results occurred by chance. In this case, the probability associated with these two factors being independent of one another is .37 (and we used CHISQ.TEST to compute it), meaning that these two dimensions are independent of one another—participation in extracurricular activities is independent of performance.

OTHER NONPARAMETRIC TESTS YOU SHOULD KNOW ABOUT

You may never need a nonparametric test to answer any of the research questions that you propose. On the other hand, you may very well find yourself dealing with samples that are very small (or at least fewer than 30) or data that violate some of the important assumptions underlying parametric tests.

Actually, a primary reason why you may want to use nonparametric statistics is a function of the measurement level of the variable you are assessing. We'll talk more about that in the next chapter, but for now, most data that are categorical and are placed in categories (such as the Sharks and Jets) or that are ordinal and are ranked (1st, 2nd, and 3rd place) call for nonparametric tests of the kind you see in Table 17.1. If that's the case, try nonparametrics on for size. Table 17.1 provides all you need to know about some other nonparametric tests: their name, what they are used for, and a research question that illustrates how each might be used. Keep in mind that the table presents only a few of the many different tests that are available.

Table 17.1   Nonparametric Tests to Analyze Data in Categories and by Ranks

Test Name	When the Test Is Used	A Sample Research Question
To analyze data organized in categories		
McNemar test for significance of changes	To examine "before and after" changes	How effective is a phone call to undecided legislators on their voting for a particular issue?
Fisher's exact test	To compute the exact probability of outcomes in a 2 × 2 table	What is the exact likelihood of getting six heads on a toss of six coins?

Test Name	When the Test Is Used	A Sample Research Question
Chi-square one-sample test (just what we focused on in this chapter)	To determine whether the number of occurrences across categories is random	Did brands Fruities, Whammies, and Zippies each sell an equal number of units during the recent sale?
To analyze data organized by ranks		
Kolmogorov-Smirnov test	To see whether scores from a sample came from a specified population	How representative is a set of judgments of certain children of those of all students at their elementary school?
The sign test, or median test	To compare the medians from two paired samples	Is the median income of people who voted for Candidate A greater than the median income of people who voted for Candidate B?
Mann-Whitney U test	To compare two independent samples	Did the transfer of learning, measured by number correct, occur faster for Group A than for Group B?
Wilcoxon rank test	To compare the magnitude as well as the direction of differences between two groups	Is preschool twice as effective as no preschool for developing children's language skills?
Kruskal-Wallis one-way analysis of variance	To compare the overall difference between two or more independent samples	How do rankings of supervisors differ among four regional offices?
Friedman two-way analysis of variance	To compare the overall difference between two or more independent samples on more than one dimension	How do rankings of supervisors differ as a function of regional office and gender?
Spearman rank correlation coefficient	To compute the correlation between ranks	What is the correlation between class rank in the senior year of high school and class rank during the freshman year of college?

REAL-WORLD STATS

Using a modern tool to explore the content of the Bible is really exciting (and clever) and a great illustration of how chi-square is used in the real world.

C. B. Houk conducted what is called a syllable–word frequency pattern analysis and used the chi-square test to identify significant differences within different chapters of Genesis (yes, that Genesis). The thesis? That the various passages were written by the same person. The analysis of the various passages argues against the thesis that the stories were developed separately given that there was no significant difference in the frequency of the occurrence of certain words and such. In other words, the same person wrote these early texts.

Want to know more? Go online or go to the library, and look for . . .

Houk, C. B. (2002). Statistical analysis of Genesis sources. *Journal for the Study of the Old Testament, 27,* 75–105.

SUMMARY

Chi-square is one of many different types of nonparametric statistics that help you answer questions based on data that violate the basic assumptions of the normal distribution or are just too small. These nonparametric tests are a very valuable tool, and even as limited an introduction as this will provide you with some assistance.

TIME TO PRACTICE

1. Using the following data, test the question of whether an equal number of Democrats, Republicans, and independents voted during the most recent election. Test the hypothesis at the .05 level of significance.

Political Affiliation		
Republican	**Democrat**	**Independent**
800	700	900

2. Using the following data, test the question of whether an equal number of boys and girls participate in soccer at the elementary level at the .01 level of significance. What's your conclusion?

Gender	
Boys	**Girls**
45	55

3. Of the following four research questions, which ones are appropriate for the chi-square test?

   a. What is the difference between the average scores of two math classes?

   b. What is the difference between the number of children who passed the math test in Class 1 and the number of children who passed the math test in Class 2?

   c. How many cars passed the CRASH Test this year versus last year?

   d. How fast can a soccer player run 100 yards compared with a football player?

4. At the Diabetes Institute, patients are classified as compliant (they take their medication as they should) or not (they don't). A new program manager has a new idea: Have some patients continuously monitor their blood sugar while telling others that they do not need to and see whether they fall into one of two categories in controlling their diet, successful or not successful. Here are the data:

Successful	Unsuccessful
60	38

So, does the program manager stay on the job or start looking?

18

Some Other (Important) Statistical Procedures You Should Know About

Difficulty Scale ☺ ☺ ☺ ☺ (moderately easy—just some reading and an extension of what you already know)

How much Excel? 📊 (just some mentions)

Throughout *Statistics for People Who (Think They) Hate Statistics, Excel 2016 Edition*, we have covered only a small part of the whole body of statistics. Partly that's because we don't have room. But more important, as you start out with your study of statistics, it's important to keep things simple and direct.

However, that does not mean that in a research article you read or in some discussion in a class, you won't come across other analytical techniques that might be important for you to know about. So, for your edification, here are 10 of those techniques, what they do, and examples of studies that used the technique to answer a question. Note that new techniques and new tools are always being developed that shed light on trends in large data sets, and if you have time, you should definitely try to fit more advanced statistics classes into your coursework. But, for now, the brief summary that follows should arm you with knowledge that will at least get you started in the galaxy of advanced statistics.

POST HOC COMPARISONS

Statisticians (rightfully so) make a big deal about the *F*-test. (Remember analysis of variance? If not, see Chapter 13 for a refresher.) The *F*-test is a robust test of the difference between two or more sample means. What that in practice means (☺) is that you can't tell whether the difference between groups 1 and 2, or 1 and 3, or 2 and 3 (or some combination) is the reason for the overall difference. But if you're smart, then you know about post hoc comparison, or tools to do an analysis after the fact. There are several of these methods; one is called Tukey HSD (or Honestly Significant Differences).

For example, Lynne Sanford Koester and Eve Lahti-Harper from the University of Montana looked at how parents "guide their infants in the regulation of emotions, language acquisition, and participation in social exchanges." They compared deaf and hearing mother–infant dyads and their level of what the researchers refer to as "intuitive parenting behaviors" when the children were 6, 9, 12, and 18 months old. In their analysis, they used the Tukey's HSD post hoc tool to examine differences among the dyads of mothers and infants.

Want to know more? Go online and find Koester, L. S., & Lahti-Harper, E. (2010). Mother–infant hearing status and intuitive parenting behaviors during the first 18 months. *American Annals of the Deaf, 155*, 5–18.

MULTIVARIATE ANALYSIS OF VARIANCE

You won't be surprised to learn that there are many different renditions of analysis of variance (ANOVA), each one designed to fit a particular "the means of more than two groups being compared" situation. One of these, multivariate analysis of variance (MANOVA), is used when there is more than one dependent variable. So, instead of looking at just one outcome, the researcher uses more than one outcome or dependent variable. If the dependent or outcome variables are related to one another (which they usually are—see the

(Really Important) Tech Talk note in Chapter 13 about multiple *t*-tests), it's hard to determine clearly the effect of the treatment variable on any one outcome; hence, MANOVA to the rescue. In effect, MANOVA allows you to determine the best combination of dependent variables.

For example, Jonathan Plucker from Indiana University examined the effects of gender, race, and grade differences on how gifted adolescents dealt with pressures at school. The MANOVA analysis that he used was a 2 × 4 × 5 (gender: male and female; race: Caucasian, African American, Asian American, and Hispanic; grade: 8 through 12) MANOVA. The *multivariate* part of the analysis was the five subscales of the Adolescent Coping Scale. By using a multivariate technique, Plucker could estimate the effects of the independent variables (gender, race, and grade) for each of the five scales, independently of one another.

Want to know more? Take a look at Plucker, J. A. (1998). Gender, race, and grade differences in gifted adolescents' coping strategies. *Journal for the Education of the Gifted, 21,* 423–436.

REPEATED MEASURES ANALYSIS OF VARIANCE

Here's another kind of analysis of variance. Repeated measures analysis of variance is very similar to any analysis of variance where, if you recall (see Chapter 13), the means of two or more groups are tested for differences. In a repeated measures ANOVA, there is one factor on which participants are tested more than once. That's why it's called *repeated*—you repeat the process at more than one point in time on the same factor.

For example, Brenda Lundy, Tiffany Field, Cami McBride, Tory Field, and Shay Largie examined same-sex and opposite-sex interaction with best friends using juniors who then became seniors in high school. One of their main analyses was ANOVA with three factors: gender (male or female), friendship (same-sex or opposite-sex), and year in high school (junior or senior year). The repeated measure is year in high school, because the measurement was repeated across the same subjects.

Want to know more? Take a look at Lundy, B., Field, T., McBride, C., Field, T., & Largie, S. (1998). Same-sex and opposite-sex best friend interactions among high school juniors and seniors. *Adolescence, 33,* 279–289.

ANALYSIS OF COVARIANCE

Here's our last rendition of ANOVA. Analysis of covariance (ANCOVA) is particularly interesting because it basically allows you to equalize initial differences between groups. Let's say you are sponsoring a program to increase running speed and want to compare how fast two groups of athletes can run a 100-yard dash. Because strength is often related to speed, you have to make some correction so that strength does not account for any differences at the end of the program. Rather, you want to see the effects of training with strength removed. You would measure participants' strength before you started the training program and then use ANCOVA to adjust final speed based on initial strength.

Michaela Hynie, John Lydon, and Ali Taradash from McGill University used ANCOVA in their investigation of the influence of intimacy and commitment on the acceptability of premarital sex and contraceptive use. They used ANCOVA with social acceptability as the dependent variable (in which they were looking for group differences) and ratings of a particular scenario as the covariate. ANCOVA would ensure that differences in social acceptability would be corrected using ratings, thus controlling one difference.

Want to know more? See Hynie, M., Lydon, J. E., & Taradash, A. (1997). Commitment, intimacy, and women's perceptions of premarital sex and contraceptive readiness. *Psychology of Women Quarterly, 21*, 447–464.

MULTIPLE REGRESSION

Often, social and behavioral sciences researchers look at how more than one variable can predict another. We touched on this in Chapter 5 and went into more depth in Chapter 16, and here's more about what is called multiple regression.

For example, it's fairly well established that parents' literacy behaviors (such as having books in the home) are related to how much and how well their children read. So, it would seem quite interesting to look at such variables as parents' age, educational level, literacy activities, and shared reading with children to see what they contribute to early language skills and interest in books. Paula Lyytinen, Marja-Leena Laakso, and Anna-Maija Poikkeus did exactly that and used stepwise regression analysis to examine the

contribution of parental background variables to children's literacy. They found that mothers' literacy activities and mothers' level of education contributed significantly to children's language skills, whereas mothers' age and shared reading did not.

Want to know more? Take a look at Lyytinen, P., Laakso, M.-L., & Poikkeus, A.-M. (1998). Parental contributions to child's early language and interest in books. *European Journal of Psychology of Education, 13,* 297–308.

LOGISTIC REGRESSION

Logistic regression is a variant on what we just mentioned, multiple regression. Basically, it is used to deal with the situation in which the outcome or dependent variable is a categorical variable, such as "like" or "dislike," and the predictors are either continuous, such as scores on a test from 1 to 100, or categorical, such as membership (belongs/does not belong). Logistic regression comes in two flavors—binary logistic regression in which there are two possible outcomes (such as "eligible" or "not eligible") and multinomial logistic regression in which more than two categories can be predicted.

For example, Stephen Shmanske looked at the factors that contribute to golf pros' decisions about which tournaments to enter. He looked at size of the winnings, the strength of the competition, and players' skills. He found that the amount of prize money is the most important factor, followed by the golfer's skill.

Want to know more? See Shmanske, S. (2009). Golf match: The choice by PGA Tour golfers of which tournaments to enter. *International Journal of Sport Finance, 4,* 114–135.

FACTOR ANALYSIS

Factor analysis is a technique based on how well various items are related to one another. Related variables are said to form clusters or factors. Each factor represents several variables, and factors turn out to be more efficient than individual variables at representing outcomes in certain studies. In using this technique, the goal is to represent those things that are related to one another by a more general name, such as a factor. And the names you assign to these groups of variables called factors are not the result of a willy-nilly process—the names reflect the variables' content and your ideas underlying how they might be related.

For example, David Wolfe and his colleagues at the University of Western Ontario attempted to understand how experiences of maltreatment occurring before children were 12 years old affected peer and dating relationships during adolescence. To do this, the researchers collected data on many variables and then looked at the relationships between all of them. Those that seemed to contain items that were related (and belonged to a group that made theoretical sense) were deemed factors, such as the factor named Abuse/Blame in this study. Another factor, named Positive Communication, was made up of 10 variables, all of which were related to each other.

Want to know more? See Wolfe, D. A., Wekerle, C., Reitzel-Jaffe, D., & Lefebvre, L. (1998). Factors associated with abusive relationships among maltreated and nonmaltreated youth. *Development and Psychopathology, 10,* 61–85.

DATA MINING

Data mining is not so much a statistical technique for testing relationships or trends as it is a tool for dealing with the huge data sets that have become commonplace in the social and behavioral sciences. Among other things, it is a way to look for patterns in sets of data. It was actually first used by the business and professional sports communities when looking at (and for) financial trends, but it is now being used by psychologists, educators, nurses, and others as well. Chapter 20, new to this 2016 edition of *Statistics for People . . .* , provides a very simple introduction to this topic. In that chapter, you'll use Excel as a tool to reveal patterns.

Data mining is exploratory in nature, sometimes secondary to the main analysis, and it is also used to explore relationships between variables from several data sets. Data mining is also sometimes referred to as data or knowledge discovery. And, as you might expect, as the technique has become more popular, new software tools have been developed to facilitate using it (which frankly was impossible before the advent of computers).

For example, for all you Gen Y and Millennials students, you well know that online shopping activity has soared over the past 10 years. One study by Pamela Norum analyzed online buying behavior among college students and used data-mining techniques to

examine the purchases of 4,688 students in nine merchandise categories. What factors play a role in online shopping (at least for these folks)? The important factors are age, gender, income, car ownership, ability to identify a secure Internet site, and compulsive buying behavior.

Want to know more? See Norum, P. S. (2008). Student Internet purchases. *Family and Consumer Sciences Research Journal, 36,* 373–388. Now, where's my iPhone?

PATH ANALYSIS

Here's another statistical technique that examines correlations but also suggests the direction, or causality, in the relationship between factors. Path analysis basically examines the direction of relationships through a postulation of some theoretical relationship between variables and then a test to see whether the direction of these relationships is substantiated by the data.

For example, Anastasia Efklides, Maria Papadaki, Georgia Papantoniou, and Gregoris Kiosseoglou examined individual feelings of difficulty experienced in the learning of mathematics. To do this, they administered several types of tests (such as those in the area of cognitive ability) and found that feelings of difficulty are mainly influenced by cognitive (problem-solving) rather than affective (emotional) factors. One of the most interesting aspects of path analysis is that a technique called structural equation modeling is used to present the results as a graphical representation of the relationship among all the different factors under consideration. You can readily see what relates to what and with what degree of strength. Then, you can judge how well the data fit the model that was previously suggested. Cool.

Want to know more? Take a look at Efklides, A., Papadaki, M., Papantoniou, G., & Kiosseoglou, G. (1998). Individual differences in feelings of difficulty: The case of school mathematics. *European Journal of Psychology of Education, 13,* 207–226.

STRUCTURAL EQUATION MODELING

Structural equation modeling (SEM) is a relatively new technique that has become increasingly popular since it was introduced in the early 1960s. Some researchers feel it is an umbrella term for techniques such as regression, factor analysis, and path analysis. Others believe that it stands on its own as an entirely separate approach. It's based on relationships between variables (like the previous three techniques we described).

The major difference between SEM and other advanced techniques, such as factor analysis, is that SEM is *confirmatory* rather than *exploratory*. In other words, the researcher is more likely to use SEM to confirm whether a certain model that has been proposed works (in other words, to ask whether the data fit that model). Exploratory techniques set out to discover a particular relationship, with less (but not no) model building beforehand.

For example, Heather Gotham, Kenneth Sher, and Phillip Wood examined the relationships among young adult alcohol-use disorders; preadulthood variables (gender, family history of alcoholism, childhood stressors, high school class rank, religious involvement, neuroticism, extraversion, psychoticism); and young adult developmental tasks (baccalaureate degree completion, full-time employment, marriage). Using SEM techniques, they found that preadulthood variables were more salient predictors of developmental tasks than a diagnosis of having a young adult alcohol-use disorder.

Want to know more? Take a look at Gotham, H. J., Sher, K. J., & Wood, P. K. (2003). Alcohol involvement and developmental task completion during young adulthood. *Journal of Studies on Alcohol, 64,* 32–42.

SUMMARY

Even though you probably will not be using these more advanced procedures anytime soon, that's all the more reason to know at least something about them, because you will certainly see them mentioned in various research publications and may even hear them mentioned in another class you are taking. By combining a passing familiarity with these techniques with your understanding of the basics (all the chapters in the book up to this one), you can feel confident of having mastered a good deal of important information about basic (and even some intermediate) statistics.

19

A Statistical Software Sampler

Difficulty Scale ☺ ☺ ☺ ☺ ☺ (a cinch!)

How much Excel? None at all!

WHAT YOU'LL LEARN ABOUT IN THIS CHAPTER

✦ Other types of software that allow you to analyze, chart, and better understand your data

Y ou need not be a nerd or anything of the sort to appreciate and enjoy what the various computer programs can do for you in your efforts to learn and use basic statistics (though if you are a nerd, there's nothing wrong with that!). The purpose of this chapter is to give you an overview of some of the more commonly used programs and some of their features and a quick look at how they work. But before we go into these descriptions, here are some words of advice.

You can find a mega listing of software programs, calculators, and more at Betty C. Jung's home page at www.bettycjung.net/Statpgms. htm, a gold mine of material on everything from basic software sites to the basics of statistical software and specialized statistical calculators. Explore all the links—you can never tell what tool you might find valuable. And, almost as always these days, Wikipedia has a listing of software programs organized by open source, public domain, freeware, and proprietary (a fancy word for "you have to pay") at http://en.wikipedia.org/wiki/List_of_statistical_packages. Make either of these your first stop, but make sure you look at both of them as you make a decision.

SELECTING THE PERFECT STATISTICS SOFTWARE

Here are some tried-and-true suggestions for making sure that you get what you want from a stats program.

1. Whether the software program is expensive (like SPSS at about $2,000 for the full package and about $30 to rent the student or academic version) or not so (like MyStat, which is free), be sure you try it before you buy it. Almost every stats program listed offers a demo (usually at its website) that you can download, and in some cases, you can even ask the maker to send you a demo version on disk or CD. These versions are often fully featured and last for up to 30 days, which gives you plenty of time to try them out.

2. Note that an increasing number of these programs cannot be purchased. Instead, they can only be rented for a period such as 6 or 12 months. At the end of that time, you will have to renew.

3. While we're mentioning price, buying directly from the manufacturer might be the most expensive way to go, especially if you buy outright without inquiring about discounts for students and faculty (sometimes called an "educational discount"). Your school bookstore may offer a discount (or have a license to distribute certain software free to students), or work with a company that distributes the software such as On The Hub (at http://onthehub.com).

4. Many of the vendors who produce statistical analysis software offer two flavors. The first is the commercial version, and the second is the academic version. They are usually the same in content but may differ (sometimes dramatically) in price. If you are going for the academic version, first find out whether it is the same as the fully featured commercial version. If not, then ask yourself if you can live with the differences. Why is the academic version so much cheaper? The company hopes that if you are a student, when you graduate, you'll move into some fat-cat job and buy the full version! There may also be a student version in which the number of cases or variables you are allowed to enter is limited. Ask, ask, ask.

5. It's hard to know exactly what you'll need before you get started, but some packages come in modules, and you don't have to buy all of the modules to get the tools you need for

the job you have to do. Read the company's brochures and website and call and ask questions.

6. Shareware is another option, and plenty of such programs are available. Shareware is a method of distributing software such that users pay for it only if they like it. Sounds like the honor system, doesn't it? Well, it is. The prices are almost always very reasonable; the shareware is often better than the commercial product; and, if you do pay, you help ensure that the clever author will continue his or her other efforts to deliver new versions that are even better than the one you have. And freeware is what it sounds like—free ware. Maybe not as ambitious as what the big boys and girls play with, but also maybe all that you need.

7. Don't buy any software that does not offer telephone technical support or, at the least, some type of e-mail or chat contact. To test this, call the tech support number (before you buy!) and see how long it takes for someone to pick up the phone. If you're on hold for 20 minutes, that may indicate that the company doesn't take tech support seriously enough to get to users' questions quickly. Or, if you e-mail and never hear back, look for another product.

8. Almost all the big stats packages do the same things—the difference is in the way that they do them. For example, SPSS, Minitab, and JMP all do a nice job of analyzing data and are acceptable. But it's the little things that might make a difference. For example, Minitab allows you to use spaces in the naming of variables while SPSS does not. Go figure.

9. Make sure you have the hardware (aka system requirements) to run the program you want to use. For example, most software is not limited by the number of cases and variables you want to analyze. The only limit is usually the size of your hard drive, which you'll use to store the data files. And if you have a slow (old) machine, then you'll likely be waiting around and watching that hourglass while your CPU does its thing. Be sure of the hardware you need to run a program before you download the demo. Same goes for the version of your Macintosh operating system or your version of Windows—make sure all is compatible.

WHAT'S OUT THERE

There are more statistical analysis programs available (more than 200) than you would ever need (or, really, want to know about). Here's a listing of some of the most popular and their outstanding features. Remember that many of these do the same thing. If at all possible, as emphasized in the preceding section, try before you buy.

A *ton* of these programs are available, some for free always and forever, some as free demos, and some that charge up front. Have some fun and tool around until you find one that works for you. We'll cover the free and open source (meaning that the underlying code is available for you to change and improve) programs and then move on to the software that has some kind of charge associated with it.

Your friends at *Statistics for People . . .* galactic headquarters like the following.

The Free Stuff and Open Source Stuff

Free is not bad and, in some cases, may be all that you need. To get a good picture of what's available, visit Free Statistical Software (http://statpages.org/javasta2.html). Keep in mind that there is the "Completely Free . . ." category (which has no strings attached), as well as the "Free, but . . ." category (which has some strings attached such as "student version," "demos," etc.).

Gnumeric Spreadsheet

Perhaps at the top of our list is the Gnumeric spreadsheet, which operates under a General Public License (or GPL). This basically means it is free and open source and you can download it from a variety of sources. This Excel-like (in both form and function) spreadsheet comes through the gracious efforts of the GNOME community, people who have dedicated time and resources to create software that is available to anyone. Don't like Excel? Turn to Gnumeric, and almost everything in this book applies equally as well. And even better, for those beloved Mac users out there (and remember that the newest version of Excel for the Mac does not support the Data Analysis tools), Gnumeric contains all the tools you need to do the same things as the Windows version of the Data Analysis tools (nice, no?).

Need more information? Go to http://en.wikipedia.org/wiki/ Gnumeric.

SSP (Smith's Statistical Package)

SSP is a simple stats package for Mac and Windows that does lots of SPSS-type (the big dog on the block) things such as calculate basic summaries; prepare charts; compare means; and do ANOVAs, chi-square tests, and regression. You can see the results of a simple *t*-test in Figure 19.1. This is a truly free package that is simple to get started with and may be all you ever need. But—Mac users beware. SSP may not be supported by the latest Mac operating system.

Need more information? Go to http://economics-files.pomona.edu/GarySmith/StatSite/SSP.html.

Figure 19.1   The Results of a Simple *t*-Test Done in SSP

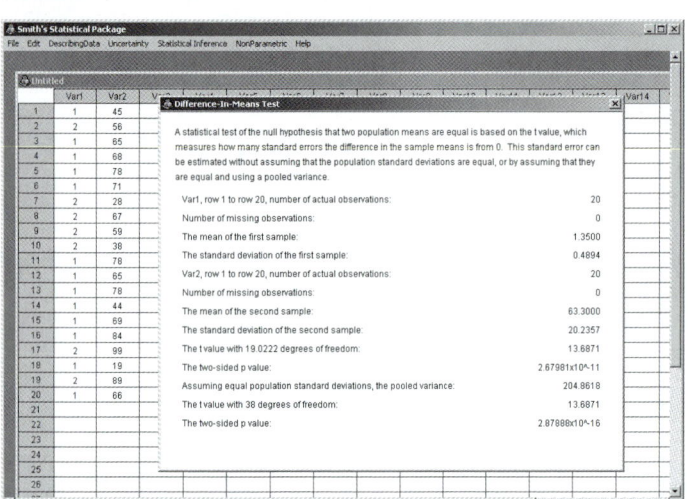

VassarStats

"Very nice" is all that we can say about this free site that handles a comprehensive assortment of statistical topics such as probabilities, frequency data, correlations and regression, ANOVA, and more. VassarStats also contains a cool set of utilities, including a Statistical Tables Calculator and a Simple Graph Maker. These handle almost everything that Excel does as described in this book.

Need more information? Go to http://vassarstats.net.

R

R is one of the up-and-coming and very popular open source programming packages from the people originally at Bell Labs. The good news is that it is all that you will ever need. The bad news is that getting started with it takes some work and the learning curve is a bit steep. If you're a beginner, R is best learned by working with someone who knows the program. Once you get the idea, your work will speed along, as will your knowledge of this very powerful tool in your arsenal.

Need more information? Go to www.r-project.org. There are plenty of links there to related sites as well, where you can get even more information on R.

PSPP

PSPP is an open source variant of the very successful (and very expensive) SPSS. Though a bit complicated to install, it's a pretty thorough, sophisticated, and complete software analysis package with an easy-to-use graphic interface.

Need more information? Go to www.gnu.org/software/pspp/.

Time to Pay

Okay, enough free stuff. Don't forget—first see what the free stuff can do, and if it's not enough, then look at these.

StatCrunch (Used to Be Called WebSTAT)

What's great about it? It's very low cost and—best of all—it's web based. No need to download software—just "fire it up," enter your data, and calculate what you want. And, because it is web based, you can use it (and your data) anywhere. Very impressive, convenient, and even fun. It's now owned and operated by Pearson Education.

Need more information? Go to www.statcrunch.com.

Cost: $24.20 for 1 year or $13.75 for 6 months

JMP

JMP (now in version 12) is billed as the "statistical discovery software." It operates on Mac, Windows, and Linux platforms and "links statistics with graphics to interactively explore, understand, and visualize data." One of JMP's features is to present a graph accompanying every statistic so you can always see the results of the analysis both as numbers and as an image. And all this is done automatically without you requesting it.

Need more information? Go to www.jmp.com/software/ or call 877-594-6567.

Cost: $1,540 for a single license for 1 year.

Minitab

This was one of the first programs available for the personal computer, and it is now in version 17 (it's been around a while!), which means that it's seen its share of changes over the years in response to users' needs. Some of the more outstanding features of this new version are

- customizable menus and toolbars;
- StatGuide™, which helps explain output;
- ReportPad™, which is a report generator;
- online tutorials;
- user-editable profiles;
- a new graphics engine; and
- lots of new multivariate tools.

Need more information? Go to www.minitab.com.

Cost: You can rent the academic version for $49.99 for 1 year or $29.99 for 6 months.

STATISTICA

StatSoft (now a part of Dell software) offers a collection of products for Windows, including STATISTICA 13. Some of the features of these powerful programs that are particularly nice are the self-prompting dialog boxes and templates (you click OK, and STATISTICA tells you what to enter); the customizable interface; the easy integration with other programs; STATISTICA Visual Basic, which allows you to access more than 11,000 functions and use this development environment to design special applications; and the ability to use macros to automate tasks.

Need more information? Go to www.statsoft.com/Products/ STATISTICA/Product-Index/ or call 918-749-1119 or e-mail sales@ software.dell.com.

Cost: There are many different options for purchase and Dell wants you to contact them for a quote. In the past, an academic license was $50 per year.

SPSS

SPSS may be the most popular big-time statistical package in use. It comes with a variety of modules that cover all aspects of statistical analysis, including both basic and advanced statistics, and a version exists for several platforms (Windows, Mac, and Linux).

One of the nicer new features included in Version 23 is new chart types and templates that are easier to work with. Figure 19.2 shows a simple bar graph created in SPSS telling you how many males and females are in a group. SPSS also features a powerful report writer. SPSS is now owned by IBM, so the good news is that deep pockets are there to fund further development; the bad news is that IBM is huge and it may be tough for SPSS customers to negotiate the bureaucracy for help. In addition, the student version may be discontinued by the time you read this, but check with your bookstore or even IBM!

Need more information? Go to www.spss.com or call 800-543-2185.

Cost: You can rent a student version (Base GradPack 23) for $73.25 for 1 year or $39.25 for 6 months, plus a one-time $4.99 "download fee."

Figure 19.2 Some Simple Statistics From SPSS

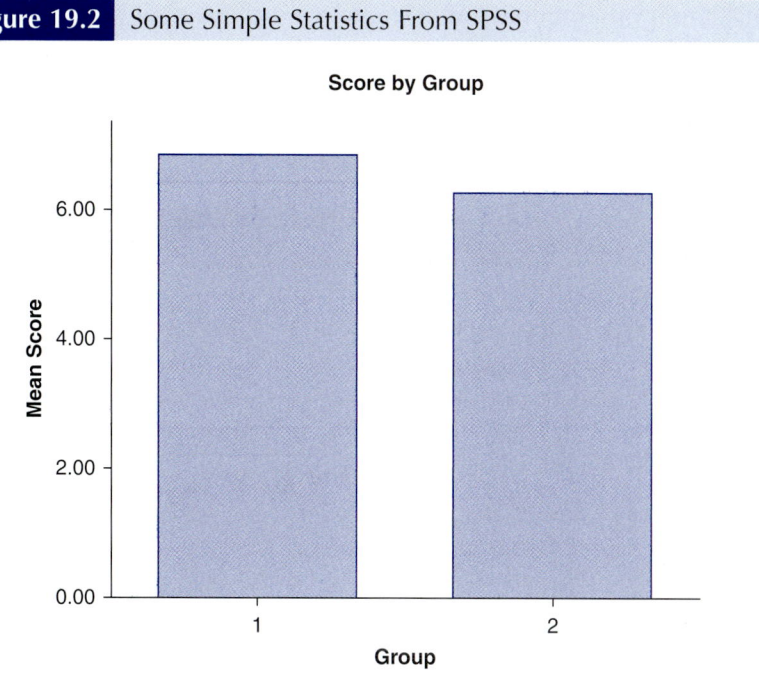

SYSTAT

SYSTAT 13.1 tends to be used by researchers in the biological and physical sciences, whereas the social and behavioral sciences researchers like SPSS (although the SYSTAT people are making an effort to appeal to social and behavioral sciences users). This package supports a strong command language so that analysis can be fine-tuned to users' needs. The latest version also sports a new interface

customizable menus. The beginner can use this stuff, but
propriate for the advanced student or professional.
information? Go to http://systat.com or call 1-800-797-
il sales@systat.com.
for the academic version, but you can download
..ch is a free version of SYSTAT and probably does lots
what you need.

STATISTIX for Windows

Version 10 of STATISTIX (only for Windows) is as powerful as the
other programs described here, but it also offers a menu-driven
interface that makes it particularly easy to learn to use, provides free
technical support, and—ready for this?—gets you a real, 400-page
paper manual. And when you call technical support, you talk with
the actual programmers who know what they're talking about (my
question was answered in 10 seconds!). All around, a good deal.

Need more information? Go to www.statistix.com or call 800-933-
7879 or e-mail sales@statistix.com.

Cost: $395 for the academic version.

SUMMARY

That's the end of Part IV and just about the end of *Statistics for People
Who (Think They) Hate Statistics, Excel 2016 Edition*. But read on! The
next chapter provides an introduction to data mining, and then Chapter
21 includes the 10 best Internet sites in the universe for information
about statistics.

20

(Mini) Data Mining

An Introduction to Getting the Most Out of Your BIG Data

B y the time you are reading this fourth edition of *Statistics for People Who (Think They) Hate Statistics, Excel 2016 Edition*, the amount of data that scientists, politicians, businesspeople, and just about everyone deals with will already be astronomical, and still it will be growing and growing and growing. It's not called BIG data for nothing!

How big? Well, these days, information is measured in terms of **exabytes** or about 1,152,921,504,606,846,976 bytes (with each byte representing a 1 or a 0) or about 1 quintillion bytes. And, there are about 1,000 exabytes of information out there now (and that amount is growing rapidly). That's a lot of stuff.

Why so much data, and what can we do with it? Technological advances allow for more interconnectedness among institutions and people (see the Internet of Things soon to be playing on your local desktop!), and this same technology allows for the collection of every single piece of data that is available, if privacy and other concerns can be addressed (and the jury is surely still out on those questions). Think *The Internet of Everything*.

You'd be surprised at how much data is "Big" and how much of it is all around us . . .

- Health care records
- Social media interactions
- Detailed analysis of sporting events
- What you purchased online, when you bought it, what it cost, and what you might be interested in purchasing next
- Human genome mapping
- Weather data analysis and prediction
- Traffic patterns
- Even such seemingly innocuous things as how many Twinkies are sold each year (okay, okay . . . 500 *million*)

ness, business, business—it loves big data because the
ng to sell products and services believe (somewhat
at these reams of data can be analyzed to understand
h is what analyzing big data is all about) of consum-
the most micro of levels. In turn, the results of the
information can be used to predict, and understand,
influence consumer buying habits.

All of these data are invaluable, but there is so much information
that it is very difficult to make sense out of it. What's needed is tools
that can look for patterns, and that's where data mining (and Excel)
come in.

Okay, so big data it is, and there are tons of jobs for those who have the
quantitative skills to dig into it (these folks are often referred to as
"quants"). But do be aware: *Big* data is no substitute for *good* data, and
we have a tendency to think that bigger is better (which, by the way, is
only true on Thanksgiving). So, while big data will surely come your
way in one form or another, the same questions need to be asked about
it as about all data sets, including where the data came from, are they
valid and reliable, who collected them and with what intentions or
purposes, and so on. We suspect that in the years to come, the analysis
of big data will yield remarkable findings in many areas, but we also
suspect that the possible pitfalls of big data, and its uses, will need to be
addressed as well.

This chapter provides a very general introduction to using Excel
for **data mining** (which is looking for patterns in large data sets)
and discusses different functions that can help you deal with large
data sets and examples of each of these functions. The chapter also
contains a brief introduction to pivot tables and cross-tabulation
tables, which are tables that can be rearranged with a click of a
mouse button to view information in unique ways.

Now here are the big caveats for this chapter.

First, this chapter is an introduction to how to work with
large data sets using Excel. Whatever you read here can be used
with small data sets as well, but we want to show you how these
tools can help make sense out of very large data sets. Smaller
data sets can almost always be examined visually to look for
trends or patterns.

Second, Excel also offers a Data Mining Add-In (much like the Data Analysis tools), but it only works when accompanied by a version of specialized server software that is beyond the scope of this book and many of the Excel installations that users of this book have available. So, for now, we'll be working with some basic functions and the data exploration capabilities of Excel.

This chapter deals with the simple question of how to make sense of data sets that are very large. Our goal is to make these data sets more manageable through the use of tools that allow us to easily extract the information that we want.

OUR SAMPLE DATA SET—WHO DOESN'T LOVE BABIES?

Basically, BIG data is a very large collection of either cases or variables, but usually both. Conceptually, big data represents a data set that is too large to just "eyeball" and get a sense of what trends might be present, what outliers might be in the set, or what important patterns may be less than obvious but are there.

For illustrative purposes, we have selected a database titled *Baby Names: Beginning 2007* from www.data.gov. This is a database from New York State containing more than 35,000 (big enough?) baby names. Baby names are displayed by the year of birth, the name of the county or borough where the mother resided according to the child's birth certificate, the child's gender, and the frequency with which the name appears in the population. The variables in the database are these:

- Year of birth
- First name
- County of birth
- Sex
- Count (or number of times that name appears)

For example, in Figure 20.1 you can see the first few sample records. If you want to download this data set and follow along, you can get it from the author. Just send an e-mail request to njs@ku.edu.

The First Few Records in the Baby Names Database

	B	C	D	E
	First Name	**County**	**Sex**	**Count**
	DOMINIC	CAYUGA	M	6
	ADDISON	ONONDAGA	F	14
	2012 JULIA	ONONDAGA	F	15
5	2012 WILLIAM	WESTCHESTER	M	41
6	2012 AMELIA	ONONDAGA	F	15
7	2012 LILY	ONONDAGA	F	15
8	2012 AIDAN	WESTCHESTER	M	16
9	2012 STEVEN	WESTCHESTER	M	16
10	2012 MAX	WESTCHESTER	M	16
11	2012 BENJAMIN	WESTCHESTER	M	40
12	2012 JUSTIN	WESTCHESTER	M	39

Thousands of databases, like the Baby Names database, are available to the public, and there are plenty of places you can look for them. Some databases allow for a search (only), such as the Grand Comics Database (at http://comics.org), and other databases contain actual data that you can download, usually presented in a variety of formats. In this case, Baby_Names was available for downloading as an *.xls* Excel file from data.gov, where you can find more than 100,000 data sets in categories such as health, weather, consumer, and scientific research among many others). Gee, it's just kind of fun to browse through this huge collection. Many of these (like Baby_Names) are available in Excel format and downloadable with a single click.

SOME EXCEL DATA-EXPLORING FUNCTIONS

There are many Excel functions that can be used to extract answers from large (or small) databases. The two such functions discussed below are just a tiny sample of all the functions you might find useful, presented here to give you some insight into how Excel can help manage a big data set and help you make sense out of entries that otherwise would be overwhelming in their complexity and size.

For each function, we will define what the function does, explain the syntax or format, and then provide an example that answers a particular question.

If you want to use a specific function but cannot find it, use the Insert Function key on the ribbon and then, in the dialog box, enter the name of the function in the Search area and click Go. Note: You have to enter the complete name—Excel won't guess at what it thinks you mean.

THE DAVERAGE FUNCTION

What DAVERAGE Does

DAVERAGE is an Excel database function that computes the average within a specified field where certain conditions (called criteria) are met. You're probably not surprised to learn that DAVERAGE stand for *database average*. For example, what's the average number of babies across all counties, born in 2007?

What DAVERAGE Looks Like

Here's the syntax for the DAVERAGE function:

$$=DAVERAGE(database, field, criteria),$$

where

database	is the range of cells that are contained in the database;
field	is the name of the column (in quotes) or the number of the column in which the desired information is located; and
criteria	defines the range of cells that contain the criterion or criteria that have to be met in order for the function to include that information.

Because database functions deal with criteria, we created a separate row at the top of the worksheet in cells G1 through K1 containing the criteria that could be used to answer our question, as shown in Figure 20.2.

...hing Criteria for the DAVERAGE Function

E	F	G	H	I	J	K
...unt		Year	First Name	County	Sex	Count
5			2007			
5						

...E *Function*

...ere are the steps we followed to use the DAVERAGE function to find out, on average across all counties, how many babies were born in 2007.

1. Click cell G4, since that will be the location for which the DAVERAGE function will return the results.

2. Click the Formula tab. Then click the Insert Function button on the left side of the ribbon and select All in the Insert Function dialog box.

3. Scroll down until you see the DAVERAGE function and double-click on DAVERAGE. You will see the DAVERAGE dialog box, as shown in Figure 20.3.

Figure 20.3 The DAVERAGE Dialog Box

Function Arguments

DAVERAGE

Database   = reference
Field   = number
Criteria   = text

=

Averages the values in a column in a list or database that match conditions you specify.

Database   is the range of cells that makes up the list or database. A database is a list of related data.

Formula result =

Help on this function   OK   Cancel

4. Click in the Database range box and then click in the intersection of rows and columns at the top left of the worksheet (a time-saver). Excel will automatically enter the range of cells from 1 to 65536, or in other words, all the possible cells in the worksheet.

5. In the Field range box, specify the field that contains what you want averaged, which in this case is Count (but according to Excel rules, this must be entered using quotes as "Count").

6. In the Criteria range, enter the criteria on which count values will be selected. Here, these are cells G1 and G2. The completed dialog box is shown in Figure 20.4.

Figure 20.4 The Completed DAVERAGE Dialog Box

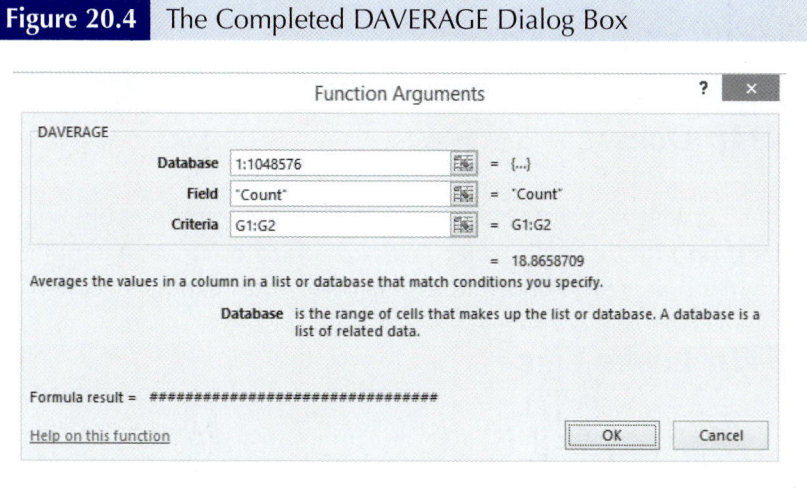

In Figure 20.5, you can see that the average number of babies born in 2007, across all names and all counties, is 18.8658709 or 18.87.

Figure 20.5 Output of the DAVERAGE Function

	A	B	C	D	E	F	G	H	I	J	K
1	Year	First Name	County	Sex	Count		Year	First Name	County	Sex	Count
2	2007	YOEL	NASSAU	M	5		2007				
3	2007	YAEL	NASSAU	F	5						
4	2007	ZISSY	ROCKLAND	F	5		18.8658709				

Formula bar: G4 =DAVERAGE(1:1048576,"Count",G1:G2)

Now, to take our example one step further, how about using DAVERAGE to return the average number of female babies born only in 2007? As you probably recognize, we are adding a second criterion.

Simple; all that needs to be done is . . .

Add an F (for female) to the criteria table in cell J2 and change the DAVERAGE syntax in cell G4 to G1:J2, as you see in Figure 20.6. In this way, two criteria are applied to determine the average number of babies across names and counties born in 2007 who are females. The result? The average is 16.86.

Figure 20.6   Using More Than One Criterion With DAVERAGE

	A	B	C	D	E	F	G	H	I	J	K
							Year	First Name	County	Sex	Count
1	Year	First Name	County	Sex	Count					F	
2	2007	YOEL	NASSAU	M	5		2007				
3	2007	YAEL	NASSAU	F	5						
4	2007	ZISSY	ROCKLAND	F	5		16.85676216				

G4   =DAVERAGE(1:1048576,"Count",G1:J2)

THE COUNTIF FUNCTION

What COUNTIF Does

COUNTIF is an Excel database function that counts the number of cells on a range of cells that meet certain criteria. For example, in how many counties were babies born with the name David?

What COUNTIF Looks Like

Here's the syntax for the COUNTIF function:

=COUNTIF(range,criteria),

where

range   is the range of cells within which you want to count; and

criteria   is the condition(s) you want to meet.

Using the COUNTIF Function

Here are the steps we followed to use the COUNTIF function to find out the number of counties in which the name David appears:

1. Enter the COUNTIF function in cell G1. This brings up the COUNTIF dialog box, as you can see in Figure 20.7.

Figure 20.7   The COUNTIF Dialog Box

Function Arguments   ? ×

COUNTIF

Range [   ] = reference

Criteria [   ] = any

=

Counts the number of cells within a range that meet the given condition.

Range   is the range of cells from which you want to count nonblank cells.

Formula result =

Help on this function   OK   Cancel

2. Click in the Range box and then click in the title of the column with the data you're interested in. Here, you're interested in first names, so click on the B at the top of Column B (another time-saver). Excel will automatically enter the range of cells B:B or, in other words, all the possible cells in Column B.

3. In the Criteria range box, specify the field that contains what you want counted, which in this case is the name "David" (you need the quotes). You can see the complete COUNTIF dialog box in Figure 20.8.

Figure 20.8 The Completed COUNTIF Dialog Box

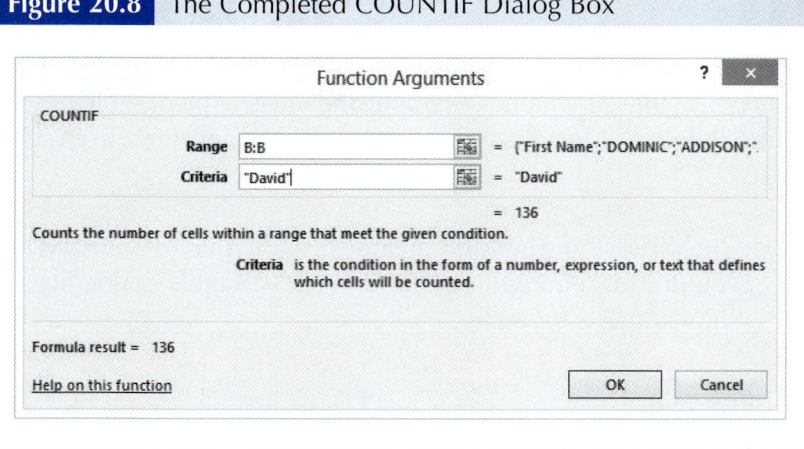

4. Click OK, and as you can also see in Figure 20.8, the name David appears across all counties 136 times.

You can use COUNTIF on multiple criteria as well. For example, if you wanted to find out the number of times that both David and Emily appear, just repeat the function in the same cell as follows:
=COUNTIF(B:B, "David")+COUNTIF(B:B, "Emily")
And in case you're interested (which we hope you are), David *and* Emily appear in 299 counties.

PIVOT TABLES AND CROSS-TABULATION: FINDING HIDDEN PATTERNS

Once you have the "raw" information organized in a worksheet as you have seen throughout this chapter, it's time to think about how you might "mine" that information, looking for patterns that can help you make important decisions. To this end, you can use a **pivot**

table, a specially designed table that allows you to easily visualize and manipulate rows and columns as well as the contents of cells.

There are many different ways to create, use, and modify pivot tables in Excel. We'll show you examples of the ways we think are the most direct and easiest to use and understand.

Creating a Pivot Table

When pivot tables first became a feature of spreadsheet programs such as Excel, creating and using them was tedious and time-consuming. Fortunately, with newer versions of Excel, a pivot table is only a few clicks away. After that, manipulating the table is as simple as dragging the title of a row or a column, or the contents of cells, to a new location.

Let's use the baby names example and create a pivot table to look at the number of female and male names that appeared from 2007 to 2012.

1. Click Insert on the Ribbon and then click Pivot Table. When you do this, you will see the Create PivotTable dialog box, as shown in Figure 20.9.

Figure 20.9	The Create PivotTable Dialog Box

Create PivotTable   ?   ×

Choose the data that you want to analyze
  ◉ Select a table or range
     Table/Range: |
  ○ Use an external data source
        Choose Connection...
     Connection name:
Choose where you want the PivotTable report to be placed
  ○ New Worksheet
  ◉ Existing Worksheet
     Location: [   ]
Choose whether you want to analyze multiple tables
  ☐ Add this data to the Data Model

                          OK   Cancel

2. In the Table/Range space, enter the range of the cells you want to use to create the pivot table. In this case, enter A1:E35218.

3. Determine whether you want the pivot table to be located on a new worksheet or someplace in an existing one; click the appropriate button and enter the appropriate location. In our example, we want our pivot table located in a new worksheet to keep things clean.

4. Click OK, and you will see the PivotTable Fields selection area on the right, as shown in Figure 20.10. You'll use this area to select and control the presentation of different fields.

Figure 20.10 The Pivot Table Fields Area

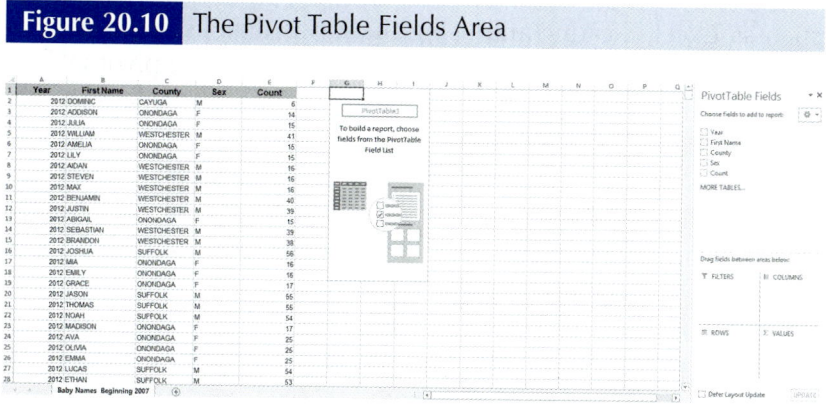

5. Click on the box next to the Year field to select it and then drag the Year field to the Column area. When you do that, you'll see columns created by year, as shown in Figure 20.11.

Figure 20.11 Creating Columns in a Pivot Table

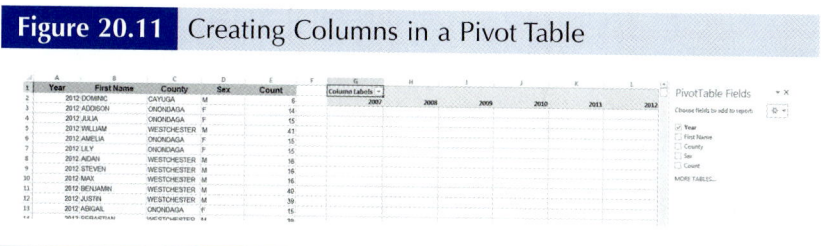

6. Drag the field named Sex to the Rows area.

7. Drag the field named Count to the Values area. When you have completed steps 4, 5, and 6, you should see the new pivot table, as shown in Figure 20.12.

Figure 20.12 A Pivot Table Organized by Year and Sex

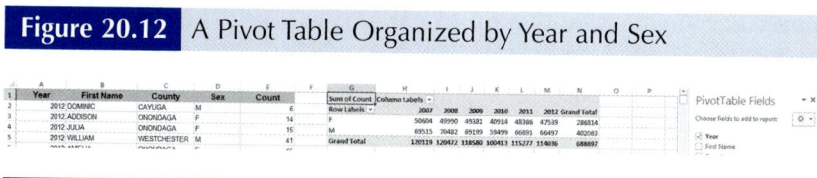

The default formula for the VALUES area of the PivotTable Fields is Sum, which gives you the totals of rows and columns. But, if you want another descriptor, such as Average, click on the small down triangle (▼), select Value Field Settings, and then select the way you want the data summarized. Options include Sum, Count, Average, Mix, etc.

That was easy and fast. And now, by dragging and arranging rows and columns as we see fit, we can organize the data any way that we want, given the information available and the fields in which the original data were organized.

For example, if you wanted to see a table that revealed use of first names by year, drag the field named First Name to the ROWS area and the field named Year to the COLUMNS area. You can see the result in Figure 20.13. And, if you want to create a table with rows or columns encompassing more than one variable, just drag those to columns or rows as the question you're asking dictates.

Cross-tabulation tables or cross-tabs (for short), which we have just created, summarize categorical data (such as year or sex in the Baby Names database we have been working with) to create a table with row and column totals as well as cell counts. These data can then be used with techniques such as chi-square (see Chapter 17) to test for the independence of whatever variables are being examined.

Figure 20.13   A First Name–by–Year Pivot Table

Your ability to change the variables or fields included in a pivot table is only limited by what variables or fields you first define with row and column headings when you enter the original data. So, as a general rule, be as granular (a fancy word for *detailed*) as possible, since you never know what you'll want to explore in your table until the time comes for exploration.

Want Excel to suggest some pivot tables for you? Simple. Click on the Recommended Pivot Tables on the Insert tab. Excel will show the Recommended Pivot Tables box with a listing of the pivot tables it thinks you might want to see. A simple click selects the one you want, and then you can modify it as you see fit.

Modifying a Pivot Table

You may have noticed that when you first create a pivot table, a new set of options opens on the Excel screen (along the top) named "PIVOTTABLE TOOLS" Under this heading are two menus, ANALYZE, with options for analyzing the contents of the pivot table, and DESIGN, with options for changing the way the table looks.

If you click on the DESIGN tab, as shown in Figure 20.14, you can work with row and column headers, change the appearance of the table (such as by including or excluding row and column totals), and more. For example, in Figure 20.15 we selected one of the many PivotTable Styles available. This doesn't do anything dramatic—just changes the table's appearance. You can also work with many different elements of a pivot table by right-clicking anywhere in the table and then clicking Pivot Table Options.

Figure 20.14 Using the Design Options for Pivot Tables

Clicking the Table option on the Insert tab (be sure that you have selected the table you are working with) provides many of the same options for designing a simple table as are available under the Pivot Table Options we just explored.

Figure 20.15	Changing the Pivot Table Style

Sum of Count	Year						
First Name	2007	2008	2009	2010	2011	2012	Grand Total
APRIL					5	11	16
AUGUST	10	10	26	18	10	37	111
AADEN		21	18				39
AALIYAH	138	152	193	154	252	221	1110
AARON	459	455	423	404	417	472	2630
AAYAN			12			10	22
ABBY	16	16				10	42
ABDIEL					10		10
ABDOULAYE					10		10
ABDUL		13	13		12		38
ABDULLAH	26	11	23	10	32	18	120
ABEL						17	17
ABIGAIL	692	682	699	624	665	694	4056
ABRAHAM	178	222	171	226	250	208	1255
ABRAM					5		5
ADA		18	6	12	15	11	62
ADALYN					5		5
ADALYNN						6	6

SUMMARY

It would be very difficult to cover even an introduction to data mining in an introductory book, but in this chapter and in this last part of *Statistics for People . . .*, we wanted you to see how Excel can help you search for patterns in big data sets using Excel functions and the pivot table tools.

TIME TO PRACTICE

1. Using Chapter 20 Data Set 1, create a cross-tabs table that shows average score (ranging from 1 to 100) by proficiency level (ranging from 1 to 5) for all 500 students.

2. Using Chapter 20 Data Set 2, create a cross-tabs table that shows the number of level-4 athletes who are female among 1,000 students. In the table, under Gender, 1 = male and 2 = female. Pivot table time!

PART V

Ten Things You'll Want to Know and Remember

Snapshots

"The Internet's got him ... Reboot! REBOOT!"

21

The Ten (or More) Best (and Most Fun) Internet Sites for Statistics Stuff

Of course you use the Internet. It's probably your first stop when you want to find out about something new. Well, just like recipes, music-sharing apps, and the latest scores, a ton of material on statistics is available for those who are new to (and those who are not so new to) its study and application. If you're not yet using the Internet as a specific tool in your learning and research activities, you are missing out on an extraordinary resource.

What's available on the Internet will not make up for a lack of studying or motivation—nothing will do that—but you can certainly find a great deal of information that will enhance your whole college experience. And this doesn't even begin to include all the fun you can have!

So, now that you're a certified novice statistician, here are some Internet sites that you might find very useful should you want to learn more about statistics.

Although the locations of websites on the Internet are more stable than ever, they still can change frequently. The URL (the uniform resource locator, what we all call the "web address") that worked today might not work tomorrow. If you don't get to where you want to go, use Google or some other search engine and search on the name of the website—perhaps there's a new URL or another web address that works.

HOW ABOUT STUDYING STATISTICS IN STOCKHOLM?

The World Wide Web Virtual Library: Statistics is the name of the page, and indeed it is a virtual worldwide library. The site (from the

good people at the University of Florida at www.stat.ufl.edu/vlib/
statistics.html) includes information on just about every facet of the
topic, including data sources, job announcements, departments,
divisions and schools of statistics (descriptions of programs all over
the world), statistical research groups, institutes and associations,
statistical services, statistical archives and resources, statistical software vendors and software, statistical journals, mailing list archives,
and related fields. Tons of great information is available here. Make
it a stop along the way.

CALCULATORS GALORE!

Want to draw a histogram? How about a table of random numbers? A sample size calculator? The Statistical Calculators page
at http://calculators.stat.ucla.edu from the very good people at
University of California–Los Angeles has just about every type
(more than 15) of calculator and table you could need. Enough
to carry you through any statistics course that you might take
and even more. Very, very cool stuff. This site is sometimes down
for technical reasons, but there are referrals to other links and
other calculators.

For example, you can click on the Random Permutations link
and complete the two boxes, and you get the number of permutations you want (as you see in Figure 21.1 for two random
permutations of 100 integers). This is very handy when you need a
table of random numbers for a specific number of participants so
you can assign them to groups.

You can find a huge assortment of calculators at http://bettycjung
.net/Statpgms.htm, mentioned in Chapter 19, as well.

Figure 21.1   Generating a Set of Random Numbers

Statistics Calculators

Random Permutations

80 100 98 6 57 96 82 90 85 73 8 61 29 39 30 4 32 59 88 92 24 5 23 86 11 9 17 71 70 49 15 54 97 76 31 63 33 10 94 58 67 48 3 91
44 7 28 93 25 81 87 1 72 36 22 18 77 47 84 46 62 26 50 53 74 42 14 75 64 65 45 79 37 68 78 43 83 13 41 40 99 19 51 38 66 52 95
12 34 21 89 56 20 16 60 2 69 27 55 35
72 46 80 74 59 98 9 3 38 50 66 12 31 17 16 62 43 22 58 36 41 8 26 14 91 5 61 97 73 57 63 47 18 55 89 95 24 82 70 51 37 100 28
33 88 27 64 23 77 83 20 96 76 11 92 78 49 42 52 1 48 45 6 35 32 30 67 86 69 25 10 7 44 19 4 79 65 2 75 94 71 39 53 15 40 90 29
84 56 93 68 60 54 13 87 34 81 21 99 85

UCLA Department of Statistics
Last updated: 15-Mar-2002
Access count is: 30052, since 18-Mar-2002
Maintained by: webstaff [webstaff@ucla.edu]

WHO'S WHO AND WHAT'S HAPPENED

The History of Statistics page located at http://anselm.edu/ homepage/jpitocch/biostats/biostatshist.html contains portraits and bibliographies of famous statisticians and a time line of important contributions to the field of statistics. So, do names like Bernoulli, Galton, Fisher, and Spearman pique your curiosity? How about the development of the first test between two averages during the early 20th century? It might seem a bit boring until you have a chance to read about the people who make up this field and their ideas—in sum, pretty cool ideas and pretty cool people.

Of course, Wikipedia at http://en.wikipedia.org/wiki/History_ of_statistics does a great job of introducing the history of this topic, as does eMathZone at http://www.emathzone.com/tutorials/ basic-statistics/history-of-statistics.html.

IT'S ALL HERE

SurfStat Australia (http://surfstat.anu.edu.au/surfstat-home/) is the online component of a basic stats course taught at the University of Newcastle, Australia, but it has grown far beyond just the notes originally written by Annette Dobson in 1987 and updated over several years' use by Anne Young, Bob Gibberd, and others. Among other things, SurfStat contains a complete interactive statistics text. Besides the text, there are exercises, a list of other statistics sites on the Internet, and a collection of Java applets (cool little programs you can use to work with different statistical procedures).

HYPERSTAT

This online tutorial with 18 lessons, at http://davidmlane.com/ hyperstat/index.html, offers nicely designed and user-friendly coverage of the important basic topics. What we really like about the site is the glossary, which uses hypertext to connect different concepts to one another. For example, in Figure 21.2, you can see topics that are hyperlinked (the live underlined words) to others. Click on any of those and zap! You're there (or at least on your way).

Figure 21.2	Sample HyperStat Screen

DATA? YOU WANT DATA?

There are data all over the place, ripe for the picking. Here are just a few. What to do with these? Download them to be used as examples in your work or as examples of analysis that you might want to do. You can use these as models:

- Statistical Reference Datasets at http://itl.nist.gov/div898/strd/
- United States Census Bureau (a huge collection and a gold mine of data courtesy of American FactFinder) at http://fact-finder2.census.gov/faces/nav/jsf/pages/index.xhtml
- The Data and Story Library, with great annotations of the data, at http://lib.stat.cmu.edu/DASL/ (look for the "stories" link)
- Tons of economic data sets provided by Growth Data Sets at www.bris.ac.uk/Depts/Economics/Growth/datasets.htm

Even more data sets are available through the federal government (besides the Census Bureau and others highlighted above). Your tax money supports these resources, so why not use them? For example, there's FedStats (at http://fedstats.sites.usa.gov), where more than 70 agencies in the US government publish statistics of interest to the public. The Federal Interagency Council on Statistical Policy maintains this site to provide easy access to the full range of statistics and information produced by these agencies for public use. Here you can find country profiles contributed by the CIA; public school student, staff, and faculty data (from the National Center for Education Statistics); and the Atlas of United States Mortality (from the National Center for Health Statistics). What a ton of data!

And most states have their data available for the clicking. We got the data for demonstration purposes for Chapter 20 from a data.gov website at http://catalog.data.gov/dataset?q=baby+names&sort=score+-desc%2C+name+asc. We clicked on the CSV option (which allows us to open the data set in Excel) and went from there.

MORE AND MORE RESOURCES

The University of Michigan's Research Guides site (http://guides.lib.umich.edu) has hundreds and hundreds of resource links, including to information on banking; book publishing; the elderly; and, for those of you with allergies, pollen count. Browse or search for exactly what you need—either way, you are guaranteed to find something interesting.

ONLINE STATISTICAL TEACHING MATERIALS

You're so good at this statistics stuff that you might as well start helping your neighbor and colleague in class. If that's the case, turn to Teaching Statistics: A Bag of Tricks at www.stat.columbia.edu/~gelman/bag-of-tricks/, brought to us by Andrew Gelman and Deborah Nolan. You can also find more about teaching statistics at Vanderbilt University (http://cft.vanderbilt.edu/guides-sub-pages/teaching-statistics/).

AND, OF COURSE, YOUTUBE . . .

Yes, you can now find stats stuff on YouTube in the form of Statz Rappers (www.youtube.com/watch?v=JS9GmU5hr5w), a group of talented young men and women who seem to be having a great time making just a bit of fun of their stats course—a very fitting stop on this path of what the Internet holds for those interested in exploring statistics. But there's also much more serious information. See, for example, www.youtube.com/watch?v=HvDqbzu0i0E from Khan Academy.org—another cool place that is full of thousands—yes, thousands—of video tutorials on everything from algebra to economics to investing and of course (you guessed it) statistics!

22 The Ten Commandments of Data Collection

Now that you know how to analyze data, you would be well served to hear something about collecting them. The data collection process can be a long and rigorous one, even if it involves only a simple, one-page questionnaire given to a group of students, parents, patients, or voters. The data collection process may very well be the most time-consuming part of your project. But as many researchers do, you will also use this time to think about the upcoming analysis and what it will entail.

Here they are: the ten commandments for making sure your data get collected in such a way that they are usable. Unlike the original Ten Commandments, these should not be carved in stone (because they can certainly change), but if you follow them, you can avoid lots of aggravation.

Commandment 1. As you begin thinking about a research question, also begin thinking about the type of data you will have to collect to answer that question. Interview? Questionnaire? Paper and pencil? Find out how other people have done it in the past by reading the relevant journals in your area of interest and consider doing what they did.

Commandment 2. As you think about the type of data you will be collecting, think about where you will be getting the data. If you are using the library for historical data or accessing files of data that have already been collected, such as census data (available through the US Census Bureau and some online sites), you will have few logistical problems. But what if you want to assess the interaction between newborns and their parents? The attitude of teachers toward unionizing? The age at which people over 50 think they are old? All of these questions require people to provide the answers, and finding people can be tough. Start now.

Commandment 3. Make sure that the data collection forms you use are clear and easy to use. Practice on a set of pilot data so you can make sure it is easy to go from the original scoring sheets to the data collection form.

Commandment 4. Always make a duplicate copy of the data file and keep it in a separate location. Keep in mind that there are two types of people: those who have lost their data and those who will. Keep a copy of data collection sheets in a separate location. If you are recording your data as a computer file, such as a spreadsheet, be sure to make a backup!

Commandment 5. Do not rely on other people to collect or transfer your data unless you have personally trained them and are confident that they understand the data collection process as well as you do. It is great to have people help you, and company helps keep the morale up during those long data collection sessions. But unless your helpers are competent beyond question, you could easily sabotage all your hard work and planning.

Commandment 6. Plan a detailed schedule of when and where you will be collecting your data. If you need to visit three schools and each of 50 children needs to be tested for a total of 10 minutes at each school, that is 25 hours of testing. That does not mean you can allot 25 hours from your schedule for this activity. What about travel from one school to another? What about the child who is in the bathroom when it is his turn, and you have to wait 10 minutes until he comes back to the classroom? What about the day you show up and Cowboy Bob is the featured guest . . . and on and on. Be prepared for anything and allocate 25% to 50% more time in your schedule for unforeseen happenings.

Commandment 7. As soon as possible, cultivate possible sources for your subject pool. Because you already have some knowledge in your own discipline, you probably also know of people who work with the type of population you want or who might be able to help you gain access to these samples. If you are in a university community, it is likely that hundreds of other people are competing for the same subject sample that you need. Instead of competing, why not try a more out-of-the-way (maybe 30 minutes away) school district or social group or civic organization or hospital, where you might be able to obtain a sample with less competition?

Commandment 8. Try to follow up on subjects who missed their testing session or interview. Call them back and try to reschedule. Once you get in the habit of skipping possible participants, it becomes too easy to cut the sample down to too small a size. And you can never tell—the people who drop out might be dropping out for reasons related to what you are studying. This can mean that your final sample of people is qualitatively different from the sample with which you started.

Commandment 9. Never discard the original data, such as the test booklets, interview notes, and so forth. Other researchers might want to use the same database, or you may have to return to the original materials for further information.

And number 10? Follow the previous 9 commandments. No kidding!

APPENDIX A

Excel-erate Your Learning

All You Need to Know About Excel

If you only have a little experience with Excel, this is the place to start. We've listed 50 of the most important and useful tasks you should start off mastering to make using Excel for simple data analysis a breeze.

Our advice is to open a new or practice worksheet where no damage can be done and enter a good deal of data (or use one of the data sets we review in the previous chapters). Then practice, practice, practice. And here's the best tip you'll ever get about Excel: Try everything and have no fear. You can't hurt anything, and you'll only learn and have fun.

One of the best things about the newer versions of Excel (including 2016) is the Quick Access Toolbar.

You could always customize toolbars in Excel, but now you can create kind of a summary toolbar right above the Excel Ribbon (which is the set of tabs at the top of the screen). You can customize this to your heart's content to make using Excel faster and easier, and that's where we will start.

To add an icon to the Quick Access Toolbar, follow these steps:

1. Click on the File tab, select Options, and then click Customize Ribbon.

2. Highlight the command you want to use on the left side of the screen and highlight the tab and menu where you want it to be available on the right side of the screen.

3. Click the Add button to add the command to the list on the right.

4. Click OK, and the button for the command will appear in the Quick Access Toolbar. No more hunting through tabs and menus—just click what you want. Figure A.1 shows you a sample Quick Access Toolbar with commands for New, Save, Save As, AutoFit, Open, Close, Undo, and Redo. Pretty cool.

Figure A.1	A Simple Quick Access Toolbar: Customizable and a Great Time-Saver

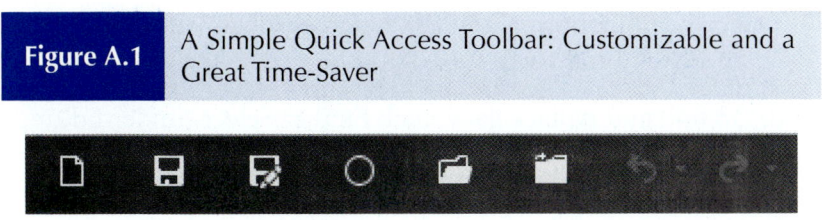

JUST THE BASICS

1. To create a new worksheet, click the File tab and then click New or use the Ctrl+N key combination.

2. To open an existing worksheet, click the File tab and then click Open or use the Ctrl+O key combination.

3. To save a worksheet, click the File tab and then click Save or use the Ctrl+S key combination.

4. To save a worksheet under a different name, click the File tab and then click Save As.

5. Need help? Press the F1 key or click the question mark on the upper right of the spreadsheet.

6. Screw up? Use the Ctrl+Z key combination to reverse the last operation you asked Excel to perform, be it simple data entry or a huge calculation.

ENTERING DATA IN A WORKSHEET

7. To enter data in a worksheet, click on the cell, type in the data, and press Enter.

8. To enter data in a series, enter the first value in the series, enter the second value, highlight both of them, and drag the latest value in the series to the last cell.

FINDING AND REPLACING DATA

9. To find data in a worksheet, click the Home tab, click Find & Select (under Editing) and click Find or use the Ctrl+F

key combination in any tab, enter the data you want to find, and click Find Next.

10. To find and replace data, click Find & Select (under Editing) and click Replace or use the Ctrl+H key combination in any tab, enter the data you want to find and what you want to replace it with, and then click Find Next.

EDITING A WORKSHEET

11. To select a cell, click on that cell. To select the entire worksheet, click on the empty box next to Column A and Row 1.

12. To edit a cell, click on that cell, press the F2 key, and make the edits in the cell or the formula bar or double-click on that cell and make the changes you want.

13. To select a row or column, click on the heading for that row (a number) or that column (a letter).

14. To insert a row or column, right-click on the column letter or row number and click. You can also use the Insert and Delete buttons on the Home tab under the Cells category.

15. To copy data from one cell or a range of cells, highlight the data to be copied, right-click → Copy, click on the cell in which you want the data copied, and right-click → Paste. You can also use the Clipboard category on the Home tab to accomplish the same thing using individual commands.

16. To copy data from one cell or a range of cells, you can also highlight the data to be copied, place the mouse pointer on the selection border so that the pointer appears as a hand, press the Ctrl key, and drag the data to the new location.

17. To replace data, click on the cell, type the new data, and press Enter.

18. To cut data from one cell or a range of cells, highlight the data to be cut and right click → Cut or press the Delete key.

19. To format a number, select the cell, right-click Format Cells, and click the Number tab. Select the format and click OK.

WORKING WITH A WORKSHEET'S APPEARANCE

20. To make rows or columns adjust to fit the data in a worksheet, highlight the entire worksheet, click the Home tab, click in the Cells category option, and click AutoFit Column Width or AutoFit Row Height.

21. To change the format of data, highlight the cells you want to change, right-click Format Cells, and make the changes.

22. To change the default font, click the File Tab, click the Options category, and select the font and the font size.

23. To add borders to a cell, highlight the cells you want to change and then click the border change you want on the drop-down menu of the Borders button located in the Font category.

24. To add shading to a cell, click the Home tab and then, in the Font category, click the little Paint Bucket drop-down menu to pick the color you want.

25. To change the margins of a worksheet, click File tab → Print → Page Setup and define the margins.

26. To add a header or a footer to a worksheet, click the Insert tab, select the Text category, click Header & Footer, and enter the text for the header and/or footer. Then click on any area outside of the header or footer.

27. To show or hide gridlines, click the View tab and click the Gridlines box in the Show category.

28. To bold data, highlight the cells and click the Bold button in the Font category on the Home tab or use the Ctrl+B key combination.

29. To italicize data, highlight the cells and click the Italics button in the Font category on the Home tab or use the Ctrl+I key combination.

30. To change the alignment of text, highlight the left, center, or right alignment button in the Alignment category on the Home tab.

31. To change the number of decimal places in a number, click on the Increase Decimal or Decrease Decimal icons in the Number category on the Home tab.

32. To get rid of empty rows between data, sort the data and then delete the empty rows at the end.

33. Use the Wrap Text option on the Ribbon to break text where you want it in any cell and create a new line.

WORKING WITH CELLS AND VALUES

34. To name a range of cells, select the cells you want to name, right-click, click Define Name, provide a name, and click OK.

35. To create a formula, click the cell in which you want the results of the formula returned, type an equal sign (=), type the formula, and press Enter.

36. To enter a function, click the cell in which you want the results of the function returned, click the Formulas tab, click the group of functions containing the function you want to use, and select the function.

37. To sort data, select the cells you want to sort, click the Data tab, and select sort by Ascending (low to high) or Descending (high to low).

38. To hide columns or rows, select the column or row you want to hide, click the View tab in the Window category, and click Hide.

39. To unhide columns or rows, select the column or row adjacent to the one that is hidden, click the View tab in the Window category, and click Unhide.

40. To square a number in a formula, use the ^ sign; for example, type =2^2. To find the square root, use ½ as the power; for example, type 2^(1/2) or 2^1/2.

USING THE DATA ANALYSIS TOOLS

41. To use the Data Analysis tools, click the Data tab, click Data Analysis in the Analysis category, and double-click the analysis you want to do.

CREATING AND USING CHARTS

42. To create a chart, highlight the data, including the column and row labels; click the Insert tab; and in the Charts category, click the type of chart you want to create.

43. To resize a chart, drag on the chart handles horizontally, vertically, or diagonally.

44. To change chart title, labels, or other information about the chart, click the Layout tab under Chart Tools and click the information you want to change.

45. To print only a chart, click on the chart to highlight it, click the File button, and click Print.

46. To change the format of a chart element, click on that element, such as major or minor tick marks; make the changes you want; and click OK.

47. To copy a chart to another application, highlight it, press the Ctrl+A key combination, press Ctrl+C, go to the new application, and press Ctrl+V.

PRINTING WORKSHEETS

48. To print a worksheet, click the File tab and then click Print.

49. To preview a worksheet, click the File tab, click Print Preview, and you will see the preview.

50. To print nonadjacent sets of cells in a worksheet, hold down the Ctrl button as they are selected and then print them.

APPENDIX B

Tables

TABLE B.1: AREAS BENEATH THE NORMAL CURVE

How to use this table:

1. Compute the z score based on the raw score and the mean of the sample.

2. Read to the right of the z score to determine the percentage of the total area underneath the normal curve that is the area between the mean and computed z score.

Here's an example:

The average score on an exam is 78 with a standard deviation of 7. What is the area under the curve for a raw score of 82? For a raw score of 82, the corresponding z score is 0.71. Using Table B.1, we find the corresponding area under the normal curve to be 50 + 26.11 or 76.11.

Table B.1 Areas Beneath the Normal Curve

z score	Area Between the Mean and the z score	z score	Area Between the Mean and the z score	z score	Area Between the Mean and the z score	z score	Area Between the Mean and the z score	z score	Area Between the Mean and the z score	z score	Area Between the Mean and the z score	z score	Area Between the Mean and the z score	z score	Area Between the Mean and the z score
0.00	0.00	0.50	19.15	1.00	34.13	1.50	43.32	2.00	47.72	2.50	49.38	3.00	49.87	3.50	49.98
0.01	0.40	0.51	19.50	1.01	34.38	1.51	43.45	2.01	47.78	2.51	49.40	3.01	49.87	3.51	49.98
0.02	0.50	0.52	19.85	1.02	34.61	1.52	43.57	2.02	47.83	2.52	49.41	3.02	49.87	3.52	49.98
0.03	1.20	0.53	20.19	1.03	34.85	1.53	43.70	2.03	47.88	2.53	49.43	3.03	49.88	3.53	49.98
0.04	1.60	0.54	20.54	1.04	35.08	1.54	43.82	2.04	47.93	2.54	49.45	3.04	49.88	3.54	49.98
0.05	1.99	0.55	20.88	1.05	35.31	1.55	43.94	2.05	47.98	2.55	49.46	3.05	49.89	3.55	49.98
0.06	2.39	0.56	21.23	1.06	35.54	1.56	44.06	2.06	48.03	2.56	49.48	3.06	49.89	3.56	49.98
0.07	2.79	0.57	21.57	1.07	35.77	1.57	44.18	2.07	48.08	2.57	49.49	3.07	49.89	3.57	49.98
0.08	3.19	0.58	21.90	1.08	35.99	1.58	44.29	2.08	48.12	2.58	49.51	3.08	49.90	3.58	49.98
0.09	3.59	0.59	22.24	1.09	36.21	1.59	44.41	2.09	48.17	2.59	49.52	3.09	49.90	3.59	49.98
0.10	3.98	0.60	22.57	1.10	36.43	1.60	44.52	2.10	48.21	2.60	49.53	3.10	49.90	3.60	49.98
0.11	4.38	0.61	22.91	1.11	36.65	1.61	44.63	2.11	48.26	2.61	49.55	3.11	49.91	3.61	49.98
0.12	4.78	0.62	23.24	1.12	36.86	1.62	44.74	2.12	48.30	2.62	49.56	3.12	49.91	3.62	49.98
0.13	5.17	0.63	23.57	1.13	37.08	1.63	44.84	2.13	48.34	2.63	49.57	3.13	49.91	3.63	49.98
0.14	5.57	0.64	23.89	1.14	37.29	1.64	44.95	2.14	48.38	2.64	49.59	3.14	49.92	3.64	49.98
0.15	5.96	0.65	24.22	1.15	37.49	1.65	45.05	2.15	48.42	2.65	49.60	3.15	49.92	3.65	49.98
0.16	6.36	0.66	24.54	1.16	37.70	1.66	45.15	2.16	48.46	2.66	49.61	3.16	49.92	3.66	49.98
0.17	6.75	0.67	24.86	1.17	37.90	1.67	45.25	2.17	48.50	2.67	49.62	3.17	49.92	3.67	49.98
0.18	7.14	0.68	25.18	1.18	38.10	1.68	45.35	2.18	48.54	2.68	49.63	3.18	49.93	3.68	49.98
0.19	7.53	0.69	25.49	1.19	38.30	1.69	45.45	2.19	48.57	2.69	49.64	3.19	49.93	3.69	49.98
0.20	7.93	0.70	25.80	1.20	38.49	1.70	45.54	2.20	48.61	2.70	49.65	3.20	49.93	3.70	49.99
0.21	8.32	0.71	26.11	1.21	38.69	1.71	45.64	2.21	48.64	2.71	49.66	3.21	49.93	3.71	49.99
0.22	8.71	0.72	26.42	1.22	38.88	1.72	45.73	2.22	48.68	2.72	49.67	3.22	49.94	3.72	49.99
0.23	9.10	0.73	26.73	1.23	39.07	1.73	45.82	2.23	48.71	2.73	49.68	3.23	49.94	3.73	49.99
0.24	9.48	0.74	27.04	1.24	39.25	1.74	45.91	2.24	48.75	2.74	49.69	3.24	49.94	3.74	49.99
0.25	9.99	0.75	27.34	1.25	39.44	1.75	45.99	2.25	48.78	2.75	49.70	3.25	49.94	3.75	49.99
0.26	10.26	0.76	27.64	1.26	39.62	1.76	46.08	2.26	48.81	2.76	49.71	3.26	49.94	3.76	49.99
0.27	10.64	0.77	27.94	1.27	39.80	1.77	46.16	2.27	48.84	2.77	49.72	3.27	49.94	3.77	49.99
0.28	11.03	0.78	28.23	1.28	39.97	1.78	46.25	2.28	48.87	2.78	49.73	3.28	49.94	3.78	49.99
0.29	11.41	0.79	28.52	1.29	40.15	1.79	46.33	2.29	48.90	2.79	49.74	3.29	49.94	3.79	49.99
0.30	11.79	0.80	28.81	1.30	40.32	1.80	46.41	2.30	48.93	2.80	49.74	3.30	49.95	3.80	49.99
0.31	12.17	0.81	29.10	1.31	40.49	1.81	46.49	2.31	48.96	2.81	49.75	3.31	49.95	3.81	49.99
0.32	12.55	0.82	29.39	1.32	40.66	1.82	46.56	2.32	48.98	2.82	49.76	3.32	49.95	3.82	49.99

(Continued)

Table B.1 (Continued)

z score	Area Between the Mean and the z score	z score	Area Between the Mean and the z score	z score	Area Between the Mean and the z score	z score	Area Between the Mean and the z score	z score	Area Between the Mean and the z score	z score	Area Between the Mean and the z score	z score	Area Between the Mean and the z score	z score	Area Between the Mean and the z score
0.33	12.93	0.83	29.67	1.33	40.82	1.83	46.64	2.33	49.01	2.83	49.77	3.33	49.95	3.83	49.99
0.34	13.31	0.84	29.95	1.34	40.99	1.84	46.71	2.34	49.04	2.84	49.77	3.34	49.95	3.84	49.99
0.35	13.68	0.85	30.23	1.35	41.15	1.85	46.78	2.35	49.06	2.85	49.78	3.35	49.96	3.85	49.99
0.36	14.06	0.86	30.51	1.36	41.31	1.86	46.86	2.36	49.09	2.86	49.79	3.36	49.96	3.86	49.99
0.37	14.43	0.87	30.78	1.37	41.47	1.87	46.93	2.37	49.11	2.87	49.79	3.37	49.96	3.87	49.99
0.38	14.80	0.88	31.06	1.38	41.62	1.88	46.99	2.38	49.13	2.88	49.80	3.38	49.96	3.88	49.99
0.39	15.17	0.89	31.33	1.39	41.77	1.89	47.06	2.39	49.16	2.89	49.81	3.39	49.96	3.89	49.99
0.40	15.54	0.90	31.59	1.40	41.92	1.90	47.13	2.40	49.18	2.90	49.81	3.40	49.97	3.90	49.99
0.41	15.91	0.91	31.86	1.41	42.07	1.91	47.19	2.41	49.20	2.91	49.82	3.41	49.97	3.91	49.99
0.42	16.28	0.92	32.12	1.42	42.22	1.92	47.26	2.42	49.22	2.92	49.82	3.42	49.97	3.92	49.99
0.43	16.64	0.93	32.38	1.43	42.36	1.93	47.32	2.43	49.25	2.93	49.83	3.43	49.97	3.93	49.99
0.44	17.00	0.94	32.64	1.44	42.51	1.94	47.38	2.44	49.27	2.94	49.84	3.44	49.97	3.94	49.99
0.45	17.36	0.95	32.89	1.45	42.65	1.95	47.44	2.45	49.29	2.95	49.84	3.45	49.98	3.95	49.99
0.46	17.72	0.96	33.15	1.46	42.79	1.96	47.50	2.46	49.31	2.96	49.85	3.46	49.98	3.96	49.99
0.47	18.08	0.97	33.40	1.47	42.92	1.97	47.56	2.47	49.32	2.97	49.85	3.47	49.98	3.97	49.99
0.48	18.44	0.98	33.65	1.48	43.06	1.98	47.61	2.48	49.34	2.98	49.86	3.48	49.98	3.98	49.99
0.49	18.79	0.99	33.89	1.49	43.19	1.99	47.67	2.49	49.36	2.99	49.86	3.49	49.98	3.99	49.99

TABLE B.2: *T* VALUES NEEDED FOR REJECTION OF THE NULL HYPOTHESIS

How to use this table:

1. Compute the *t* value test statistic.

2. Compare the obtained *t* value with the critical value listed in this table. Be sure you have calculated the number of degrees of freedom correctly and you have selected an appropriate level of significance.

3. If the obtained value is greater than the critical or tabled value, the null hypothesis (that the means are equal) is not the most attractive explanation for any observed differences.

4. If the obtained value is less than the critical or table value, the null hypothesis is the most attractive explanation for any observed differences.

Here's an example:

For a test of the difference between two groups, the table tells us that the critical value for a one-tailed test with 18 degrees of freedom tested at the .01 level is 2.553. The obtained value is 1.64, indicating that the null hypothesis cannot be rejected.

Table B.2   *t* Values Needed for Rejection of the Null Hypothesis

df	One-Tailed Test			df	Two-Tailed Test		
	0.10	0.05	0.01		0.10	0.05	0.01
1	3.078	6.314	31.821	1	6.314	12.706	63.657
2	1.886	2.92	6.965	2	2.92	4.303	9.925
3	1.638	2.353	4.541	3	2.353	3.182	5.841
4	1.533	2.132	3.747	4	2.132	2.776	4.604
5	1.476	2.015	3.365	5	2.015	2.571	4.032
6	1.44	1.943	3.143	6	1.943	2.447	3.708
7	1.415	1.895	2.998	7	1.895	2.365	3.5
8	1.397	1.86	2.897	8	1.86	2.306	3.356
9	1.383	1.833	2.822	9	1.833	2.262	3.25
10	1.372	1.813	2.764	10	1.813	2.228	3.17
11	1.364	1.796	2.718	11	1.796	2.201	3.106
12	1.356	1.783	2.681	12	1.783	2.179	3.055
13	1.35	1.771	2.651	13	1.771	2.161	3.013
14	1.345	1.762	2.625	14	1.762	2.145	2.977
15	1.341	1.753	2.603	15	1.753	2.132	2.947
16	1.337	1.746	2.584	16	1.746	2.12	2.921
17	1.334	1.74	2.567	17	1.74	2.11	2.898
18	1.331	1.734	2.553	18	1.734	2.101	2.879
19	1.328	1.729	2.54	19	1.729	2.093	2.861
20	1.326	1.725	2.528	20	1.725	2.086	2.846
21	1.323	1.721	2.518	21	1.721	2.08	2.832
22	1.321	1.717	2.509	22	1.717	2.074	2.819
23	1.32	1.714	2.5	23	1.714	2.069	2.808
24	1.318	1.711	2.492	24	1.711	2.064	2.797
25	1.317	1.708	2.485	25	1.708	2.06	2.788
26	1.315	1.706	2.479	26	1.706	2.056	2.779
27	1.314	1.704	2.473	27	1.704	2.052	2.771

df	One-Tailed Test			df	Two-Tailed Test		
	0.10	0.05	0.01		0.10	0.05	0.01
28	1.313	1.701	2.467	28	1.701	2.049	2.764
29	1.312	1.699	2.462	29	1.699	2.045	2.757
30	1.311	1.698	2.458	30	1.698	2.043	2.75
35	1.306	1.69	2.438	35	1.69	2.03	2.724
40	1.303	1.684	2.424	40	1.684	2.021	2.705
45	1.301	1.68	2.412	45	1.68	2.014	2.69
50	1.299	1.676	2.404	50	1.676	2.009	2.678
55	1.297	1.673	2.396	55	1.673	2.004	2.668
60	1.296	1.671	2.39	60	1.671	2.001	2.661
65	1.295	1.669	2.385	65	1.669	1.997	2.654
70	1.294	1.667	2.381	70	1.667	1.995	2.648
75	1.293	1.666	2.377	75	1.666	1.992	2.643
80	1.292	1.664	2.374	80	1.664	1.99	2.639
85	1.292	1.663	2.371	85	1.663	1.989	2.635
90	1.291	1.662	2.369	90	1.662	1.987	2.632
95	1.291	1.661	2.366	95	1.661	1.986	2.629
100	1.29	1.66	2.364	100	1.66	1.984	2.626
Infinity	1.282	1.645	2.327	Infinity	1.645	1.96	2.576

TABLE B.3: CRITICAL VALUES FOR ANALYSIS OF VARIANCE OR F-TEST

How to use this table:

1. Compute the F value.

2. Determine the number of degrees of freedom for the numerator $(k - 1)$ and the number of degrees of freedom for the denominator $(n - k)$.

3. Locate the critical value by reading across to locate the degrees of freedom in the numerator and down to locate the degrees of freedom in the denominator. The critical value is at the intersection of this column and row.

4. If the obtained value is greater than the critical or tabled value, the null hypothesis (that the means are equal to one another) is not the most attractive explanation for any observed differences.

5. If the obtained value is less than the critical or tabled value, the null hypothesis is the most attractive explanation for any observed differences.

Here's an example:

For a test of the difference between the means of four groups, each with 20 participants, the table gives the critical value with 3 and 15 degrees of freedom tested at the .05 level as 3.29. The obtained value is 2.87, indicating that the null hypothesis cannot be rejected and there is no overall difference among the three means.

Table B.3 Critical Values for Analysis of Variance or *F*-Test

df for the Denominator	Type I Error Rate	*df* for the Numerator					
		1	2	3	4	5	6
1	.01	4052.00	4999.00	5403.00	5625.00	5764.00	5859.00
	.05	162.00	200.00	216.00	225.00	230.00	234.00
	.10	39.90	49.50	53.60	55.80	57.20	58.20
2	.01	98.50	99.00	99.17	99.25	99.30	99.33
	.05	18.51	19.00	19.17	19.25	19.30	19.33
	.10	8.53	9.00	9.16	9.24	9.29	9.33
3	.01	34.12	30.82	29.46	28.71	28.24	27.91
	.05	10.13	9.55	9.28	9.12	9.01	8.94
	.10	5.54	5.46	5.39	5.34	5.31	5.28
4	.01	21.20	18.00	16.70	15.98	15.52	15.21
	.05	7.71	6.95	6.59	6.39	6.26	6.16
	.10	4.55	4.33	4.19	4.11	4.05	4.01
5	.01	16.26	13.27	12.06	11.39	10.97	10.67
	.05	6.61	5.79	5.41	5.19	5.05	4.95
	.10	4.06	3.78	3.62	3.52	3.45	3.41
6	.01	13.75	10.93	9.78	9.15	8.75	8.47
	.05	5.99	5.14	4.76	4.53	4.39	4.28
	.10	3.78	3.46	3.29	3.18	3.11	3.06
7	.01	12.25	9.55	8.45	7.85	7.46	7.19
	.05	5.59	4.74	4.35	4.12	3.97	3.87
	.10	3.59	3.26	3.08	2.96	2.88	2.83
8	.01	11.26	8.65	7.59	7.01	6.63	6.37
	.05	5.32	4.46	4.07	3.84	3.69	3.58
	.10	3.46	3.11	2.92	2.81	2.73	2.67
9	.01	10.56	8.02	6.99	6.42	6.06	5.80
	.05	5.12	4.26	3.86	3.63	3.48	3.37

(Continued)

Table B.3 (Continued)

df for the Denominator	Type I Error Rate	df for the Numerator					
		1	2	3	4	5	6
10	.10	3.36	3.01	2.81	2.69	2.61	2.55
	.01	10.05	7.56	6.55	6.00	5.64	5.39
	.05	4.97	4.10	3.71	3.48	3.33	3.22
11	.10	3.29	2.93	2.73	2.61	2.52	2.46
	.01	9.65	7.21	6.22	5.67	5.32	5.07
	.05	4.85	3.98	3.59	3.36	3.20	3.10
12	.10	3.23	2.86	2.66	2.54	2.45	2.39
	.01	9.33	6.93	5.95	5.41	5.07	4.82
	.05	4.75	3.89	3.49	3.26	3.11	3.00
13	.10	3.18	2.81	2.61	2.48	2.40	2.33
	.01	9.07	6.70	5.74	5.21	4.86	4.62
	.05	4.67	3.81	3.41	3.18	3.03	2.92
14	.10	3.14	2.76	2.56	2.43	2.35	2.28
	.01	8.86	6.52	5.56	5.04	4.70	4.46
	.05	4.60	3.74	3.34	3.11	2.96	2.85
15	.10	3.10	2.73	2.52	2.40	2.31	2.24
	.01	8.68	6.36	5.42	4.89	4.56	4.32
	.05	4.54	3.68	3.29	3.06	2.90	2.79
16	.10	3.07	2.70	2.49	2.36	2.27	2.21
	.01	8.53	6.23	5.29	4.77	4.44	4.20
	.05	4.49	3.63	3.24	3.01	2.85	2.74
17	.10	3.05	2.67	2.46	2.33	2.24	2.18
	.01	8.40	6.11	5.19	4.67	4.34	4.10
	.05	4.45	3.59	3.20	2.97	2.81	2.70
18	.10	3.03	2.65	2.44	2.31	2.22	2.15
	.01	8.29	6.01	5.09	4.58	4.25	4.02
	.05	4.41	3.56	3.16	2.93	2.77	2.66
19	.10	3.01	2.62	2.42	2.29	2.20	2.13
	.01	8.19	5.93	5.01	4.50	4.17	3.94

_df_ for the Denominator	Type I Error Rate	_df_ for the Numerator					
		1	2	3	4	5	6
	.05	4.38	3.52	3.13	2.90	2.74	2.63
	.10	2.99	2.61	2.40	2.27	2.18	2.11
20	.01	8.10	5.85	4.94	4.43	4.10	3.87
	.05	4.35	3.49	3.10	2.87	2.71	2.60
	.10	2.98	2.59	2.38	2.25	2.16	2.09
21	.01	8.02	5.78	4.88	4.37	4.04	3.81
	.05	4.33	3.47	3.07	2.84	2.69	2.57
	.10	2.96	2.58	2.37	2.23	2.14	2.08
22	.01	7.95	5.72	4.82	4.31	3.99	3.76
	.05	4.30	3.44	3.05	2.82	2.66	2.55
	.10	2.95	2.56	2.35	2.22	2.13	2.06
23	.01	7.88	5.66	4.77	4.26	3.94	3.71
	.05	4.28	3.42	3.03	2.80	2.64	2.53
	.10	2.94	2.55	2.34	2.21	2.12	2.05
24	.01	7.82	5.61	4.72	4.22	3.90	3.67
	.05	4.26	3.40	3.01	2.78	2.62	2.51
	.10	2.93	2.54	2.33	2.20	2.10	2.04
25	.01	7.77	5.57	4.68	4.18	3.86	3.63
	.05	4.24	3.39	2.99	2.76	2.60	2.49
	.10	2.92	2.53	2.32	2.19	2.09	2.03
26	.01	7.72	5.53	4.64	4.14	3.82	3.59
	.05	4.23	3.37	2.98	2.74	2.59	2.48
	.10	2.91	2.52	2.31	2.18	2.08	2.01
27	.01	7.68	5.49	4.60	4.11	3.79	3.56
	.05	4.21	3.36	2.96	2.73	2.57	2.46
	.10	2.90	2.51	2.30	2.17	2.07	2.01
28	.01	7.64	5.45	4.57	4.08	3.75	3.53
	.05	4.20	3.34	2.95	2.72	2.56	2.45

(Continued)

Table B.3 (Continued)

df for the Denominator	Type I Error Rate	df for the Numerator					
		1	2	3	4	5	6
	.10	2.89	2.50	2.29	2.16	2.07	2.00
29	.01	7.60	5.42	4.54	4.05	3.73	3.50
	.05	4.18	3.33	2.94	2.70	2.55	2.43
	.10	2.89	2.50	2.28	2.15	2.06	1.99
30	.01	7.56	5.39	4.51	4.02	3.70	3.47
	.05	4.17	3.32	2.92	2.69	2.53	2.42
	.10	2.88	2.49	2.28	2.14	2.05	1.98
35	.01	7.42	5.27	4.40	3.91	3.59	3.37
	.05	4.12	3.27	2.88	2.64	2.49	2.37
	.10	2.86	2.46	2.25	2.14	2.02	1.95
40	.01	7.32	5.18	4.31	3.91	3.51	3.29
	.05	4.09	3.23	2.84	2.64	2.45	2.34
	.10	2.84	2.44	2.23	2.11	2.00	1.93
45	.01	7.23	5.11	4.25	3.83	3.46	3.23
	.05	4.06	3.21	2.81	2.61	2.42	2.31
	.10	2.82	2.43	2.21	2.09	1.98	1.91
50	.01	7.17	5.06	4.20	3.77	3.41	3.19
	.05	4.04	3.18	2.79	2.58	2.40	2.29
	.10	2.81	2.41	2.20	2.08	1.97	1.90
55	.01	7.12	5.01	4.16	3.72	3.37	3.15
	.05	4.02	3.17	2.77	2.56	2.38	2.27
	.10	2.80	2.40	2.19	2.06	1.96	1.89
60	.01	7.08	4.98	4.13	3.68	3.34	3.12
	.05	4.00	3.15	2.76	2.54	2.37	2.26
	.10	2.79	2.39	2.18	2.05	1.95	1.88
65	.01	7.04	4.95	4.10	3.65	3.31	3.09
	.05	3.99	3.14	2.75	2.53	2.36	2.24

df for the Denominator	Type I Error Rate	*df* for the Numerator					
		1	2	3	4	5	6
	.10	2.79	2.39	2.17	2.04	1.94	1.87
70	.01	7.01	4.92	4.08	3.62	3.29	3.07
	.05	3.98	3.13	2.74	2.51	2.35	2.23
	.10	2.78	2.38	2.16	2.03	1.93	1.86
75	.01	6.99	4.90	4.06	3.60	3.27	3.05
	.05	3.97	3.12	2.73	2.50	2.34	2.22
	.10	2.77	2.38	2.16	2.03	1.93	1.86
80	.01	3.96	4.88	4.04	3.56	3.26	3.04
	.05	6.96	3.11	2.72	2.49	2.33	2.22
	.10	2.77	2.37	2.15	2.02	1.92	1.85
85	.01	6.94	4.86	4.02	3.55	3.24	3.02
	.05	3.95	3.10	2.71	2.48	2.32	2.21
	.10	2.77	2.37	2.15	2.01	1.92	1.85
90	.01	6.93	4.85	4.02	3.54	3.23	3.01
	.05	3.95	3.10	2.71	2.47	2.32	2.20
	.10	2.76	2.36	2.15	2.01	1.91	1.84
95	.01	6.91	4.84	4.00	3.52	3.22	3.00
	.05	3.94	3.09	2.70	2.47	2.31	2.20
	.10	2.76	2.36	2.14	2.01	1.91	1.84
100	.01	6.90	4.82	3.98	3.51	3.21	2.99
	.05	3.94	3.09	2.70	2.46	2.31	2.19
	.10	2.76	2.36	2.14	2.00	1.91	1.83
Infinity	.01	6.64	4.61	3.78	3.32	3.02	2.80
	.05	3.84	3.00	2.61	2.37	2.22	2.10
	.10	2.71	2.30	2.08	1.95	1.85	1.78

TABLE B.4: VALUES OF THE CORRELATION COEFFICIENT NEEDED FOR REJECTION OF THE NULL HYPOTHESIS

How to use this table:

1. Compute the value of the correlation coefficient.

2. Compare the value of the correlation coefficient with the critical value listed in this table.

3. If the obtained value is greater than the critical or tabled value, the null hypothesis (that the correlation coefficient is equal to zero) is not the most attractive explanation for any observed differences.

4. If the obtained value is less than the critical or tabled value, the null hypothesis is the most attractive explanation for any observed differences.

Here's an example:

For a two-tailed test at the .05 level for the significance of a correlation coefficient equal to .61 with $n = 50$ and $df = 50 - 2$ or 48 (and we use 45 in the table to be conservative), the critical value is .2875. The research hypothesis that there is a relationship between the two variables is supported.

Table B.4	Values of the Correlation Coefficient Needed for Rejection of the Null Hypothesis

df	One-Tailed Test		df	Two-Tailed Test	
	.05	.01		.05	.01
1	.9877	.9995	1	.9969	.9999
2	.9000	.9800	2	.9500	.9900
3	.8054	.9343	3	.8783	.9587
4	.7293	.8822	4	.8114	.9172
5	.6694	.8320	5	.7545	.8745
6	.6215	.7887	6	.7067	.8343
7	.5822	.7498	7	.6664	.7977
8	.5494	.7155	8	.6319	.7646
9	.5214	.6851	9	.6021	.7348
10	.4973	.6581	10	.5760	.7079
11	.4762	.6339	11	.5529	.6835
12	.4575	.6120	12	.5324	.6614
13	.4409	.5923	13	.5139	.6411
14	.4259	.5742	14	.4973	.6226
15	.412	.5577	15	.4821	.6055
16	.4000	.5425	16	.4683	.5897
17	.3887	.5285	17	.4555	.5751
18	.3783	.5155	18	.4438	.5614
19	.3687	.5034	19	.4329	.5487
20	.3598	.4921	20	.4227	.5368
25	.3233	.4451	25	.3809	.4869
30	.2960	.4093	30	.3494	.4487
35	.2746	.3810	35	.3246	.4182
40	.2573	.3578	40	.3044	.3932
45	.2428	.3384	45	.2875	.3721
50	.2306	.3218	50	.2732	.3541
60	.2108	.2948	60	.2500	.3248
70	.1954	.2737	70	.2319	.3017
80	.1829	.2565	80	.2172	.2830
90	.1726	.2422	90	.2050	.2673
100	.1638	.2301	100	.1946	.2540

TABLE B.5: CRITICAL VALUES FOR THE CHI-SQUARE TEST

How to use this table:

1. Compute the χ^2 value.

2. Determine the number of degrees of freedom for the rows ($R - 1$) and the number of degrees of freedom for the columns ($C - 1$). If your table is one dimensional, then you have only columns.

3. Locate the critical value by locating the degrees of freedom in the titled (*df*) column, and under the appropriate column for level of significance, read across.

4. If the obtained value is greater than the critical or tabled value, the null hypothesis (that the frequencies are equal to one another) is not the most attractive explanation for any observed differences.

5. If the obtained value is less than the critical or tabled value, the null hypothesis is the most attractive explanation for any observed differences.

Here's an example:

For a test of the independence among six groups, the table shows that the critical value with 5 degrees of freedom tested at the .01 level is 15.09. The obtained value is 11.64, indicating that the null hypothesis cannot be rejected and the frequencies of occurrence within the six groups are not independent of one another.

Table B.5	Critical Values for the Chi-Square Test

df	Level of Significance		
	.10	**.05**	**.01**
1	2.71	3.84	6.64
2	4.00	5.99	9.21
3	6.25	7.82	11.34
4	7.78	9.49	13.28
5	9.24	11.07	15.09
6	10.64	12.59	16.81
7	12.02	14.07	18.48
8	13.36	15.51	20.09
9	14.68	16.92	21.67
10	16.99	18.31	23.21
11	17.28	19.68	24.72
12	18.65	21.03	26.22
13	19.81	22.36	27.69
14	21.06	23.68	29.14
15	22.31	25.00	30.58
16	23.54	26.30	32.00
17	24.77	27.60	33.41
18	25.99	28.87	34.80
19	27.20	30.14	36.19
20	28.41	31.41	37.57
21	29.62	32.67	38.93
22	30.81	33.92	40.29
23	32.01	35.17	41.64
24	33.20	36.42	42.98
25	34.38	37.65	44.81
26	35.56	38.88	45.64
27	36.74	40.11	46.96
28	37.92	41.34	48.28
29	39.09	42.56	49.59
30	40.26	43.77	50.89

APPENDIX C

Data Sets

CHAPTER 2 DATA SET 1

	Score 1	Score 2	Score 3
	3	34	154
	7	54	167
	5	17	132
	4	26	145
	5	34	154
	6	25	145
	7	14	113
	8	24	156
	6	25	154
	5	23	123
Mean	5.6	27.6	144.3
Median	5.5	25.0	149.5
Mode	5.0	34.0	154.0

CHAPTER 2 DATA SET 2

Day	Class 1	Class 2	Class 3
Monday	23	32	17
Tuesday	15	44	12
Wednesday	34	15	27
Thursday	32	44	19
Friday	33	36	23

CHAPTER 2 DATA SET 3

Student	Fondant	Cupcakes	Icing	Assembly	Texture
1	1	1	6	5	3
2	5	2	3	2	7
3	7	4	4	2	1
4	1	4	3	4	3
5	5	5	1	5	7
6	6	6	6	4	5
7	2	6	3	5	4
8	5	1	6	3	6
9	7	2	3	5	2
10	3	3	5	6	5

CHAPTER 3 DATA SET 1

Height	Weight
53	156
46	131
54	123
44	142
56	156
76	171
87	143
65	135
45	138
44	114
57	154
68	166

(Continued)

(Continued)

Height	Weight
65	153
66	140
54	143
66	156
51	173
58	143
49	161
48	131

CHAPTER 3 DATA SET 2

No Intervention	Intervention
18	17
16	15
17	21
15	24
16	12
14	16
22	14
21	25
7	19
24	24
23	21
19	25
12	9
20	9
23	13

CHAPTER 4 DATA SET 1

Comp Score
12
15
11
16
21
25
21
8
6
2
22
26

Comp Score
27
36
34
33
38
42
44
47
54
55
51
56

Comp Score
53
57
49
45
45
47
43
31
12
14
15
16
22

Comp Score
29
29
54
56
57
59
54
56
43
44
41
42
7

CHAPTER 5 DATA SET 1

Correct	Attitude
17	94
13	73
12	59
15	80
16	93
14	85
16	66
16	79
18	77
19	91

CHAPTER 5 DATA SET 2

Years of Training	Successful Outcomes
1	9
9	1
1	8
4	7
3	6
3	7
7	9
9	5
7	5
6	6
6	7
1	4

CHAPTER 5 DATA SET 3

Wash	Number	Infect
2	4	1
4	2	2
2	4	2
3	4	3
4	5	1
5	5	1
4	2	5
3	5	4
2	4	2

CHAPTER 6 DATA SET 1

Fall Results	Spring Results
21	7
38	13
15	35
34	45
5	19
32	47
24	34
3	1
17	12
32	41
33	3
15	20
21	39
8	46
3	30
16	26
34	43
50	20
14	22
14	25
3	50
4	17
42	32
28	46
40	10
40	48
12	11
5	23

CHAPTER 6 DATA SET 2

Observation Period	Judge 1 Rating	Judge 2 Rating
1	1	1
2	1	1
3	1	1

(Continued)

(Continued)

Observation Period	Judge 1 Rating	Judge 2 Rating
4	1	1
5	0	0
6	0	0
7	1	0
8	0	1
9	0	1
10	1	0
11	1	0
12	0	0
13	0	0
14	1	0
15	1	0
16	1	1
17	0	1
18	0	0
19	1	0
20	1	1
21	1	1
22	1	0
23	0	0
24	0	1
25	0	0
26	1	1
27	1	0
28	0	1
29	1	0
30	0	1
31	1	0
32	0	0
33	1	1
34	0	1
35	0	0
36	1	0
37	1	1
38	1	0
39	0	1
40	0	0

Observation Period	Judge 1 Rating	Judge 2 Rating
41	0	1
42	1	1
43	0	1
44	1	0
45	1	0
46	1	0
47	1	1
48	0	0
49	0	1
50	0	0

CHAPTER 8 DATA SET 1

z Score
1.5
2.1
0.7
0.4
2.0
1.6
0.4
0.8
0.5
1.7

CHAPTER 10 DATA SET 1

61		57		92		89		58	
78		74		60		61		71	
73		76		93		57		74	
92		62		100		60		92	
71		91		65		51		50	
83		53		53		99		73	
58		60		54		77		63	
78		97		66		74		59	
94		55		73		58		93	

(Continued)

(Continued)

94		99		92		94		93	
72		57		64		91		54	
89		64		93		59		51	
88		57		93		73		69	
66		98		76		98		63	
83		51		83		81		71	
71		89		70		86		92	
53		100		52		61		71	
87		81		86		75		97	
66		61		55		86		72	
87		68		70		88		92	
								74	

CHAPTER 10 DATA SET 2

Class 1	Class 2	Class 3	Class 4	Class 5	Class 6	Class 7	Class 8	Class 9	Class 10
78	81	96	85	88	78	90	79	96	86
77	78	97	90	88	82	86	93	87	89
78	93	88	88	94	92	82	89	92	94
83	81	78	75	77	96	83	93	84	75
79	82	88	89	84	99	87	80	85	77
82	83	93	89	85	81	89	96	79	85
77	83	77	85	82	96	95	99	89	76
83	92	80	89	82	100	99	87	90	89
93	97	87	83	96	93	92	75	80	93
86	86	89	98	81	75	80	95	99	86

CHAPTER 10 DATA SET 3

June 2015 Sales (Week #1)
$22,402
$37,205
$33,931
$35,347
$39,892

June 2015 Sales (Week #1)
$22,705
$37,290
$28,060
$25,047
$28,541
$33,301
$38,738
$34,655
$26,029
$22,329
$27,007
$29,143
$20,961
$26,025

CHAPTER 11 DATA SET 1

Group 1	Group 2
7	5
3	4
3	4
2	5
3	5
8	7
8	8
5	8
8	9
5	8
5	3
4	2
6	5
10	4
10	4
5	6

(Continued)

(Continued)

Group 1	Group 2
1	7
1	7
4	5
3	6
5	4
7	3
1	2
9	7
2	6
5	2
2	8
12	9
15	7
4	6

CHAPTER 11 DATA SET 2

Males	Females
9	3
8	5
4	1
9	2
3	6
8	4
10	3
8	6
9	7
8	9
10	7
7	3
6	7
12	6
	8
	8

CHAPTER 11 DATA SET 3

Urban	Rural
6.5	7.9
9.9	4.3
6.8	6.8
4.8	6.5
4.0	3.3
5.3	13.2
8.0	9.3
4.2	1.3
7.0	6.7
6.0	5.3
9.3	2.4
6.4	4.3
9.0	1.0
5.6	3.5
6.6	
5.0	

CHAPTER 11 DATA SET 4

Sales	Main Street Store	Mall Store
Week 1	$3,453	$2,542
Week 2	$5,435	$3,221
Week 3	$3,656	$1,423
Week 4	$4,543	$1,656
Week 5	$4,543	$4,324
Week 6	$1,232	$3,234
Week 7	$4,543	$2,312
Week 8	$5,643	$1,324
Week 9	$4,354	$2,178
Week 10	$6,342	$5,468
Week 11	$4,355	$2,432
Week 12	$3,232	$2,123
Week 13	$6,532	$1,543
Week 14	$3,234	$1,121
Week 15	$3,545	$4,231

CHAPTER 11 DATA SET 5

Game	Brutes	Opponents
1	215	231
2	143	452
3	202	181
4	163	171
5	324	442
6	151	275
7	151	243
8	225	216
9	199	354
10	185	332
11	232	202
12	244	355

CHAPTER 12 DATA SET 1

Before Recycling	After Recycling
20	23
6	8
12	11
34	35
55	57
43	76
54	54
24	26
33	35
21	26
34	28
33	31
54	56
23	22
33	35
44	41
65	56

Before Recycling	After Recycling
43	34
53	51
22	21
34	31
32	33
44	38
17	15
28	27

CHAPTER 12 DATA SET 2

Before Intervention	After Intervention
1.3	6.5
2.5	8.7
2.3	9.8
8.1	10.2
5.0	7.9
7.0	6.5
7.5	8.7
5.2	7.9
4.4	8.7
7.6	9.1
9.0	8.4
7.6	6.4
4.5	7.2
1.1	5.8
5.6	6.9
6.2	5.9
7.0	7.6
6.9	7.8
5.6	7.3
5.2	4.6

CHAPTER 12 DATA SET 3

Before Treatment	After Treatment
45	46
46	44
32	47
34	42
33	45
21	32
23	36
41	43
27	24
38	41
41	38
47	31
41	22
32	36
22	36
34	27
36	41
19	44
23	32
22	32

CHAPTER 12 DATA SET 4

Team	First Game Rushing	Last Game Rushing
1	252	289
2	188	254
3	196	193
4	274	102
5	289	227
6	272	202
7	110	150
8	283	244
9	265	260
10	264	254

CHAPTER 13 DATA SET 1

<15 Hours Practice	15–25 Hours Practice	More Than 25 Hours Practice
58.7	64.4	68
55.3	55.8	65.9
61.8	58.7	54.7
49.5	54.7	53.6
64.5	52.7	58.7
61	67.8	58.7
65.7	61.6	65.7
51.4	58.7	66.5
53.6	54.6	56.7
59	51.5	55.4
	54.7	51.5
	61.4	54.8
	56.9	57.2

CHAPTER 13 DATA SET 2

	High School 1	High School 2	High School 3	High School 4	High School 5
2003	67	82	94	65	88
2004	68	87	78	65	87
2005	65	83	81	45	86
2006	68	73	76	57	88
2007	67	77	75	68	89
2008	71	74	81	76	87
2009	78	76	79	77	81
2010	76	78	89	72	78
2011	72	76	76	69	89
2012	77	86	77	58	87

CHAPTER 13 DATA SET 3

Store	Fall	Winter	Spring	Summer
1	$64,866	$51,382	$67,480	$67,282
2	$55,848	$70,963	$68,719	$64,741
3	$74,985	$71,475	$50,981	$64,963
4	$71,215	$64,265	$65,634	$59,487
5	$67,414	$74,796	$57,839	$74,481

CHAPTER 14 DATA SET 1

	High Impact	Low Impact
Male	76	88
	78	76
	76	76
	76	76
	76	56
	74	76
	74	76
	76	98
	76	88
	55	78

	High Impact	Low Impact
Female	65	65
	90	67
	65	67
	90	87
	65	78
	90	56
	90	54
	79	56
	70	54
	90	56

CHAPTER 14 DATA SET 2

	Treatment 1	Treatment 2	Treatment 3
Severity 1	6	6	2
	6	5	1
	7	4	3
	7	5	4
	7	4	5
	6	3	4
	5	3	3

	Treatment 1	Treatment 2	Treatment 3
	6	3	3
	7	4	3
	8	5	4
	7	5	5
	6	5	3
	5	6	1
	6	6	2
	7	7	4
	8	6	3
	9	5	5
	8	7	4
	7	6	2
	7	8	3
Severity 2	7	7	4
	8	5	5
	8	4	6
	9	3	5
	8	4	4
	7	5	4
	6	4	6
	6	4	5
	6	3	4
	7	3	2
	7	4	1
	6	5	3
	7	6	2
	8	7	2
	8	7	3
	8	6	4
	9	5	3
	0	4	2
	9	4	2
	8	5	1

CHAPTER 14 DATA SET 3

	Before Intervention	After Intervention
Nutrition Level 1	53	3
	7	7
	9	5
	7	4
	6	6
	7	5
	8	7
	8	6
	9	6
	8	5
Nutrition Level 2	10	4
	10	6
	6	7
	8	8
	7	7
	9	6
	5	9
	6	5
	8	7
	9	8
Nutrition Level 3	8	7
	7	6
	6	5
	6	8
	7	9
	9	7
	8	6
	4	5
	7	6
	8	7

CHAPTER 14 DATA SET 4

	Quartile 1	Quartile 2	Quartile 3	Quartile 4
Level 1 Participation	2	4	4	4
	4	4	3	4
	2	4	4	1
	1	4	3	3
	1	3	4	4
	3	1	1	2
	3	2	4	2
	4	2	4	4
	3	2	3	3
	3	4	4	3
Level 2 Participation	1	2	3	3
	3	2	4	1
	3	4	4	3
	3	2	2	3
	4	1	4	3
	1	3	4	3
	2	1	4	4
	1	4	4	4
	1	4	4	3
	4	2	2	4
Level 3 Participation	3	1	4	3
	2	1	4	1
	1	4	4	3
	2	3	4	4
	3	1	3	2
	4	4	1	3
	3	2	3	1
	4	1	3	4
	3	2	1	4
	1	2	4	3

CHAPTER 15 DATA SET 1

Motivation	GPA		Motivation	GPA
1	3.4		6	2.6
6	3.4		7	2.5
2	2.5		7	2.8
7	3.1		2	1.8
5	2.8		9	3.7
4	2.6		8	3.1
3	2.1		8	2.5
1	1.6		7	2.4
8	3.1		6	2.1
6	2.6		9	4
5	3.2		7	3.9
6	3.1		8	3.1
5	3.2		7	3.3
5	2.7		8	3
6	2.8		9	2

CHAPTER 15 DATA SET 2

Number of Books	Educational Level
68	11
345	15
276	16
756	12
43	6
546	14
58	6
187	14
286	9
93	8
376	11

Number of Books	Educational Level
623	18
876	12
28	4
289	15

CHAPTER 15 DATA SET 3

Risk	Number of Factors	Progress
4	3	42
10	1	98
4	3	43
4	3	73
10	2	17
3	3	71
10	2	39
3	2	68
3	2	50
6	1	36
6	2	56
6	1	42
10	1	22
9	2	25
8	1	31
7	2	3
1	2	42
4	2	39
3	1	56
1	2	2

(Continued)

(Continued)

Risk	Number of Factors	Progress
6	2	97
3	3	54
2	2	1
1	2	4
3	3	10

CHAPTER 16 DATA SET 1

Time	Correct
14.5	5
13.4	7
12.7	6
16.4	2
21.0	4
13.9	3
17.3	12
12.5	5
16.7	4
22.7	3

CHAPTER 16 DATA SET 2

Health	Sweets	Gender	BMI
92	1	1	21
76	4	2	23
84	4	2	25
56	6	1	31
73	6	2	22
48	8	2	28
98	2	1	22
96	4	1	23
70	6	1	26
27	8	2	35

Health	Sweets	Gender	BMI
63	7	1	27
49	5	2	29
72	5	2	26
57	8	2	27
66	7	1	25
98	2	2	19
69	7	1	32
84	3	1	27
78	8	1	28
55	6	1	26

CHAPTER 16 DATA SET 3

Years of Training	Chef's Score
7	78
6	89
15	96
9	87
8	89
2	57
15	69
16	84
7	78
6	89
15	96
9	87
8	89
2	57
15	69
16	84
10	92
9	75
11	83
12	88
6	65
12	88

CHAPTER 20 DATA SET 1

Here's the beginning of the data set (the first four cases) . . .

Proficiency Level	Score
2	83
3	75
3	54
2	63

. . . but it is pretty large and too big to fit in this appendix (it would just take up too much room), so head over to the book's website at http://edge.sagepub.com/salkindexcel4e/ to find it.

CHAPTER 20 DATA SET 2

This one is even bigger (1,000 cases!) and is available at http://edge .sagepub.com/salkindexcel4e/.

APPENDIX D

Answers to Practice Questions

CHAPTER 1A

1a–1d.

Figure 1a.16 Answers to Questions 1a to 1d

	A	B
1	Formula	Result
2	=3+5	8
3	=(10-5)*7	35
4	=(5+6+7+8)/4	6.5
5	=3^2+4^2+5^2	40

CHAPTER 2

1. By hand . . .

	Score 1	Score 2	Score 3
Mean	5.6	27.6	144.3
Median	5.5	25.0	149.5
Mode	5	25, 34	154

Figure 2.17 shows you what the Excel worksheet could look like. Keep in mind that there are two modes in the set of data named Score 2 (they are 34 and 25), but Excel will show only one, in this case 34.

Figure 2.17	Using Excel to Compute the Mean, Median, and Mode for the Data From Question 1

	A	B	C	D
1		Score 1	Score 2	Score 3
2		3	34	154
3		7	54	167
4		5	17	132
5		4	26	145
6		5	34	154
7		6	25	145
8		7	14	113
9		8	24	156
10		6	25	154
11		5	23	123
12	Mean	5.6	27.6	144.3
13	Median	5.5	25	149.5
14	Mode	5.0	34.0	154.0

2. You could use the mode or the median, but the mean (the AVERAGE in Excel terms) is the best measure because it is the most precise given that the variable (number of hand raises) is not categorical and there are no extreme values.

3. Here's what your response might look like:

As usual, the Chicken Littles [the mode] led the way in sales. The total amount of food sold was $303, for an average of $2.55 for each special.

4. You use the median when you have extreme scores, which would disproportionately bias the mean. One situation in which the median is preferable to the mean is when you are studying income and reported incomes vary widely. Because

they vary so much, you want a measure of central tendency that is insensitive to extreme scores. Another example is when you have an extreme score or an outlier; for example, you are measuring the speed with which a group of adolescents can run 100 yards and there are one or two exceptionally fast (or slow) individuals. [Your examples may well vary from these, but you should capture the idea of using the median when an outlier(s) is present.]

5. Here are five examples:

Most popular car in the high school parking lot as measured by brand name

Most disliked football opponent in the school's conference as measured by like/dislike

Least successful testing outcome as measured by number of students who failed on each of five tests (pass/fail)

Least favorite flavor of salsa by brand name as measured by preferred/not preferred

Favorite pizza by store name as measured by favorite/not favorite

6. Means for the quarter by month are shown in Figure 2.18. We inserted the AVERAGE function in only one cell and then copied it across Row 2 and then copied it down Column E.

Figure 2.18	Havefun.com's Third-Quarter Mean Sales by Toy and by Month

	A	B	C	D	E
1	Toy	July Sales	August Sales	September Sales	Average Sales
2	Slammer	$12,345.00	$ 14,453.00	$ 15,435.00	$ 14,077.67
3	Radar Zinger	$31,454.00	$ 34,567.00	$ 29,678.00	$ 31,899.67
4	Potato Gun	$ 3,253.00	$ 3,121.00	$ 5,131.00	$ 3,835.00
5	Average Sales	$15,684.00	$ 17,380.33	$ 16,748.00	$ 16,604.11

7. As you can see in Figure 2.19, the median sales for each toy can be found in Cells F1 through F3. Guess which function we used? ☺

Figure 2.19	Havefun.com's Third-Quarter Median Sales by Month

	A	B	C	D	E
1	Toy	July Sales	August Sales	September Sales	Average Sales
2	Slammer	$12,345.00	$ 14,453.00	$ 15,435.00	$ 14,077.67
3	Radar Zinger	$31,454.00	$ 34,567.00	$ 29,678.00	$ 31,899.67
4	Potato Gun	$ 3,253.00	$ 3,121.00	$ 5,131.00	$ 3,835.00
5	Median Sales	$12,345.00	$ 14,453.00	$ 15,435.00	$ 14,077.67

8. You would use the median since it is insensitive to extreme scores.

9.

	12/1 Through 12/7	12/8 Through 12/15	12/16 Through 12/23
Mean	19.25	15.50	17.25
Median	13.50	13.00	17.00

At least for the week of 12/1 through 12/7, the median is a more representative measure of central tendency because there is one extreme data point, 38, for the 15- to 19-year-old group. For the week of 12/16 through 12/23, the mean seems appropriate. And for the week of 12/8 through 12/15, the value of 24 could be seen as an outlier—it's your call whether the mean or the median better represents the center of the data!

10. Figure 2.20 shows you the Excel output, somewhat modified to appear more readable and more attractive.

Figure 2.20	The Descriptive Statistics Output

Student		Fondant		Cupcakes		Icing	
Mean	5.50	Mean	4.20	Mean	3.40	Mean	
Standard Error	0.957	Standard Error	0.727	Standard Error	0.600	Standard Error	
Median	5.500	Median	5.000	Median	3.500	Median	
Mode	#N/A	Mode	5	Mode	1	Mode	
Standard Deviation	3.028	Standard Deviation	2.300	Standard Deviation	1.897	Standard Deviation	
Sample Variance	9.167	Sample Variance	5.289	Sample Variance	3.600	Sample Variance	
Kurtosis	-1.200	Kurtosis	-1.453	Kurtosis	-1.438	Kurtosis	
Skewness	0.000	Skewness	-0.304	Skewness	0.132	Skewness	
Range	9	Range	6	Range	5	Range	
Minimum	1	Minimum	1	Minimum	1	Minimum	
Maximum	10	Maximum	7	Maximum	6.000	Maximum	
Sum	55	Sum	42	Sum	34.000	Sum	
Count	10	Count	10	Count	10.000	Count	

CHAPTER 3

1. The range is the most convenient measure of dispersion because it requires you only to subtract one number (the lowest value) from another number (the highest value). It's imprecise because it does not take into account the values that fall between the highest and the lowest values in a distribution. Use the range when you want an imprecise estimate of the variability in a distribution.

2.

High Score	Low Score	Inclusive Range	Exclusive Range
7	6	2	1
89	45	45	44
34	17	18	17
15	2	14	13
1	1	1	0

3. The range is 30. The unbiased sample standard deviation equals 10.19. The biased estimate equals 9.60. The difference is due to dividing by a sample size of 8 (for the unbiased estimate) as compared with a sample size of 9 (for the biased estimate). The unbiased estimate of the variance is 103.78, and the biased estimate is 92.25.

4. The unbiased standard deviation is 12.10, and the unbiased variance is 146.23.

5. The biased estimates are 11.47 for the standard deviation and 131.61 for the variance.

6. Unbiased estimates are always larger for two reasons (closely related, of course). First, the denominator in the formula for computing the unbiased estimate contains the value $n - 1$, rather than the value of n, so the resulting value of the fraction will always be bigger. More important, because we want to be conservative, the unbiased estimate (based on a sample that does not give us as much information as the entire population would) has to be a bit larger so we can compensate for the fact that we are looking only at the small part of the entire population.

7. Figure 3.6 shows you the data and the computed standard deviation and variance. We used both the unbiased functions (STDEV.S and VAR.S) and the biased functions (STDEV.P and VAR.P) to compute the values. After the fact, you can, of course, just look at the formula bar and examine the cell's contents to see the function's syntax.

	Figure 3.6	Computing the Unbiased and Biased Standard Deviation and Variance

	A	B	C
1		Height	Weight
2		53	156
3		46	131
4		54	123
5		44	142
6		56	156
7		76	171
8		87	143
9		65	135
10		45	138
11		44	114
12		57	154
13		68	166
14		65	153
15		66	140
16		54	143
17		66	156
18		51	173
19		58	143
20		49	161
21		48	131
22	STDEV.S	11.44	15.65
23	VAR.S	130.78	245.00
24	STDEV.P	11.15	15.26
25	VAR.P	124.24	232.75

8. First, the facts . . . (and we used the Descriptive Statistics option on the Analysis ToolPak, which is the most efficient way to fly in this case). The average number of folks flying on a morning flight is 244 (actually 244.33), and the average number flying on an evening flight is 296 (actually 296.5).

The standard deviation for morning flights is 61.74 and for evening flights is 47.35.

You can compute just about any measures of central tendency and variation and make some sense of them. For example, more people fly in the evening than the morning (which might mean more one-way tickets are purchased, etc.), and the number of people tends to be more consistent (a lower standard deviation) when it comes to evening flights. (There are a lot more descriptive things we could compute that might be of interest too, such as a comparison of cities by time of day.)

9. As you can see in Figure 3.7, the nicely cleaned up results from using the Descriptive Statistics option (from the Analysis ToolPak) reveal that the average intervention score for the No Intervention group (17.80) is only slightly larger than the average score for the Intervention group (17.60). The standard deviations are also similar: 4.68 for the No Intervention group and 5.60 for the Intervention group.

Figure 3.7	Comparison of Reading Intervention With No Intervention: Analysis ToolPak Results

	A	B	C	D	E	F	G
1	No Intervention	Intervention					
2	18	17		*No Intervention*		*Intervention*	
3	16	15					
4	17	21		Mean	17.80	Mean	17.60
5	15	24		Standard Error	1.21	Standard Error	1.45
6	16	12		Median	18	Median	17
7	14	16		Mode	16	Mode	21
8	22	14		Standard Deviation	4.68	Standard Deviation	5.60
9	21	25		Sample Variance	21.89	Sample Variance	31.40
10	7	19		Kurtosis	0.45	Kurtosis	-1.29
11	24	24		Skewness	-0.73	Skewness	-0.09
12	23	21		Range	17	Range	16
13	19	25		Minimum	7	Minimum	9
14	12	9		Maximum	24	Maximum	25
15	20	9		Sum	267	Sum	264
16	23	13		Count	15	Count	15

10. This is a bit of a trick question because you probably would not choose to do such a thing. The standard deviation is the gold standard for reporting variability in reports. But that's not to say that reporting the variance would be incorrect—it just may not be preferred.

CHAPTER 4

1a. Here's the frequency distribution.

Class Interval	Frequency
55–59	7
50–54	5
45–49	5
40–44	7
35–39	2
30–34	3
25–29	5
20–24	4
15–19	5
10–14	3
5–9	3
0–4	1

Figure 4.29   Histogram of Data in Chapter 4 Data Set 1

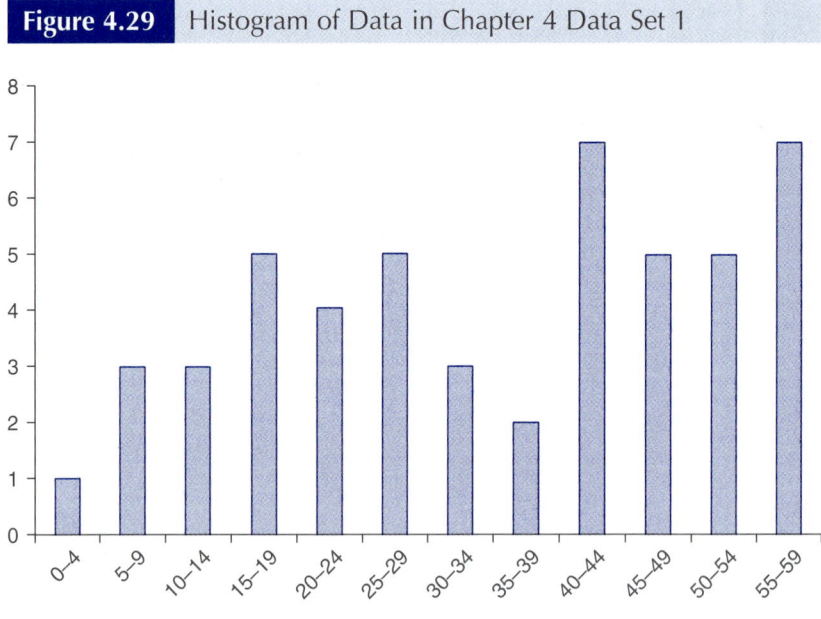

1b. We settled on a class interval of 5 because it fit the criteria that we discussed in this chapter for deciding on a class interval. Specifically, we wanted a class interval with a range of 2, 5, 10, or 20, and we wanted to cover the range of data with 10 to 20 intervals. Choosing an interval of 5 allowed us to use 12 intervals.

1c. The distribution is negatively skewed because the mean is less than the median.

2a. A line chart, which tracks changes over time

2b. A pie chart, which allows one to see relative percentages of a whole

2c. A bar chart, which is especially good at displaying categorical or nominal data

3a. Pie, to show proportions

3b. Line, to show change over time

3c. Bar or column, to display categorical data

3d. Line, to show change as stimulus is repeated

3e. Bar or column, to display categorical data

 4. On your own!

5. You can see the results in Figure 4.30. This is marginally over the top as far as cute goes, but it does make the point that you can use images to effectively transmit meaning. To quickly change the chart type, right-click inside the chart and select Change Chart Type and then make your choice.

Figure 4.30   A Chart That Uses Images as Its Bars

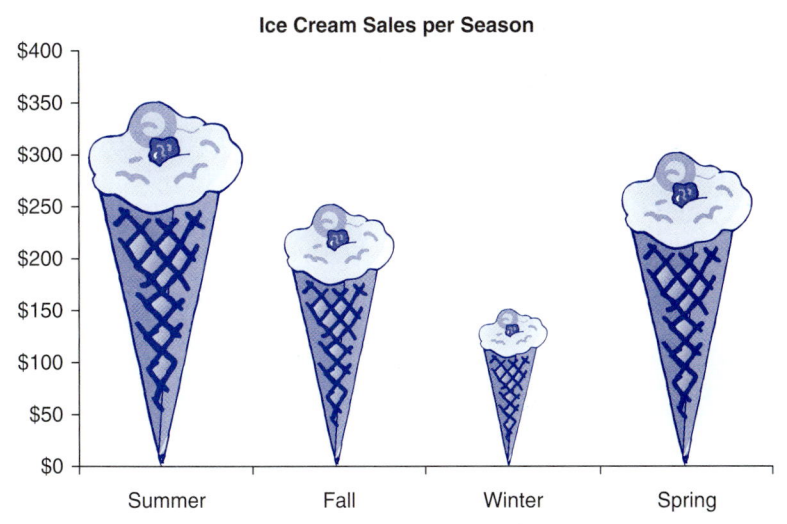

6. We did this using Excel and the chart editor, and the result is as uninformative as it is ugly. This pie chart revised by Dr. Frankenstein now appears as Figure 4.31.

Figure 4.31   A Really, Really Ugly Chart Brought to You by Chart Junk

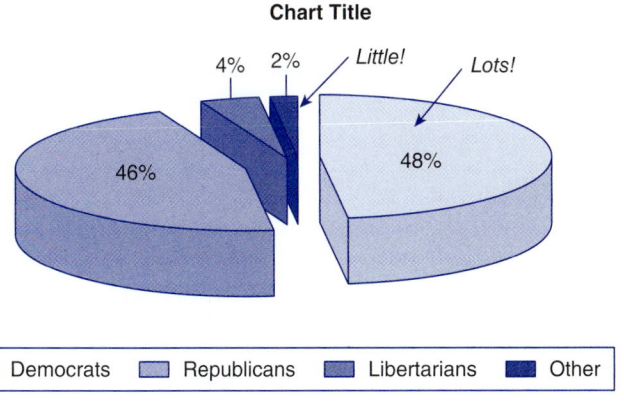

7. Your chart could look like the one shown in Figure 4.31 with data that we created, but don't get excited if it does not look exactly the same. Just try to include as many of the elements as you can that Question 7 asks for.

CHAPTER 5

1a. $r = .596$.

1b. From the answer to 1a, a positive value for r, you already know that the correlation is direct. But from the scatterplot shown in Figure 5.13, you can predict it to be such (even if you didn't know the sign of the coefficient), because the data points group themselves from the lower-left corner of the graph to the upper-right corner and assume a positive slope.

| Figure 5.13 | A Scatterplot of Problems Correct and Attitude Toward Test Taking Showing a Positive Relationship |

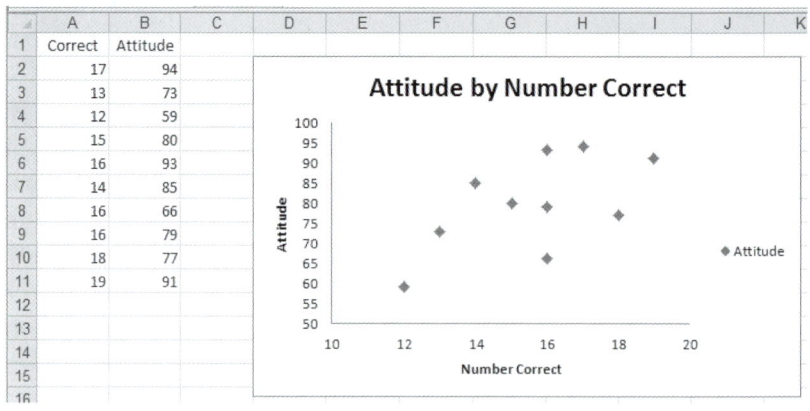

2a. $r = .269$.

2b. According to Table 5.2, the general strength of the correlation of this magnitude is weak. The coefficient of determination is .2692, and .072 (or 7.2%) of the variance is accounted for. The subjective analysis (weak) and the objective one (7.2% of the variance accounted for) are consistent with one another.

3. The correlation is $-.45$, which means the more training the doctors have, the better the outcomes (remember that 1 is good and 10 is not) and that the less training the doctors

have, the worse the outcomes. Squaring .45 results in a value of .20, meaning 20% of the variability in one variable is accounted for by the other. It does not seem that the amount of training a doctor has had and the outcomes of this procedure share a lot.

4. Here is one example (yours is probably different): Two variables that may not be correlated would be number of children in a family and average number of children in the neighborhood per household. These two variables just don't share enough in common (the key point your explanation should include).

5. The correlation matrix is shown in Figure 5.14, and as you can see, between Wash and Number, the correlation is not very strong (technically, nonexistent), and it is even weaker between Wash and Infect. However, between Number and Infect, the correlation is quite strong. What this could mean is that the number of washings has much more to do with reducing infections than the quality of washing. Quality of washing and infections no more cause each other than the rooster's crowing causes the sun to rise. They may happen simultaneously, but neither produces the other's outcome.

Figure 5.14	Correlation Matrix: Hand-Washing Efficiency, Hand-Washing Frequency, and Hospital-wide Infections

	A	B	C	D	E	F	G	H
1	Wash	Number	Infect			Wash	Number	Infect
2	2	4	1		Wash	1		
3	4	2	2		Number	-0.07625	1	
4	2	4	2		Infect	0.026958	-0.42931	1
5	3	4	3					
6	4	5	1					
7	5	5	1					
8	4	2	5					
9	3	5	4					
10	2	4	2					

6a. .8

6b. Very strong

6c. 1 − .64, or 36% (.36)

7. To examine the relationship between ethnicity and political affiliation, you would use the phi coefficient because both variables are nominal in nature. To examine the relationship between club membership and high school GPA, you would use the point biserial correlation because one variable is nominal (club membership) and the other is interval (GPA).

8. Variables that share something with one another are usually correlated with one another. Examples include level of education acquired and lifetime earnings, weight and level of blood sugar, and happiness with surgical outcomes and expectations. You cannot conclude that a change in one variable causes a change in the other because correlations reflect associations and not causality. Too many things happen "coincidentally"—like ice cream and crime. Remember?

9. The legislator may be very well-intentioned, but he or she may also be mistaken. The statement implies that teenage pregnancy may be caused by dropping out of school (and we sure know that's not the case ☺). In fact, these two variables are just related to one another, and the relationship might very well be a function of what they share in common (such as family income level and other important variables related to both early pregnancy and dropout rates).

10. The correlation is .64, meaning that increases in budget and increases in the number of clients served are positively related to one another. From a descriptive perspective, a bit more than 36% of the variance is shared between the two variables.

11.

+.36

−.45

+.47

−.62

+.71

12. This is easy to explain. Most children begin walking between 18 and 24 months because of normal development, and they will do so if parents wave (or don't wave) garlic over their cribs. Thus, most parents who do the garlic-waving intervention will see their child take his or her first steps on schedule, but we promise—garlic doesn't cause walking.

CHAPTER 6

1. Do this one on your own.

2. First, test–retest . . . You want to examine the stability of a test score over time, and you would need to do that, for example, if you were testing children's skills in August when the school year begins and again in May when it ends. As far as parallel forms, you may want to give two groups of adolescents a test of the same phenomenon, expressed in one form through paper-and-pencil writings and in another form through the use of word processing software. You want to compare the two and make sure that the evaluating tool is reliable (as a first step).

3. Since this is a test–retest situation, we use the CORREL or the PEARSON function or the Data Analysis ToolPak Correlation option to calculate a correlation of .84, a value that is healthy and indicates a high degree of reliability.

4. The test–retest reliability is less than .14 (actually .138), giving this vocational test a pretty low claim to any reliability.

5. Each judge had 50 observations, and the judges agreed 19 times for an interrater reliability coefficient of 19/50, or .38—not that terrific. No substitutions from the menu allowed.

6. A test can be reliable but not measure what it is supposed to; that is, it can be reliable but not valid. In order for a test to be valid, however, it has to do the same thing consistently (which is reliability). If it does not, how can one say it does what it is supposed to do? One can't, my good friend.

7. Ah, the million-dollar question. If one does not use an instrument that is reliable and valid, how does one know that the hypothesis is not being (or is being) supported? Perhaps the poor quality of the instrumentation is yielding positive or negative results.

8. Concurrent validity assesses how well a test reflects current performance of a particular construct, trait, characteristic, or ability, while predictive validity predicts future performance. An example of concurrent validity would be to see how accurately a test assesses proper weight-lifting technique, while predictive validity might look at how well a questionnaire predicts weight-lifting success in competition.

9. This is just a little bit of a trick question. Construct validity is hard to establish because constructs are difficult to define, theoretically as well as empirically. And if the construct is difficult to define and it's tough to design measurements of that construct, establishing validity is difficult as well. Establishing construct validity begins with a very well thought through theoretical argument and a good foundation as to what the construct is, why it is important to the field, and how it might be assessed. Only then can the assessment tool be designed and administered and then the effort at establishing construct validity begun.

CHAPTER 7

Questions 1 and 2 are specific to your own interests. So, although there are no right answers, there are plenty of wrong ones! But, to get a jump on these first two questions, try to find studies that are close to your professional interest and ones that you find engaging to read.

3. Your answers may indeed be different from the ones below, but the ones that follow should provide you some guidelines about what's correct.

3a. *Null:* Children with short attention spans, as measured by the Attention Span Observation Scale, will have the same frequency of out-of-seat behavior as those with long attention spans.

Directional: Children with short attention spans, as measured by the Attention Span Observation Scale, will have a higher frequency of out-of-seat behavior than those with long attention spans.

Nondirectional: Children with short attention spans, as measured by the Attention Span Observation Scale, will differ in the frequency of out-of-seat behavior from those with long attention spans.

3b. *Null:* There is no relationship between the overall quality of a marriage and the quality of spouses' relationships with their siblings.

Directional: There is a positive relationship between the overall quality of a marriage and the quality of spouses' relationships with their siblings.

Nondirectional: There is a relationship between the overall quality of a marriage and the quality of spouses' relationships with their siblings.

3c. *Null:* Pharmacological treatment combined with traditional psychotherapy has the same effect in treating anorexia nervosa as does traditional psychotherapy alone.

Directional: Pharmacological treatment combined with traditional psychotherapy is more effective in treating anorexia nervosa than is traditional psychotherapy alone.

Nondirectional: Pharmacological treatment combined with traditional psychotherapy differs in effectiveness from traditional psychotherapy alone in the treatment of anorexia nervosa.

3d. *Null:* Participation in early reading programs makes no difference in later reading scores.

Directional: Children who participate in an early intervention reading program will have higher reading scores when entering sixth grade than those children who do not participate.

Nondirectional: Children who participate in an early intervention reading program will have different reading scores when entering sixth grade from those of children who do not participate.

4. This is pretty much on your own, but remember that the more complete and clear the research hypothesis, the more likely it is to adhere to the criteria that we specified during that discussion. Clear and simple—that's what you want.

5. There are many difficulties that are associated with poorly written hypotheses. To begin with, poorly written hypotheses are difficult to test because ambiguous terms might be used and posited relationships are unclear. If a research hypothesis does not clearly state what's being tested and how, there's very little confidence we can place in the outcome (and even less generalizability).

6. The null hypothesis is a statement of equality, and one of its most important purposes is that it is a starting point for any research endeavor in which the "null" state is one of equality. That is, when we know nothing else about the relationship between variables, the only fair conclusion we can reach is that their values are equal. The null differs from the research hypothesis in that the research hypothesis is a statement of inequality.

7. In the most general of terms, chance is the effect of the many factors on your outcome variable you have not accounted for. All the reasons why two variables might be related, other than what you hypothesize, can be related to chance. Our job? Always, to minimize the degree to which chance can explain outcomes rather than the variables we are interested in studying.

8. If you're at the beginning of exploring a question (which then becomes a hypothesis) and you have little knowledge about the outcome (which is why you are asking the question and performing the tests in the first place), then the null is the perfect starting point because it is a statement of equality. It basically says, "Given no other information about the relationships that I am studying, I should start at the beginning where I know very little." The null is the perfect, unbiased, and objective starting point because it is the place where everything is thought to be equal unless proved otherwise. To assume anything else would be to adopt a biased stance to start with—not a desirable state when beginning a research project.

9. Possible answers are as follows:

a. Null hypothesis: There is no difference between the amount of money spent on food by undergraduate student-athletes and other undergraduate students. $H_0: \mu_{us} = \mu_{sa}$	a. Research hypothesis: Undergraduate student-athletes spend more money on food than do other undergraduate students. $H_1: \bar{X}_{us} < \bar{X}_{sa}$
b. Null hypothesis: There is no difference between white and brown rats in the average amount of time taken to get out of a maze. $H_0: \mu_W = \mu_B$	b. Research hypothesis: There is a difference between white and brown rats in the average amount of time taken to get out of a maze. $H_1: \bar{X}_W \neq \bar{X}_B$
c. Null hypothesis: The effects of Drug A on a disease are not different from the effects of Drug B. $H_0: \mu_A = \mu_B$	c. Research hypothesis: Drug A has stronger effects on a disease than Drug B. $H_1: \bar{X}_A > \bar{X}_B$
d. Null hypothesis: There is no difference between the time used to complete a task when Method 1 is used as compared with Method 2. $H_0: \mu_1 = \mu_2$	d. Research hypothesis: There is a difference between the time used to complete a task when Method 1 is used as compared with Method 2. $H_1: \bar{X}_1 \neq \bar{X}_2$

CHAPTER 8

1a. In a normal curve, the mean, median, and mode are equal to one another; the curve is symmetrical about the mean; and the tails are asymptotic.

1b. Height and weight are examples, as are intelligence and problem-solving skills.

2. A z score is a standard score (and is comparable to other scores of the same type) because it is based on the degree of variability within its respective distribution of scores. Because a z score is always a measure of the distance between the mean and some point on the x-axis (regardless of the mean and standard deviation differences from one distribution to the next), the same units are used (units of standard deviations), and they can be compared with one another.

3. The z score, or any standard score for that matter, allows you to compare scores from different distributions using the same metric. In other words, for the most part, the characteristics of a distribution don't matter—standard scores derived from different distributions are comparable.

   A good example is when you compare raw scores from different testing situations and the scores are converted to standard scores for the comparison.

4a. $z = (55 - 50)/5 = +1.00$.

4b. $z = (50 - 50)/5 = 0$.

4c. $z = (60 - 50)/5 = +2.00$.

4d. $z = (58.5 - 50)/5 = +1.7$.

4e. $z = (46 - 50)/5 = -0.8$.

5. If the mean is 40 and the standard deviation equal to 5, the corresponding raw score of $z = 1.5$ is . . .

$$X = 5(1.5) + 40 = 47.5$$

And the corresponding t score is . . .

$$t = 50 + 10(z) = 65$$

6a. The probability of a score falling between a raw score of 70 and a raw score of 80 is .5646. A z score for a raw score of 70 is −0.78, and a z score for a raw score of 80 is +0.78. The area from the mean to a *z* score of 0.78 is 28.23%. The area between the two scores is 28.23 times 2, or 56.46%.

6b. The probability of a score falling above a raw score of 80 is .2177. A *z* score for a raw score of 80 is 0.78. The area between the mean and a *z* score of 0.78 is 28.23%. The area below a *z* score of 0.78 is .50 + .2823, or .7823. The difference between 1 (the total area under the curve) and .7823 is .2177.

6c. The probability of a score falling between a raw score of 81 and a raw score of 83 is .068. A *z* score for a raw score of 81 is 0.94, and a *z* score for a raw score of 83 is 1.25. The area from the mean to a *z* score of 0.94 is 32.64%. The area between the mean and a *z* score of 1.25 is 39.44%. The difference between the two is .3944 − .3264 = .068, or 6.8%.

6d. The probability of a score falling below a raw score of 63 is .03. A *z* score for a raw score of 63 is −1.88. The area between the mean and a *z* score of −1.88 is 46.99%. The area below a *z* score of 1.88 is 1 − (.50 + .4699) = .03.

7. This is easier than you think. Just enter the following formula, which uses the NORM.S.DIST function in any cell, and press Enter:

=NORM.S.DIST(2,TRUE)-NORM.S.DIST(1,TRUE)

And the magic answer is 0.135905122.

8. You can see what the results should be in Figure 8.11, where the formula shown was copied down from B2 to B11.

Figure 8.11   Using the NORMAL.S.DIST Function to Compute the Probability of *z* Scores

	B2			*fx*	=NORM.S.DIST(A2,TRUE)	
	A	B	C	D	E	F
1	z Scores	Probability				
2	1.5	0.933193				
3	2.1	0.982136				
4	0.7	0.758036				
5	0.4	0.655422				
6	2.0	0.977250				
7	1.6	0.945201				
8	0.4	0.655422				
9	0.8	0.788145				
10	0.5	0.691462				
11	1.7	0.955435				

9. Well, we know that the top 90% of the distribution is represented by a z of about 1.29, so we can plug in the values for $X = zs + \bar{X}$ which is $X = 1.29(5.5) + 78 = 85.095$. Let's round this number and say that Jake needs a score of at least 85 to get his certificate.

10. Understanding the role that the central limit theorem plays in inferential statistics is critical to understanding how populations that may not have all the characteristics of a normal distribution can still be treated as such. Multiple selections of samples will result in the values of those samples resembling a normal distribution.

11. It doesn't make sense because raw scores are not comparable to one another when they belong to different distributions. A raw score of 80 on the math test when the class mean is 40 is just not comparable to an 80 on the essay-writing skills test on which everyone got the one answer correct. Distributions, like people, are not always comparable to one another. Not everything (or everyone) is comparable to everything else.

12. Here's the info with the z scores filled in.

Math			
Class Mean	81		
Class Standard Deviation	2		
Reading			
Class Mean	87		
Class Standard Deviation	10		
Raw Scores			
	Math Score	Reading Score	Average
Noah	85	88	86.5
Talya	87	81	84
z Scores			
	Math Score	Reading Score	Average
Noah	2	0.1	1.05
Talya	3	–0.6	1.2

Noah has the higher average raw score (86.5 vs. 84 for Talya), but Talya has the higher average z score (1.2 vs. 1.05 for Noah). Remember that we asked who the better student was relative to the rest of the class, which requires the use of a standard score (we used *z* scores). But why is Talya the better student relative to Noah? Because on the test where there is the lowest variability (Math with *sd* = 2), Talya really stands out with a *z* score of 3. That puts her ahead.

13. And this really is a fun, and somewhat provocative question.

Everything we know about probability and its application to real-world events tells us that no matter how unlikely it is for an event to occur, there is always, always, always a chance that it will—maybe a really small chance, but still a chance. That's why the tails of the distribution curve never touch the *x*-axis. And that's why there is always a chance for rain, no matter the conditions or the forecast.

And even though one might predict a 100% chance of rain, if it's not actually raining, there's always that very small chance that it will not. Fun ideas to think about, no?

CHAPTER 9

1. The concept of significance is crucial to the study and use of inferential statistics because significance (reflected in the idea of a significance level) sets the level at which we can be confident that the outcomes we observe are "truthful" and to what extent these outcomes can be generalized to the larger population from which the sample was selected.

2a. Level of significance refers only to a single, independent test of the null hypothesis and not to multiple tests.

2b. No, no, and no. It is impossible to set the error rate to zero because it is not possible to ensure that we would not reject a null hypothesis when it is actually true. There's always a chance.

2c. The level of risk that you are willing to take to reject the null hypothesis when it is true has nothing to do with the meaningfulness of the outcomes of your research. You can have a highly significant outcome that is meaningless, or have a relatively high Type I error rate (.10) but a very meaningful finding.

3. Chance is reflected in the degree of risk (Type I error) that we are willing to take in the possible rejection of a true null hypothesis.

4a. Reject the null since the probability of this outcome is less than .05 (or what you would expect by chance alone). In other words, the relationship is significant.

4b. Fail to reject the null since there is no relationship. In other words, consumption of coffee and GPA are not related.

4c. Fail to reject the null since there is no relationship between the variables. In other words, work hours and job satisfaction are unrelated to one another.

5. At the .01 level, less room is left for errors or mistakes because the test is more rigorous. In other words, it is "harder" to find an outcome that is sufficiently removed from what you would expect by chance (the null hypothesis) when the probability associated with that outcome is smaller (such as .01) rather than larger (such as .05).

6. This is a bit tricky, but here goes. Since you can never directly test the null (remember that nulls are for populations and research hypotheses are for samples), you can't reject what you do not test. But, in light of results of the test of the research hypothesis, you can fail to reject the null or, in other words, accept the research hypothesis as the clearest explanation of the observed outcomes.

7. The critical value is a cutoff at which less extreme values occur by chance (if the null is "correct"), and more extreme values indicate that an outcome is due to something other than chance.

8. The obtained value is the result of applying a statistical test to evaluate the probability that an outcome occurred by chance rather than being the result of some systematic change as a result of the research.

9. Here's the order of the steps through the flowchart, starting at the top:

The two groups are independent; one is not a sample and the other a population.

Differences between groups on one or more variables are being examined.

Different participants are being tested.

Two groups are being tested.

The *t*-test for independent samples is needed.

10a. The area under the curve represents outcomes that are so unlikely, we attribute them to something other than chance—perhaps the treatment.

10b. As the test becomes more rigorous, the area becomes smaller, and the defining line where the area begins moves to the right. There's less room for error (of the Type I kind) and, hence, the area is smaller.

CHAPTER 10

1. The one-sample Z-test is appropriate to use when the mean of a sample is being compared with the mean of a population and the null hypothesis is that there is no difference.

2. Quite interestingly, the Z in Z-test is a kind of standard score just as the simple z score is. Its similarity to a simple z score or to any other standard score lies in the fact that it is comparable across distributions, having as its denominator the standard error of the mean. This is a form of deviation about the means of all the means of a distribution rather than just one mean, but like the simple z-score that is standardized on one mean, the value from a Z-test is comparable across distributions as well. This is why the values of areas underneath the normal curve are useful—they provide comparability across different events!

3a. $H_1 : \bar{X}_{\text{Chocolate-Only Diet}} \neq \mu_{\text{Chocolate-Only Diet}}$

3b. $H_1 : \bar{X}_{\text{Rate This Season}} \neq \mu_{\text{Rate Last 50 Seasons}}$

3c. $H_1 : \bar{X}_{\text{Costs Last Year}} \neq \mu_{\text{Costs Last 20 Years}}$

4. Here's the math:

$$SEM = \frac{2.35}{\sqrt{15}} = .60$$

$$z = \frac{16 - 15}{.60} = 1.66$$

This value of 1.66, when checked against the chart in Appendix B, is not extreme enough for us to conclude that the number of flu cases in Butterfield is any different from the number occurring around the state. Don't forget to wash your hands.

5. Using the Z.TEST function, you find that the likelihood that Mark's class scored higher than the other 10 classes is .76—not bad, but not that exceptional, right?

6. Joe must be doing something right. The likelihood that his sales exceeded the average for the 20 other restaurants (which is $29,927) is .99. According to the data we have, his sales are exceptional.

CHAPTER 11

1. The mean for boys equals 7.93, and the mean for girls equals 5.31. The obtained t value is 3.006, and the critical t value at the .05 level for rejection of the null hypothesis for a one-tailed test (boys *more* than girls, remember?) is 1.701. Conclusion? Boys raise their hands significantly more!

2. Now this is very interesting. We have the same exact data, of course, but a different hypothesis. Here, the hypothesis is that the number of times is *different* (not more or less), necessitating a two-tailed test. So, using Table B.2 and looking at the .01 level for a two-tailed test, we find that the critical value is 2.764. The obtained value of 3.006 (same results as when you did the analysis for Question 1) does exceed what we would expect by chance, and given this hypothesis, there is a difference. Note that given the same data, a one-tailed finding, as in Question 1, need not be as extreme as a two-tailed finding for the researcher to reach the same conclusion (that the research hypothesis is supported).

3. We used the T.TEST function and got a value of .254. No muss, no fuss—that's the exact probability that these two groups of scores are different as a function of residence. And guess what? We don't need to know the exact value of the t-test outcome. And what else? They absolutely don't differ from one another.

4. And the results of the two-store comparison are (and remember, we made it appear a bit prettier than the plain output) . . .

t-Test: Two-Sample Assuming Equal Variances		
	Main Street Store	Mall Store
Mean	4,626.17	4,580.67
Variance	94,771.79	38,936.61
Observations	12	12
Pooled Variance	66,854.20	
Hypothesized Mean Difference	0.00	
df	22.00	
t Stat	0.43	
P(T<=t) one-tail	0.34	
t Critical one-tail	1.72	
P(T<=t) two-tail	0.67	
t Critical two-tail	2.07	

Because the probability associated with the difference of $45.50 (4,626.17 − 4,580.67) is .67, obviously the stores are not different. (And remember, this is a two-tailed test because the boss only wants to know whether there is a difference and not in what direction it is.) All is well—the stores are doing equally well (or poorly!).

5. The coach is history, but only if you think yards gained is important, right? If so, buy him out for $12 million and move on. Why? Well, the Brutes averaged about 202 yards while their opponents averaged about 287. There's a significant difference at the .007 level for a one-tailed test. However, you'd better be sure that the fans, including the alumni groups, think that yards gained is the most important criterion to judge success. Sounds like it could be, but other measures may be just, or more, important—such as games won ☺.

6. The finding would still be useful, but the statistical significance of a difference always has to be considered within the context of the question being asked. A statistically significant difference with a nonmeaningful effect size indicates that the difference, while not due to chance, may be conceptually weaker than the statistical evidence on its own would dictate. That's why statistics is a thinking person's sport—the numbers alone never tell the whole story.

CHAPTER 12

1. A *t*-test for independent means tests two distinct and different groups of participants, and each group is tested once. A *t*-test for dependent means tests one group of participants, and each participant is tested twice.

2. The mean before the recycling program was 34.44, and the mean after was 34.80. There is an increase in recycling. Is the difference across the 25 districts significant? The obtained *t* value is 0.234, and with 24 degrees of freedom, the difference is not significant at the .01 level (in fact, the probability of this value occurring by chance alone is .408)—the level at which the research hypothesis is being tested. Conclusion: The recycling program does not result in an increase in paper recycled.

3a. Independent

3b. Independent

3c. Dependent

3d. Independent

3e. Dependent

4. There was an increase in level of satisfaction, from 5.48 to 7.60, which results in a *t* value of 3.893. This difference has an associated probability level of .001. It's very likely that the social service intervention worked (pretty well, in fact).

5. When you compare dependent groups (and you are in effect comparing one group to itself given only one factor that changes, the treatment, for example), the standard is higher because the comparison is more rigorous—less room for error given that the comparison is so exact with little wiggle room.

6. Yes for Jack! The *t* value is 3.34, which is significant at the .003 level. The average sales before the training were $61,849.08, and afterward they were $83,850.83. Smart Jack.

7. We did it the Excel way, and you can see the output in Figure 12.7.

Figure 12.7	The Results of a Simple t-Test Between Paired or Dependent Means

t-Test: Paired Two Sample for Means

	Level of Tolerance Before Treatment	Level of Tolerance After Treatment
Mean	32.85	36.95
Variance	81.92	55.00
Observations	20	20.00
Pearson Correlation	0.18	
Hypothesized Mean Difference	0.00	
df	19	
t Stat	-1.73	
P(T<=t) one-tail	0.05	
t Critical one-tail	1.73	
P(T<=t) two-tail	0.10	
t Critical two-tail	2.09	

And our conclusion? Yes for the intervention. The level of tolerance went from 32.85 to 36.95, and this difference is significant at the .05 level.

8. Clearly, the first week with a mean gain of 239.3 yards went better than the last week of 217.5 yards. There goes the bowl game bid.

CHAPTER 13

1. Here is the table filled in with some possible examples:

Design	Grouping Variable(s)	Test Variable
Simple ANOVA	Four levels of hours of training: 2, 4, 6, and 8 hours	Typing accuracy
	Three age-groups: 20-, 25-, and 30-year-olds	Strength
	Six levels of job types	Job performance
Two-factor ANOVA	Two levels of training and gender (2 × 2 design)	Typing accuracy
	Three levels of age (5, 10, and 15 years) and number of siblings	Social skills
Three-factor ANOVA	Curriculum type (Type 1 or Type 2), GPA (above or below 3.0), and activity participation (participates or not)	ACT scores

2. As you can see in Figure 13.7, an abbreviated output from the Data Analysis tools, the means for the three groups are 58.05 seconds, 57.96 seconds, and 59.03 seconds, and the probability of this F value ($F_{(2,33)}$ = 0.160) occurring by chance is .85, far above what we would expect due to the treatment. Our conclusion? The number of hours of practice makes no difference in how fast these athletes swim!

Figure 13.7 Abbreviated Output From the Data Analysis Tools

Anova: Single Factor

SUMMARY

Groups	Count	Sum	Average	Variance
<15 Hours Practice	10	580.50	58.05	29.88
15-25 Hours Practice	13	753.50	57.96	22.68
More than 25 Hours Practice	13	767.40	59.03	31.08

ANOVA

Source of Variation	SS	df	MS	F	P-value	F crit
Between Groups	8.87	2	4.43	0.16	0.85	3.28
Within Groups	914.06	33	27.70			
Total	922.9322222	35				

3. There certainly is a difference. The results of the analysis are $F_{(2,48)}$ = 63.36, $p < .000$, which means that the likelihood of there being a difference due to anything other than the format is very, very low. And, if you look at the overall means of the three groups . . .

Group	Average
Color	7.06
Black-and-White	4.53
Combination	8.76

. . . it's clear that the treatment labeled Combination is the most effective.

4. There's definitely an overall difference among the five high schools given that the F value is 17.73 and the associated probability level is way smaller than .01 (it's actually .000000008). High School 5 has the highest graduation rate (86.00%), and High School 4 has the lowest graduation rate (65.20%). You can see all this in Figure 13.8.

Figure 13.8	A One-Way Analysis of Variance

SUMMARY

Groups	Count	Sum	Average	Variance
High School 1	10	709	70.90	21.88
High School 2	10	792	79.20	24.62
High School 3	10	806	80.60	38.49
High School 4	10	652	65.20	94.62
High School 5	10	860	86.00	13.11

ANOVA

Source of Variation	SS	df	MS	F	P-value	F crit
Between Groups	2733.28	4	683.32	17.73	0.00	2.58
Within Groups	1734.50	45	38.54			
Total	4467.78	49				

5. OK, it's a bit of a trick question. The *highest* sales were in the fall, but since there is no significant difference between sales across the four seasons (the *F* value is significant at the .73 level), you would be safe in concluding that sales were equal across seasons. It all depends how you define "best," right?

CHAPTER 14

1. Easy. Factorial ANOVA is used only when you have more than one factor or independent variable! And, actually, not so easy an answer to get (but if you get it, you really understand the material) when you hypothesize an interaction.

2. Here's one of many different possible examples. There are three levels of the factor named Treatment (or Sample) and two levels of the factor named Severity of Illness (or Column).

		Treatment		
		Drug #1	Drug #2	Placebo
Severity of Illness	Severe			
	Mild			

3. And the edited source table looks like this:

Source of Variation	ANOVA				
	SS	df	MS	F	p-value
Sample	0.075	1	0.075	0.037	0.848
Column	263.517	2	131.758	64.785	0.000
Interaction	3.150	2	1.575	0.774	0.463
Within	231.850	114	2.034		
Total	498.592	119			

And our conclusions? In this data set, there is no main effect for Severity of Illness, there is a main effect for Treatment, and there is no interaction between the two main factors.

4a. Well, it sort of worked—but in the wrong direction. There is a significant main effect for intervention, but the average score before the treatment was 7.4 and the after-intervention score was 6.23.

4b. No-go for the nutrition education program: There was no difference among the averages of the three levels, with an F value of 1.79 and a level of significance equal to .176.

4c. As far as an interaction between the intervention and the nutrition education program, there was none, as evidenced by the F value of 1.59 and a Type I error rate of .212.

4d. All in all, if you want folks to increase their score on a test of healthy eating (which hopefully is a valid indicator meaning they are eating better), then this dietary intervention is not the way to go. In addition, the type of education they received didn't make any difference. Okay, we used two sentences.

5. Here's the edited source table from the Data Analysis tools, and as you can see, students should put their energy into good grades (Columns, $F = 3.94$, $p < .01$) rather than participation in after-school activities (Sample, $F = 1.04$, $p < .36$).

Source of Variation	SS	df	MS	F	p-value
Sample	2.47	2	1.23	1.04	0.36
Columns	14.07	3	4.69	3.94	0.01
Interaction	3.53	6	0.59	0.49	0.81
Within	128.60	108	1.19		
Total	148.67	119			

CHAPTER 15

1a. With 18 degrees of freedom ($df = n - 2$) at the .01 level, the critical value for rejection of the null hypothesis is .516. There is a significant correlation between speed and strength, and the correlation accounts for 32.15% of the variance.

1b. With 78 degrees of freedom at the .05 level, the critical value for rejection of the null hypothesis is .183 for a one-tailed test (a one-tailed test was used because the research hypothesis is that the relationship is indirect or negative). There is a significant correlation between number correct and time, and approximately 20% of the variance is accounted for.

1c. With 48 degrees of freedom at the .05 level, the critical value for rejection of the null hypothesis is .273 for a two-tailed test (we used Table B.4). There is a significant correlation between number of friends a child has and GPA, and the correlation accounts for 13.69% of the variance.

2a. and b. We used the Data Analysis tools to compute the correlation between motivation and GPA as .434, significant at the .017 level using a two-tailed test. Figure 15.2 shows the final output from the analysis. Now, note that there's no probability level displayed—you still have to go to Table B.4 in the appendix to determine the Type I error rate.

Figure 15.2 Correlation Data Analysis Tools Output for Chapter 15 Data Set 1

	A	B	C	D	E	F
1	Motivation	GPA				
2	1	3.4			Motivation	GPA
3	6	3.4		Motivation	1	
4	2	2.5		GPA	0.43	1

2c. True. The more motivated you are, the higher your GPA. This is true because a significant correlation exists between the variables. But (and this is a big *but*), studying more does not *cause* you to be more highly motivated, nor does being more highly motivated *cause* you to study more.

3. Many examples could be given. Let's use the number of hours you study and your performance on your first test in statistics. These variables are not causally related. For example, some classmates may have studied for hours but done poorly because they never understood the material, and other classmates may have done very well without any studying because they had learned some of the same material in another class. Just imagine if we forced someone to stay at his or her desk and study for 10 hours each of 4 nights before the exam. Would that ensure that student would get a good grade? Of course not. Just because the variables are related does not mean that one causes the other.

4. The correlation between Number of Books and Educational Level is .56, which with 8 degrees of freedom is significant at the .05 level for a one-tailed test. But as for dropping off lots of books and looking for change in educational level . . . don't bet your remaining student loan money on it. And by this time you should know why: Things that are related don't (necessarily) cause one another.

5. For a two-tailed test with 23 degrees of freedom (25 − 2), a value of .42 shows the research hypothesis to be supported (yep, Table B.4 again). In this case, the output you see in Figure 15.3 shows that a higher risk category is significantly associated with a higher number of risk factors but there are no other significant correlations. The conclusion? An experimental study may be called for that looks at these significant factors as casual agents.

Figure 15.3	Analysis of Correlations Among Risk for Juvenile Detention, Number of Risk Factors, and Progress Made 10 Years After Intervention

	A	B	C	D	E	F	G	H
1	Risk	Number of Factors	Progress			*Risk*	*Number of Factors*	*Progress*
2	4	1	80		Risk	1		
3	2	2	81		Number of Factors	0.422823775	1	
4	5	2	22		Progress	-0.161463523	0.007323398	1

CHAPTER 16

1a. The regression equation is $Y' = -0.216 \times$ number correct + 17.310.

1b. $Y' = -0.216(8) + 17.310 = 15.582$.

1c.

Time (Y)	# Correct (X)	Y'	Y – Y'
15.5	5	16.13	–1.6
13.4	7	15.70	–2.3
12.7	6	15.92	–3.2
16.4	2	16.77	–0.4
21.0	4	16.35	4.7
13.9	3	16.56	–2.7
17.3	12	15.63	2.7
12.5	5	16.13	–3.6
16.7	4	16.35	0.4
22.7	3	16.56	6.1

The standard error is 3.59 (and we got that from the Data Analysis tools output we used to compute the regression equation in 1a.

2a. The other predictor variables should not be related to any other predictor variable. Only when they are independent of one another can they each contribute unique information to predicting the outcome or dependent variable.

2b. Examples of predictor variables would be living arrangements (single or in a group) and access to health care (high, medium, or low). You probably thought of others.

2c. Presence of Alzheimer's disease = (level of education)X_1 + (general physical health)X_2 + (living arrangements)X_3 + (access to health care)X_4 + a. (Of course, use your predictor variables in place of "living arrangements" and "access to health care.")

3. Regardless of what you are predicting, there's a real cost associated with too many predictors. First, it costs time and money to collect so much data, and second, it is very difficult to find so many variables that are conceptually related to one

other that are not empirically related as well. In other words, you're collecting information that overlaps greatly with what you may already have. The big problem? How do you know which variables actually contribute to the prediction?

4. This one you do on your own.

5a. You could compute the correlation between the two variables, which is .204. According to the information in Chapter 5, the magnitude of such a correlation is quite low. You could thus conclude that the number of wins over the previous 10 years is not a very good predictor of whether a team has won a Super Bowl during that same period.

5b. Many variables are categorical by nature (gender, race, social class, and political party) and cannot be measured easily on a scale from 1 to 100, for example. Using categorical variables allows us more flexibility. In this case, we studied the categorical win/loss variable.

5c. Some other predictor variables might be number of All-American players, win–loss record of coaches, and home game attendance.

6. The standard error of estimate or prediction is a measure of how well the prediction model works—that is, how little or how much the predicted scores (the outcome or dependent variable) differ from actual scores. So, if the correlation is low, then the prediction has to be somewhat poor and the standard error of estimate high.

7. The clear winner is that all three variables acting together have a correlation of .885, which is pretty high, and account for 74% (.738) of the variance. And that contribution of all three as predictors is highly significant. Cool beans, but . . . keep in mind that you have to decide how much overlap there is between the three. After all, they may be measuring similar outcomes.

8. Take a look at the results here. While years of training might not have a causal effect on how good a chef is, it sure does predict it!

Regression Statistics	
Multiple R	0.48
R Square	0.23
Adjusted R Square	0.17
Standard Error	10.23
Observations	14

ANOVA					
	df	**SS**	**MS**	**F**	**Significance F**
Regression	1	383.45	383.45	3.66	0.08
Residual	12	1255.98	104.67		
Total	13	1639.43			

	Coefficients	**Standard Error**	**t Stat**	**P-value**	**Lower 95%**	**Upper 95%**	**Lower 95.0%**	**Upper 95.0%**
Intercept	67.97	7.54	9.01	0.00	51.53	84.41	51.53	84.41
Years of Training	1.37	0.71	1.91	0.08	−0.19	2.92	−0.19	2.92

CHAPTER 17

1. Here's the worksheet for computing the chi-square value:

Category	*O* (observed frequency)	*E* (expected frequency)	*D* (difference)	$(O - E)^2$	$(O - E)^2/E$
Republican	800	800	0	0	0.00
Democrat	700	800	100	10,000	12.50
Independent	900	800	100	10,000	12.50
Chi-Square					25.00

With 2 degrees of freedom at the .05 level, the critical value needed for rejection of the null hypothesis is 5.99. The obtained value of 25 allows us to reject the null and conclude that there is a significant difference in the numbers of people who voted as a function of political party.

2. Here's the worksheet for computing the chi-square value:

Category	*O* (observed frequency)	*E* (expected frequency)	*D* (difference)	$(O - E)^2$	$(O - E)^2/E$
Boys	45	50	5	25	0.5
Girls	55	50	5	25	0.5
Chi-Square					1.0

With 1 degree of freedom at the .01 level of significance, the critical value needed for rejection of the null hypothesis is 6.64. The obtained value of 1.00 means that the null cannot be rejected and there is no difference between the numbers of boys and girls who play soccer.

3. Chi-square would be appropriate for Questions 3b and 3c because the data that are collected are categorical in nature (pass/fail in both cases). Questions 3a and 3d deal with data that are continuous (average scores and speed, respectively).

4. As you can see in Figure 17.6, the job is hers to keep, with the likelihood being pretty low (about 2.6%) that there's no difference in the proportion of those who succeeded and those who did not.

Figure 17.6	The CHISQ.TEST Value for the New Diabetes Management Program

	D1		▾ (	*fx*	=CHISQ.TEST(A2:B2,A3:B3)	
	A	B	C	D	E	
1	Successful	Unsuccessful		0.026261		
2	60	38				
3	49	49				

CHAPTER 20

Here's the completed pivot table shown in Figure 20.16 with an average score of 73.27.

Figure 20.16	A Simple Cross-Tabs Table Showing Score by Proficiency Level for 500 Participants

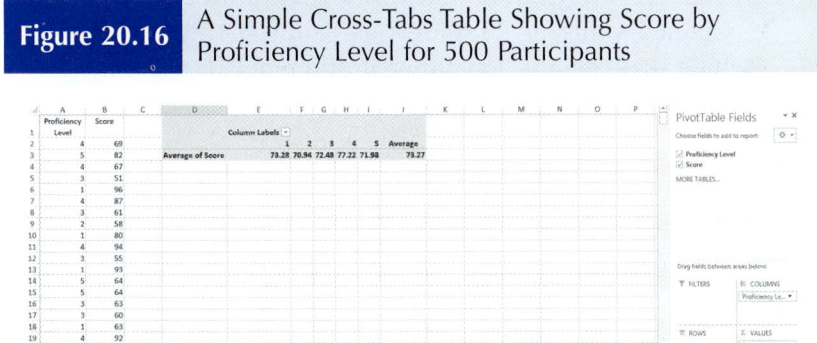

In Figure 20.17, you can see that among the 500 students, there are 128 level-4 females.

Figure 20.17	A Two-Dimensional Cross-Tabs Table With the Count for Level-4 Females Among 1,000 Athletes

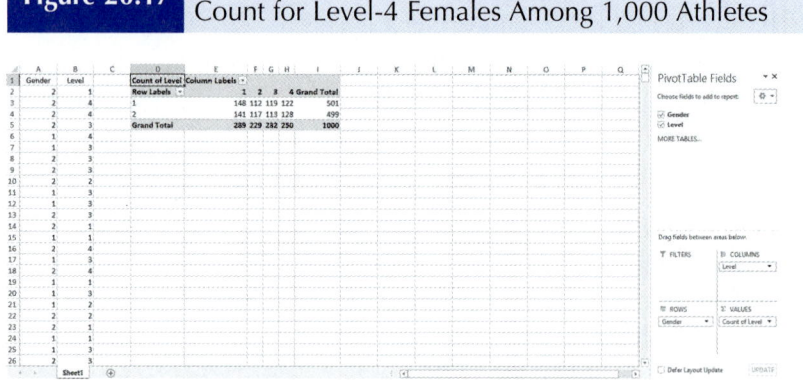

APPENDIX E

Math: Just the Basics

I f you're reading this, then you know you may need a bit of help with your basic math skills. Lots of people need such help, especially after coming back to school after a break. There's nothing wrong with taking this little side trip before you continue working in *Statistics for People Who (Think They) Hate Statistics*.

You already have most of the skills you need to work the examples in this book and to complete those at the end of the chapters. For example, you can add, subtract, multiply, and divide. You also probably know how to use a calculator to compute the square root of a number.

The confusion begins when we start dealing with equations and the various operations that can take place within parentheses, like these → ( ), and brackets, like these → [ ].

That's where we will spend most of our time and show you examples so you better understand how to work through what appear to be complex operations. Once they are reduced to their individual parts, completing them is a cinch.

THE BIG RULES—SAY HELLO TO BODMAS

Sounds like an alien life form or something from the Borg, right?

Nope. It is simply an acronym that indicates the order in which operations take place in an expression or an equation.

BODMAS goes like this . . .

B is for brackets, such as [ ], or sometimes parens (short for parentheses), like this ( ), both of which are sometimes present in an expression or equation.

O is for order or power, as in raise 4 to the order of 2 or 4^2.

D is division, as in $6 \div 3$ or $6/3$.

M is multiplication, as in 6 × 3.

A is addition, as in 2 + 3.

S is subtraction, as in 5 − 1.

You perform these operations in the above order. For example, the first thing you do is work within brackets (or parentheses), then take numbers to a power (such as squaring), then divide, then multiply, and so on. If there's nothing to square, skip the *O* step, and if there's nothing to add, skip the *A* step. If both brackets and parens are present, do the brackets first, and then the parentheses.

For example, take a look at this expression:

$$(3 + 2) \times 2 = ?$$

Using the BODMAS acronym, we know that . . .

1. The first thing we do is any operation within brackets or, in this case, parentheses. So, 3 + 2 = 5.

2. Moving on, the next available step is multiplying 5 times 2 for a total of 10, and 10 is the answer.

Here's another:

$$(4/2 \times 5) + 7 = ?$$

And here's what we do:

1. First is the division of 4 by 2, which equals 2.

2. Then that 2 is multiplied by 5 to get a value of 10.

3. Finally, 10 is added to 7 for a sum of 17—the answer.

Let's get a bit fancier and look at an equation with an exponent:

$$(10^2 \times 3)/150 = ?$$

Here's what we do:

1. Look inside the brackets or parentheses (as always for the first step).

2. Within these parentheses, first square 10 to get 100.

3. Then, still inside the parentheses, multiply 100 by 3 and arrive at 300.

4. Now every operation inside the parentheses is done, so divide 300 by 150. The answer is 2.

Let's add another layer of complexity when we have more than one set of brackets or parentheses. All you need to remember is that when there are parentheses inside brackets, we always work from inside out. Here we go . . .

$$[(15 \times 2) - (5 + 7)]/6 = ?$$

1. 15 times 2 is 30.

2. 5 plus 7 is 12.

3. 30 − 12 is 18.

4. 18 divided by 6 is 3.

THE LITTLE RULES

Just a few more. You see negative and positive numbers used throughout the book, and you need to know how they act when combined in different ways.

When multiplying negative and positive numbers, the following is true:

1. A negative number multiplied by a positive number (or a positive number multiplied by a negative number) always, always, always equals a negative number. For example . . .

$-3 \times 2 = -6$

or

$4 \times -5 = -20$

2. A negative number multiplied by another negative number results in a positive number. For example . . .

$-4 \times -3 = 12$

or

$-2.5 \times -3 = 7.5$

And a negative number divided by a positive number results in a negative number. For example . . .

$-10/2 = -5$

or

$25/-5 = -5$

And finally, a negative number divided by a negative number results in a positive number. For example . . .

$-10/-5 = 2$

Practice makes perfect, so here are 10 problems to practice with. The answers follow just afterward. If you can't get the right answer, review the order of operations above and also ask someone in your study group to review where you might have gone wrong.

Here we go . . .

1. $75 + 10 =$
2. $104 - 50 =$
3. $50 - 104 =$
4. 42×-2
5. -50×-60
6. $25/5 - 6/3$
7. $6,392 - (-700)$
8. $(510 - 500)/-10$
9. $[(40^2 - 207) - (80^2 - 400)]/35 \times 24$
10. $([(502 - 300) - 25] - [(242 - 100) - 50])/20 \times 30$

Answers

1. 85
2. 54
3. -54
4. -84
5. 3,000
6. 3
7. 7,092

8. −1

9. −3.6

10. 5,172

Want some more help and more practice? Take a look at these sites:

www.webmath.com

www.math.com/homeworkhelp/BasicMath.html

www.purplemath.com

www.khanacademy.org

There's nothing worse than starting a course and being so anxious that any meaningful learning just can't take place. Thousands of students less well prepared than you have succeeded, and you can as well. Reread the Chapter 1 tips on how to approach the material in this course—and good luck!

APPENDIX F

The Reward

The Brownie Recipe

What the heck is a brownie recipe doing in an introductory statistics book? Good question.

In all seriousness, you have probably worked hard on this material, whether for a course, as a review, or just for your own edification. And, because of all your effort, you deserve a reward. Here it is. The recipe is based on several different recipes and some tweaking, and it's all your author's and he is happy to share it with you. There, the secret is out.

Right out of the pan, not even cooled, these brownies are terrific with ice cream. Once they've aged a bit, they get very nice and chewy and are great from the fridge. If you freeze them, note that it takes more calories to defrost them in your mouth than are contained in the brownies themselves, so there is a net loss. Eat as many frozen as you want. ☺

1 stick (8 tablespoons) butter

4 ounces unsweetened chocolate (or more)

½ tablespoon salt

2 eggs

1 cup flour

2 cups sugar

1 tablespoon vanilla

2 tablespoons mayonnaise (I know)

6 ounces chocolate chips (or more)

1 cup whole walnuts (optional)

How to do it . . .

1. Preheat oven to 325 °F.

2. Melt unsweetened chocolate and butter in a saucepan.

3. Mix flour and salt together in a bowl.

4. Add sugar, vanilla, nuts, mayonnaise, and eggs to melted chocolate-butter stuff and mix well.

5. Add all of #4 to flour mixture and mix well.

6. Add chocolate chips.

7. Pour into an 8″ × 8″ greased baking dish.

8. Bake for about 35 to 40 minutes or until tester comes out clean.

NOTES . . .

- I know about the mayonnaise thing. If you think it sounds weird, then don't put it in. These brownies are not delicious for nothing, though, so leave out this ingredient at your own risk.
- Use good chocolate—the higher the fat content, the better. And you can use up to 6 ounces of unsweetened chocolate and even more of the chocolate chips.

GLOSSARY

Analysis of variance

A test for the difference between two or more means. A simple analysis of variance (or ANOVA) has only one independent variable, whereas a factorial analysis of variance tests the means of more than one independent variable. One-way analysis of variance looks for differences among the means of more than two groups.

Arithmetic mean

A measure of central tendency that sums all the scores in the data sets and divides by the number of scores.

Asymptotic

The quality of the normal curve such that the tails never touch the x-axis.

AVERAGE

A function that returns the mean of its arguments.

Average

The most representative score in a set of scores.

Bell-shaped curve

A distribution of scores that is symmetrical about the mean, median, and mode and has asymptotic tails.

Bivariate correlation

A correlation between two variables.

Cell

The intersection of a row and a column.

Central limit theorem

States that a large number of independent observations or samples will be distributed approximately normally and that the greater the number of observations or samples, the more normal their distribution will be.

Chi-square

A nonparametric test that allows you to determine whether what you observe in a distribution of frequencies would be what you would expect to occur by chance.

CHISQ.DIST

A function that returns the probability of an outcome given the degrees of freedom and the value of the chi-square statistic.

CHISQ.TEST

A function that returns the test for independence.

Class interval

The upper and lower boundaries of a set of scores used in the creation of a frequency distribution.

Coefficient of alienation

The amount of variance unaccounted for in the relationship between two variables.

Coefficient of determination

The amount of variance accounted for in the relationship between two variables.

Coefficient of nondetermination

See Coefficient of alienation.

Concurrent validity

A type of validity that examines how well a test outcome is consistent with a criterion that occurs in the present.

Confidence interval

The best estimate of the range of a population value or parameter that can be calculated given the sample value or statistic.

Construct validity

A type of validity that examines how well a test reflects an underlying construct.

Content validity

A type of validity that examines how well a test samples a universe of items.

CORREL

A function that returns the correlation coefficient between two data sets.

Correlation coefficient

A numerical index that reflects the relationship between two variables.

Correlation matrix

A set of correlation coefficients.

Criterion

Another term for the outcome variable.

Criterion validity

A type of validity that examines how well a test reflects some criterion that occurs either in the present (concurrent) or in the future (predictive).

Critical value

The value necessary for rejection (or nonacceptance) of the null hypothesis.

Cross-tabulation table

A table that summarizes categorical data using rows and columns.

Cumulative frequency distribution

A frequency distribution that shows frequencies for class intervals along with the cumulative frequency for each.

Data

Records of observations or events such as test scores, grades in math class, or response times.

Data mining

The process of examining large data sets to establish patterns.

Data point

An observation; the intersection of two values.

Data set

A set of data points.

Degrees of freedom

A value that is different for different statistical tests and approximates the sample size of a number of individual cells in an experimental design.

Dependent variable

The outcome variable or the predicted variable in a regression equation.

Descriptive statistics

Values that describe the characteristics of a sample or population.

Direct correlation

A positive correlation where the values of both variables change in the same direction.

Directional research hypothesis

A research hypothesis that includes a statement of inequality.

Effect size

A measure of the magnitude (and not necessarily the size) of the difference between two statistics such as group means.

Error in prediction

The difference between the actual score (Y) and the predicted score (Y').

Error of estimate

See Error in prediction.

Error score

The part of a test score that is random and contributes to the unreliability of a test.

Exabyte

A very large number of bytes or binary 1s and 0s.

Factorial analysis of variance

An analysis of variance with more than one factor or independent variable.

Factorial design

A research design in which there is more than one treatment variable.

F.DIST

A function that returns the F probability distribution.

FORECAST

A function that returns a value along a linear trend.

Formula

A series of cell references and operators that produces a particular outcome.

Formula bar

The location on the spreadsheet below the toolbars where cell contents are revealed.

FREQUENCY

A function that returns a frequency distribution as a vertical array.

Frequency distribution

A method for illustrating the distribution of scores within class intervals.

Frequency polygon

A graphical representation of a frequency distribution.

F.TEST

A function that returns the result of an F-test.

Function

A predefined formula.

GEOMEAN

A function that returns the geometric mean.

Goodness-of-fit test

See One-sample chi-square.

Histogram

A graphical representation of a frequency distribution.

Hypothesis

An if–then statement of conjecture that relates variables to one another.

Independent variable

The treatment variable that is manipulated or the predictor variable in a regression equation.

Indirect correlation

A negative correlation in which the values of variables move in opposite directions.

Inferential statistics

Tools that are used to infer characteristics of a population from results based on a sample.

Interaction effect

The outcome in which the effect of one factor is differentiated across another factor.

INTERCEPT

A function that computes the location where the regression line crosses the y-axis.

Internal consistency reliability

A type of reliability that examines the one-dimensional nature of an assessment tool.

Interrater reliability

A type of reliability that examines the consistency between raters.

Interval level of measurement

The level of measurement that stipulates there is an equal interval or distance between various points along some underlying continuum.

KURT

A function that returns the kurtosis of a data set.

Kurtosis

The quality of a distribution such that it is flat or peaked.

Leptokurtic

The quality of a normal curve that defines its peakedness.

Line of best fit

The regression line that best fits the actual scores and minimizes the error in prediction.

Linear relationship

A correlation that is best expressed as a straight line.

LINEST

A function that returns the parameters of a linear trend.

Main effect

In analysis of variance, when a factor or an independent variable has a significant effect upon the outcome variable.

Mean

A type of average in which scores are summed and divided by the number of observations.

Mean deviation

The average deviation of all scores from the mean of a distribution.

Measurement

The assignment of values to outcomes following a set of rules.

Measures of central tendency

The mean, median, and mode.

MEDIAN

A function that returns the median of the given numbers.

Median

The point at which 50% of the cases in a distribution fall below the point and 50% fall above.

Midpoint

The central point in a class interval.

Mode

The most frequently occurring score in a distribution.

MODE.MULT

A function that returns multiple modes when they occur in a data set.

MODE.SNGL

A function that returns the most common value in a data set.

Multiple regression

A statistical technique in which several variables are used to predict one.

Nominal level of measurement

The level of measurement that stipulates data are categorical in nature.

Nondirectional research hypothesis

A hypothesis that posits no direction but only a difference.

Nonparametric statistics

Distribution-free statistics.

Normal curve

See Bell-shaped curve.

NORM.S.DIST

A function that returns the standard normal cumulative distribution.

Null hypothesis

A statement of equality between sets of variables, numbers, text, or logical values.

Observed score

The score that is recorded or observed.

Obtained value

The value that results from the application of a statistical test.

Ogive

A visual representation of a cumulative frequency distribution.

One-sample chi-square

A chi-square test that includes only one dimension.

One-tailed test

A directional test.

One-way analysis of variance

See Analysis of variance.

Ordinal level of measurement

The level of measurement that stipulates that data can be, and are, ranked.

Outliers

Those scores in a distribution that are noticeably more extreme than the majority of scores. Exactly which score is an outlier is usually an arbitrary decision made by the researcher.

Parallel forms reliability

A type of reliability that examines the consistency across different forms of the same test.

Parametric statistics

Statistics used for making an inference from a sample to a population.

PEARSON

A function that returns the Pearson product-moment correlation coefficient.

Pearson product-moment correlation

See Correlation coefficient.

Percentile point

The point at or below where a score appears.

Pivot table

A table in which the rows and columns can be rearranged and data extracted.

Platykurtic

The quality of a normal curve that defines its flatness.

Population

All the possible subjects or cases of interest.

Power

A construct that has to do with how well a statistical test can detect and reject a null hypothesis when it is false.

Predictive validity

A type of validity that examines how well a test outcome is consistent with a criterion that occurs in the future.

Predictor variable

The variable that predicts an outcome.

QUARTILE.INC

A function that returns the quartile of a data set.

Range

The highest score minus the lowest score and a gross measure of variability. *Exclusive* range is the highest score minus the lowest score. *Inclusive* range is the highest score minus the lowest score plus 1.

Ratio level of measurement

The level of measurement that stipulates there is an absolute zero to the scale.

Regression equation

The equation that defines the points and the line that are closest to the actual scores.

Regression line

The line drawn based on the values in the regression equation.

Reliability

The consistency of a test over time or across forms.

Research hypothesis

A statement of inequality between two variables.

Sample

A subset of a population.

Sampling error

The difference between sample and population values.

Scales of measurement

Different ways of categorizing measurement outcomes.

Scatterplot, or scattergram

A plot of paired data points.

Significance level

The risk set by the researcher for rejecting a null hypothesis when it is true.

Simple analysis of variance

See Analysis of variance.

Single-factor analysis of variance

See Analysis of variance.

SKEW

A function that returns the skewness of a distribution.

Skew, or skewness

The quality of a distribution that defines the disproportionate frequency of certain scores. A longer right tail than left corresponds to a smaller number of occurrences at the high end of the distribution; this is a *positively* skewed distribution. A shorter right tail than left corresponds to a larger number of occurrences at the high end of the distribution; this is a *negatively* skewed distribution.

SLOPE

A function that returns the slope of the linear regression line.

Source table

A listing of sources of variance in an analysis of variance summary table.

Standard deviation

The average deviation from the mean.

Standard error of estimate

A measure of accuracy in prediction.

Standard score

See z score.

STANDARDIZE

A function that returns a normalized value.

Statistical significance

See Significance level.

Statistics

A set of tools and techniques used to organize, describe, and interpret information.

STDEV.P

A function that calculates standard deviation based on the entire population.

STDEV.S

A function that estimates standard deviation based on a sample.

STEYX

A function that returns the standard error of the predicted *y* value for each *x* in the regression.

T.DIST

A function that returns the *t* distribution.

Test of independence

See Two-sample chi-square.

Test statistic value

See Obtained value.

Test–retest reliability

A type of reliability that examines consistency over time.

TREND

A function that returns values along a linear trend.

True score

The unobservable part of an observed score that reflects the actual ability or behavior.

T.TEST

A function that returns the probability associated with a *t*-test.

Two-sample chi-square

A chi-square test that uses two dimensions.

Two-tailed test

A test of a nondirectional hypothesis in which the direction of the difference is of little importance.

Type I error

The probability of rejecting a null hypothesis when it is true.

Type II error

The probability of accepting a null hypothesis when it is false.

Unbiased estimate

A conservative estimate of a population parameter.

Validity

The quality of a test such that it measures what it says it does.

VAR.P

A function that calculates variance based on the entire population.

VAR.S

A function that estimates variance based on a sample.

Variability

The amount of spread or dispersion in a set of scores.

Variance

The square of the standard deviation and another measure of a distribution's spread or dispersion.

Workbook

A collection of worksheets.

Worksheet

A single Excel spreadsheet.

Y prime, or Y'

The predicted Y value.

z score

A raw score that is adjusted for the mean and standard deviation of the distribution from which the raw score comes.

Z.TEST

A function that calculates the probability that a data point belongs to a population.

INDEX